HARMFUL THOUGHTS

HARMFUL THOUGHTS

ESSAYS ON LAW, SELF, AND MORALITY

MEIR DAN-COHEN

PRINCETON UNIVERSITY PRESS
PRINCETON AND OXFORD

Copyright © 2002 by Princeton University Press

Published by Princeton University Press, 41 William Street, Princeton, New Jersey 08540

In the United Kingdom: Princeton University Press, 3 Market Place, Woodstock, Oxfordshire OX20 1SY

Library of Congress Cataloging-in-Publication Data

Dan-Cohen, Meir.
    Harmful thoughts : essays on law, self, and morality / Meir Dan-Cohen.
        p. cm.
    Includes bibliographical references and index.
    ISBN 0-691-09006-8 (alk. paper) — ISBN 0-691-09007-6 (pbk. : alk. paper)
    1. Law—Philosophy. 2. Law and ethics. I. Title.
    K246 .D36 2002
    340′.1—dc21   2001038754

British Library Cataloging-in-Publication Data is available

This book has been composed in Sabon and Futura

Printed on acid-free paper. ∞

Printed in the United States of America

10 9 8 7 6 5 4 3 2 1
10 9 8 7 6 5 4 3 2 1
(Pbk.)

FOR ANNI

CONTENTS

ACKNOWLEDGMENTS

Few debts are as gratifying as those incurred in the course of one's academic work, and even fewer so conveniently require not to be discharged but just to be recognized. It is with great pleasure and gratitude that I list the following friends and colleagues, for whose comments, suggestions, and objections, regarding at least one and often a number of these essays, I am deeply indebted: Bruce Ackerman, John Coons, Melvin Eisenberg, Claire Finkelstein, George Fletcher, Chaim Gans, Ruth Gavison, Kent Greenawalt, Miriam Gur-Arye, Russell Hardin, Paul Hoeber, Sanford Kadish, Christopher Kutz, Andrei Marmor, Michael Moore, Philippe Nonet, Andrea Peterson, Richard Pildes, Robert Post, Eric Rakowski, Andrzej Rapaczynski, Joseph Raz, Edward Rubin, Daniel Rubinfeld, Samuel Scheffler, Phillip Selznick, Yoram Shachar, Leon Sheleff, Marjorie Shultz, M. B. E. Smith, Stephen Sugarman, Cass Sunstein, Jan Vetter, Jeremy Waldron, and Frank Zimring.

I would also like to thank various copyright holders for their permission to use previously printed material:

"Law, Community, and Communication" is a revised version of the Duke Law Journal Lecture, delivered in the spring of 1989 and published in the *Duke Law Journal* 1989:1654.

"Decision Rules and Conduct Rules: On Acoustic Separation in Criminal Law" was published in the *Harvard Law Review* 97 (1984): 625. Copyright 1984 by The Harvard Law Review Association.

"In Defense of Defiance" was published in *Philosophy and Public Affairs* 23 (1994): 24. Copyright 1994 by Princeton University Press.

"Conceptions of Choice and Conceptions of Autonomy" was published in *Ethics* 102 (1992): 221. Copyright 1992 by The University of Chicago Press.

"Defending Dignity" is based on a lecture given at the Center for Ethics and the Professions at Harvard University in April 2000 and contains material from "Basic Values and the Victim's State of Mind," *California Law Review* 88 (2000): 759. Copyright 2000 by The California Law Review Association.

"Harmful Thoughts" was published in the *Journal of Law and Philosophy* 18 (1999): 379. Copyright 1999 by Klueger Publishers.

An earlier version of "Responsibility and the Boundaries of the Self" was published in the *Harvard Law Review* 105 (1992): 959. Copyright 1992 by The Harvard Law Review Association.

"Interpreting Official Speech" was published in *Law and Interpretation,* ed. Andrei Marmor (Oxford: Oxford University Press, 1995). Copyright 1995 by Oxford University Press.

"The Value of Ownership" was published in the *Journal of Political Philosophy* 9 (2001): 404. Copyright 2001 by Blackwell Publishers.

For the most part I have made only minor stylistic changes in the previously published essays.

INTRODUCTION

The following essays were written by a number of quite different writers over a long period of time. Binding the essays in one volume does not guarantee them greater unity than that guaranteed to their several authors by the mere fact that at different times they have all occupied the same body. Nonetheless, it is hoped that in both cases a measure of unity or at least coherence has been attained. The unity, such as it is, is both substantive and temperamental. The purpose of this introduction is accordingly to track some interrelated themes and to confess some idiosyncrasies of philosophic temper that are displayed in these essays.

Not surprisingly, the substantive themes echo their time, which has been marked in relevant respects by two salient intellectual trends. One took place within liberal thinking. It is the ascendance of a deontological, for the most part Kantian, approach, largely as a response to a growing disaffection with utilitarianism. In this process Kant has come to mean different things to different people, providing a wide platform on which many antagonists find a foothold. But broadly speaking, Kant is enlisted to the liberal cause mostly through the centrality to his moral theory of the idea of a free will. A liberal sensibility that celebrates individual choice can easily assimilate Kantian ideas by embracing autonomy as its fundamental value and voluntariness as the ground of moral and legal responsibility. Another dominant strain in contemporary Kantian liberalism is an insistence on communication or dialogue as a medium for forging principles of justice or fair terms of social cooperation, an insistence inspired at least in part by Kant's uplifting fantasy of the Kingdom of Ends.

The Kantianism absorbed into the liberal canon is, however, a dera-
cinated one, cut off from its metaphysical roots. Kant's own version of
autonomy, voluntariness, and the Kingdom of Ends is grounded in a
metaphysic that few contemporary normative Kantians espouse. Central
to it is the idea of the noumenal self, whose autonomy consists in moral
self-legislation and whose freedom is a matter of wholesale exemption
from laws of nature, which for this purpose comprise not just physics
but what we ordinarily think of as psychology as well. Membership in
the Kingdom of Ends is correspondingly limited to such abstractly conceived entities whose universally valid rationality is not hindered by any
real-world distortion or aberration.

Although the noumenal self is of little contemporary appeal and liberal Kantians have for the most part deserted it, no single conception of
the self has come to replace it. Liberal writers disagree about the most
adequate description of the self and about its most important or essential characteristics. But this very disagreement testifies to a deeper agreement that some such description and some such characteristics exist
and provide a necessary, if mostly implicit, foundation or backdrop for
moral and legal theory. However, the second intellectual trend reflected
in these essays consists in a large body of thought that can be understood as questioning this widely shared premise. This trend is vastly
more ramified than the first, and hence less amenable to a short summary. Nonetheless, a salient, perhaps dominant, theme can be discerned.
The view that "man has no essence" and must create his own, though
originating at least as far back as the fifteenth century,[1] was given new
impetus and significance in the twentieth. For many writers in this vein
human self-constitution depends crucially on language or discourse and
takes place in the medium of meaning. The insight that the meanings we
create create us undergirds some of the most influential and otherwise
diverse schools of thought of the recent past, such as existentialism,
postmodernism, and communitarianism.

My main interests lie in the intersection of these two trends. The
normative orientation of these essays is broadly Kantian, with Kant's
noumenal self replaced by a socially constructed one: the self as the
largely unintended by-product of individual actions and collective practices, including those of law and morality, whose primary orientation is
not the creation of a self but the accomplishment of some individual or
collective goals. For the most part, these goals and their pursuit provide
practical philosophy with its subject matter. The substitution I propose
suggests a shift or an addition of focus. It draws attention to the role of
our various normative engagements not just in responding to a preexisting self but also in shaping it.

Replacing within a Kantian perspective the noumenal self with a self that is socially constructed has a number of other corollaries, three of which seem to me of particular importance. First, there is a shift from a metaphysically underwritten freedom of choice to a more somber recognition of the contingency of meaning. Imagination rather than will becomes the dominant capacity that makes a normative assessment of the actual an intelligible activity. Second, there is a corresponding shift of emphasis from personal autonomy to human dignity as the preeminent Kantian value and from volition to *identification* as the key to responsibility. Third, the noumenal self connotes a realm of true morality that can be coherently conceived as transcending and therefore separate from the messy real-world domains of law and politics. Absent such metaphysical division, coercion and the good moral will are doomed to an uncomfortable coexistence on the same stage, and the line between inner, authentic motivation and external compulsion must be drawn within a single medium that is at once psychological and socially constructed throughout. Relatedly, the legitimating potential of communication or dialogue is hampered by the vicious cycle in which it moves: what we say depends on who we are and where we stand, which depend in turn on the very same social, political, and legal formations that communication is expected to legitimate.

The result of these reflections can be described as an insider's critique of liberalism. Insider's, inasmuch as the Kantian normative outlook as well as the raw materials with which I work—moral intuitions, legal doctrines, and court decisions—are all ingredients of what I take to be the dominant liberal culture broadly conceived. These factors provide a matrix for the questions I raise and the theories I develop. But the approach is critical, sometimes revisionary, all the same, since abandoning the safe if exotic haven of a metaphysically grounded noumenal self in favor of the contingency and indeterminacy of a socially constructed one throws into question some of liberalism's fundamental assumptions. These concern, as the book's three subdivisions indicate, the problem of coercion and its bearing on the nature of legal communication; the basic values to which liberalism is committed; and the constitution through normative practices of the legal and moral subject, or, in the prevailing idiom, the self. I'll say a few words about each.

Ubiquity of coercion and its bearing on the nature of legal discourse or communication, and relatedly on the rule of law and law's authority, are the main concerns of the essays in part 1. Political philosophy begins, soundly enough, by marking the state's coercion as a prime evil and then struggles to redeem it through one or another justification. The tacit belief is that a satisfactory justification will solve the problem of coercion, so that at least within the parameters defined by the favored account the exercise of coercion ought no longer trouble the collective conscience or disturb the good citizen's sleep. The essays in this part do not share such complacency. They are prompted by the belief that the abominations perpetrated in the name of the law are never fully rectified by the practical imperatives that may necessitate them, and that the problem of coercion is posed anew each time legal brutality is employed. A lesser evil is still an evil. As a result, law, like politics, is routinely implicated in the moral predicament of "dirty hands." Coping with this predicament is a central feature of law and the legal profession that legal theory must recognize.

Chapter 1 criticizes as excessively high minded a liberal jurisprudence that portrays legal discourse as striving exclusively toward moral truth. Appropriating and modifying the sociological concept of *role distance,* the chapter highlights the impersonal way in which legal actors enact their roles and reveals their avowedly strategic forms of communication as weapons deployed within what is sometimes a literally life-and-death agon. In a coercion-saturated environment, speech is the continuation of force by other, and milder, means. Chapter 2 strikes a similar note. It uses a communicative model to distinguish between the inner discourse of law, which I call *decision rules,* and the messages law conveys to the general public through *conduct rules.* In light of this distinction the essay questions the viability of the rule of law ideal of full transparency. The volume and complexity of legal communications make such transparency an illusory goal. Better realize that different messages are conveyed to different audiences to serve different purposes. The functional equivalence between force and speech is posited once again, displayed in the law's own reliance on *strategies of selective transmission* that can help accomplish various legal goals while reducing reliance on brute force. The third essay considers an even more fundamental conflict in which law's coerciveness is inescapably embroiled. Obedience to law can be itself a communicative action expressing deference to law's authority and respect for the government. But the pervasiveness of coercion that backs up law's authority perforce replaces an appeal to the citizens' good will with intimidation, thus depriving law-abiding behavior of the morally expressive significance it might otherwise have. In this sense, the very fact of law's coerciveness undercuts law's normativity.

The essays in part 2 revolve around some of liberalism's basic normative commitments. These include autonomy, the harm principle, and, relatedly, an aversion to thought control. The first two essays deal with the problematics of choice, a theme that is also central to the theory of responsibility developed in chapter 7. Chapter 4 examines the connection between choice and autonomy. According to the dominant model of rational choice, agents rank the members of a choice-set in light of their preferences. This model, I argue, is ill suited to account for the conception of autonomy that is relevant to some of the most important aspects of our life, such as morality, creativity, and most importantly the formation of our own identity. A categorical affirmation of, or identification with, a particular option we face or a feature of our life better captures the essence of autonomy as it bears on these regions. Chapter 5 questions the primacy of autonomy as well as welfare in our considered moral judgments and legal practices. It urges instead the priority of dignity over these other liberal values. Such priority is not only faithful to Kant's own moral theory, but is also better able to capture our moral intuitions than do the other values liberalism entertains, as well as to accommodate divergent moral views with which many legal systems are increasingly confronted. The eponymous chapter 6 tackles another liberal shibboleth, aversion to thought control, an aversion allegedly supported by the harm principle. I question this support by demonstrating the potential harmfulness of mental states. A self that is constituted by meanings is also susceptible to changes in them. Other people's attitudes and states of mind can accordingly affect a person's identity all by themselves, without the mediation of action or expression. Somewhat paradoxically, this observation issues in an argument, based on a dignity-based right to know important facts that bear upon one, in favor of the liberal willingness to extend First Amendment protection to forms of offensive expression such as hate speech.

Issues of human identity and conceptions of self crop up at many points throughout this book, but in part 3 they assume center stage. The basic goal is the same in all three essays: to trace in different normative settings, respectively concerning responsibility, legal interpretation, and private property, the implications of a view of self as the resultant of practical engagements and social practices and not just as their subject. Chapter 7 pursues this goal in search of a theory of responsibility. Dominant conceptions of responsibility ground it in human beings' possession of a free will and their capacity for self-control. But as I pointed out earlier, outside of the Kantian metaphysics of the noumenal self, the idea of free will runs into the conundrum of determinism, and self-control is not even a factor when strict or collective responsibility is ascribed. Putting matters of choice and control to one side, the theory I propose depicts ascriptions and denials of responsibility as *constitutive practices* that help determine the self's composition and boundaries. Law's coerciveness assumes special significance in this context, providing a powerful incentive to contract the self's boundaries and to enact a "minimal" self in order to escape the nasty incidents of legal responsibility. Chapter 8 focuses on the aspects of one's identity that are constituted by social roles. Relying on the concept of *role distance* (which I mentioned earlier in connection with the first essay), I distinguish between *proximate* roles with which one identifies and that are integral parts of the self, and *distant* roles that are enacted in an impersonal manner. This distinction serves as the basis for a novel understanding of the age-old debate concerning the relevance of legislators' intention in statutory interpretation. Our practices of interpretation, I argue, specifically the varying significance we assign to speakers' intentions, are among the factors that determine whether a role is perceived and enacted as proximate or distant. The ambiguity concerning the proper interpretive significance of legislative intent can be seen, accordingly, as part of the social construction of *official* roles and as determinations of the degree of distance with which such roles are properly enacted. Finally, in chapter 9, I outline a conception of property as the extension of the physical dimension of the self. The extension depends on the use of the personal pronoun *I*. Due to the self's *articulate self-awareness,* the use of *I* plays a constitutive role in fixing the self's composition and boundaries; and in light of the view of the self as socially constructed, the content of this pronoun is determined by the social occasions and practices in which it is properly used. The latter often put within the scope of the pronoun not just the body but other objects as well. Consequently, the normative significance of objects we own is on a par with that of the body: the scope and the ramifications of various values that apply to individuals, such as autonomy and dignity, depend on how the boundaries of the self are drawn and on what is thought to fall within them.

I indicated at the outset that in addition to the substantive themes I have just adumbrated, these essays as well as the authorial selves that composed them are united by a shared philosophic temper. Matters of temperament are usually best left for the reader to judge, but in the present case it does seem to me advisable, if only out of fairness, to alert the reader to what may be a departure from a prevailing norm, so as to set the right expectations. As most commonly practiced these days, practical philosophy begins in faith. The enterprise of elaborating suggestions about how the world ought to be is an essentially optimistic endeavor, in which at least two hopeful assumptions are implicitly made: that the world will listen and that it will improve as a result. It has correspondingly become fashionable to present and interpret pronouncements made within this activity as stating the writer's views about how things ought to be. This picture has two important stylistic implications. One is a rather high-voltage polemic animus that characterizes much writing in this area. The other is a certain earnestness that puts a lid on the theoretic imagination to keep it within the bounds of common sense.

Only so can theory remain a viable interlocutor in the public arena and participate in the same discourse in which other actors—politicians, lawyers, and the media—engage.

I do occasionally indulge in the kind of enterprise I have just described, but for the most part I remain somewhat skeptical about its aspirations and assumptions. As a result, I do not really conceive of myself as promulgating views and defending them. Of course, like other people I too am occasionally beset by views, which sometime issue in actions, many of which I come to regret. But all of this is rather private and of interest, if at all, to very few close souls. I prefer accordingly to think of these essays not as expressing views but as exhibiting ideas. The main difference, as I see it, between views and ideas concerns the role of the will, which is central to the former and absent from the latter. Even if ultimately both views and ideas seek to prevail, views are propelled to battle by someone's will, whereas ideas must conduct their own fight. More likely, though, this entire agonistic metaphor does not fit ideas at all. Their main ambition is to shed light or to provoke further thinking, and they will be let down if they do not; but their disappointment will be of one who failed in one's mission or whose good services were spurned, not the defeat of a frustrated and vanquished will.

This antiview view has predictable effects along the two stylistic dimensions I distinguished. The polemically minded reader will be quite disappointed. If there is a general normative message in this book, it is more in the nature of a keen sense of the dead-ends we run into and the slipperiness of the ground we tread than of a confident vision of how things ought to be. The effects on the relationship of the theories and arguments I propound to commonsense views and beliefs is perhaps even more pronounced and may also be more unsettling. How far from common sense are our theories allowed to venture? Though by general philosophical standards the answer exhibited by these essays is not at all extravagant (nothing analogous to, say, *monads* is to be found anywhere here), compared to the standards that dominate in contemporary practical theorizing, I do sometimes stray quite far afield. I say this not as an apology but as a caveat. Theories, I believe, must be answerable to common sense by way of accounting for it, not by way of being part of it. Understanding requires perspective and perspective, distance. One way to gain perspective when trying to comprehend large terrains of common sense is to leap high up into the air. To be sure, one cannot and probably would not wish to maintain that position for long; but with luck, one may glimpse a worthwhile vista from up there.

I have so far accentuated in this introduction the commonalities among the essays, but my concluding comment concerns a feature that divides them. Some of the essays initially appeared in law reviews and others in philosophy journals, and the difference of venue bespeaks a difference in methodology and argumentative style. Members of the respective audiences who read this book will likely find more congenial the essays that belong to their own genre. Binding the essays together, however, implies a hope for some synergistic added value that is more likely to be realized if such professional boundaries, with the resistances and habits of thought they cultivate, can be breached.[2]

Notes

1. The well-known text is by Giovanni Pico della Mirandola, *Oration on the Dignity of Man,* trans. A. Robert Caponigri (Washington, D.C.: Regency Gateway, 1956).

2. But since the essays can also profitably be read separately and out of order, I leave intact a few minor redundancies in the argument, especially between chapters 1 and 8.

PART 1
COERCION AND COMMUNICATION

CHAPTER ONE
LAW, COMMUNITY, AND COMMUNICATION

I follow the fashion of listing no more, and no less, than three items in a title. If it were not for this fashion, my title would have included two more items—interpretation and organization. I shall relate these concepts in the following way: I shall pair community with interpretation and organization with communication. An important strand in contemporary legal and social theory—I have in mind primarily the work of Ronald Dworkin in this country and Jürgen Habermas in Europe—is fixated on the first couple consisting of community and interpretation. In this it gives us only a partial representation of social reality and, specifically, of law; it paints only half, and probably the less significant half, of the picture. But drawing attention to the other elements in the picture, those I call organization and communication, does not simply supplement it. Rather, the fuller painting, I hope to show, bears scant resemblance to the partial rendering by Dworkin and others who belong in his mold. The linchpin that holds together the various terms I want to relate is yet another concept—role distance—which I borrow, with some modifications, from the work of the sociologist Erving Goffman.[1] Let me then start by describing this linchpin.

1. Role Distance, Community, and Organization

The term *role distance* belongs to the vocabulary of the self as well as to the vocabulary of social role, and serves as a bridge between the two. It is part of a dramaturgical imagery of the self, according to which the self consists, at least in part, of the social roles that it enacts. The special insight that the concept of role distance imports into this picture relates to the self's capacity to locate itself, metaphorically speaking, at variable distances from the different roles that it occupies. Identification with a role is a matter of degree, and depending on the degree of identification, a given role may be more or less integrated with and constitutive of a particular self. This is the basic idea, and though my account of it must remain simplified, let me add a few further details.

Exactly what identification with a role or detachment from it consists of is a difficult matter, but the following criterion provides at least a proxy or approximation. When I fully identify with a role, when the role distance, to further exploit the spatial metaphor, is down to zero, I enact the role "transparently"—that is, without an explicit awareness of the role's requirements and the fact that I fulfill them. By contrast, the presence of role distance is marked by self-consciousness: by an explicit awareness that I engage in playacting; that I enact a certain role by responding to its requirements and expectations.

Identification and detachment are not fixed properties of roles: the distance between a person and a role can shrink or expand; it can fluctuate over time. It is also not the case that some roles must be worn tightly, whereas others are kept at a distance by all their takers. I can become at times self-conscious about, and distanced from, every one of my roles, just as it seems that every role can in principle be enacted transparently by someone. Still a certain degree of uniformity in the style of enacting different roles exists, and so some generalization regarding role distance is possible. Some roles call for greater identification than others. Certain roles are in general more likely to be enacted at a distance than other roles. So it is meaningful, though not altogether accurate, to speak in general terms about "detached" or "distant" as opposed to "nondetached" or "proximate" roles. What I shall have to say depends, at any rate, on the soundness of this distinction.

Role distance, as I said, is the linchpin that links the various concepts I want to relate. I will use role distance first to distinguish two types of collectivity or social structure: *community* and *organization*. The juxtaposition is of course familiar. It immediately brings to mind Ferdinand Tönnies' distinction between *Gemeinschaft* and *Gesellschaft*,[2] and I mean to capitalize on this association. But for my present purposes, I first want to draw the distinction exclusively in terms of the concept of role distance. I will define a community as *a social union of nondetached roles.* In other words, a community is a collectivity whose roles do not allow their holders to maintain a distance from those roles. By contrast, an organization is *a social union of detached roles;* it is a collectivity whose roles allow or even call for distance. These definitions are admittedly stipulative, but they are not arbitrary. I would like to get at least provisional assent to them, and I hope to earn it by an illustration and an explanation.

Consider the role of a parent—a role within a collectivity, the family, which in its ideal form I take to be the paradigm of what I call community. Contrast this role with that of say an AT&T operator, who performs what I take to be a quintessentially organizational role. Let me now draw attention to a few aspects of this opposition.

First notice that there are pretty clear social norms that regulate role distance in these instances. To be a parent, characteristically, is to enact a nondetached role. Since there is no distance between me and my role as a father, since I fully identify with that role, the imperatives that guide me in discharging it are in an important sense internal to me. I simply do what I think best in a certain regard, for example in matters that pertain to my child's education, or behavior, or welfare. We can say that in doing so my conduct as father is fully autonomous. This is not because I can treat my child with unfettered discretion, let alone arbitrarily. Quite the contrary. The demands of my role as father often are circumscribed narrowly, mandating a very specific attitude or course of action. Still, these imperatives do not compromise my autonomy but rather express it, since they follow from *me*; they shape or constitute an aspect of my own identity, that of parent.

Nor should it be thought that my autonomy in going about my fatherly role depends on my doing so cheerfully and enthusiastically. Many a parent would flunk *this* test when getting up to attend to a screaming baby in the middle of the night, and yet their autonomy in performing the parental role is not thereby the least bit diminished. This conclusion derives, by close analogy, straight from Kant. The strain we feel in performing our moral duties, according to Kant, results from their frequent conflict with our inclinations. Still, this is in an important sense an internal struggle between different parts or aspects of the self. When we do follow morality, despite our inclinations, we act autonomously because we heed an internal, not an external, call. So also in the case of the parent. One's identification with the role and one's autonomous execution of its demands are not undercut but rather are put to the test by temptations and pressures that lead away from the role's requirements. Another way of making the same point, a way that also has clear Kantian overtones and will serve us later, is this: in enacting a nondetached role, my will is identical (within the role's domain) with the role's requirements. There is therefore no question of providing me with some external motivation to perform the various aspects of my parental role—for example, to get up to my crying baby—since an internal motivation is already provided in the assumption that I enact parenthood as a nondetached role. In that case I simply *will* the role's various imperatives, although my will on occasion may have to prevail over such impediments as my desire to go on sleeping.

Moreover, since there is no question of motivation to behave in accordance with the precepts of a nondetached role, there is a fortiori no question of coercion to do so. It is not that coercion is pragmatically unnecessary, but rather that it is conceptually out of place. Coercion becomes intelligible in this context only when the premises of my depiction of (the idealized) parental role already have been vitiated—that is, when a gap has been opened between the person and his or her role as parent, so that compliance with the role's requirements is put into question for the first time.

A telephone operator's role contrasts with the parent's in all these respects. It would be utterly appropriate for the operator to keep the role at a distance. He can be an accomplished operator even though he just, as it were, goes through the motions of an operator (as long as, of course, he goes through them well enough). Since the operator need not identify with his role, its imperatives are external to him. The main difference between the roles of parent and operator is not that the latter role's demands are more narrowly defined on any particular occasion than are the former's. The difference, instead, lies in the source relative to the self of the guidance provided by the role. Insofar as the role that I enact is a detached one, I experience the role's imperatives as external, and thus potentially as constraints. Potentially, because the role's requirements may coincide, of course, in general or in any specific instance with my wants and desires. But this coincidence is, in principle, adventitious; it is not an essential part of my relationship to a detached role.

It follows that unlike a nondetached role, a detached one presents starkly the problems of motivation, autonomy, and coercion. Since I keep the role at a distance—outside of me—the role's requirements do not, in and of themselves, become *my* reasons or motivations for complying with them. The various tasks that compose the telephone operator's role, such as answering the numerous phone calls and operating the electronic switchboard, are not the things the operator himself has any reason or desire to do. (The crucial point here is that it makes perfectly good sense to refer to the "operator himself," meaning the operator qua person, aside from this particular role. By contrast, it ordinarily would be clumsy to separate a person from, say, the parent that he is.) If the operator is to perform his tasks, he must be motivated somehow, bribed or coerced, to do so. The most common combination used to this effect contains elements of both kinds of inducement. Performing a detached role is therefore not, as such, a display of autonomy. I say as such, because depending on a more detailed theory of autonomy, as well as on the nature of the second-order reasons one may have for enacting the detached role, its enactment may count as autonomous after all. But the individual's very engagement in the tasks of a telephone operator does not purport to express the operator's own will in the way that properly discharging parental duties is ordinarily supposed to be a manifestation of the parent's will.

The telephone operator is a member of an *organization*, AT&T in my example, simply in the sense, and by virtue of the fact, that he holds a detached role in that collectivity. For this reason, he in principle must be bribed or coerced if he is to perform the role's requirements. But don't those who do the bribing or coercing have to do so willfully, out of identification with *their* roles, and thus exemplify a communal type of participation in AT&T? And, if so, isn't there a contradiction in describing AT&T both as an organization and a community?

My answer to both questions is negative. First, it is not really necessary for anyone at AT&T, including those who see to it that the operator perform his tasks, to identify with their roles. Putting aside the historical question of how AT&T came to be, the organization presently can consist entirely of detached roles, all of which depend on some external source of motivation for implementation by their holders. Although it is not required that some of AT&T's roles be nondetached, however, there would be no contradiction in terms of my proposed scheme if, in fact, some roles were to be enacted so. It is altogether possible for AT&T to comprise some roles—upper echelon management, perhaps—that are to be held with no elbow room, with no personal distance. In my terminology, AT&T would then provide a community for the holders of those roles, whereas it would continue to be an organization for its other role holders.

Why do some collectivities call for and some attain identification, whereas others engender or condone role distance? Like other social questions, this one too can be investigated descriptively or normatively. The normative investigation can be *conventional* in character—it can look for the source of various claims to role identification or role distance in a society's existing value system—or it can be *critical*, in the sense of trying to assess or ground such claims from the perspective of some ideal normative scheme. A complete theory of social structures in terms of variations in role distance would have to tackle these various issues at the different levels, but that is not an enterprise in which I can engage here. Instead, I will settle for only some crude and speculative observations that will serve me in my present argument.

The main hypothesis is this: there is a rough correlation in our society between role distance, as both norm and reality, and a form of social organization that we can loosely call *bureaucratic*. Social entities fitting under this heading are marked by their large size, formal and hierarchical structure, and a relatively well and narrowly defined set of goals. It is primarily with regard to such entities—AT&T is a paradigm example—that role distance is engendered and condoned. We also can glimpse in passing an explanation, albeit a highly speculative one, for the prominence of role distance in bureaucratic organizations. By isolating the self from the organizational role, role distance shields the self to a degree from the blatant instrumentalism of these organizations. At the same time, role distance gives those organizations as well as their members a certain flexibility and adaptability that are likely to be conducive to the organization's operational success. Detached roles can be, if necessary, redefined or reassigned without thereby playing havoc with the selves of the roles' individual bearers.

If my hypothesis is sound, my characterization of community and organization in terms of role distance will be roughly coextensive with our ordinary use of those two labels, based upon some general structural features that distinguish the two types of collectivity. My proposed characterization, however, lays emphasis on what, at least for my present purposes, deserves the greatest attention: the radically different relationship to the self that various collectivities can and ought to bear.

One final observation. Role distance is a normative as well as descriptive concept. One's appropriate distance from various roles is regulated normatively and, as I said, is amenable to assessment on both conventional and ideal grounds. In all of this, role distance must be sharply distinguished from *alienation,* which is a malady of the self. In the conceptual scheme that I propose, alienation is an *inappropriate* role distance—that is, it is distance from what is supposed to be one's *communal* role. So understood, alienation contrasts with what would be the self's opposite disease: misplaced identification with what ought to be a distanced, organizational role. The name of this disease is *bad faith*.[3]

2. Interpretation and Communication

I turn now to the second pair of concepts that I want to juxtapose: interpretation and communication. I begin with a caveat: the way in which I'm going to use these terms may create confusion, and I shall try to avoid it by the following clarifications. I borrow the notion of interpretation directly from Ronald Dworkin's writings, primarily *Law's Empire,*[4] where this concept is already shaped to suit our legal concerns as the centerpiece of a theory that Dworkin calls "law as interpretation."[5] However, it seems to me we can better understand Dworkin's conception of interpretation, as well as appreciate its shortcomings, if we view it in the light of an important distinction drawn by Jürgen Habermas in his theory of communicative action.[6] Habermas sharply distinguishes between two kinds of discursive social action: *communicative action* and *strategic communication*. In communicative action, the participants are oriented toward reaching agreement through understanding. In strategic communication, by contrast, participants are oriented toward success; they have a specific goal determined antecedently to their discursive behavior that the latter is designed to promote. My claim is that Habermas' notion of communicative action—that is, discourse oriented toward agreement through understanding—is closely related to Dworkin's idea of interpretation.[7] I shall not be able to defend fully this claim here, though I trust that it does not seem particularly controversial to those familiar with the relevant writings. At any rate, I shall have to rest my case mainly on one central factor common to both notions. The engine that drives Dworkin's interpretation as well as Habermas' communicative action, or to shift the metaphor, the beacon that attracts them both, is truth, or perhaps more accurately, a shared belief in its attainability. I propose to treat interpretation and communicative action as one pole, which, following Dworkin's usage, I shall call *interpretation,* of an opposition that has the notion of strategic communication, or simply *communication,* as the other pole.

The terms interpretation and communication are convenient labels for the polarity that I want to describe, but as I warned already, and for reasons that I hope are now clearer, my use of these terms is potentially misleading. Both terms are characterizations of discourse, and thus both pertain to communication. My derivation of the notion of interpretation in part from Habermas' concept of communicative action underscores this obvious fact. Still, my proposed usage—juxtaposing interpretation with communication—has a substantive justification in addition to its convenience. It helps bring out the internal relationship between interpretation and community that I have anticipated at the outset. My point is this: though the program of interpretation does characteristically involve a plurality of participants, it is evident in both Dworkin's and Habermas' depiction of it that the existence of a plurality is not essential to the proper analysis and understanding of interpretation under ideal conditions. This is so for the following reason. Those ideal conditions, which, as Professor Dworkin is at pains to emphasize, point to the fact that interpretation takes place in the context of community, secure a degree of cognitive alignment and motivational coordination among the participants so as to make their plurality insignificant. As embodied in Dworkin's famous allegory of Judge Hercules, interpretation in principle can be understood successfully on a monological model, as though the discourse under consideration took place within an individual's internal forum in which the interlocutors are all figments of the interpreter's own imagination.[8] In deploying competing views and arguments, these imaginary speakers serve a purely heuristic purpose in the unified search for truth and understanding.[9]

In terms of the metaphor of role distance and the idea of community to which it gives rise, the picture is this: when individuals fully participate in community, when they efface all distance between themselves and their communal roles, then the system of interlocking roles, which is the community, constitutes a configuration of partially intermingled personal identities. Partially, because the individual identities intermingle only along the dimension or within the domain that defines and bounds the particular community that these individuals share. But insofar as matters concerning the community go, the members occupy a common space, which is fully continuous with each member's private space. We plausibly can imagine their public discourse as taking place within a single member's private forum precisely because the relevant zone of that private forum is continuous with the community's public space.

This, I believe, is the picture that underlies and best explains the concept of interpretation as articulated by Dworkin and Habermas. This picture links up with a number of important features of interpretation that I shall now consider.

Recall the examples of parent and telephone operator. Dworkin derives his description of law as interpretation from an analysis of interpretation in the context of another social practice: courtesy.[10] In order to keep the following comments as parallel as I can to Dworkin's discussion, I shall also begin by placing my protagonists, the parent first, in a similar context. Suppose that someone had just helped my four-year-old daughter to cross the street, as I happen to walk by. Being in general a polite fellow, I wonder (this of course is just a way of speaking) whether courtesy makes any demands on me in these circumstances. The answer is plain, and so I say to the benefactor something like, "Thank you for helping my daughter." The first thing to notice about this situation is this: my expression of gratitude is strictly a matter of performing my role as father. After all, the benefactor has not rendered any help directly to *me*. It is only by virtue of my parental role, and as an aspect of it, that it is appropriate and necessary that I thank the helper under these circumstances. But it is equally important to notice that once I have ascertained that it is incumbent upon a father to express gratitude under these circumstances, no further question about motivation—that is, why did *I* express gratitude—arises. This motivation is already provided for (though it is not invariably guaranteed) by my general tendency to excel at what I take myself to be—by my striving to be the best at what I am. In this case, my general tendency to be a polite person is sufficient to secure my performance of such a speech act, because my being a father is simply the aspect of my personal identity that pertains to the situation at hand.

Suppose now that the above episode happens when I'm in my wife's company. As we are approaching the helping person, my wife urges me to thank the stranger for her help. I demur: "It was none of this woman's business to help our daughter go where we didn't want her to go," I argue. It is now open to my wife to persuade me that I have taken the wrong attitude; that gratitude and its expression are due. I may be persuaded by her reasons, or I may defer to her judgment, which, in matters of courtesy, I consider superior to mine. All of this possible interaction comports with the spirit of community and counts as an exercise in interpretation. A good test of this conclusion is whether I can imagine the same dialogue occurring "in my head," with me deploying my wife's arguments on her behalf and then duly considering them. There is however one thing that my wife decidedly cannot do and still remain within the interpretive enterprise. She cannot, when all fails, squeeze my elbow and mutter through clenched teeth: "Thank her or I'll break your arm!" As Habermas insists, interpretation proceeds on the participants' shared assumption of their mutual desire to reach the truth, to the discovery of which they all have an equal claim. Understanding, both in the sense of improved comprehension and increasing agreement, is the exclusive concern of this form of discursive activity. Forcing assent by coercive measures cannot promote interpretation; it can only undercut it and convert it into a form of the antinomous category—strategic communication. Observe also that resort to coercion suspends community. If I act on my wife's threat and thank my child's benefactor for that reason, I act apart from, and despite, my own understanding of my role as father. I am propelled by external motivation, with whose source I do not identify. By issuing the threat, my wife herself has stepped out of our shared communal space and has instead installed herself as the final arbiter of an enterprise that I am no longer expected to share.

Let us return now to the original version of my story to observe another aspect of my thanking my daughter's benefactor. An important aspect or consequence of the fact that I identify with my fatherly role is that by making the appropriate utterance— "Thank you for helping my daughter"—I express my gratitude. In doing so I abide by what speech act theorists refer to as the *condition of sincerity*, which in this case simply means that my utterance truthfully conveys my sense of gratitude. I'll have more to say later about the significance of this observation.

Now contrast the episode above with another familiar display of politeness. Recall our second protagonist, the AT&T operator. If courtesy were measured by the frequency with which one utters words of politeness, that operator would surely be a world champion in the field. As anyone who has ever needed his or her assistance knows, the operator concludes each exchange, no matter how short or trivial (and these exchanges tend to be both) by proclaiming: "Thank you for using AT&T." Now, on the face of it, this utterance is on all fours with my "Thank you for helping my daughter," addressed to her benefactor. Still, the differences are striking. We can mark them by looking again at the elements of motivation, coercion, and sincerity that we have considered before.

The point about motivation can perhaps best be made by noticing that, unlike the case of the grateful father, the operator's recitation of thanks bears no relationship to a personal disposition toward politeness or its absence. This feature of the situation follows from, and testifies to, the fact that the politeness evinced by the operator remains external to him. Both in the case of the parent and the operator, the relevant script is written into their respective roles. But, unlike the parent's role, the operator's role, including the particular script we consider, remains at a distance. The fact that the role of operator mandates an expression of gratitude on certain specified occasions, has in itself no hold over the role-player. There must be some other source of motivation to compel his utterance of the required text. Such motivation can be provided for, consistent with the organizational nature of the role, in the form of either bribery or coercion. A recalcitrant operator surely will be threatened with dismissal if he fails to perform the incantation, irrespective of the earnestness of his belief that the required practice is silly and inappropriate for him or for the role he holds. Or imagine the operators going on partial strike, their union decreeing: "No more of this 'thank you' silliness until we get a raise." It would seem altogether appropriate for AT&T to meet the union's demands by actually paying the operators to perform that particular aspect of their task. Moreover, as our example clearly demonstrates, the point of the organizational speech act is essentially instrumental and therefore strategic. On the prevailing understanding of corporate legitimacy, the avowed point of the operator's polite refrain must not be the expression of gratitude, but rather the business purpose of trying to secure customers' continued patronage of the firm.

Finally, observe that the norm of sincerity does not belong in this language game. Professor John Searle, a leading speech act theorist, supports the claim that the requirement of sincerity is a condition for the successful performance of a speech act by observing that "it is linguistically unacceptable (though not self-contradictory) to conjoin the explicitly performative verb with the denial of the expressed psychological state."[11] One cannot well say, "Thank you, but I'm not really grateful." However in the operator's case, we can find an opposite and equally instructive oddity. It would be quite ludicrous for the overly zealous telephone operator to say "Thank you for using AT&T," and then add, "and I really mean it." The oddity would not be removed even if the particular operator happened in fact to experience a sense of gratitude, born of either misplaced identification with AT&T or a belief that his own livelihood is secured by the customer's patronage. The conclusion that the norm of sincerity does not apply in this context is both a product, and evidence, of an organizational setting marked by role distance and discourse that is essentially communicative—that is, to use Habermas' description, oriented toward success and strategic in nature.

I hope I have said enough to give at least a rough idea of how variations in role distance give rise to two kinds of social collectivity—community and organization—and, respectively, to two forms of discourse: truth-seeking, understanding-oriented *interpretation* and strategic, success-oriented *communication*. It is now time to place law in this framework.

3. Legal Roles and Legal Discourse

In this short space, we shall not be able to derive from the framework I have proposed all the answers concerning law that it potentially might yield; but we can get a head start by first using this framework to help us formulate some questions about law. The suggested framework permits us to pose in three different and, I think, mutually illuminating ways what is essentially the same question. Do the various legal actors perform their respective roles in a detached or nondetached fashion? Does law take place in the context of community or organization? Is legal discourse an exercise in interpretation or communication? The general answer to each of these questions (or more precisely to the three formulations of the one question) seems to me to be plainly, both. If, however, I were pressed to choose, I believe that the concepts of role distance, organization, and communication are more central to law than the opposing terms. Here are some considerations that support, as well as clarify, this hypothesis.

Lawyers

Much of contemporary jurisprudence, notably Dworkin's, revolves around adjudication. Thus, the courtroom will be a natural place for us to begin the legal part of our journey. But whereas Dworkin and others preoccupy themselves with the role of a judge, I propose a provisional shift of focus: to direct our spotlight first on the lawyers. Although the judge has the final word in the courtroom, it is the lawyers who do most of the talking. As we investigate legal discourse, the lawyers deserve more of our attention: How are we to characterize and understand their role and their discourse?

We can get a clue by recalling the problem we just raised when we put the AT&T operator's thanks to the test of sincerity. Analogously, try to imagine a lawyer presenting a compelling legal argument, only to be greeted at the end of his speech with the judicial question: "Very persuasive, but do you really believe what you've just said?" A judge probing into the lawyer's sincerity would be breaching some of the fundamental rules of the game. The point here, as in the operator's case, is not that the one protagonist or the other—the operator or the lawyer—might lack the psychological state that his or her speech act ostensibly expresses. This fact, in itself, would be utterly inconsequential. The point is that in both situations the norm of sincerity does not at all apply. This conclusion accounts for the indisputable oddity, in both cases, of inquiring about or affirming the psychological state that other speakers, using the same language under different circumstances, would be expected to possess. This is not to say, of course, that the lawyer can get away in court with absolutely any argument; there are limits to what the lawyer is allowed to say, limits that shape and restrict his or her speech. But sincerity has nothing to do with these limits. The condition of adequacy of a lawyer's speech act is not a pure heart, but only a straight face.

Lawyers routinely say, and indeed are expected to say, things they are not supposed to believe. Are they therefore irredeemable liars or dissemblers? Perhaps so. But their ultimate salvation, if there is to be any, lies in role distance. When arguing before a court, the lawyer typically performs a highly detached role. As with the telephone operator, the lawyer's role involves a script (or rather, in this case, a range of scripts), which the lawyer is motivated to utter simply by being paid to do so. We must further investigate the shape and the point of this arrangement. But we can already observe that it is only a picture such as this that can take lawyers off the moral hook and preserve their rectitude by maintaining a space—visible and generally recognized—between their person and their role, and thus between their beliefs and their utterances.[12]

What is the point of a role that systematically engages its holders in the performance of insincere speech acts? There is a conventional answer to this query: we should not consider a single lawyer's speech in isolation, but rather we should view it as part of a process. And the process, unlike its component parts viewed separately, *is* designed to attain legal truth. By pitting one-sided lawyers against each other, the process assures that each side of the coin is presented meticulously for the judge to inspect and make the right decision.

The premise that underlies this conventional account—that legal truth will best emerge out of the opposition between two deliberate efforts to distort it—raises, of course, many difficult problems.[13] But I shall not challenge this premise here. Instead, I want to suggest that even if we grant its validity, grounds remain for dissatisfaction with the account of litigation that rests on it. First, this account assigns to the lawyer a function that is best understood as a "latent function": one that ought to be hidden from the lawyer himself. On the premise we granted, truth is best served when each lawyer acts *as if* he or she were devoted to his or her client's cause. But if the lawyer took seriously the notion that all this is done only in the service of his real function—to attain the truth—he might be tempted, consciously or unconsciously, to cheat against his assigned role by himself glimpsing the truth and smuggling it into his presentation, thereby undermining the process that his one-sidedness is supposed to serve. The acceptance of the proposed account of a lawyer's role by the lawyers themselves accordingly would be self-defeating. Evidence abounds that lawyers, in fact, do not construe their role in light of the conventional account. Which lawyer, for example, would ever celebrate his or her latest defeat in court by toasting the victory of truth?

The second inadequacy of the proposed account is that it explains only some, but not all, of the prominent features of lawyers' discourse. Even if presenting one-sided *arguments* can be thought plausibly to promote truth, it is much more difficult to maintain such optimism with regard to other aspects of the lawyer's performance. I have in mind practices such as *courtroom tactics* or *litigation strategies*. These terms do not, after all, describe some devious practices of shady lawyering; they are part and parcel of the prevailing conception of a lawyer's role, and they can feature unabashedly in any law school's curriculum.

We need an account of the lawyer's role that encompasses these additional features and serves, without self-destruction, the lawyers themselves in the construal of their task. Such an account is, of course, readily available. It is simply that the lawyer's role is designed to help his or her client win a lawsuit. Insofar as litigation is concerned, this is the lawyer's primary function; occasional lame references to the lawyer as an "officer of the court" can neither mask nor change this overwhelming reality.[14] We must dwell longer on this characterization of the lawyer's role, but we can first draw out its implications for the kind of discourse in which lawyers engage. Their discourse is a paradigmatic case of strategic, success-oriented communication. It is geared toward the attainment of a preconceived goal—a favorable outcome for one's client. In speaking, the lawyer is acutely aware of the identity of his or her audience—the judge or the jury. The latter's disposition and attitude, inasmuch as he can ascertain them, strategically guide both the style and the content of the lawyer's speech.[15]

The account of lawyering that I have just outlined is so obvious that we may fail to be puzzled by it, but it is important for my argument that we are. However, our perceptions and beliefs in this area are sufficiently mixed that it should not be difficult, I hope, to provoke the requisite puzzlement. Think of it this way: Here is the judge heroically laboring at the altar of truth, while being constantly diverted by two characters who view it as their legitimate purpose to deflect her, each one trying to sway the judge in his preferred direction. The same incongruity can be stated in different terms. The judge, Professor Dworkin tells us, engages in an Herculean effort at *interpretation*. She is trying to divine the right answer to the legal problem by (ideally) constructing a comprehensive theory of law that would best fit the extant legal materials and present them in the most attractive moral light. But the other discussants, from whom she seeks assistance and illumination, instead of joining the interpretive effort, overtly adopt a communicative mode and, by using various discursive tactics and strategies, try to extract a favorable result from the judge.

This dissonant mixture of discursive styles is no doubt puzzling, but we can start toward a solution by observing how far removed the circumstances of a trial are from conditions that, according to Habermas, ought to characterize truly interpretive discourse. The participants in the latter enterprise each have an equal claim to interpretive truth. They are motivated to reach common understanding, and their mutual accommodation is free from coercion. But this picture is a poor model for the trial in which, at the end of the day, the judge's interpretive conclusion will prevail, even in the face of lingering disagreement, as a result of the superiority not of reason but of brute force. Faced with the prospect of an unwelcome (and perhaps unwarranted) interpretation forced on them by the judge, the litigants' response is not surprising. They resort to an expert in strategic communication—a lawyer—to make right the discursive imbalance and to reduce the likelihood that coercive measures will be visited upon them.

So far, we have answered two of the three questions posed with regard to the lawyer's role: we have characterized it as a *detached* role and the lawyer's speech as a species of *communication*. The remaining task is to identify and characterize the collectivity within which the lawyer's role is defined and in relationship to which this role is enacted.

The answer is evident: The lawyer's role is defined by and is a constituent of the municipal legal system and, as such, this role belongs, as does the legal system itself, to the state. We should not be misled by the fact that a lawyer typically is not an employee of the state and is not, in this sense, a public official. Nothing of importance for our purposes hangs on this formality, as is evidenced by the fact that nothing in our understanding of the lawyer's role changes on those occasions—think of the prosecutor or the public defender—in which the lawyer is a state employee. Whether on the government's payroll or not, the lawyer is, if you like, an official of the legal system (which is not to say that he acts as an officer of the *court*), and, in this important sense, his role belongs to the collectivity whose legal systems it is, namely to the state. The point is worth stressing because it provides a crucial link to the following conclusion. Seen from the perspective of the lawyer's role, the state is, in my proposed definition, an *organization,* that is, a union of detached roles. The relationships that it defines among its members (I am still talking only about lawyers in court) are *external* relationships, mediated but also separated by the visible gaps between the selves involved, between people in their "personal" capacity, on the one hand, and the clusters of tasks, duties, and expectations (discursive or otherwise) that make up those people's detached roles, on the other. It is in its capacity as an organization that we can best understand the state cultivating a breed of speakers who are exempt from the norm of sincerity and one of whose tasks consists in the use of communicative strategies to defend individuals against the state's own coercive power.

A further question that naturally arises—Why *should* the state uphold such an arrangement?—would take us further afield into political theory than we can here venture. I only want to remove the air of paradox from what appears as a self-defeating interpretation of the lawyer's role from the state's perspective. In principle, there is nothing paradoxical about observing different roles in an organization working at what look like cross-purposes. This might mean only that the organization's purpose is more complex than we initially thought, or that the organization does indeed serve conflicting purposes, such that the interactions among conflicting roles are the way the organization reaches a compromise or an accommodation.

We have been dealing so far exclusively with the lawyer's role, and it was only in regard to this role that we considered the state as an organization. But we now can expand our vision, and observe the state in a more cinemascopic fashion, unrestricted by any particular role that it assigns. In terms of our twofold classification, what sort of entity is it? The case for classifying the state as an organization is overwhelming.[16] We cannot fully examine this case here, but it will suffice if I mention two prominent features of the state that strongly argue in favor of this classification: bureaucracy and coercion. We often think of the state as a vast bureaucracy or, perhaps more accurately, as a conglomerate of bureaucracies—all impersonal, goal-oriented, self-perpetuating organizations. As I have said before, such entities inspire distance, and we tend to experience our interactions with them, in whatever role or capacity, as remote and external. The state is also the quintessential coercive collectivity. It often addresses us by means of threats, backed by the most brutal force. Reliance on such external motivation for compliance with the state's demands both fosters and reflects distance. It is at once a recognition and a consolidation of the fact that one's actual continued assent is not required or expected as a condition of one's playing a role in a collective enterprise. When we contemplate the state under both of these aspects—bureaucracy and coercion—we think of an organization, of a collectivity whose claims are external to us and from whose clutches we flee by maintaining a distance between our engagements with it, on the one hand, and our true selves, on the other.[17]

These aspects are, of course, not the only aspects under which the state can be contemplated. The state is not *just* bureaucracy and coercion. To be an American, for example, is not only to stand in a certain relationship to the American government and to be subject to its coercive threats. It also means to share important bonds of language, culture, history, and morality with a vast number of other people. *American* is accordingly a summary reference to a composite role or perhaps even more accurately, a cluster of roles, many of which are nondetached, inextricable constituents of an American's innermost identity. The state is therefore also the social union of these nondetached roles and, to that extent, a community.

But the organizational aspects of the state cannot be ignored. These aspects of the state are especially relevant in connection to law. Law characteristically provides the context or the medium within which we encounter the state as government, that is to say, in its bureaucratic and coercive capacities.[18]

Judges

With these observations we can now move to what will be the last stage of our inquiry: a consideration of the judicial role. We shall again proceed in terms of the three questions we posed before, trying to characterize in terms of our dichotomies the kind of role, discourse, and collectivity that pertain to judging.

I have just summarized a case for the communal conception of the state, and it is along these lines that Dworkin's theory of adjudication, and of law, gains whatever plausibility it has. The judge is rooted in a common culture and a shared morality and is the exponent of an evolving tradition. She is, in Professor Owen Fiss' idiom,[19] the articulator of our (that is, the community's) public values. She engages in what is a quintessentially interpretive venture, of which Dworkin's analysis is as good as we have ever had: the judge tries to express in her decision the best vision of the community's tradition that she can divine. In doing so, there is no space, as Professor Stanley Fish is right to insist,[20] between the judge's personal and judicial views on the matter. There is no space, because her judicial views *are* her personal views, just as being a judge is being simply who she is at the relevant time and with regard to the relevant issues. Seen in this light, the judge's interpretive utterances are marked by sincerity: they convey her genuine vision, conditioned but not separated by her role, of the proper disposition of the case, supported by what she takes to be the best arguments and the right principles.

This is an ennobling, almost beatific, picture of the judicial role, and it is valid as far as it goes. But it does not go very far. It starts to come apart as soon as the judge looks down from these interpretive heights at the litigants and recalls the bearing that the conclusions she reaches will have on them. The judge must then realize that in the litigants' ears, her interpretive pronouncements are liable to be converted into hard-edged communication, as they come down not just clothed in the state's authority, but also backed by its superior physical force. That is an essential part of the legal context—the acceptance of the judge's decision by the litigants is not conditional upon their reaching an agreement on the merits of her position, an agreement discursively worked out through the free flow of unconstrained, truth-oriented speech. On the contrary, the parties' assent is ultimately secured through brute force. We have already observed the implications of this all-important fact for the lawyer's role. But this fact is significant in shaping the judge's role as well. Even if the judge sets out to perform a feat of Dworkinian interpretation in the context of community, she then must convey her interpretive conclusions to the litigants. And in doing so, she must shift, as we have just observed, into an altogether different discursive mode. The judge presents the litigants with a nondebatable proposition; the ultimate purpose of the judge's utterances is to secure compliance, not to generate agreement; and her speech act is accompanied by a threat of force. In short, we have here the makings of strategic communication that stands in sharp contrast to the interpretive soliloquy in which the judge may have engaged before.

We have now come up with a composite, two-stage depiction of judicial discourse. First, the judge engages in Dworkinian interpretation in which, as you remember, she is instructed to scan all relevant legal texts and construct a theory that fits them best, while presenting them in the most attractive moral light. Having reached in this way a conclusion that she believes to be right, the judge then faces the additional task of writing an opinion—that is, addressing the parties in a way designed to secure their compliance with the results of the interpretive exploration.

But a moment's reflection will reveal that this two-stage process, with its promise of peaceful coexistence between interpretation and communication in the judicial role, is highly problematic. It faces an obvious difficulty: If the actual judicial pronouncements—the judicial opinions—are crafted strategically, with an eye to communicative exigencies, then it makes no sense to take these same opinions at face value as the texts that ought to guide and to ground the interpretive efforts during the first stage. Once we allow communicative concerns to enter into judicial speech, we cannot maintain the interpretive stage intact. When legal material becomes infected with strategic, success-oriented considerations, it no longer can plausibly be held up as the repository of the community's accumulated wisdom and ideals. The text was designed with a motive ulterior to that of discovering the truth and conveying it so as to promote understanding and foster agreement. Now as a truth-seeking interpreter, I must somehow see through the rhetorical devices and the strategic intentions. Using the judicial text as rendered as the object of my interpretation is bound to lead me astray.

I have focused so far on the relation in which the judge stands to the parties, but the communicative exigencies of his role do not stop here. In articulating our public values, to use again Fiss' phrase, judges do not view themselves, nor are they viewed by others, as contributing to the public's enlightenment along lines essentially similar to, say, moral philosophers or legal scholars. The judge's proffered articulations do not engage in discursive competition with the other sources, and his claim to interpretive superiority is not put to the test of general assent. A judicial pronouncement is presented as unconditionally valid; it must be followed whether or not we concede its truth or accept its authority. In either case, it is backed up by the state's force, ready to descend on those who resist the judicial interpretation and would opt for a different articulation.

The fact that the state's power underwrites the judge's pronouncements reveals their true discursive point. Judicial utterances are supposed to secure certain forms of conduct, not only to highlight or recommend their desirability. These utterances are therefore success- rather than truth-oriented; they are communicative rather than interpretive. And, given the coercive background against which judicial speech is uttered, the more successful it is in inducing compliance, the less need there may be to resort to the coercive measures that back it up.

The judge's communicative task is not a simple one, and we cannot hope to do justice to its complexities in the present essay. Let me just mention very briefly two of the difficulties with which judicial communication must cope: the multiplicity of audiences, and the variability of contexts. In the case of interpretive discourse, these issues do not arise. As I said earlier, interpretive activity can be understood in essentially monological terms: no special attention need be paid to the audience and the context. The speaker shares a common context with the hearer and tacitly assumes the hearer to have the same linguistic and cognitive dispositions as his own. Thus, context and audience recede into the background and are taken for granted. By contrast, the judge can take neither audience nor context for granted. First, to make her pronouncement stick, the judge must consider the possibility that she addresses a multiplicity of audiences, whose responses to a given utterance might vary considerably. I have no space to explore this issue any further here; all I can do is drop a footnote to Professor Sadurski's helpful illustrations of what he calls the "strategy of reassurance" in which the Supreme Court engages when it affirms in general terms a dominant moral view while actually deciding the case in accordance with a more controversial moral position.[21] The Court here is playing to different audiences, and its rhetoric involves a difficult balancing act that tries to respond to their contrasting dispositions and expectations.

Variability of context is a problem that results primarily from the temporal dimension of judicial opinions. The judge projects her vision into an indefinite future and thus must intend it to exert its force under changing circumstances. If her vision is to command compliance in the long run, the judge must be sensitive to the contextual shifts under which her opinion will necessarily operate. Again here I can do no more than give an illustrative reference, this time to Professor Blasi's view of First Amendment doctrine—as designed with times of political emergency in the judge's mind[22]—and to the illuminating exchange between Blasi and Professor Christie about the role of strategic considerations of this kind in judicial opinions.[23]

Characterizing judicial speech as communicative provides the answer to one of the three questions concerning the judicial role that we have posed. Let me now turn to a brief consideration of the other two. The judge's utterances, I have observed, are presented to us as nonoptional, nonnegotiable propositions; from the outset they are assured victory in the competition for legal truth. But why do judges claim infallibility, which they do not in fact possess and which is backed by force they do not fully control? The only satisfactory answer I can see is that they do not. Or, perhaps more cautiously, that they ought not. So if some do, they suffer from a massive case of bad faith. As with the lawyer's escape from the charge of dissembling, the judge's defense from what otherwise would be spectacular hubris lies also in role distance. An implicit claim to infallibility is written into the judicial role, but it does not attach to the judge qua person. In other words, we—this includes judges as well—must at all times be aware of the difference between the judge in his or her personal and official capacities. The rather sharp line between the two can be erased and the distance between them eliminated, only at the cost of the judge ascribing to him- or herself awesome, and rather grotesque, omnipotence and omniscience.

Insofar as the judge's is a distant role, to that extent his is also an organizational rather than a communal function. This conclusion is not surprising. It is eminently consistent with the bureaucratic and coercive aspects of the state that are inextricably connected with the judicial role. It is an avowed purpose of this social structure to secure order and promote cooperation, if need be by force, in the face of recalcitrance, moral diversity, and disagreement. This is an agenda far removed from the spirit of community and fraternity that underlies and motivates Dworkin's theory of law. And it is in relation to this agenda that the judicial role must be understood.[24]

Conclusion

I cannot examine here other legal role players, most importantly citizens in their capacity as litigants and in other capacities, and I shall end with the two following observations. First, by describing judging, as well as lawyering, in terms of role distance, strategic communication, and organization, I do not mean to deny that important aspects of these roles are better understood in the vocabulary of identification, interpretation, and community. As I said at the outset, I take interaction between both polarities to provide a key to a proper understanding of law. So my stressing the pole that I did is mostly reactive, to right an imbalance in present-day jurisprudence that Dworkin's theory mainly creates. My second and related observation is this. The terms I used to characterize one pole—identification, community, and interpretation—are likely to sound to many ears as friendly terms, whereas the other three—distance, organization, and strategic communication—will sound as hostile ones. The tone with which I have used these terms may indeed have contributed to this impression. I therefore should clarify that I do not intend to endorse the former pole and condemn the latter one. To be sure, there is a great temptation to envision utopias conceived exclusively in terms of the friendly categories.[25] But short of utopia, we must contend with both poles. There is need and value in distance as well as identification, organization as well as community, communication as well as interpretation, although of course there is room for much disagreement concerning the desirable proportions between the two sets in our imperfect, nonutopian world. My main point is a much more limited one, and it is independent of our attitude to the two contrasting poles of social life. It can be put, somewhat tendentiously, this way: we should be wary of a fable that likens the operation of the judicial system to an exercise in the composition of a chain novel,[26] and of a legal theory that considers literary criticism as an adequate model for the legal enterprise. It is quite a strange novel that has the execution of some of its intended readers as its denouement. This prospect, while no doubt concentrating the readers' minds, may put a strain on their interpretive skills that is quite unfamiliar in literary circles.

Notes

1. See Erving Goffman, "Role Distance," in *Encounters: Two Studies in the Sociology of Interaction* (Indianapolis: Bobbs-Merrill, 1961), 83.

2. See Ferdinand Tönnies, *Community and Society,* trans. and ed. C. P. Loomis (East Lansing: Michigan State University Press, 1957).

3. This expression is borrowed from Jean-Paul Sartre, *Being and Nothingness,* trans. Hazel E. Barnes (New York: Simon and Schuster, 1966), 86.

4. Ronald M. Dworkin, *Law's Empire* (Cambridge: Harvard University Press, 1986).

5. See Ronald M. Dworkin, "Law as Interpretation," in *The Politics of Interpretation,* ed. W. J. T. Mitchell (Chicago: University of Chicago Press, 1983), 287.

6. See Jürgen Habermas, *Communication and the Evolution of Society*, trans. Thomas McCarthy (Boston: Beacon Press, 1979), chap. 1, and *The Theory of Communicative Action*, trans. Thomas McCarthy (Boston: Beacon Press, 1981), chap. 3.

7. See Ronald M. Dworkin, *Taking Rights Seriously* (Cambridge: Harvard University Press, 1977), chap. 4; Dworkin, *Law's Empire*.

8. Compare Frank I. Michelman, "The Supreme Court, 1985 Term—Foreword: Traces of Self-Government," *Harvard Law Review* 100 (1986): 4, at 73: "The judge, as Dworkin envisions him, represents ... by his own practical reason our missing dialogue."

9. The case with Habermas is more complicated. His advocacy of and contribution to a "formal-pragmatic" approach to a theory of meaning is presented by him in part as a reaction against the monological conception characteristic of "formal semantics." He draws in this context on the "intuitively accessible distinction between thinking in propositions in abstraction from speaker-hearer relations and imagining interpersonal relations." *Theory of Communicative Action*, 440–41. However the dialogical component that Habermas deems essential for the understanding of communicative action is on his view consistent with and is satisfied by the *imaginative* assumption by the solitary thinker of "the roles of proponent and opponent as a communicative relation in his thought." Ibid. This description comports with my characterization in the text of the essentially monological nature of interpretation. But the issue (regarding Habermas' position) is difficult, and I cannot do it full justice here.

10. Dworkin, *Law's Empire*, 46–49.

11. John R. Searle, *Expression and Meaning* (New York: Cambridge University Press, 1979), 4–5.

12. My view of the lawyer's role is accordingly antithetical to the one suggested by Professor Charles Fried in "The Lawyer as Friend: The Moral Foundations of the Lawyer-Client Relation," *Yale Law Journal* 85 (1976): 1060 (arguing that an attorney is a legal friend who makes his client's interests his own insofar as necessary to preserve the client's autonomy within the law). I side instead with Fried's critics, according to whom, "Most lawyers are free-lance bureaucrats." Edward A. Dauer and Arthur A. Leff, "The Lawyer as Friend," *Yale Law Journal* 86 (1977): 573, at 581.

13. Such problems are discussed, for example, in Jerome Frank, *Courts on Trial: Myth and Reality in American Justice* (Princeton: Princeton University Press, 1949), chap. 6.

14. Compare Mirjan R. Damaska, *The Faces of Justice and State Authority: A Comparative Approach to the Legal Process* (New Haven: Yale University Press, 1986), 143: "The invocation of counsel as officer of the court is designed to constrain the excessive amalgamation of the lawyer's interest with that of his client and to forestall the transformation of privately managed litigation into a melee of self-seeking."

15. This characterization of lawyers' speech should be distinguished from a related one proposed by Joseph Raz. The latter is based on his distinction between *committed* and *detached* normative statements. Committed statements are made by those who accept the validity of a normative system. Detached statements do not imply such acceptance: the speaker makes them from the point of view of someone who accepts the system's validity, without being himself so committed. According to Professor Raz, the lawyer advising her client is a good example of such detached, noncommitted speech. But notice that detached speech can still be sincere: in the usual case, the lawyer would be expected to convey to her client her sincere view of the legal situation (whether or not she also *accepts* it as sound or authoritative). By contrast, the strategic communication that I ascribe to the lawyer in court is "detached" in a stronger sense, in that it is exempt from the norm of sincerity altogether. See Joseph Raz, *Practical Reason and Norms* (London: Hutchinson, 1975), 170–77, and *The Authority of Law: Essays on Law and Morality* (Oxford: Clarendon Press, 1979), 153–77. As Raz points out, the distinction is present, albeit in a less crystallized form, in Kelsen's writings. The description of Raz's distinction in the language of *committed* versus *detached* statements is introduced in H. L. A. Hart, "Legal Duty and Obligation," in *Essays on Bentham: Studies in Jurisprudence and Political Theory* (Oxford: Clarendon Press, 1982), 127, at 153–55.

16. For an exploration of some legal-theoretical implications of applying to the state an organizational perspective, see Meir Dan-Cohen, *Rights, Persons, and Organizations: A Legal Theory for Bureaucratic*

Society (Berkeley and Los Angeles: University of California Press, 1986), 163–98.

17. For a similar conception of the state and its relation to the self see Peter Gabel, "The Phenomenology of Rights-Consciousness and the Pact of the Withdrawn Selves," *Texas Law Review* 62 (1984): 1563, at 1563.

18. There is of course considerable literature warning against the fallacy and the danger of conceiving of the state in excessively communal terms. A well-known example is Robert Nisbet, *The Quest for Community* (New York: Oxford University Press, 1953).

19. See Owen M. Fiss, "The Supreme Court, 1978 Term—Foreword: The Forms of Justice," *Harvard Law Review* 93 (1979): 1.

20. Stanley Fish, "Still Wrong after All These Years," *Law and Philosophy* 6 (1987): 401, at 412.

21. Wojciech Sadurski, "It All Comes Out in the End: Judicial Rhetoric and the Strategy of Reassurance," *Oxford Journal of Legal Studies* 7 (1987): 258.

22. Vincent Blasi, "The Pathological Perspective and the First Amendment," *Columbia Law Review* 85 (1985): 449 (arguing that courts should interpret the First Amendment to provide maximum protection when intolerance of unorthodox ideas is prevalent and government is likely to stifle dissent).

23. George C. Christie, "Why the First Amendment Should Not Be Interpreted from the Pathological Perspective: A Response to Professor Blasi," *Duke Law Journal* 1986:683 (advocating that judges should consider legal argument, rather than a theory of societal good, in deciding cases); Vincent Blasi, "The Role of Strategic Reasoning in Constitutional Interpretation: In Defense of the Pathological Perspective," *Duke Law Journal* 1986:696 (advocating the use of strategic reasoning to safeguard "core" constitutional commitments in First Amendment cases).

24. For a compelling expression of a vision of law and of the judicial role that accentuates their coerciveness see Robert M. Cover, "The Supreme Court, 1982—Foreword: Nomos and Narrative," *Harvard Law Review* 97 (1983): 4, and "Violence and the Word," *Yale Law Journal* 95 (1986): 1601.

25. Such a temptation is one of the themes in Peter Gabel and Duncan Kennedy, "Roll Over, Beethoven," *Stanford Law Review* 36 (1984): 1.

26. See Dworkin, *Law's Empire*, 228–38.

CHAPTER TWO

DECISION RULES AND CONDUCT RULES: ON ACOUSTIC SEPARATION IN CRIMINAL LAW

It is an old but neglected idea that a distinction can be drawn in the law between rules addressed to the general public and rules addressed to officials. The neglect of this idea results, I think, from a widely accepted but oversimplified conception of the relationship between the two kinds of rules. This common view tends to understate both the analytical soundness and the jurisprudential significance of the distinction. In what follows, I criticize the prevailing view and offer another one in its place. The proposed account takes seriously the distinction between the two kinds of rules and is intended to help us appreciate and investigate their relative independence and the complexity of their interrelations. This account also provides guidelines for apportioning rules of law between the two categories and demonstrates the ability of such a classification to illuminate some problem areas in the law.

Although the distinction between the two types of rules is of quite general validity, I limit both my claims and my illustrations to the criminal law. My immediate purpose is to use the distinction to shed light upon a number of difficult issues and perplexing decisions in this area. If I succeed in doing so, my exercise will also have demonstrated the utility of the distinction and suggested its possible usefulness in other fields. The latter outcome, however, will have been an incidental benefit rather than the direct purpose of this study.

1. The Separation between Decision Rules and Conduct Rules

The Prevailing Conception—a Critique

The distinction between the two types of legal rules that I have in mind can be traced in modern times back to Bentham. As Bentham observed:

> A law confining itself to the creation of an offence, and a law com-
> manding a punishment to be administered in case of the commis-
> sion of such an offence, are two distinct laws; not parts (as they
> seem to have been generally accounted hitherto) of one and the
> same law. The acts they command are altogether different; the
> persons they are addressed to are altogether different. Instance, *Let
> no man steal;* and, *Let the judge cause whoever is convicted of
> stealing to be hanged.*[1]

Yet the relation between the two sets of laws is, according to Bentham, a close one. Bentham argued that

> though a simply imperative law, and the punitory law attached to
> it, are so far distinct laws, that the former contains nothing of the
> latter, and the latter, in its direct tenor, contains nothing of the
> former; yet by *implication,* and that a necessary one, the punitory
> does involve and include the import of the simply imperative law
> to which it is appended. To say to the judge, *Cause to be hanged
> whoever in due form of law is convicted of stealing,* is, though not
> a direct, yet as intelligible a way of intimating to men in general
> that they must not steal, as to say to them directly, *Do not steal:*
> and one sees, how much more likely to be efficacious.[2]

The distinction Bentham drew between the two types of rules appears to be sound and, at least with respect to some laws, intuitively obvious. Bentham's account of the distinction, however, supposes too simple a relation between the two kinds of rules. If we are to generalize from Bentham's example, we must conclude that the laws addressed to officials (which I shall call *decision rules*) necessarily imply the laws addressed to the general public (which I shall call *conduct rules*). The view that decision rules *imply* conduct rules naturally leads to the widely accepted conclusion that a single set of rules is in principle sufficient to fulfill both the function of guiding official decisions and that of guiding the public's behavior. Such a reductionist position can assume either of two forms. One view deems the law to consist primarily of decision rules and rele-gates conduct rules to the status of mere implications. A second view, the converse of the first, focuses on conduct rules that are "applied" or "enforced" by the courts.

Hans Kelsen was a noted proponent of the first version; he attempted, rather counterintuitively, to collapse the distinction between decision and conduct rules by treating all laws only as directives to officials. Citing as an example the provision, "One shall not steal; if somebody steals, he shall be punished," Kelsen stated:

> If it is assumed that the first norm which forbids theft is valid only if the second norm attaches a sanction to theft, then the first norm is certainly superfluous in an exact exposition of law. If at all existent, the first norm is contained in the second, which is the only genuine legal norm.[3]

This position has been effectively criticized by H. L. A. Hart, who argued that it obscures "the specific character of law as a means of social control": by eliminating the independent function that the substantive rules of the criminal law have in guiding behavior, Kelsen's view fails to account for the difference between a fine and a tax. The difference, Hart pointed out, lies precisely in the fact "that the first involves, as the second does not, an offence or breach of duty in the form of a violation of a rule set up to guide the conduct of ordinary citizens."[4]

The opposite reductionist view—which focuses on conduct rules and portrays the role of courts (and other officials) as one of "applying" or "enforcing" those rules[5]—is equally untenable. Norms are commonly understood to be both actor-specific and act-specific. A norm addresses itself to certain subjects or groups of subjects and guides them with respect to a certain type of action.[6] For example, the law against theft, seen as a conduct rule, has the general public as its norm-subject and the (forbidden) act of stealing as its norm-act. Thus, when we loosely say that the judge, in imposing punishment on the thief, "applies" the rule forbidding stealing, we must realize that the judge is not guided or bound by that rule: he is not, in his capacity as judge, one of the rule's norm-subjects, nor does his act (that of imposing punishment) correspond to the norm-act (not stealing) that is specified by the rule. As long as our normative arsenal contains only conduct rules, we must deem the judge to be normatively unguided or uncontrolled in the act of passing judgment.[7] We can successfully account for the normative constraints that the law imposes on judicial decision-making only if we impute to the legal system an additional relevant norm whose norm-subject is the judge and whose norm-act is the act of judging or imposing punishment.

Once we introduce such separate norms into our description of the legal system, we can give a more precise and satisfactory account of the normative situation involved in the preceding example. When we say that the judge "applies" (or "enforces") the law of theft, we mean that he is guided by a decision rule that has among its conditions of application (1) the existence of a certain conduct rule (in our example, the rule against stealing), and (2) the violation of that conduct rule by the defendant.[8]

The inclusion of decision rules and conduct rules in the description of law draws attention to the potential independence of these two sets of rules and opens up for investigation the nature of their relationship. That relationship may, of course, accord with the one in the preceding paragraph's example: judges can indeed be guided exclusively by a decision rule that tells them to "apply" the conduct rules of the system in the sense I have described. But such a relationship, though possible, is not a necessary one, and it should not be taken for granted. Instead, the insistence on the conceptual separation of conduct rules and decision rules compels an explicit examination of the various normative considerations that should guide judicial and other official decision-making—an examination that allows for the possibility of decision rules that do not mandate the application of conduct rules.

In this way, the distinction between conduct rules and decision rules exposes an important ambiguity in the seemingly obvious proposition that the role of judges and other officials is to apply the law. The language of "law application" obscures the complexity that inheres in the operation of two different norms in each case of "application." That judges and other officials must (from a legal point of view) follow the law in rendering their decisions remains a truism, provided we understand the proposition to refer to the decision rules that are addressed to judges and are binding on them. The judges' task with regard to conduct rules is not, however, similarly obvious. The proper relationship between decision rules and their corresponding conduct rules is not a logical or analytical matter.[9] Rather, it is a normative issue that must be decided in accordance with the relevant policies and values.

The distinction between conduct rules and decision rules cannot, accordingly, be abolished without loss. We therefore need an account of the two kinds of rules that preserves the distinction between them and that depicts their interrelationship more accurately than does the prevailing view. I now propose such an alternative account.[10]

The Model of Acoustic Separation

The distinction between conduct rules and decision rules can best be understood through a simple thought experiment. Imagine a universe consisting of two groups of people—the general public and officials. The general public engages in various kinds of conduct, while officials make decisions with respect to members of the general public. Imagine further that each of the two groups occupies a different, acoustically sealed chamber. This condition I shall call *acoustic separation*. Now think of the law as a set of normative messages directed to both groups. In such a universe, the law necessarily contains two sets of messages. One set is directed at the general public and provides guidelines for conduct. These guidelines are what I have called conduct rules. The other set of messages is directed at the officials and provides guidelines for their decisions. These are decision rules.[11]

The specific conduct rules that such a system would maintain would depend upon what conduct lawmakers deemed desirable—desirable, that is, in terms of the policies underlying the legal system. Similarly, the content of the decision rules of the system would be determined by the kinds of decisions that were deemed desirable in this sense.

The categories of conduct rules and decision rules, as defined in our imaginary universe, will help us to analyze real legal systems as well. In the real world, too, we may speak of messages that convey normative information regarding conduct to the general public, and we may distinguish such messages from ones aimed at guiding the decisions of officials.[12] A fundamental difference exists, however, between the imagined universe and the real world: the condition of acoustic separation, which obtained in the former by stipulation, seems to be absent from the latter. In the real world, the public and officialdom are not in fact locked into acoustically sealed chambers, and consequently each group may "hear" the normative messages the law transmits to the other group.

This lack of acoustic separation has three obvious ramifications for the relationship between the two sets of rules. First, conduct rules and decision rules may often come tightly packaged in undifferentiated mixed pairs. Such packaging would not, of course, be possible in the imagined universe; there the law would necessarily consist of two separate sets of rules, each transmitted to one or the other of the two constituent bodies. This pattern of separation would prevail in the imaginary universe even if the rules in the two sets were identical in content. But such radical separation is unnecessary in the real world. As Bentham pointed out, a single statutory provision may simultaneously guide both conduct and decision and may thus function as both a conduct rule and a decision rule. A criminal statute, to use Bentham's example, conveys to the public a normative message that certain behavior should be avoided, coupled with a warning of the sanction that will be applied to those who engage in the prohibited conduct. The same statutory provision also speaks to judges: it instructs them that, upon ascertaining that an individual has engaged in the forbidden conduct, they should visit upon him the specified sanction. The actual rules of a legal system are, accordingly, of three kinds. Any given rule may be a conduct rule, a decision rule, or both. The mere linguistic form in which a legal rule is cast does not determine the category to which it belongs. In order to classify a rule and discern the subject to whom its normative message is addressed, we must conceive of the rule in the imaginary universe characterized by acoustic separation, and then decide—in light of the policies underlying the legal system—whether the rule would in that universe be a directive to the general public, to officials, or to both.

The second difference between the real world and our imaginary universe is that, in the imaginary universe, acoustic separation ensures that conduct rules cannot, as such, affect decisions; similarly, decision rules cannot, as such, influence conduct. The two sets of rules are independent.[13] Not so in the real world. Here, officials are aware of the system's conduct rules and may take them into account in making decisions. By the same token, because individuals are familiar with the decision rules, they may well consider those rules in shaping their own conduct. We may say, therefore, that reality differs from the imagined world in that real-world decision rules are likely to have conduct side effects, just as real-world conduct rules are likely to have decisional side effects. To determine whether a given rule that affects conduct is merely a decision rule with a conduct side effect or instead an independent conduct rule, we can perform the same thought experiment that helped us to classify the rule in the first place: we can ask whether the rule would operate in the imagined universe as an independent conduct rule, deliberately and separately transmitted to the general public. The answer would again depend on the general policies and values that the legal system sought to promote. The same procedure would also enable us to discover whether the effects of a rule on decisions are mere side effects or are instead the products of an independent decision rule that is just conjoined with a conduct rule.

Third, the possibility that conduct or decision rules may have such unintended side effects creates the potential for conflict between decision rules and conduct rules in the absence of acoustic separation. A decision rule conflicts with a conduct rule if the decision rule conveys, as a side effect, a normative message that opposes or detracts from the power of the conduct rule. Conversely, a conduct rule conflicts with a decision rule when the messages it sends decision makers contradict the decision rule. Such conflicting messages are impossible under conditions of acoustic separation. Because officials and the public each receive only the messages specifically directed to them and meant to guide their respective activities, neither group is in danger of receiving conflicting messages addressed to the other.[14]

An example to clarify the foregoing remarks may at this point be overdue. For centuries criminal lawyers have been troubled by the question whether duress should operate as a defense to a criminal charge.

Some have maintained that, even when external pressures impel an individual toward crime, the law should by no means relax its demand that the individual make the socially correct choice. If anything, the opposite is the case: "[It] is at the moment when temptation to crime is strongest that the law should speak most clearly and emphatically to the contrary."[15] Proponents of the defense, by contrast, have emphasized the unfairness of punishing a person for succumbing to pressures to which even his judges might have yielded.[16] These conflicting arguments seem to impale the law on the horns of an inexorable dilemma. The law faces a hopeless trade-off between the competing values of deterrence and compassion (or fairness); whichever way it resolves the question of duress, it must sacrifice one value to the other.

The impasse dissolves, however, if we analyze the problem in terms of the distinction between conduct rules and decision rules and consider to which of the two categories the defense of duress properly belongs. To answer this question, we resort to our mental experiment: we locate duress in the imaginary world of acoustic separation. When we do so, it becomes obvious that the policies advanced by the defense would lead to its use as a decision rule—an instruction to the judge that defendants who under duress committed acts that would otherwise amount to offenses should not be punished. Just as obviously, no comparable rule would be included among the conduct rules of the system: knowledge of the existence of the defense of duress would not be permitted to shape individual conduct; conduct would be guided exclusively by the relevant criminal proscriptions.

Viewed as a decision rule only, duress does not present the imaginary legal system with the dilemma described above. Under conditions of acoustic separation, the values at stake in the debate over duress do not clash. Eliminating the defense from the conduct rules addressed to the public allows the system to reap the benefits of maximum obedience to the law. At the same time, preserving duress as a decision rule ensures fairness and allows decision makers to express compassion in imposing punishment. The ability of acoustic separation to resolve the dilemma to which duress gives rise in the real world allows us to diagnose that dilemma as a case of conflict between conduct rules (the norms defining criminal offenses) and a decision rule (the defense of duress). According to our analysis, such a conflict occurs because of the behavioral side effects that the decision rule of duress is likely to have in the absence of acoustic separation: it is likely to convey to people who know about it a normative message that points in the opposite direction from, and thus detracts from the force of, the proscriptions against various criminal offenses.

The example of duress demonstrates that, although the policies underlying an actual legal rule may require that the rule be only a decision rule or only a conduct rule, such a rule is likely in the real world to have both decisional and conduct effects and hence to defeat (at least in part) its underlying purposes. Perceived tensions in the law may in many cases be born of the law's inability to pursue the option, available in the imaginary universe characterized by acoustic separation, of having different decision and conduct rules.

I do not mean to deny that there are often good reasons for maintaining complete harmony between a conduct rule and its corresponding decision rule. One obvious reason for such harmony is that conduct rules often guide behavior by indicating the nature of future court decisions relative to that behavior. The expectations that such conduct rules raise may in most cases be reason enough for using a decision rule that accords with the conduct rule. But we should notice two things. First, harmony between decision rules and conduct rules, even when it obtains, is not a logical matter, but rather a normative one. Second, although the reasons for maintaining such harmony may well hold in many cases, they do not hold in all. For instance, the argument that fairness requires the fulfillment of well-founded expectations is often inapplicable in the criminal law. When decision rules are more lenient than the relevant conduct rules, as in our duress example, no one is likely to complain about the frustration of an expectation of punishment.[17]

Strategies of Selective Transmission

Acoustic separation has functioned thus far as an heuristic device for distinguishing conduct rules from decision rules and for diagnosing possible tensions in the law that are caused by policies best served when decision rules differ from conduct rules. I would like now to challenge the assumption that acoustic separation is an entirely imaginary construct and to suggest that it is not as alien to the real world as we have heretofore assumed.

Officials and the public are not in fact hermetically sealed off from each other, but neither are they completely intermingled. As soon as a society can be differentiated into a "public" and an "officialdom," it has probably reached a condition of partial acoustic separation. Partial acoustic separation obtains whenever certain normative messages are more likely to register with one of the two groups than with the other. Societies differ in their degree of acoustic separation. But just as it would be difficult to find a society displaying complete acoustic separation, it would be equally difficult to find one in which such separation were wholly absent. We are also likely to discover that, within any given society, the degree of acoustic separation varies with respect to different groups of the population and different issues.[18]

If this empirical hypothesis is correct, actual legal systems may exhibit, to a greater extent than one might otherwise have expected, some features of the legal system of our imaginary universe. More specifically, actual legal systems may in fact avail themselves of the benefits of acoustic separation by engaging in *selective transmission*—that is, the transmission of different normative messages to decision makers and to the general public.[19] Furthermore, because the acoustic separation that actually obtains in any given society is likely to be only partial, the law may attempt to segregate its messages by employing special measures to increase the probability that a certain normative message will reach only the constituency for which it is intended.[20] I shall refer to these techniques as *strategies of selective transmission*.[21]

The term strategies calls for an explanation. My use of the term should not be understood to connote deliberate, purposeful human action. Imputing to the law strategies of selective transmission does not, therefore, imply a conspiracy view of lawmaking in which legislators, judges, and other decision makers plot strategies for segregating their normative communications more effectively. Instead, strategies of selective transmission may be the kinds of strategies without a strategist that Michel Foucault describes in his analysis of power.[22] Such strategies take the form of social phenomena, patterns, and practices that look like (that is, are amenable to an illuminating interpretation as) tactics for promoting certain human interests or values; yet it may well be the case "that no one is there to have invented them, and few who can be said to have formulated them."[23] I am accordingly making no general claim regarding the level of self-consciousness or of intentionality at which lawmakers rely on acoustic separation and employ strategies of selective transmission. Nor shall I propose any causal explanation of the origins and evolution of acoustic separation or selective transmission.[24]

2. Application of the Model to Criminal Law

On the basis of the foregoing discussion, the following hypothesis may now be stated: we may expect the law to engage in selective transmission (1) under conditions of partial acoustic separation, and (2) in pursuit of policies that are best served by decision rules that differ from the corresponding conduct rules. In this part, I undertake to illustrate this hypothesis by examining several doctrines and opinions in criminal law. Such an exercise has a triple purpose—to support the hypothesis, to clarify and elaborate the concepts of acoustic separation and selective transmission, and to demonstrate the ability of these concepts to cast new light on some troubling issues and decisions in the criminal law. Before I turn to the specific applications of the model, however, I must doubly qualify their role: they are meant neither to prove nor to endorse the law's attempt to segregate its normative messages through acoustic separation.

With regard to the first qualification, the thesis of this article (like that of much other jurisprudential theorizing) is in part impervious to and in part incapable of empirical proof. The part that is impervious to empirical evidence is the analytical structure, which suggests, on the basis of the imaginary construct of an acoustically separated legal universe, the logical independence of decision rules and conduct rules and the *potential* utility of this independence. The other part of my thesis—that the law can be seen to exploit situations of partial acoustic separation and to resort to strategies of selective transmission—is incapable of empirical proof, because it claims not the status of a falsifiable causal theory, but only the more modest one of a plausible and occasionally illuminating *interpretation.*[25] Such an interpretation is illuminating insofar as it lends coherence to and makes sense of certain legal phenomena by placing them in a functionally rational pattern. The burden that the following illustrations must carry is not, therefore, the burden of proof. Rather, it is the lesser burden of demonstrating that the proffered interpretation is *sound:* that it is, in other words, illuminating in the cases to which it applies; and that it is *rewarding:* that it makes sense of a sufficient number of significant cases to justify the labors of elaborating and mastering a new analytical structure.

The second qualification regarding the role of the following applications is that the demonstration that certain legal practices, doctrines, and decisions may fruitfully be interpreted as instances of selective transmission is not meant to imply endorsement of such a strategy. Identifying such instances may serve as much to warn as to express approval and endorsement. In any event it is clear that, until we have revealed the possibility and potential uses of acoustic separation, we cannot reckon with them. For the time being, I wish to suspend any discussion of the desirability and legitimacy of the law's reliance on acoustic separation to segregate its normative messages; these issues are taken up in part 3.

Criminal Defenses

Necessity and Duress

The defense of necessity as a pure decision rule. The defense of duress, as we have already seen,[26] can be analyzed as a decision rule that would, in a world of acoustic separation, be conveyed only to officials; it would not be part of the conduct rules addressed to the general public. Unlike duress, which is commonly seen as a mere excuse, necessity is often thought of as a justification for otherwise criminal conduct: by violating a statute under circumstances of necessity, an actor is said to have chosen the lesser of two evils—he has done the right thing.[27] The law, it may be argued, should encourage rather than discourage such actions. It is possible, therefore, that in contrast with the defense of duress, the necessity norm would be included not only among the imaginary legal system's decision rules, but also among its conduct rules. But this would not necessarily be so. At least in some cases, the test of necessity should be the actor's willingness to face, as an alternative to the ill consequences of abiding by the law, the threat of criminal punishment unmitigated by the prospect of legal reprieve.

This test seems particularly pertinent when the source of the necessity is the actor's self-interest—when he breaks the law in order to avert an allegedly greater evil to himself. In such situations actors are prone, deliberately or in good faith, to exaggerate the danger to be averted and to underestimate the evil involved in disobeying the law. The prospect of a defense to a future criminal charge is likely to enhance the tendency to exaggerate the sense of necessity of protecting one's own interests. By contrast, the prospect of punishment (undiminished by the availability of a defense) can be seen here to place an objectively determined price tag on the option of violating the law. The willingness of the individual to pay the price of his transgression lends credence to the claim of necessity by helping to assure the judge that the evil averted by the transgression was compelling.

This reasoning suggests that the defense of necessity, when based on self-interest, may be allowed most confidently in situations in which the actor did not know of its availability at the time of his criminal conduct. Accordingly, necessity defenses arising out of situations of self-interest resemble the defense of duress in that they too should be governed by rules that in a world of acoustic separation would be conveyed solely to officials. The law's resistance to allowing or expanding the defense of necessity may thus be interpreted as reflecting concern with the undesirable behavioral side effects that a decision rule allowing such a defense would likely have in the real world.[28]

The conflicts between the conduct rules of the criminal law and a decision rule allowing the defense of duress or necessity need not, however, be as acute as I have indicated. Such conflicts may in fact be mitigated in the real world by partial acoustic separation, just as they would be eliminated in the imaginary world by complete acoustic separation. What I mean to suggest is simply that the arguments against recognizing duress, and those for constricting the scope of the necessity defense, may well exaggerate the extent to which the general public is likely to be familiar with the defenses and to be influenced by them in its conduct. The greater the degree of acoustic separation in a given society or area of conduct, the stronger is the case for allowing such defenses. These observations suggest a possible interpretation of two salient features of the defenses of duress and necessity—their notorious vagueness and their variable application.

Vagueness as a means of selective transmission. Courts and commentators have recognized the vague and open-ended quality of the defenses of duress and necessity.[29] Such vagueness makes a mockery of the standards of clarity and specificity that criminal statutes are generally required to meet.[30] Yet as Professors Mortimer and Sanford Kadish point out, "no court would conceivably hold a penal code unconstitutionally vague because it recognized a lesser-evil defense"[31]—nor, it may be confidently added, would any court strike down a penal code because it recognized a defense of duress.

Insofar as the characterization of these defenses as decision rules is sound, it suggests a simple explanation for judicial toleration of their vagueness. Far from being a defect, the failure of the rules to communicate to the public a clear and precise normative message is, in light of the policies underlying the defenses, a virtue. These policies do not require that the availability of the defenses be generally known; indeed, in many cases they require that the availability of the defenses *not* be known. In other words, vagueness can be interpreted as a strategy of selective transmission that helps approximate in the real world the conditions of acoustic separation that would obtain in the imaginary world.[32]

There are two ways in which the vagueness of standards such as those defining the defenses of necessity and duress can serve as a vehicle of selective transmission. First, the indeterminacy of the standards makes it less likely that ordinary citizens will be able to rely on them with any degree of confidence. Second, even if the standards were to attain a more definite meaning by spawning a body of decisional law, this law, because of its sheer volume and complexity, would probably elude the legally untutored citizen.[33] As long as the standard for a particular defense is sufficiently vague, and the body of decisions interpreting the standard sufficiently broad and varied, the danger that the defense will seriously modify individual behavior governed by the various conduct rules of the criminal law is reduced.[34]

Variable application. The second aspect of the defenses of necessity and duress for which we may now offer an explanation is their variable application. The preceding remarks would lead us to expect some correspondence between the willingness of a court to allow the defenses and the degree of acoustic separation that the court perceives to obtain in various situations: the higher the degree of acoustic separation, the more willing a court will probably be to adopt a decision rule allowing a defense. The factors that determine the degree of acoustic separation can be conveniently divided into two sets. In the first set are factors relating to the legal sophistication and other characteristics of the actors likely to engage in a given activity. The second set comprises factors concerning the circumstances under which the offense in question is normally committed. For example, the period of prolonged deliberation that commonly precedes certain offenses allows the actor to obtain through legal advice knowledge of relevant decision rules; low emotional involvement in the forbidden conduct increases the effectiveness of that knowledge in shaping behavior and further reduces acoustic separation.

The typical situation that gives rise to a defense of duress or necessity involves an actor of no special legal sophistication caught in circumstances of emergency, high pressure, and emotion. The likelihood that the actor is aware of the defense or able to act on such awareness is in these circumstances at its lowest. Allowing the defense under such conditions of high acoustic separation (enhanced, as we observed, by the defenses' vague formulation) creates little risk of undesirable behavioral side effects. In some cases that might give rise to the defenses, however, special circumstances or the special characteristics of the individuals involved indicate a lower degree of acoustic separation. The law can be seen to respond to such situations by disallowing or curtailing the defenses. Let me consider three examples.

First, cases involving prison escapes exhibit a low degree of acoustic separation because of the nature of the actors involved. In a series of cases, courts have been faced with prison escapes prompted by threats of homosexual rape or death directed at the escapees. Courts have for many years virtually refused to allow such threats to serve as a defense to the charge of escape.[35] In recent cases in which courts have recognized in principle a defense of necessity (or duress) to prison escape, they have nevertheless tended to place unusually restrictive conditions on the use of the defense.[36] The concerns underlying the courts' grudging attitude toward defenses to escape are vividly conveyed by the leading decision of *People v. Lovercamp:*[37] "However, before *Lovercamp* becomes a household word in prison circles and we are exposed to the spectacle of hordes of prisoners leaping over the walls screaming 'rape,' we hasten to add that the defense of necessity to an escape charge is extremely limited in its application."[38] The necessity defense in prison escape cases is narrowly circumscribed, it seems, because of the courts' belief that the relevant constituency—that of prison inmates—is highly attuned to legal pronouncements affecting it; thus, any decision rule concerning prisoners is very likely to create significant behavioral side effects. The result is that the courts define their decision rule more narrowly than may be justified by the policies and values underlying it.

A second set of situations involves the duty to testify. *People v. Carradine*,[39] which dealt with this duty, illustrates the legal effects of the second group of factors responsible for low acoustic separation—factors relating to the circumstances under which the defense (in this case, duress) is likely to be invoked. Georgia Carradine, the defendant, refused to testify in a homicide trial out of fear for her life and her children's lives. In rejecting this fear as an excuse the court said: "[Fear] is not a valid reason for not testifying. If it's a valid reason then we might as well close the doors."[40]

Here, as in the situation of prison escape, the court's position is based on a special concern about the effect that allowing a defense will have on people's future conduct.[41] It was certainly not the severity of the offense involved that gave pause to the *Carradine* court: duress has generally been allowed as a defense to much graver charges than the failure to testify.[42] Rather, the court's apocalyptic view of the likely results of allowing fear to excuse noncompliance with the law in such cases must rest on an assessment of the special circumstances under which the offense of failure to testify is typically committed. The decision about whether to testify is of a distinctively legal character: it is a decision about whether to participate in the legal process. It therefore focuses the individual's attention on the relevant legal duty in a way that most offenses do not. This decision is probably also the product of prolonged deliberation, in the course of which the individual may seek legal advice about the scope of her duty and the likely legal consequences of a failure to testify. Furthermore, because the duty to testify and the accompanying threats by defendants or their associates arise in fairly standard circumstances, courts' rulings in this area are easily generalizable.

These factors are apt to result in the failure of selective transmission. A court's decision to allow fear of reprisal to excuse witnesses from the duty to testify is likely to register with and shape the conduct of many potential witnesses. The *Carradine* court's position may accordingly be understood to reflect both the court's belief that a decision rule of duress is liable to generate considerable behavioral side effects, and its assessment that the cost to society of the subsequent corrosive effect on the duty to testify outweighs the considerations of fairness and compassion that support a decision rule allowing such a defense.[43]

Finally, a similar analysis can help rationalize the vagaries of the "act at your peril" rule that is followed in some situations of necessity. One such situation involves a citizen's use of deadly force to apprehend an escaping felon: "If the private citizen acts on suspicion that a [violent or otherwise serious] felony has been committed, he acts at his own peril. For the homicide to be justifiable, it must be established that his suspicion was correct."[44]

Seen as a conduct rule, such a provision is extremely defective and is subject to the charge, raised by the Model Penal Code's commentary, that "it does not prescribe a workable standard of conduct; liability depends upon fortuitous results."[45] This charge loses its force, however, if the "act at your peril" formula is interpreted not as a conduct rule, but rather as a decision rule. Resorting once again to the idea of a universe of acoustic separation can help us uncover the considerations that might underlie such a decision rule.

In determining whether to allow citizens to use deadly force against escaping felons, lawmakers may conclude that the danger to innocent people of this unprofessional use of force outweighs its possible law enforcement benefits. This judgment would lead lawmakers in the imaginary world to devise a conduct rule flatly forbidding citizens to use deadly force against suspected criminals. But the lawmakers might at the same time feel that it is unfair to punish a citizen who has successfully apprehended a dangerous felon through the use of deadly force: not only has the citizen in fact avoided the perils giving rise to the conduct rule (she has not injured any innocent party), but she has also rendered society a service that is not merely tolerated in, but indeed expected of, its police force. This sentiment naturally leads to an "act at your peril" decision rule—one that instructs judges not to impose punishment when deadly force has been successfully used to apprehend an escaping felon.

The conduct rule that unequivocally proscribes the use of deadly force and the decision rule that allows a qualified defense predicated on the actual success of the use of force can coexist without conflict in the imaginary world. In the real world, however, decision makers must choose between the two rules. The Model Penal Code, which flatly denies a defense even for the successful user of deadly force against escaping felons,[46] may be understood to pursue the logic of the conduct rule. By contrast, the "act at your peril" approach taken by some courts may be understood as an adoption of the corresponding decision rule. Focusing in this way on the decision rule rather than on the conduct rule may not be unreasonable in light of the degree of acoustic separation likely to obtain in such situations: the typical case in which the defense is asserted involves neither the legally sophisticated actor nor the cool and prolonged reflection that would make the availability of a defense the source of considerable and undesirable behavioral side effects.[47]

In contrast to some courts' application of the "act at your peril" rule regarding the use of deadly force against escaping felons is the resolute refusal by the Supreme Court of California to follow a similar rule in the case of *People v. Ceballos.*[48] This case dealt with an assault charge based on the injuries sustained by a would-be burglar who activated a trap gun installed by the defendant Ceballos. Invoking the "act at your peril" rule, Ceballos argued in his defense that his victim was in fact an intruder whom Ceballos could have shot with impunity.

The analogy between the installation of trap guns and the use of deadly force against escaping felons is clear. In both cases, the general policy disfavoring such practices is based on the notion that the dangers involved outweigh the possible benefits. The argument for a qualified defense is also similar in the two situations: the particular defendant has in fact avoided the dangers and successfully accomplished something that society considers beneficial.[49]

Still, refusing to allow the defense in trap gun cases may be consistent with allowing it in cases involving the use of deadly force against escaping felons, because the respective degrees of acoustic separation in the two situations differ. Whereas people who shoot escaping felons typically do so on the spur of the moment, people who install trap guns presumably do so under circumstances that permit effective inquiry into the relevant legal ramifications. Consequently, the court's refusal to allow even a qualified defense in trap gun cases—a refusal based on the notion that "the use of such [deadly mechanical] devices should not be encouraged"[50]—has a firmer basis than would a similar refusal in cases involving the use of force against escaping felons. It should not be surprising, then, that the considerations underlying the desirable conduct rule may prevail in trap gun cases while the considerations underlying the decision rule determine the outcome in situations involving use of deadly force against fleeing felons.

The common thread that links the prison escape, duty-to-testify, and trap gun situations is low acoustic separation. Judicial reluctance to allow a defense to criminal charges in these situations may accordingly be explained in part by the undesirable behavioral side effects that such a defense might have. Conversely, the greater latitude given to duress or necessity in other situations may reflect a tacit belief that adopting such decision rules will not send a significantly counterproductive message to the public. The degree of acoustic separation may thus be seen as a variable essential to a complete account of the shifting boundaries of those defenses.

Ignorance of the Law

If one were to take a poll and ask about the legal significance of ignorance of law, most nonlawyers would very likely answer by citing the maxim that "ignorance of the law is no excuse."[51] The results of the poll, if my guess is correct, might attest to a successful legal feat of selective transmission. By reciting the maxim, courts reinforce the popular belief that it accurately describes the law. But the maxim, far from being an exhaustive statement of the law, is in reality a mere starting point for a complex set of conflicting standards and considerations that allow courts to avoid many of the harsh results that strict adherence to the maxim would entail.[52] If one were to state the law on the question whether ignorance of law is ever a valid defense, one would have to consider the various distinctions set out in the following list.

Factors that weigh against allowing the defense	Factors that favor allowing the defense
The offense is *malum in se*	The offense is *malum prohibitum*[53]
The charge is based on a statutory provision	The charge is based on a regulation[54]
The subject matter is likely to be legally regulated	The subject matter is not likely to be legally regulated[55]
The statute in question serves an important purpose	The statute in question does not serve an important purpose[56]
Mens rea is not negated by the ignorance of law	*Mens rea* is negated by the ignorance of law[57]
The offense charged is a general-intent crime	The offense charged is a specific-intent crime[58]
The ignorance pertains to a criminal law	The ignorance pertains to a non-criminal law[59]
The defendant relied on a non-authoritative source of law	The defendant relied on an authoritative source of law[60]
The charge is based on an action	The charge is based on an ommision[61]

The list presents distinctions that courts rely upon as reasons for decisions allowing or disallowing a defense of ignorance of law. The presence of any of the circumstances listed in the left-hand column counts as a reason to deny the defense, whereas a circumstance from the right-hand column supports the defense. The list is not meant to be complete; other considerations may be found in various decisions. Moreover, the several pairs of elements are related in numerous ways: some overlap partially, others may be mutually exclusive, and so on. The main point is that the law is not reducible to any simple rule. Rather, it consists of an entire array of decisional variables that give rise to almost endless permutations. The complexity of this set of decisional rules stands in sharp contrast to the simplicity and straightforwardness of the rule that ignorance of the law is no excuse. My suggestion is that we may understand this contrast to reflect the rift between conduct rules and decision rules. Such a suggestion is supported by both the content and the form of the respective rules.

Consider the question of ignorance of law in a world of acoustic separation. Plainly, the purpose of the relevant conduct rule would be to encourage people to be diligent in their efforts to know the law. At the same time, considerations of justice might motivate decision makers to give great effect to the defense of ignorance of law and to acquit whenever a bona fide ignorance of the law negated the culpability that would otherwise have attached to an act.[62] Absent acoustic separation, these rules would be in conflict: the force of the duty to know the law would probably be severely compromised by public knowledge of the existence of a decision rule that excused offenses committed in ignorance of the law. In a world of partial acoustic separation, however, the law might try to serve the policies of both the conduct rule and the decision rule by approximating as closely as possible the imaginary world's complete acoustic separation. It would do so by attempting to convey to the general public a firm duty to know the law and by simultaneously instructing decision makers to excuse violations in ignorance of the law if fairness so required. It would also attempt to keep those two messages separate by employing a strategy of selective transmission.

The actual legal situation comports with this hypothesis both in content and in form. The clear behavioral implication of the rule that "ignorance of the law is no excuse" is that one had better know the law. The clarity and simplicity of this phrase make it a highly suitable form of communication to the legally untutored. On the other hand, the complexity of the set of decisional variables that actually guide courts in this area makes obscure to the public, but not to courts, the instruction that the demands of justice be served in cases in which ignorance of the law breeds innocence.

Criminal Offenses

The Dual Function of Laws Defining Criminal Offenses

Our examples thus far all concern criminal defenses, which seem to belong quite naturally in the camp of decision rules. Laws defining criminal offenses, by contrast, would seem to be the paradigmatic examples of conduct rules: the obvious point of the various rules defining offenses, unlike that of rules creating defenses, is to convey to the public a normative message consisting of a description of some proscribed or prescribed mode of behavior coupled with a threatened sanction. It is also obvious, as Bentham pointed out,[63] that once the distinction between conduct rules and decision rules is introduced, statutes defining offenses turn out to be decision rules as well as conduct rules: they specify for the courts some of the preconditions to the imposition of punishment. What may be less evident, however, is that it is not logically necessary for the conduct rule and the decision rule, normally conjoined in a single law, to overlap fully. Reverting to our imaginary universe helps us to conceive of that possibility: under conditions of complete acoustic separation, the conduct prohibited and the punishment threatened may differ from the conduct actually punished and the punishment actually imposed.

Are there any reasons for the law to avail itself of the possibility of using different decision and conduct rules in defining criminal offenses? The following considerations suggest an affirmative answer.[64] The criminal law, one might argue, is (in part) an embodiment of (part of) the community's morality. One of the functions of criminal laws is to reinforce that morality by encouraging behavior in accordance with specific moral precepts.[65] To the extent that criminal laws merely embody extant moral norms, the possibility of conflict between moral and legal duties is eliminated.[66] Correspondence between moral and legal duties would also take the sting out of Holmes' "bad man" theory of criminal law[67] — the theory that criminal law should be understood to address those who generally seek to escape their social obligations and who are motivated to abide by such obligations only insofar as the obligations are backed by the threat of legal sanction. When the "bad man" consulted a law embodying such a correspondence, he would find himself confronted with the full-fledged moral precepts he had hoped to evade.

But concerns other than reinforcement of community morality motivate decision rules. Primary among such concerns is the need to shape, control, and constrain the power wielded by decision makers. To attain this aim, the rules governing official decision-making must be characterized by a greater degree of precision and determinacy than can normally be expected of the community's moral precepts. Accordingly, whereas a conduct rule may be fully coextensive with the relevant moral precept, the corresponding decision rule need not be. Instead, the decision rule should define, as clearly and precisely as possible, a range of punishable conduct that is unquestionably within the bounds of the community's relevant moral norm.[68]

Another, though related, argument for having different decision and conduct rules address the same criminal offense starts from the assumption that the good person is one who would want to make sure that her conduct did not violate any moral precept. In case of doubt, she would therefore tend to interpret broadly her duties and the moral constraints they imposed upon her. I call this metaprinciple about the proper interpretation of moral duties the "safe-side principle," because it requires that we always try to be on the safe side (morally speaking) in discharging our moral duties.[69] Adopting the safe-side principle would lead to different decision and conduct rules based on the same moral duty. Imagine that a person wants to take a particular action but suspects that it might be prohibited by a moral precept. The safe-side principle ought to lead him to decide against taking the action. But assume that he does take it, and that a judge is called upon to decide whether to punish him for so acting. As is everyone else, the judge is bound by the safe-side principle. This principle requires her to be quite sure that the defendant well deserves any suffering that she proposes to inflict upon him. In other words, the judge must be confident that the defendant has in fact violated the moral precept, and she must resolve any doubts on the matter by deciding against punishment. It follows, therefore, that the safe-side principle will lead her to adopt a decision rule different from the conduct rule that the principle should have led the defendant to adopt. More specifically, the defendant should have acted on a broad version of the moral precept, whereas the judge should base her decision on a narrow version thereof.

We may conclude that in a world of perfect acoustic separation the law, while promulgating conduct rules that were fully coextensive with the relevant moral precepts, might at the same time apply decision rules that were more precisely defined and narrowly drawn than the corresponding conduct rules. The law would thus avoid the charge that it is directed at the "bad people" in the community without risking unjust punishment or giving free reign to the personal and discretionary power of decision makers.[70]

In actual legal systems, in which complete acoustic separation does not obtain, laws defining criminal offenses serve to convey both conduct rules and decision rules. The discussion of the relation between these two sets of rules in our imaginary legal universe may nonetheless illuminate the tension inherent in actual criminal laws, a tension born of the fact that the same legal provisions must in actuality fulfill two different functions and satisfy the different and sometimes conflicting substantive and formal requirements associated with those functions. To be coextensive with our morality, the laws that define offenses must often be broadly drawn and open ended; to serve as decision rules that adequately constrain judges, the laws must be narrow and precise.

But as in the case of criminal defenses, the reference to acoustic separation does not merely serve to aid us in diagnosing sources of tension in the law. It also sharpens our ability to perceive what may be seen as strategies employed by the law to resolve or relax the tension by drawing on the partial acoustic separation that exists in reality.

In the next subsection I argue that the use of ordinary language in the definitions of criminal offenses can be seen as such a strategy of selective transmission, and I show that this view may improve our understanding of the *mens rea* component of criminal liability. Then, in the following subsection, I apply the notion of partial acoustic separation to some nagging problems in the doctrine of vagueness.

Mens Rea and the Use of Ordinary Language

Ordinary language and selective transmission. Numerous offenses are defined in terms current in ordinary language. The legal system frequently employs statutory definitions or judicial interpretations to give these terms technical legal meaning that diverges from their ordinary meaning. This peculiar combination of ordinary language and technical definition is especially puzzling in a system of normative communication. If the law intends to convey its message through ordinary language, the employment of technical legal definitions that distort the meaning of that language does not make sense. If, on the other hand, the intended normative message is best expressed through technical definitions, the law may do better to coin a technical vocabulary (as in fact it frequently does) rather than use misleadingly familiar terms. The puzzle would be solved, however, if the law intended not one or the other, but both: to convey both the normative message expressed by the common meaning of its terms and the message rendered by their technical legal definitions.[71]

I want to suggest that an interpretation that imputes to the law such a double meaning is, in some cases, quite plausible. The ordinary language of a law defining an offense frames the conduct rule that the law conveys to the general public; the technical legal definitions give content to the decision rule conveyed by the same law. Furthermore, the method by which these double messages are conveyed is well suited to the task of selective transmission. By framing its imperatives in familiar language, the law reinforces the layperson's ordinary moral beliefs without arousing his suspicion, as the use of esoteric terminology might do, that his legal duties do not coincide with what he takes his moral duties to be. At the same time, the technical legal definitions of the ordinary terms are familiar to the professional decision maker. The occasional complexity of the legal definitions, although an additional barrier for the layperson, creates no special problems for the lawyer, familiar as she is with a technical and esoteric professional language.[72]

Ordinary language and the concept of mens rea. This view of the role of ordinary language in facilitating the operation of criminal laws as both conduct rules and decision rules derives support from the resolution it offers of a persistent problem concerning the nature of *mens rea.* The problem is most directly associated with and best illustrated by the famous English case of *Regina v. Prince.*[73] Prince was charged under a Victorian statute that provided that "[w]hosoever shall unlawfully take or cause to be taken any unmarried girl, being under the age of sixteen years, out of the possession and against the will of her father or mother, ... shall be guilty of a misdemeanor."[74] Even though Prince had reasonably believed that the girl (who in fact was fourteen) was eighteen years old, the court disallowed the defense of mistake of fact and upheld Prince's conviction. Lord Bramwell's opinion deserves (and has received)[75] greatest attention, and it merits quotation at some length.

> Let us remember what is the case supposed by the statute. It supposes that there is a *girl*—it does not say a woman, but a girl—something between a child and a woman; it supposes she is in the *possession* of her father or mother, or other person having lawful *care or charge* of her; and it supposes there is a *taking,* and that that taking is *against the will* of the person in whose possession she is. It is, then, a *taking* of a *girl,* in the *possession* of some one, *against his will.* I say that done without lawful cause is wrong, and that the legislature meant it should be at the risk of the taker whether or no she was under sixteen. I do not say that taking a woman of fifty from her brother's or even father's house is wrong. She is at an age when she has a right to choose for herself; she is not a girl, nor of such tender age that she can be said to be in the *possession* of or under the *care or charge* of anyone. I am asked where I draw the line; I answer at when the female is no longer a girl in anyone's possession.
>
> But what the statute contemplates, and what I say is wrong, is the taking of a female of such tender years that she is properly called a *girl,* can be said to be in another's *possession,* and in that other's *care or charge.* ... This opinion gives full scope to the doctrine of the *mens rea.*[76]

The most puzzling feature of this argument is its conclusion. How could Lord Bramwell possibly have believed that his denial of the relevance of Prince's mistake of fact concerning the girl's age was compatible with the requirement of *mens rea?* Had not Prince, reasonably and genuinely believing that the girl was eighteen years old, acted innocently and in accordance with the law's instructions?

Previous interpretations of the opinion attribute to Lord Bramwell a "spurious use of the expression *mens rea*,"[77] one that expands the term beyond its commonly accepted bounds. Lord Bramwell is commonly understood to have enunciated the so-called moral wrong doctrine, according to which Prince's criminal liability rested on his moral culpability or on the wrongfulness of his conduct as measured by community standards.[78] The mere transgression of the community's moral standards is sufficient, under this interpretation of Lord Bramwell's opinion, to provide the element of culpability required for criminal liability. Yet such an interpretation fails to account for Lord Bramwell's insistent use of the technical term *mens rea*. Moreover, because it substitutes moral culpability or wrongfulness of conduct for the more rigorous *mens rea* requirement, this view is also open to the charge, forcefully made by Professor Hughes,[79] that it would allow any immorality associated with the defendant's conduct, and not necessarily the immorality underlying the offense with which he is charged, to support a conviction.[80] To Professor Hughes, "this appears as an appallingly dangerous position which comes close to giving the jury a discretion to create new crimes."[81]

The failure of previous analyses to provide a satisfactory interpretation of Lord Bramwell's opinion is of no small consequence. *Prince* is a leading opinion in an area densely populated by numerous similar decisions dealing primarily with cases of statutory rape in which the defendant is mistaken about the victim's age. The absence of an account that reconciles the result in *Prince* with the principle of *mens rea*, as Lord Bramwell purported to do, has eroded the reach of the *mens rea* requirement by setting these decisions uneasily adrift on the "uncharted sea of strict responsibility."[82]

Yet an interpretation of *Prince* is possible that both takes seriously Lord Bramwell's use of the concept of *mens rea* and withstands criticisms such as those of Professor Hughes. The key to such an interpretation is Lord Bramwell's persistent emphasis on the statute's use of the term *girl*. According to Lord Bramwell's reading of the statute, the abduction of a *girl* constitutes the subject matter of the legal prohibition. Now the word *girl* is not a legal term, but a term of ordinary language. Lord Bramwell argues, in effect, that the conduct rule issued by the statute in question should be understood to conform to the ordinary meaning of the statute's language, thus fully coinciding with the moral prohibition against the abduction of girls from their guardians. This interpretation of Lord Bramwell's position rests on two assumptions. One is that, at the time the opinion was written, the term girl referred as much to an eighteen-year-old as to a sixteen-year-old (and we must take Lord Bramwell's word for that). The second assumption is that the prohibition of the abduction of girls (including those who were above the statutory age) was a generally accepted moral norm in England at that time, a norm that the statute embodied but had not initiated. If these assumptions are accurate, it is not at all absurd to maintain, as Lord Bramwell did, that Prince had violated the relevant conduct rule by knowingly abducting a girl. It is, furthermore, quite reasonable to believe that at the time of the abduction Prince himself saw the matter in precisely this way—that he realized, in other words, that he was committing a moral and legal wrong.

Prince's guilt resided in his violation of the moral rule that was expressed through the ordinary meaning of the terms of the relevant statute. The statutory definition of *girl,* which diverged from the ordinary usage, was no part of the conduct rule issued by the statute, but only an element of the decision rule conveyed by that statute. Whereas the ordinary citizen, who was guided exclusively by the conduct rule that embodied the relevant moral norm, was neither likely nor expected to know of or act on the statutory definition, the judge was required both to know of it and to give it effect in his decisions. Indeed, Lord Bramwell gave effect to the statutory definition by insisting that the defendant be punished only if the girl had, in fact, been under age.

It should not be difficult to discern the logic behind such a decision rule. Moral principles, as well as the terms of ordinary language in which they are couched, tend to have fuzzy edges. The applicability of the moral prohibition against the abduction of girls may well be indeterminate once a victim has reached a certain age. Different judges may place different interpretations on the term *girl* or on the extent of the prohibition, and some may err by going beyond the generally accepted bounds. The legal definition of the age at which the prohibition no longer applies serves as a restriction on judges that ensures both a degree of uniformity and, quite possibly, a degree of leniency in the interpretation of conventional morality. Furthermore, by choosing a relatively low age limit, the legislature may provide for the possibility that defendants make mistakes concerning a girl's age.

In any event, a decision rule that predicates the defendant's liability on the victim's age need not presuppose knowledge by the defendant of this rather arbitrary limitation. A defendant's mistaken belief regarding the victim's age may, consistently with the principle of *mens rea,* be deemed irrelevant to his legal duties under the conduct rule in question. An understanding of *mens rea* that is thus informed by a recognition of the dual function of criminal offenses as conduct rules and decision rules can salvage from the "uncharted sea" of strict liability the decisions that follow *Prince* in refusing to allow defenses based on mistakes regarding such facts as the age of the victim in statutory rape cases. But just as the refusal to allow such a defense need not signify the abandonment pro tanto of the principle of *mens rea,* the more recent tendency toward allowing the defense need not be taken, as is commonly done, as a measure of increased commitment to *mens rea.* Instead, both the refusal and the willingness to recognize mistake as a defense to statutory rape can be seen as responses, based on essentially identical views of *mens rea,* to different social and moral circumstances.

This conclusion finds ample textual support in a leading decision, *People v. Hernandez,*[83] that signaled a new judicial willingness to recognize the defense of mistake in statutory rape cases. A careful reading of the opinion discloses that although it recognizes mistake about the victim's age as a defense to statutory rape, its underlying logic comports rather than conflicts with Lord Bramwell's reasoning in *Prince.* This conclusion rests on the following observation. The *Hernandez* decision implies that had the statutory age of consent been considerably lower (for example, ten rather than eighteen), the defense of mistake would not have been available.[84] Furthermore, in distinguishing a prior statutory rape case in which a defense based on a mistake about the female's age had been rejected, the court pointed out that "[t]he age of consent at the time of the *Ratz* decision was 14 years, and it is noteworthy that the purpose of the rule, as there announced, was to afford protection to young females therein described as 'infants.'"[85] However, if it is supposed that the statutory age limit conclusively determines the scope of the relevant conduct rule, this attempt to distinguish between an age limit of ten (or fourteen) and a limit of eighteen must fail. A defendant's belief that his partner is eleven years old when she is in fact just under ten may be as genuine and as reasonable as a similar mistake concerning the age of a seventeen-year-old. If the requirement of *mens rea* demands exculpation in the latter case, it should, on this supposition, demand the same in the former.

The distinction the court draws between the two age limits is sound only if we revert to the view that one age limit coincides with a viable norm of conventional morality, whereas the other does not. The reason a defendant who had intercourse with a ten-year-old cannot defend himself by claiming that he reasonably believed her to be eleven is not that his mistake could not have been reasonable, but rather that it is irrelevant: regardless of his belief about the victim's age, he still must have perceived himself to be having intercourse with an infant. In our culture, the prohibition of intercourse with children is an indisputable moral norm that the laws defining the offense of statutory rape embody.[86] But when the statutory age is set at eighteen (the actual situation confronted by the *Hernandez* court), the criminal provision no longer corresponds to a viable moral prohibition. In such circumstances, the statutory age of consent conclusively determines the scope of the relevant conduct rule, and thus knowledge by the defendant that the female is below the age is indeed required by the principle of *mens rea*.

Stated more broadly and abstractly, the message implicit in the *Hernandez* decision is that statutory interpretation must take account of cultural context and prevailing moral norms. A statutory provision may be the harbinger of a new standard of behavior, the embodiment of an existing one, or the mere ghost of an expired morality. In each of these capacities, the provision relates differently to common perceptions (by shaping, reflecting, or ignoring them) and is accordingly amenable to different legal analysis, especially with regard to the nature of the *mens rea* requirement. The clear implication in *Hernandez* that mistake of fact would have been of no avail to the defendant had the statutory age of consent been lower thus radically shifts the focal point of the opinion. Rather than a reaffirmation of the principle of *mens rea,* as it is commonly understood to be, *Hernandez* is a bold statement about the link between criminal conduct rules and substantive morality. Seen in this light, *Hernandez* is a justly celebrated case, but one that has so far been celebrated for the wrong reason.

The Doctrine of Vagueness

The usefulness of the distinction between conduct and decision rules is further indicated by the distinction's ability to shed light on another problem related to defining criminal offenses: the void-for-vagueness doctrine. I do not here undertake a complete examination of this doctrine. Instead, I shall focus on some of its essential aspects and on the criticisms to which it has been most frequently subjected. I shall then suggest that vagueness doctrine withstands these criticisms more successfully when reinterpreted in light of the separation of conduct and decision rules.

Vagueness doctrine and its alleged deficiencies. Courts and commentators commonly identify two rationales for the constitutional requirement that criminal statutes meet some minimum standards of clarity and specificity.[87] One is the concern with *fair warning*: "No one may be required at peril of life, liberty or property to speculate as to the meaning of penal statutes. All are entitled to be informed as to what the State commands or forbids."[88] The other, which I shall call the *power control* rationale, is the concern with guiding and controlling judicial decision-making in order to avoid leaving "judges and jurors free to decide, without any legally fixed standards, what is prohibited and what is not in each particular case."[89]

To serve these goals, the Supreme Court has recognized two ways of curing an otherwise unconstitutionally vague statute. One is by judicial gloss: the various court decisions that interpret a statute may clarify an otherwise vague provision and enable it to pass constitutional muster.[90] The second remedy for vagueness is the requirement of scienter. Reading a statute to require scienter, the Court maintains, takes the sting out of a defendant's complaint of lack of fair warning: to be convicted, the defendant must in fact have appreciated the criminality of his conduct.[91] Both measures, however, have been criticized for their inability to remedy vagueness and ensure fair warning.

We may best introduce the argument against the adequacy of judicial gloss as a remedy for vagueness by distinguishing two different ways in which a statute may be vague: indeterminacy and inaccessibility. A statute is indeterminate when a significant number of possible situations are neither excluded by it nor included in it—when there are too many borderline cases in which the question of how or whether the statute applies admits of no single answer.[92] In cases of inaccessibility, the question whether a given situation falls under the statute is believed to have a determinate answer; the defect in the statute lies in the great difficulty of discovering what this answer is. Such difficulty obtains, for example, when, in Justice Douglas' words, the statute refers the citizen "to a comprehensive law library in order to ascertain what acts [are] prohibited."[93] Clearly, indeterminacy and inaccessibility are equally fatal to a statute's ability to serve as a normative guide.

We can now diagnose with greater precision the disease for which judicial gloss provides a remedy: that disease is, quite obviously, indeterminacy. By providing an authoritative interpretation of the statute, the courts fix the statute's meaning and dispel its indeterminacy. The nature of the criticism of the remedial use of judicial gloss should also now be clear. This criticism effectively claims that judicial gloss often remedies indeterminacy only by increasing inaccessibility.[94] Consequently, judicial gloss may cripple a statute's ability to communicate to the public a fair warning no less than did the statute's earlier indeterminacy.

This criticism is vividly corroborated by the Supreme Court's decision in *Rose v. Locke,*[95] in which the Court upheld the constitutionality of a Tennessee statute prohibiting "crimes against nature" and affirmed the application of the statute to an act of cunnilingus. The judicial gloss on which the majority based its conclusion that the challenged expression pertained to cunnilingus was the product of quite elaborate legal reasoning drawing analogies and inferences from old Tennessee opinions as well as from decisions in other jurisdictions. Couched as it is in the rhetoric of fair warning, the Court's reasoning has a surreal quality: it implies that the defendant could have been expected, before engaging in sexual activities, to canvass the law libraries of various jurisdictions in search of the relevant decisions and then to anticipate the convoluted process of legal reasoning that ultimately led even Supreme Court justices to opposite conclusions.[96] When determining the meaning of a statute requires such refined legal skills, the notion of fair warning is distorted beyond recognition.

The reliance on *mens rea* to remedy vagueness has similarly been subjected to criticism. As Professors LaFave and Scott argue:

> [S]cienter—at least as it has been traditionally defined—cannot cure vagueness in a statute or regulation. One "knowingly" commits an offense when he knows that his acts will bring about certain results (those defined in the statute in question), and whether he knows that deliberately causing such results is proscribed by statute is immaterial. Because it is knowledge of the consequences of one's actions and not knowledge of the existence or meaning of the criminal law which is relevant, it seems clear that uncertain language in a statute is not clarified by the addition of a scienter element.[97]

The two-pronged attack on the use of both judicial gloss and scienter to remedy vagueness thus amounts to the charge that, despite persistent rhetoric to the contrary, the courts in fact give short shrift to the requirement of fair warning. Relying on the preceding analysis of criminal offenses and the concept of *mens rea*, I would now like to offer an account that makes better sense of vagueness doctrine and relates it more successfully to its two underlying rationales, fair warning and power control, than these criticisms suggest is possible.

Judicial gloss as a remedy for the vagueness of decision rules. We should first observe that the two rationales underlying vagueness doctrine, fair warning and power control, do not relate to the same kinds of rules. The fair warning rationale applies exclusively to conduct rules: only when vagueness affects rules addressed to the public and meant to guide public conduct does it pose a problem of fair warning. Conversely, the power control rationale pertains to the clarity of decision rules alone: only decision rules are addressed to and acted upon by officials, and only decision rules must be clear and specific in order to constrain officials' discretion and contain their power. Vagueness, accordingly, must be examined with reference to the relevant audience. We cannot simply inquire whether a statute is vague, but instead we must always ask: vague for whom?

This restatement of the problem of vagueness removes the seeming trade-off between determinacy and accessibility on which the criticism of judicial gloss rests. To see the point more clearly, consider again the

Locke decision. The Court's opinion can now be understood to focus primarily on the vagueness of the decision rule conveyed by the statute under consideration. By fixing in advance the meaning of the pertinent decision rule, judicial gloss may serve the interest in power control insofar as it reduces the danger that personal bias and animosity will intrude (or seem to intrude) on the court's decision making—a danger that the existence of prior general decision rules is meant to mitigate. At the same time, it is clear that, when viewed as a remedy for the vagueness of decision rules, judicial gloss does not present any problem of inaccessibility. As we have already observed, legal decision makers—judges and lawyers alike—are not hampered by, but rather thrive in, "comprehensive law libraries" that would baffle the ordinary citizen. Therefore, decision rules, directed as they are to a professional audience, are no less effective or specific for being "buried" in the volumes contained in law libraries. Moreover, in cases in which the law's goals are best served by decision rules that are not known to the general public, the inaccessibility engendered by judicial gloss may be seen as a strategy of selective transmission that advances those goals.[98]

Seen in this light, *Locke*'s elaborate discussion of prior judicial interpretations of the expression "crimes against nature" no longer looks so out of place. By constraining the legal meaning of such an expression, judicial gloss can reduce the vagueness of the relevant decision rule and thus serve the power control policy that underlies vagueness doctrine in part. Judicial gloss does not, however, mitigate (and it may exacerbate) the vagueness of the conduct rule conveyed by the same criminal statute; it thus leaves the need for fair warning unattended.[99] We must now turn, therefore, to the other half of vagueness doctrine.

Mens rea as a remedy for the vagueness of conduct rules. The need for fair warning is served by the second of the courts' two remedies for vagueness: the requirement of scienter. Despite the critics' misgivings, a *mens rea* requirement can successfully correct the lack of warning created by the vagueness of a conduct rule. To appreciate how such a remedy works, we must return to the analysis of the concept of *mens rea* in the context of the *Prince* case.

It will be recalled that this analysis was based on the view that the statute conveyed a conduct rule against the abduction of girls from their guardians, a rule that used the ordinary meaning of the word *girl*. The *mens rea* requirement was held satisfied because Prince, as an ordinary speaker of the English language and as a member of a certain moral community, must have realized that the person he was taking away from her father's custody was indeed a "girl." We may now generalize this illustration and say that the defendant's state of mind satisfies the *mens rea* requirement in a criminal statute if the defendant perceives the facts and the nature of his conduct in terms of the statute's ordinary-language description of them.[100]

The objection that a scienter requirement cannot dispel vagueness rests on the view that *mens rea* calls for knowledge only of facts—not of the legal categories under which they fall. We can now appreciate the fallacy of this argument: it results from an exaggeration of the distinction between knowledge of facts and knowledge of law.[101] What such a distinction overlooks is that both knowledge of facts and knowledge of law depend on the mastery and application of certain linguistic categories. When we inquire into a defendant's state of mind and ask whether she was aware of the nature of her conduct, we do so in light of a tentative or hypothetical description provided by the relevant criminal statute. We can ascertain whether the defendant possessed the requisite *mens rea* only by relating her state of mind to such a description: did her perception of the facts match the description in the statute? One can, for example, fully appreciate the fact that one's finger is pulling a small metal lever connected to a larger metal instrument and yet fail to know that one is "pulling the trigger of a gun" or that one is "shooting," let alone that one is about to "kill" someone. To say simply that *mens rea* requires knowledge only of facts obscures the crucial importance of the description against which the adequacy of that knowledge will be measured.

This is not to say that knowledge of the facts, as required by the principle of *mens rea*, calls for familiarity with technical legal terms. Most conduct rules use ordinary language to describe the proscribed conduct. Consequently, to satisfy the *mens rea* requirement, the defendant must only perceive his conduct in terms of ordinary language categories that apply to it; no special skill, but merely ordinary linguistic aptitude, is called for.

So interpreted, the requirement of *mens rea* can in fact serve the interest in fair warning by securing a correspondence between the defendant's own cognitions and the description of the proscribed conduct in the relevant conduct rule. In most cases, both the requirement of *mens rea* and that of fair warning are satisfied when the defendant acts with the awareness normally possessed by an intelligent member of a moral and linguistic community. That in the great majority of cases such awareness is taken for granted may account for the scarcity of real concern with fair warning in court decisions dealing with issues of vagueness.

Applied to the *Locke* decision, this view of *mens rea* suggests that common usage tied up with conventional morality, and not legal technicalities, will determine people's understanding of the normative message conveyed by the legal proscription against "crimes against nature." Indeed, by pointing out that "[t]he phrase has been in use among

English-speaking people for many centuries,"[102] the Court may have implied as much: ambiguities and complexities of legal usage notwithstanding, the defendant himself must have perceived his own conduct in terms of this linguistic and moral category and thus enjoyed in fact the fair warning to which he was entitled.

This analysis makes good formal sense of the Court's use of vagueness doctrine in *Locke,* but it reveals a glaring substantive inadequacy in the opinion. The tacit and crucial assumption that the expression "crimes against nature" conveys a meaningful message to ordinary people seems no longer to be tenable. The Supreme Court completely overlooked the relevance to fair warning of changes in moral outlook and their reflection in linguistic usage. This point had earlier been squarely confronted by the Supreme Court of Florida.[103] In striking down a statute similar to the one upheld in Locke, the Florida court pointed to "the transition of language over the span of the past 100 years of this law's existence." The court continued:

> The change and upheaval of modern times are of drastic proportions. People's understandings of subjects, expressions and experiences are different than they were even a decade ago. The fact of these changes in the land must be taken into account and appraised. Their effect and the reasonable reaction and understanding of people today relate to statutory language.[104]

The phrase "crimes against nature" today sounds quaint to many people (surely to many young people), just as the idea that oral sex is a sin or a crime may strike them as bizarre. We can therefore no longer assume with any confidence that, in engaging in oral sex, people will perceive themselves to be committing an "unnatural act" or a "crime against nature." Such expressions, whose linguistic vitality has expired and whose moral connotations are no longer valid, give no fair warning to the ordinary person.[105]

The analysis of vagueness doctrine I have suggested is summarized in the following table.

Kind of Rule	The Interest Served by Its Clarity	The Language in Which It Is Conveyed	The Cure for Its Vagueness
Conduct rule	Fair warning	Ordinary language	Scienter (*mens rea*)
Decision rule	Power control	Legal language	Judicial gloss

3. The Legitimacy of Selective Transmission

In numerous situations, as we have seen, the law can be understood to segregate its normative messages, either by relying on the existing degree of acoustic separation or by employing strategies of selective transmission, in ways that serve certain social policies and values. In the examples I have chosen, the law manages to maintain higher degrees of both deterrence and leniency than could otherwise coexist. I have so far delayed, however, consideration of the legitimacy of selective transmission even when its goals are generally thought desirable.[106] Indeed, the practice may seem to be such a blatant violation of the ideal of the rule of law—an ideal deeply ingrained in our political and legal culture— that its illegitimacy may well be viewed as beyond dispute.

Notice, however, that we would probably not be similarly surprised (though we would perhaps be no less disturbed) by the disclosure of analogous practices in politics. Although candor and openness must be highly valued in political life as well as in the law, the prevailing ethos of politics acknowledges the occasional infringement of these values. Moral philosophers often depict the politician as a person faced, more regularly and intensely than are persons from other walks of life, with the moral predicament described as the problem of dirty hands[107]—the confrontation with moral dilemmas whose resolution calls for actions that remain morally distasteful even when they are the right thing to do in the service of the greater good.[108]

In contrast to the political ethos embodied in the metaphor of dirty hands, the ideal of the rule of law expresses an ethos of law as an area of public life particularly committed to the values of openness and candor. Central to the rule of law is the requirement that the laws be clearly stated and publicly proclaimed. The alarm likely to follow the realization that selective transmission may circumvent these requirements accordingly seems well founded. It is thus surprising to discover that, as I try to show in the next section, the standard arguments in support of the rule of law do not in fact rule out selective transmission. Later, generalizing from the illustrations in part 2, I observe that the law's own violence and brutality may suggest a general rationale for selective transmission: in some circumstances selective transmission can mitigate or serve as a substitute for the violent means that the law frequently employs.

These two claims—that selective transmission is not inconsistent with the rule of law and can reduce the law's brutality—do not add up to an endorsement of selective transmission. They only clear the way for evaluating competing substantive moral considerations, an endeavor I do not undertake. But by clearing the way for such a project, my argument suggests that the law faces and cannot easily escape moral dilemmas similar to those found elsewhere in political and social life. The desirability of candor is, on some occasions, no less an issue for the law than it is for the politician. In this respect, I conclude, law and politics resemble each other more than their contrasting ethoses, embodied respectively in the ideal of the rule of law and in the metaphor of dirty hands, might lead one to expect.[109]

Acoustic Separation and the Rule of Law

As it is commonly understood, the ideal of the rule of law requires, among other things, that "[t]he law ... be open and adequately publicized"[110] as well as clearly stated. Selective transmission bent on hiding parts of the law from the public flies in the face of this requirement and therefore seems to violate the rule of law. Selective transmission, however, does not impede and may sometimes even advance the values associated with the rule of law. To demonstrate this point, I briefly examine four clusters of arguments that are commonly adduced in defense of the rule of law in general and the publicity and clarity of law in particular.

First, by insisting on the specificity and clarity of law, the rule of law is said to limit officials' discretion and thereby to curb their potential arbitrariness. The rule of law reduces the danger that officials may indulge their self-interest or give vent in their decisions to personal animosities or prejudices. Thus, the availability of clear, generally applicable, and binding guidelines secures for individuals a measure of formal justice—primarily a degree of equality before the law—and ensures that the substantive goals the law is supposed to pursue will not be thwarted by the whim or ineptitude of individual decision makers. But as the discussion of vagueness doctrine demonstrated in some detail,[111] this concern with power control is utterly compatible with selective transmission. The ability of decision rules to guide decisions effectively and thus to limit official discretion and arbitrariness does not depend on broad dissemination or easy accessibility of those rules to the general public. If anything, the opposite is true: the clarity and specificity of decision rules, and hence their effectiveness as guidelines, may be enhanced by the use of a technical, esoteric terminology that is incomprehensible to the public at large.[112]

The second cluster of arguments for the rule of law is even more strictly formal and instrumental. Like the sharpness of a knife, to use Raz's metaphor, conformity to the rule of law is said to be of sheer instrumental value: it endows the law with a measure of efficacy in pursuing whatever goals are assigned to it.[113] The most far-reaching version of this argument was made by Lon Fuller, whose famous allegory about

King Rex was meant to demonstrate that the principles of the rule of law, which include publicity and clarity, are necessary conditions for the successful operation, and indeed for the very existence, of a legal system.[114]

But such arguments do not apply to the kinds of decision rules that rely on the practices of selective transmission we discussed in part 2. Subjecting such decision rules to the imperatives of the rule of law, and in particular to the requirements of publicity and clarity, would tend to hinder rather than enhance the rules' efficacy in achieving their goals. Raz's view and Fuller's story of King Rex are compelling only insofar as one overlooks the possibility that some decision rules may best serve the purposes of the law by remaining concealed from public view. Thus, from the strictly instrumental perspective of the second cluster of arguments for the rule of law, publicity and clarity of decision rules are undesirable when these attributes would dull the knife and impede its usefulness.

Closely related to the instrumental arguments, but with a greater substantive component, is the third cluster of arguments for the rule of law: the utilitarian arguments. Bentham was particularly insistent on the importance of the law's publicity and clarity, and it is therefore worthwhile to focus on his views. Bentham's argument about the form that laws should take may be expressed in terms of the following syllogism.[115]

First premise: "In the arrangement of the laws, that which is best adapted for the generality of the people ought to be regarded."
Second premise: "The multitude have not leisure for profoundly studying the laws: they do not possess the capacity for connecting together distant regulations—they do not understand the technical terms of arbitrary and artificial methods."
Conclusion: "It is proper, as much as possible, not to put into a code of law any other legal terms than such as are familiar to the people."

Bentham presents the first premise of this argument as self-evident. Perhaps he has in mind only paradigmatic conduct rules. But as I have already suggested, it is not at all obvious that decision rules that are neither intended for nor addressed to "the generality of the people" should be "adapted" to the public's cognitive needs. In a different context, however, Bentham comes closer to offering an argument that, if valid, would make the first premise equally applicable to *all* laws, including decision rules. Dealing with what he terms "preappointed evidence," Bentham argues: "Not judicature only, but all human action, depends upon evidence for its conduciveness to its end: evidence, knowledge of the most proper means, being itself among the means necessary to the attainment of the end."[116]

According to this view, the requirement that the law be made known to the public is simply an instance of the broader truth that knowledge (that is, all attainable knowledge) is needed for rational human action. As Bentham would be among the first to agree, however, human action can be rational from a personal point of view and yet suboptimal in terms of social utility. According to Bentham's own assumptions about human motivation, knowledge may indeed serve an individual's own goals while diminishing rather than promoting social utility. The instances of selective transmission that I have identified deal precisely with such cases. Widespread knowledge of the defense of duress, for example, might move people to succumb to threats under circumstances in which doing so would be personally rational but socially undesirable.[117]

I conclude that, whereas utilitarian considerations such as those raised by Bentham would often favor full correspondence between conduct rules and decision rules, such considerations would not support a general principle requiring that *all* decision rules be communicated to the public.

The final and perhaps most important cluster of rationales for the rule of law includes arguments that defend the rule of law as an imperative of liberty or autonomy. Common to these arguments is the insistence that the rule of law is necessary to ensure "[p]redictability in one's environment"[118] and security in one's expectations that are essential to one's capacity to make and carry out life plans. By enhancing the individual's life-planning capacity, the rule of law expands freedom of action, secures a measure of individual liberty, and expresses respect for individual autonomy.[119]

To be sure, like utilitarian arguments, arguments from autonomy are highly relevant in determining the relationship between any particular conduct rule and the corresponding decision rule. But the protection of well-founded expectations, no matter how important to individual autonomy, does not arise with respect to all decision rules and therefore does not yield a *general* requirement that decision rules be made public.

The need for security of individual expectations is not a great obstacle to the use of selective transmission when decision rules are more lenient than conduct rules lead people to expect. I have already observed that in such cases no one is likely to feel "entrapped" by the law[120] or to complain of frustrated expectations. True, some individuals may still complain of an infringement of their autonomy by the reduction in the predictability of their environment that selective transmission brings about: had they known, for example, of the defense of duress, they would not have acted as they did, and should have done, in resisting strong pressure to commit a crime. There are two replies to this complaint. The first points to a peculiar feature of defenses such as duress:

they melt away as soon as one relies upon them. An individual who would not have committed an offense but for his knowledge of the existence of such a defense cannot, in most cases, avail himself of the defense.[121] Hiding the existence of a defense such as duress thus misleads mainly those who would, if they knew of the defense, rely upon it with the intent to eventually deny that reliance when they are brought to trial. It is doubtful that such expectations are worthy of protection.

There is a second, more general response to the complaint of the individual who is misled into obeying the law by an exaggerated fear of the legal threat. It applies not only to cases involving unknown defenses, but also, even more forcefully, to cases in which the decision rule defines an offense more narrowly than does the corresponding conduct rule.[122] Such an individual, it can be pointed out, admits to being the Holmesian "bad man," who acts out of fear of legal sanctions rather than out of deference to his duties. But essential to autonomy, at least in the Kantian sense,[123] is action motivated by deference to duty (or "reverence" to duty, in Kantian terms)[124] rather than by physical fear. In other words, the entire enterprise, central to the criminal law, of regulating conduct through deterrence, that is, through the issuance of threats of deprivation and violence, is at odds with human dignity: it appeals to individual "inclinations" (to use Kantian language) instead of to the reason and good will of moral agents. The point at which a threat of punishment has its intended effect, according to this view, is the precise point at which autonomous behaviour terminates. By obeying a law out of sheer fear of punishment rather than out of a sense of duty (when such a duty exists), an individual merely submits to a mode of regulation through intimidation; such submission is inconsistent with his claim to have acted as an autonomous moral agent. If the individual's actions fall outside the sphere of autonomy, he cannot complain of a deprivation of autonomy when he discovers that the fear that shaped his conduct was excessive and that, because of the leniency of some decision rule, he could have violated his duty with impunity.

But although he cannot rest his complaint on grounds of Kantian autonomy, an individual who has been misled by his ignorance of a lenient decision rule may still have available an argument based on the looser notion of autonomy as freedom of action or self-control. This argument points out that "predictability in one's environment" has the beneficial effect of expanding the individual's freedom of action. The ideal of "predictability in one's environment" falsely suggests, however, that the environment—to which the requirements of the rule of law might afford a measure of predictability—is not itself altered by those requirements. As some of the preceding illustrations demonstrate, quite the contrary is true: the alternative to selective transmission may sometimes be a change in the relevant legal "environment" that would diminish the degree of freedom secured by law. If, for example, the accommodation between deterrence and compassion (or fairness) offered by the possibility of selective transmission regarding the defense of duress were ruled out, the law would have to adopt one of two positions. The law could abandon the defense altogether, thereby curtailing some people's freedom of action. Alternatively, the law could preserve the defense not only as a decision rule, but also as a conduct rule—that is, as a rule that people consider in deciding whether to commit a criminal offense. But as opponents of the defense maintain, this would reduce the effectiveness of the law's protection against offensive invasions of individual freedom and unlawful curtailments of personal liberty.[125]

The relationship between the rule of law and selective transmission can be briefly summarized by reference to a single "root idea" from which, according to Professor Raz, the various arguments for the rule of law all spring. It is the basic intuition that "the law must be capable of being obeyed" and that hence "it must be capable of guiding the behaviour of its subjects. It must be such that they can find out what it is and act on it."[126] My main point is that this idea, with its seemingly unassailable logic, applies only to conduct rules: ex hypothesi, conduct rules are all one needs to know in order to obey the law. Decision rules, as such, cannot be obeyed or disobeyed by citizens; therefore, knowing them is not necessary, indeed, it is irrelevant, to one's ability to obey the law.

Acoustic Separation and the Internal Immorality of Law

The conclusion of the preceding section is largely a negative one: the options opened up by acoustic separation are not ruled out by the rule of law ideal. But the discovery that what has been called "the internal morality of law"[127] is compatible with patterns of selective transmission falls far short of justifying such strategies. The option of selective transmission is not an attractive one, and the sight of law tainted with duplicity and concealment is not pretty. Lest our lingering distaste lead us too easily to moral self-indulgence, however, we must place selective transmission in a broader context. Our assessment of the acoustic separation model as an analytical device and our attitude toward selective transmission as a normative option cannot be divorced from our moral views concerning the nature of criminal law or, indeed, from our general vision of law. These are large issues, but the narrow confines of a concluding section provide a welcome excuse for making some tentative and preliminary remarks. I will relate selective transmission first to the horrors of punishment, second to the view that punishment is a necessary evil, and third to a claim that law is an enterprise unavoidably affected with the problem of dirty hands.

The analytical merits of the acoustic separation model and the normative significance of selective transmission must be first related to law's coerciveness, where "coercion" is often a euphemism for intimidation, brutality, and violence.[128] But these features of law do not seem to have fully permeated jurisprudential thinking. To get immediately to the point, consider Professor Raz's endorsement of the conventional view of the relationship between conduct rules and decision rules: "[L]aw contains both norms guiding behaviour and institutions for evaluating and judging behaviour. The evaluation is based on the very same norms which guide behaviour."[129] Starkly missing from this statement is any recognition that the law does not just evaluate behavior, but typically uses its evaluations to justify killing, maiming, beating, or locking up the evaluated individual. The suppression of this all-important fact leads to a certain understatement of the moral awesomeness of the legal decision and to an unduly placid and benign picture of law. More generally, the conventional view of the relationship between decision rules and conduct rules, expressed in the idiom of "law application," has as its psychological, if not necessarily logical, corollary the impression that, as soon as a court finds the defendant's conduct defective relative to some standard laid down for him, punishment must inexorably follow. This conventional model does not dwell on the independent decision to carry out the legal threat and actually to impose punishment. As a result, the daunting moral significance of such a decision—a decision that sometimes, as in the case of the death penalty, assumes overwhelming proportions—recedes to the background. By contrast, the acoustic separation model brings into sharp focus the decision to impose punishment and is thus more conducive to an appreciation of the different considerations that may apply at the stage of conduct regulation (through the threat of sanctions) and at the time of the actual imposition of punishment.

By emphasizing the horror of punishment, I do not mean to deny that some system of criminal punishment is indispensable. Instead, this emphasis leads to my second point: that punishment is a necessary evil.[130] I cannot defend this view here, nor does it urgently need such a defense. Only the most thoroughgoing Kantian retributivist, who considers punishment of the guilty an unqualified, affirmative good, is likely to quarrel with this characterization. Moreover, given the inescapable incidents of convicting the innocent, even the retributivist can find only insecure satisfaction in the imposition of punishment.

The description of punishment and other forms of legal violence as necessary evils marks a tension that pervades the criminal law between the felt necessity and the perceived evil of the means used. This tension is manifested in the rift between the threat of punishment and the decision to carry out that threat. The same tension gives a sharp moral edge to more specific conflicts, such as that between the imperatives of crime prevention and compassion to the individual defendant, or that between the desirability of using the criminal law to instill new, enlightened standards of behavior in the community and the unfairness of punishing persons whose conduct comports with existing community standards that have not yet been affected by the educational efforts of the criminal law.[131] As we have seen, selective transmission may help mitigate, if not fully resolve, many acute dilemmas of this sort.

But even as it helps mitigate such dilemmas, selective transmission, because of its own unpalatableness, also compounds them. By so doing, it highlights an aspect of law reminiscent of the moral predicament of dirty hands that is commonly thought to be endemic in political life.[132]

One should be wary of too readily applying notions such as "dirty hands" to new areas. In a certain sense, all life is permeated by problems akin to that of dirty hands; by extending the notion to new situations, we risk draining it of all philosophical interest and analytical power. To avert this danger, I need to justify the application of the notion of dirty hands to the law by indicating (though not here fully elaborating) the essential similarity between the problem as it arises in the law and the problem as it appears in politics. The briefest and safest way to do so is by demonstrating that the same characteristics that have been said to make politicians particularly susceptible to the dirty hands syndrome can be found, with minor differences, in the law as well.

Michael Walzer lists three such characteristics. First, the politician presumes not "merely [to] cater to our interests," but to act "on our behalf, even in our name"; second, the politician rules over us; and third, the politician "uses violence and the threat of violence—not only against foreign nations in our defense but also against us, and again ostensibly for our greater good."[133] Substitute *law* for *politician* in each of the three propositions, and they will be no less valid. (Such a result should surprise only those who believe in the radical separation between law and politics.) Insofar as the propositions correctly capture politicians' special susceptibility to the problem of dirty hands, we should be prepared to find symptoms of that susceptibility in the law as well. Selective transmission is such a symptom. But notice that I have advisedly substituted *law,* not *lawyers,* for *politician* in Walzer's list. We find it natural, in thinking about law, to refer impersonally to the normative system rather than to individual human beings. The wielding of power and even the administering of violence and brutality by law are characteristically, probably even essentially, impersonal, stylized, and institutionalized. Consequently, and as our examination of selective transmission tends to confirm, it is reasonable to expect that the manifestations of the problem of dirty hands in the law will also be impersonal, stylized, and institutionalized. What, if any, moral significance these features have, and how, if at all, the legal version of the problem of dirty hands should affect our attitudes toward law, are important questions that I can here only broach.[134]

None of the foregoing remarks settles the question of legitimacy raised at the beginning of this part. Such a question is ultimately a matter of substantive moral judgement that the analysis presented here can help clarify but cannot resolve. All that can safely be asserted is that in a world in which murder is rampant and executions are tolerated, law, like politics, is a power game with high stakes indeed. In such a game, strategic behavior, including bluffing and other forms of deceit, must always be expected. Furthermore, the option of selective transmission can sometimes be rejected only at the cost of increased human suffering, either in the form of preventable crimes or in the form of unnecessary punishment. When the values of publicity and honesty are victorious in such instances, their victory, even if justly deserved, should be no occasion for rejoicing.

Conclusion

The analysis of selective transmission has led us from an emphasis on law's brutality, through the subsequent characterization of punishment as a necessary evil, to the diagnosis in law of the problem of dirty hands. But this is not the end of the trail. On yet a broader scale, the exposure of selective transmission is a reminder of two additional unpleasant truths, not the less distressing because platitudinous. One is that our values are in conflict and that in reconciling them we must compromise. The other is that even under the best of circumstances, in the freest of democracies, and under the most enlightened of legal systems we are still being ruled. The response to the concept of selective transmission is liable, therefore, to be such as sometimes befalls the bearer of bad tidings. Our irritation with the messenger may be in part a disguised expression of our unhappiness with the message.

Notes

1. Jeremy Bentham, *A Fragment on Government* and *An Introduction to the Principles of Morals and Legislation,* ed. W. Harrison (Oxford: Basil Blackwell, 1948), 430. Bentham was not, however, the first to draw the distinction. According to Professor David Daube, "There came a period in Talmudic law when it was assumed that the Bible had two separate statutes for each crime, one to prohibit it and one to lay down the penalty." David Daube, *Forms of Roman Legislation* (Oxford: Clarendon Press, 1956), 24.

2. Bentham, ibid., 430.

3. Hans Kelsen, *General Theory of Law and State,* trans. Anders Wedberg (Cambridge: Harvard University Press, 1945), 6. For a similar view see Alf Ross, *Directives and Norms* (London: Routledge and Kegan Paul, 1968), 91, and *On Law and Justice* (Berkeley and Los Angeles: University of California Press, 1959), 33.

4. H. L. A. Hart, *The Concept of Law* (Oxford: Clarendon Press, 1961), 39.

5. This was essentially the position held by Austin, for whom "[e]very *law* or *rule* ... is a *command.*" John Austin, *Lectures on Jurisprudence,* 3d ed. (London: J. Murray, 1869), 1:90. Although Austin distinguishes primary rights and duties that "do not arise from injuries or wrongs" from secondary (or sanctioning) rights and duties that "arise directly and exclusively from injuries or wrongs," 2:791, he insists that such a scheme "do[es] not represent a logical distinction. For a primary right or duty is not of itself a right or duty, without the secondary right or duty by which it is sustained; and e *converso.*" Ibid., 795. The role of courts with respect to both kinds of rules is that of enforcement: the distinction is between "law enforced directly by the Tribunals or Courts of Justice; and law which they only enforce indirectly or by consequence." Ibid., 791.

6. See Joseph Raz, *Practical Reason and Norms* (London: Hutchinson, 1975), 50; Ross, *Directives and Norms,* 107; Georg H. Von Wright, *Norm and Action* (New York: Humanities, 1963), 70–92.

7. Indeed, this conception of the judge's role may be an extreme form of the legal realist's view. See Hart, *The Concept of Law,* at 109–10 and 135–37, arguing that it is inaccurate and uninformative to describe as obedience the relation of a judge to the rules he uses in the determination of disputes. Raz, in *Practical Reason and Norms,* 105, also maintains that clarity of discourse about norms will be served "if every norm is conceived as guiding one act," and hence that legal theory should recognize "a distinct type of norm, power-conferring norms, guiding those acts which are the exercise of power."

8. Compare Raz, *Practical Reason and Norms,* 105, 148; and Ross, *Directives and Norms,* 113.

9. Professor Alf Ross, for example, insists on the logical identity of the two sets of rules: "From a logical point of view ... there exists only one set of rules: namely, the so called "secondary" rules which prescribe how cases are to be decided.... For we have seen that primary norms, logically speaking, contain nothing not already implied in secondary norms, whereas the converse does not hold" (*Directives and Norms,* 92)

Ross goes on, however, to distinguish between the logical and the psychological point of view: "From the psychological point of view, however, there do exist two sets of norms. Rules addressed to citizens are felt psychologically to be independent entities which are grounds for the reactions of the authorities" (Ibid). This is his response to Hart's criticism of Kelsen's position—a position that Ross shares.

10. Several typologies of rules of law draw distinctions analogous to the one between decision rules and conduct rules discussed in this essay. Relating the present distinction to the others would be, I fear, a tedious and unprofitable undertaking. Nonetheless, a brief comment on the most famous of these typologies, H. L. A. Hart's distinction between primary and secondary rules, may be in order. As Peter Hacker argues, Hart's distinction has occasioned much confusion because of the fact that "different dichotomous principles of classification are misguidedly assimilated, and wrongly thought to coincide extensionally." Hacker, "Hart's Philosophy of Law," in *Law, Morality, and Society,* ed. Peter M. S. Hacker and Joseph Raz (Oxford: Clarendon Press, 1977), 19–20. Insofar as the distinction between conduct rules and decision rules comprises one of the dichotomies underlying Hart's typology, Hart's analysis, as Hacker notes, overlooks the fact that "secondary rules ... guide behavior no less than do primary rules." Ibid., 20; see Hart, *The Concept of Law,* 77–120. I should also point out that of the typologies of rules with which I am familiar, Joseph Raz's comes closest to raising some of the issues addressed by the distinction between decision rules and conduct rules. See Joseph Raz, *The Concept of a Legal System,* 2d ed. (Oxford: Clarendon Press, 1980), 154–56.

11. But compare Hart, *The Concept of Law,* 21–22, noting the ambiguity of the statement that a law is "addressed" to someone.

12. The procedure suggested here for classifying legal rules as either conduct or decision rules should not be taken to imply the existence of a single identifiable source of legal norms, a source whose actual intentions determine the segregation of the norms into the two categories. Rather, the classification of legal rules is a scheme of interpretation based on the values and policies that the interpreter ascribes to the legal system. I do not, however, deal with the grounds for ascribing to the law

such values and policies. That a legislature in fact entertained certain intentions may, but need not, provide such grounds.

13. It is not utterly clear, nor is it of great importance, how complete the acoustic separation in the imaginary world could plausibly be made to be. Two main problems come to mind. First, would not the decisions themselves divulge to the public the decision rules? Although decision makers would not publicly give reasons for their decisions, could knowledge of the outcomes be avoided? If not, people would perhaps be able to guess decision rules from patterns of outcomes. Second, only in their capacity as officials could decision makers plausibly be said to be acoustically separated from the public. In other respects, they would be part of the public and subject to the same conduct rules. Furthermore, we would want (need) to allow for the possibility that people would undertake and resign official positions. Could we still maintain complete acoustic separation by making people "forget" the rules belonging to their other, or former, capacity? (Should we imagine a selective temporary-amnesia-inducing device in the entrance to each chamber?)

14. On practical conflict, see Hans Kelsen, *Pure Theory of Law* (Berkeley and Los Angeles University of California Press, 1967), 25–26; Von Wright, *Norm and Action,* 144–52.

15. James Fitzjames Stephen, *A History of the Criminal Law of England* (London: Macmillan, 1883), 2:107.

16. See Model Penal Code sec. 2.09 comment (Tent. Draft No. 10, 1960); George P. Fletcher, *Rethinking Criminal Law* (Boston: Little, Brown, 1978), sec. 10.3; Wayne R. LaFave and Austin W. Scott Jr., *Handbook on Criminal Law* (St. Paul: West, 1972), sec. 49.

17. See infra 71–73.

18. See infra 48–52.

19. Professor Niklas Luhmann believes that, in general, some mode of selective communication is essential to modern societies: "Under conditions [of size and complexity] that exclude the actual interaction between all members of the society, the communication system needs selective intensifiers." Niklas Luhmann, "Differentiation of Society," *Canadian Journal of Sociology* 2 (1977): 29, at 33.

20. The notions of acoustic separation and selective communication are not limited to the dichotomy between the public and officials, though that dichotomy is directly relevant to the distinction between conduct rules and decision rules on which I focus. One can think of other acoustically separated groups that afford additional opportunities for practices of selective transmission. To consider an example from the criminal law, one can interpret as an instance of selective transmission the practice of withholding from the jury information concerning its power to nullify unjust laws. See Mortimer R. Kadish and Sanford

H. Kadish, *Discretion to Disobey* (Stanford, Calif.: Stanford University Press, 1973), 45–66, for an account of jury nullification that resembles my approach); see also Alan W. Scheflin, "Jury Nullification: The Right to Say No," *Southern California Law Review* 45 (1972): 168.

21. For a discussion of specific strategies, see infra 48, 52–54, 57–62.

22. See Michel Foucault, *The History of Sexuality,* trans. Robert Hurley (New York: Pantheon, 1978).

23. Ibid., 95. A fuller quotation is worthwhile:

> [T]here is no power that is exercised without a series of aims and objectives. But this does not mean that it results from the choice or decision of an individual subject.... The rationality of power is characterized by ... tactics which ... end by forming comprehensive systems: the logic is perfectly clear, the aims decipherable, and yet it is often the case that no one is there to have invented them, and few who can be said to have formulated them: an implicit characteristic of the great anonymous, almost unspoken strategies which coordinate the loquacious tactics whose "inventors" or decision makers are often without hypocrisy.

24. From the standpoint of functionalism, strategies of selective transmission can be seen as "latent functions," but this characterization does not bring us any closer to a theory of how they originate and evolve. See Robert King Merton, "Manifest and Latent Functions," in *Social Theory and Social Structure* (Glencoe, Ill.: Free Press, 1957), 19, at 60–82; Wilbert E. Moore, "Functionalism," in *A History of Sociological Analysis,* ed. Tom Bottomore and Robert Nisbet (New York: Basic Books, 1978), 321, at 340–41.

25. For an excellent exposition of the view that radically distinguishes the methodology and expectations of the natural sciences from those of the human sciences, as well as for a discussion of the role of interpretation in the latter, see Charles Taylor, "Interpretation and the Sciences of Man," *Review of Metaphysics* 25 (1971): 3, and "Understanding in Human Science," *Review of Metaphysics* 34 (1980): 25.

26. See supra, 42–44.

27. See generally George P. Fletcher, "The Individualization of Excusing Conditions," *Southern California Law Review* 47 (1974): 25.

28. In deciding whether a particular defense would have undesirable behavioral side effects, one should take notice of the danger of overdeterrence: some people, ignorant of the defense and overly apprehensive of the legal sanction, may, in order to obey the law, succumb to hardships that they should have averted. The social benefit forgone in these cases must then be compared with the dangers of excessive reliance on

the defense were its availability known. The law's traditional resistance to allowing the defenses considered here in any but the most extreme cases may be understood to imply a belief that the benefits forgone because of overdeterrence in this area are more than offset by the danger of reduced obedience to the law that allowing these defenses would bring about.

29. See, e.g., *State v. Toscano,* 74 N.J. 421, 443, 378 A.2d 755, 766 (1977), referring to the "admittedly open-ended nature of (the person-of-reasonable-firmness) standard" of duress; Fletcher, *Rethinking Criminal Law,* sec. 7.5.1; Kadish and Kadish, *Discretion to Disobey,* 125; George P. Fletcher, "The Right Deed for the Wrong Reason: A Reply to Mr. Robinson," *UCLA Law Review* 23 (1975): 293, 312–16; Lawrence Newman and Lawrence Weitzer, "Duress, Free Will, and the Criminal Law," *Southern California Law Review* 30 (1957): 313, 314.

30. See infra 62–67.

31. Kadish and Kadish, *Discretion to Disobey,* 125.

32. Compare Fletcher, *Rethinking Criminal Law,* sec. 7.5.1, arguing that vagueness of justification and excuse defenses is acceptable on the ground that actors rarely plan the conduct that gives rise to such defenses.

33. This aspect of the strategy of selective transmission is most pronounced when the criminal code delegates the definition of defenses entirely to the courts. See, e.g., N.J. Stat. Ann. sec. 2C:3-2 (West 1982); New Jersey Criminal Law Revision Commission, *Final Report: The New Jersey Penal Code* (1971), 2:80.

34. What would amount to a more drastic strategy of selective transmission was suggested in this context by Macaulay in his proposed penal code for India. He was concerned that allowing defenses based on "the desire of self-preservation" would be widely abused and would lead people more readily into life-threatening situations. See Indian Penal Code 106 app. note B at 111 (T. Macaulay, J. MacLeod, G. Anderson, and F. Millet, eds., 1888). At the same time, he recognized the existence of circumstances of genuine necessity in which "it would be useless cruelty to punish acts done under the fear of death, or even of evils less than death." Ibid., 113. His solution was to eliminate any defense of necessity (or duress) from the code, but at the same time to relegate to government clemency the cases in which fairness demanded that no punishment be imposed. Ibid., 111–13.

35. See Note, "Intolerable Conditions as a Defense to Prison Escapes," *UCLA Law Review* 26 (1979): 1126, at 1126–28.

36. See, e.g., *People v. Lovercamp,* 43 Cal. App. 3d 823, 118 Cal. Rptr. 110 (1974); *Johnson v. State,* 379 A.2d 1129 (Del. 1977); *State v. Boleyn,* 328 So. 2d 95 (La. 1976); *People v. Hocquard,* 64 Mich. App.

331, 236 N.W.2d 72 (1975); *State v. Cross,* 58 Ohio St. 2d 482, 391 N.E.2d 319 (1979); *Commonwealth v. Stanley,* 265 Pa. Super. 194, 401 A.2d 1166 (1979), aff'd, 498 Pa. 326, 446 A.2d 583 (1982). On the unusual restrictiveness of these conditions, see *State v. Reese,* 272 N.W.2d 863, 868–70 (Iowa 1978) (McCormick, J., dissenting); and "Intolerable Conditions," 1141–45.

37. 43 Cal. App. 3d 823, 118 Cal. Rptr. 110 (1974).

38. Ibid. at 831, 118 Cal. Rptr. at 115. The same concern is echoed in most other cases adopting a similarly restrictive approach to the defense. See sources cited in note 36; see also *People v. Noble,* 18 Mich. App. 300, 170 N.W.2d 916 (1969), holding that threat of homosexual rape cannot justify prison escape, because such an excuse is too easily abused; *State v. Green,* 470 S.W.2d 565 (Mo. 1971), rejecting necessity-of-escape defense based on threatened homosexual attack because defendant had "several hours" to report threat to prison authorities, despite authorities' failure to respond to inmate's earlier requests for protection; cert. denied, 4405 U.S. 1073 (1972). Contra *People v. Harmon,* 53 Mich. App. 482, 220 N.W.2d 212 (1974).

39. 52 Ill. 2d 231, 287 N.E.2d 670 (1972).

40. Ibid. at 234, 287 N.E.2d at 672 (quoting *People v. Carradine,* No. A69-27 (Cook County, Ill. Cir. Ct. Oct. 1, 1969)).

41. This concern is the only reason given by the court for its resolute refusal to take into consideration Ms. Carradine's fear of the notorious gang to which the accused, against whom she was expected to testify, belonged. Specifically, the court did not rely on the fact that Ms. Carradine alleged no explicit threats against her, as a strict application of the doctrine of duress would probably require. The reason for the court's failure to note the absence of such allegations may have been that Ms. Carradine did not technically raise the defense of duress, but rather relied on the alleged facts of duress (that is, her fear of reprisal by the gang) as extenuating circumstances that should have reduced the prison term imposed on her for contempt of court.

42. See, e.g., *D'Aquino v. United States,* 192 F.2d 338, 357–65 (9th Cir. 1951) (treason); *Ross v. State,* 169 Ind. 388, 82 N.E. 781 (1907) (arson); *Nall v. Commonwealth,* 208 Ky. 700, 271 S.W. 1059 (1925) (burglary); *State v. St. Clair,* 262 S.W.2d 25 (Mo. 1953) (robbery); *State v. Ellis,* 232 Or. 70, 374 P.2d 461 (1962) (kidnapping).

43. Duress was, however, allowed as a defense to perjury in, for example, *Hall v. State,* 136 Fla. 644, 679–84, 187 So. 392, 407–9 (1939), and more recently in the English case of *Regina v. Hudson,* [1971] 2 All E.R. 244 (C.A.).

44. *Commonwealth v. Chermansky,* 430 Pa. 170, 174, 242 A.2d 237, 240 (1968). But compare *Commonwealth v. Klein,* 372 Mass.

823, 363 N.E.2d 1313 (1977), which declined to follow an act-at-your-peril rule.

45. Model Penal Code sec. 3.06 comment 15 (Tent. Draft No. 8, 1958).

46. See ibid. sec. 3.07(2)(b) and comment 3.

47. It is possible, of course, to conceive of more lenient decision rules than "act at your peril" that might be adopted in the imaginary universe. For example, we might opt for a rule that commanded acquittal when the defendant acted under a genuine belief that her victim was a fleeing felon and that shooting him would not jeopardize the safety of others. The adoption of such a decision rule would be premised on the notion that such a defendant would be innocent of any wrongdoing even if she in fact shot the wrong person. Under this interpretation, the promulgation in the real world of an "act at your peril" rule should be understood as a compromise between the imaginary system's conduct rule and its decision rule, a compromise intended to reduce the likelihood of behavioral side effects that the more lenient rule might have. The interpretation described in the text, however, is somewhat more ambitious in that it attempts to explain the "act at your peril" rule not as a mere compromise, but as the product of a coherent substantive position. This position condemns as at least reckless any shooting by a citizen, no matter how well intentioned, but sees as pertinent the "moral luck" involved in the actual happy outcome of the defendant's misconduct. See Bernard Williams, "Moral Luck," in *Moral Luck* (New York: Cambridge University Press, 1981), 20.

48. 12 Cal. 3d 470, 526 P.2d 241, 116 Cal. Rptr. 233 (1974).

49. That society considers such an outcome beneficial is attested to by the considerable latitude given police in the use of deadly force against escaping felons and by the defense that ex hypothesi would have been available to Ceballos had he shot at the burglar himself.

50. *Ceballos,* 12 Cal. 3d at 477, 526 P.2d at 244, 116 Cal. Rptr. at 236.

51. "Almost the only knowledge of law possessed by many people is that ignorance of it is no excuse (ignorantia juris non excusat)." Glanville Williams, *Textbook of Criminal Law* (London: Stevens, 1978), 405.

52. "Examination shows that ... from the earliest times, the numerous exceptions reduce the rule to a mere guideline for the courts. Nevertheless, *ignorantia juris* is usually cited out of its context as an irrefutable legal verity." Vera Bolgár, "The Present Function of the Maxim Ignorantia Iuris Neminem Excusat—a Comparative Study," *Iowa Law Review* 52 (1967): 636, 640. The writer attributes this tendency to a "recurring and inexplicable phenomenon of human thinking"—"persistent reliance on maxims in full ignorance of their truth." Ibid. at 639.

53. The distinction between offenses that are *malum in se* and those that are *malum prohibitum* is significant in this context because of its influence on the interpretation courts give to the term "willfully" in the relevant statute. See, e.g., *United States v. Murdock*, 290 U.S. 389 (1933), in which the Court infers a requirement of bad faith or evil intent from a statutory prohibition of "willful" failure to pay taxes; *Potter v. United States*, 155 U.S. 438, 445–48 (1894), inferring necessity of both knowledge and "bad intent" from requirement of "willful" act or omission; *United States v. Ehrlichman*, 376 F. Supp. 29, 35 (D.D.C. 1974), where the defense is rejected because acts were *malum in se*.

54. Whether the difference between ignorance of a statute and ignorance of a regulation matters depends upon the interpretation of the language of the statute under which a regulation is promulgated: the statute is sometimes interpreted to require knowledge by defendants of the regulation, in which case ignorance of the regulation becomes a valid defense. The Third Circuit endorsed this reasoning in *United States v. Boyce Motor Lines*, 188 F.2d 889, 890–91 (3d Cir.), aff'd, 342 U.S. 337, 342 (1951), but the Supreme Court's affirmance left the point ambiguous. For other cases on the subject, see *United States v. Lizarraga-Lizarraga*, 541 F.2d 826, 828 (9th Cir. 1976); *United States v. Chicago Express*, 235 F.2d 785, 786 (7th Cir. 1956); *St. Johnsbury Trucking Co. v. United States*, 220 F.2d 393, 395 (1st Cir. 1955); compare *United States v. International Minerals & Chem. Corp.*, 402 U.S. 558, 565 (1971), holding that when dangerous products, devices, or substances are involved, the probability of regulation is so great that possessors of such products are thereby put on notice regarding the existence of regulations governing them.

55. *International Minerals*, 402 U.S. at 564–65; *United States v. Freed*, 401 U.S. 601, 609 (1970); ibid., 616 (Brennan, J., concurring); *Lambert v. California*, 35 U.S. 225, 229 (1957); *Reyes v. United States*, 258 F.2d 774, 784 (9th Cir. 1958).

56. *Lambert*, 355 U.S. at 229; *Reyes*, 258 F.2d at 784–85.

57. *State v. Sawyer*, 95 Conn. 34, 110 A. 461 (1920); *Long v. State*, 44 Del. 262, 65 A.2d 489 (1949); *State v. Collins*, 15 Del. 536, 41 A. 144 (1894).

58. *Hargrove v. United States*, 67 F.2d 820 (5th Cir. 1933); *Long*, 44 Del. at 278–79, 65 A.2d at 497; *Collins*, 15 Del. at 539–40, 41 A. at 145.

59. For a detailed discussion of this distinction, see Glanville L. Williams, *Criminal Law—the General Part*, 2d ed. (London: Stevens, 1961), secs. 106–17.

60. *Cox v. Louisiana*, 379 U.S. 559, 568–75 (1965); *Raley v. Ohio*,

360 U.S. 423, 437–40 (1959). Compare *United States v. Ehrlichman,* 546 F.2d 910 (D.C. Cir. 1976), holding that presidential assistant's good-faith belief in legality of unconstitutional search is no defense to prosecution for such search (cert. denied, 426 U.S. 1120 [1977]), with *United States v. Barker,* 546 F.2d 940 (D.C. Cir. 1976), which allowed as a defense a subordinate operative's reasonable, good-faith reliance on apparent authority of presidential assistant.

61. *Lambert v. California,* 355 U.S. 225, 228–29 (1957); compare *Hayes v. United States,* 258 F.2d 774, 784 (8th Cir. 1958) (distinguishing *Lambert* on the ground, inter alia, that failure to register while crossing the border is not a mere omission).

62. As is so often the case, Holmes provides a stark and often-cited formulation of the issue: "It is no doubt true that there are many cases in which the criminal could not have known that he was breaking the law, but to admit the excuse at all would be to encourage ignorance where the law-maker has determined to make men know and obey, and justice to the individual is rightly outweighed by the larger interests on the other side of the scales." Oliver Wendell Holmes, *The Common Law* (Boston: Little, 1881), 48.

63. See Bentham, *A Fragment on Government,* 430.

64. The more common view holds such a possibility to be inconceivable: "The official evaluation of behaviour by the primary organs [that is, courts] must *of course* coincide with the guidance given by the system to ordinary individuals. If the system judges an individual to be doing what he ought not to do this entails that its norms guide him not to do that act, and *vice versa.*" Raz, *Practical Reason and Norms,* 142 (emphasis added).

65. Professor David Daube depicts such a relation between certain criminal provisions and their underlying moral norms and shows how this relation is reflected in the form of some ancient criminal statutes: "It would, then, be absurd for a lawgiver to say: 'Murder is forbidden: if anyone violates this decree, he shall be put to death.' The sensible form in this case is the other, which, so to speak, takes the prohibition of murder for granted and concentrates on making clear what will happen if you disregard it: 'If a man murders another man, he shall be put to death.'" Daube, *Forms of Roman Legislation,* 4. This view of the relation between the "core" criminal offenses and their moral counterparts is typical of natural-law thinkers and was most clearly stated by Richard Hooker. See Richard Hooker, *Of the Laws of Ecclesiastical Polity* (Cambridge: Harvard University Press, 1977), vol. 1, chap. 10, sec. 10. Hooker's position is cited and critically discussed in John Finnis, *Natural Law and Natural Rights* (Oxford: Clarendon Press, 1980), 281–83.

66. The possibility of conflict is eliminated, of course, only with respect to conventional morality or to whatever other moral system the law embodies.

67. See Oliver Wendell Holmes, "The Path of the Law," in *Collected Legal Papers* (New York: Harcourt Brace, 1920), 167, at 169–79.

68. This analysis presupposes the view that the normativity of law does not depend on its coerciveness. For an example of this view, see Raz, *Practical Reason and Norms*, 157–61; compare Finnis, *Natural Law*, 346–47, on the controversy that evolved in the fifteenth through seventeenth centuries around the "purely penal law theory" of the nature of the obligation imposed by criminal law.

69. The safe-side principle makes sense only when the agent is confronted with a single moral duty that constrains the pursuit of her self-interest. It is obviously of no help in resolving a conflict between competing moral duties. The criminal law, however, typically deals with the former situation.

70. A similar argument may apply to the part of the definition of the offense that specifies the punishment. On grounds of general deterrence, the conduct rule may issue a harsh threat, while the decision rule, on utilitarian or other humanitarian grounds, may specify a more lenient penalty. Under complete acoustic separation, considerations of general deterrence would not require that the decision rule impose any punishment at all. For the proposition that deterrence does not directly justify punishment, but only the threat of punishment, see J. D. Mabbott, "Punishment," *Mind* 48 (1939): 152, at 152.

71. On the broad implications of the distinction between ordinary and specialized language in the law, see Bruce Ackerman, *Private Property and the Constitution* (New Haven: Yale University Press, 1977), 10–20 and passim.

72. Compare Professor Glanville Williams' comment on the phenomenon considered here: "The lawyer has much the same need for a technical jargon as the scientist, but he is uncomfortable in trying to achieve it. This is because he believes that the law, which governs all men, should be intelligible to all men, and should therefore speak their language, with all its imperfections.... Our ancestors made use of bizarre legal words like withernam, replevin and trover, but this would now be frowned upon. The best we can do is to take common expressions and give them an extra sharpness for legal purposes. The word 'reckless' is a good example." Williams, *Textbook of Criminal Law*, 68.

73. 2 L.R.-Cr. Cas. Res. 154 (1875).

74. Offences Against the Person Act, 1861, 24 and 25 Vict., chap. 100, sec. 55.

75. See, e.g., Peter Brett, *An Inquiry into Criminal Guilt* (London: Sweet and Maxwell, 1963), 149; J. Edwards, *Mens Rea in Statutory Offences* (London: Macmillan, 1955), 58–63; Fletcher, *Rethinking Criminal Law,* sec. 9.3.3, pp. 723–27; Williams, *Criminal Law—the General Part,* sec. 69, pp. 185–99.

76. 2 L.R.-Cr. Cas. Res. at 174–75.

77. Williams, *Criminal Law—the General Part,* sec. 83, p. 241.

78. Ibid., sec. 69, p. 188, and the sources cited in note 75.

79. Graham Hughes, "Criminal Responsibility" (book review), *Stanford Law Review* 16 (1964): 470, 480–81.

80. See, e.g., *White v. State,* 44 Ohio App. 331, 185 N.E. 64 (1933), upholding a conviction under a statute prohibiting a husband from abandoning his pregnant wife, despite the defendant's alleged ignorance of the pregnancy, on the grounds that abandoning a wife—pregnant or not—is a wrong and a violation of the defendant's civic duty.

81. Hughes, "Criminal Responsibility," 480. This criticism is specifically directed at Brett's interpretation. See Brett, *Inquiry into Criminal Guilt.* To Professor Fletcher, Lord Bramwell's position exemplifies the view that "wrongdoers ... must assume the risk that things will turn out worse than they expected." Fletcher, *Rethinking Criminal Law,* sec. 9.3.3, p. 727. Fletcher characterizes this view as "one of the more insidious arguments in criminal law." Ibid. Glanville Williams likewise criticizes Lord Bramwell's analysis. See Williams, *Criminal Law—the General Part,* sec. 69, 189–90. Jerome Hall dismisses *Prince,* as well as the cases of statutory rape that follow its lead, as decisions in which "sexual morality has over-ridden established principles of the criminal law." Jerome Hall, "Interrelations of Criminal Law and Torts" (part 2), *Columbia Law Review* 43 (1943): 967, 995.

82. Williams, *Criminal Law—the General Part,* sec. 69, p. 197. For a sample of the decisions, see *Miller v. State,* 16 Ala. App. 534, 79 So. 314 (1918); *Anderson v. State,* 384 P.2d 669 (Alaska 1963); *State v. Superior Court,* 104 Ariz. 440, 454 P.2d 982 (1969); *Manship v. People,* 99 Colo. 1, 58 P.2d 1215 (1936); *Brown v. State,* 23 Del. 159, 74 A. 836 (1909); *Simmons v. State,* 151 Fla. 778, 10 So. 2d 436 (1942); *Holton v. State,* 28 Fla. 303, 9 So. 716 (1891); *People v. Lewellyn,* 314 Ill. 106, 145 N.E. 289 (1924); *Heath v. State,* 173 Ind. 296, 90 N.E. 310 (1910); *People v. Doyle,* 16 Mich. App. 242, 167 N.W.2d 907 (1969).

83. 61 Cal. 2d 529, 393 P.2d 673, 39 Cal. Rptr. 361 (1964).

84. See ibid. at 534 n. 3, 393 P.2d at 676 n. 3, 39 Cal. Rptr. at 364 n. 3.

85. Ibid. at 533, 393 P.2d at 675, 39 Cal. Rptr. at 363 (distinguishing *People v. Ratz,* 115 Cal. 132, 46 P. 915 (1896)).

86. What about the defendant who, in a world of only partial acoustic

separation, actually inquires about the statutory definition before engaging in sex and seeks to rely on the statutory age limit? The crux of the legal advice he should get is: you had better leave children alone! The lawyer can render this advice in more conventional form by telling the client that, although the statutory age limit is indeed ten (in our hypothetical), the client acts at his peril and will be convicted notwithstanding his reasonable belief that the child was over ten if the child turns out to be under that age. Alternatively, the lawyer can, in line with my present suggestion, tell the client that the law really forbids intercourse with infants altogether, even though it may sometimes fail to punish such intercourse (for example, when the infant turns out to be over ten years of age). Under either version of the legal advice, the imaginary scrupulous law abider will have little ground to protest a criminal conviction when he makes a mistake concerning his victim's age. He has either knowingly gambled and lost (under the first version), or with equal awareness he has transgressed the relevant legal (and moral) norm (under the second version). The main point, however, is that under the conditions of acoustic separation assumed by my argument, such a scrupulous law abider is indeed an unlikely figure: with regard to many core criminal offenses people are by and large familiar with and guided by the relevant moral norms rather than by the details of their statutory articulations.

87. For a general analysis of vagueness doctrine, see LaFave and Scott, *Handbook on Criminal Law*, sec. 11; Note, "The Void-for-Vagueness Doctrine in the Supreme Court," *University of Pennsylvania Law Review* 109 (1960): 67.

88. *Lanzetta v. New Jersey*, 306 U.S. 451, 453 (1939).

89. *Giacco v. Pennsylvania*, 38 U.S. 399, 402–3 (1966).

90. *Winters v. New York*, 333 U.S. 507, 517–20 (1948); *Fox v. Washington*, 236 U.S. 273 (1915).

91. *United States v. National Dairy Prods. Corp.*, 372 U.S. 29, 36–37 (1963); *Boyce Motor Lines v. United States*, 342 U.S. 337, 342 (1952).

92. An example of indeterminacy is the statute declared unconstitutional in *United States v. Cohen Grocery Co.*, 255 U.S. 81 (1921), which purported to punish "any unjust or unreasonable rate or charge in handling or dealing in or with any necessaries," ibid. at 89 (quoting Act of Aug. 10, 1917, chap. 53, sec. 4, 40 Stat. 276, 277, as amended by Act of Oct. 22, 1919, chap. 80, sec. 2, 41 Stat. 297, 298). On the notion of indeterminacy generally, see Granville L. Williams, "Language and the Law" (part 2), *Law Quarterly Review* 61 (1945): 179.

93. *Screws v. United States*, 325 U.S. 91, 96 (1945). A famous example of inaccessibility is the alleged practice of the emperor Caligula to "post the regulations up, but in an awkwardly cramped spot and

written so small that no one could take a copy." Suetonius, *The Twelve Caesars,* trans. Robert Graves (Baltimore: Penguin, 1957), 170, cited in *Screws,* 325 U.S. at 96.

94. See *Rose v. Locke,* 423 U.S. 48, 54–55 (1975) (Brennan, J., dissenting); *Franklin v. State,* 257 So. 2d 21, 23 (Fla. 1971); "Void-for-Vagueness Doctrine," 73–74.

95. Ibid.

96. On the basis of its interpretation of prior decisions, the dissent in *Locke* reached a conclusion opposed to the majority's—namely, that Tennessee law did not consider cunnilingus a crime against nature. See ibid. at 55–58 (Brennan, J., dissenting).

97. LaFave and Scott, *Handbook on Criminal Law,* sec. 11, p. 86 (footnotes omitted). For similar criticisms of the reliance on scienter to cure vagueness, see *Boyce Motor Lines v. United States,* 342 U.S. 337, 345 (1952) (Jackson, J., dissenting); Rex Collings, "Unconstitutional Uncertainty—an Appraisal," *Cornell Law Quarterly* 40 (1955): 195, 227–31.

98. See supra, 48.

99. "Common law definitions are of course resorted to when the forbidden conduct is not defined. This may supply the deficiency for a *legal* understanding of a vague statute, but it cannot meet the constitutional requirement that the language of the statute be understandable to the common man." *Franklin v. State,* 257 So. 2d 21, 23 (Fla. 1971) (footnote omitted). That judicial gloss has little to do with fair warning is made abundantly clear by decisions that rely on judicial interpretations given to the statute after the defendant's alleged criminal act. See, e.g., *United States v. Vuitch,* 402 U.S. 62, 71–72 (1971); *Winters v. New York,* 333 U.S. 507, 514–15; see also "Void-for-Vagueness Doctrine," at 72–75 and nn. 30–38.

100. It must be emphasized that this statement pertains only to the part of the criminal law that codifies aspects of conventional morality. In the case of regulatory offenses, particularly those addressed to some professional subgroup of the population, the *mens rea* requirement may be met if the language of the regulation, understood in the sense in which that language is used by the professional subgroup, indicates to its audience the nature of the proscribed conduct. See LaFave and Scott, *Handbook on Criminal Law,* sec. 11, p. 85 and n. 26.

101. See, e.g., *Boyce Motor Lines v. United States,* 34 U.S. 337, 345 (1957) (Jackson, J., dissenting): "[T]he knowledge requisite to knowing violation of a statute is factual knowledge as distinguished from knowledge of the law."

102. *Rose v. Locke,* 423 U.S. 48, 50 (1975).

103. *Franklin v. State,* 257 So. 2d 21 (Fla. 1971).

104. Ibid., 23.

105. According to Professor Douglas Hay's fascinating account of the criminal law in eighteenth-century England, the entire system of criminal justice placed critical reliance on what amounts to the selective transmission of conduct rules and decision rules. In the absence of a police force, the criminal law depended on in terrorem legislation (mostly in the form of threats of capital punishment) coupled with de facto leniency. This reliance was made possible and partially disguised by "the opacity of the law," and by a broad use of the low-visibility pardon power of the king. See Hay, "Property, Authority, and the Criminal Law," in D. Hay, P. Linebaugh, J. Rule, E. P. Thompson, and C. Winslow, *Albion's Fatal Tree* (New York: Pantheon, 1975), 17.

Professor P. S. Atiyah suggests an essentially similar account of the role played by equity in contract law: "[H]istorically [Equity] may have been especially useful when its existence and extent was not widely known among the mass of the people. If equitable rules are applied on a regular and uniform basis so that they come to supplant the legal rules altogether, then the deterrent effect of the legal rules may be greatly weakened. Who will pay his debts punctually if everybody knows that the legal sanction for failing to do so is, as a matter of course, disregarded by Courts of Equity?" Atiyah, "Judges and Policy," *Israel Law Review* 15 (1980): 346, 361. "It is, therefore, not surprising that attempts were made to conceal the likelihood of equitable relief or mercy being available, and rather to emphasize the threat itself." P. S. Atiyah, *The Rise and Fall of Freedom of Contract* (Oxford: Clarendon Press, 1979), 193. Professor Atiyah comments that "there was a strong elitist tradition in English law until relatively recent times. Saying one thing, and doing another, or keeping quiet about powers of mercy or Equity, was an important contribution to the mystique of the law. The process helped to reconcile the relatively free political condition of Englishmen with the fact that they had no political power." Atiyah, *Rise and Fall*, 361.

106. Selective transmission can be used for clearly illegitimate purposes. For example, a decision rule may impose punishment (most likely out of a desire for vengeance or moral retribution) for conduct not prohibited by a corresponding conduct rule. Courts' refusal to allow evidence of the defendant's intoxication to negate *mens rea* even in offenses in which intent is required can be interpreted as imposing low-visibility punishment for the intoxication itself in the absence of an explicit criminal prohibition against it.

107. See Thomas Nagel, "Ruthlessness in Public Life," in *Mortal Questions* (New York: Cambridge University Press, 1979), 75; Williams, "Moral Luck," 547; Walzer, "Political Action: The Problem of Dirty

Hands," in *War and Moral Responsibility*, ed. Marshall Cohen, Thomas Nagel, and Thomas Scanlon (Princeton: Princeton University Press, 1974), 62; see also Hannah Arendt, "Truth and Politics," in *Philosophy, Politics, and Society*, ed. P. Laslett and W. Runcirnan, 3d ser. (New York: Barnes and Noble, 1967), 104; Max Weber, "Politics as a Vocation," in *From Max Weber: Essays in Sociology*, ed. and trans. H. H. Gerth and C. Wright Mills (New York: Oxford University Press, 1946), 77. *Dirty Hands* is the title of Sartre's play that deals with this moral issue. See Jean-Paul Sartre, *No Exit and Three Other Plays,* trans. L. Abel (New York: Vintage, 1956).

108. In one form or another, the problem of dirty hands appears in all regimes, democracies included. In a well-functioning democracy, however, duly elected officials who are answerable to the electorate or to some representative body are perhaps less likely than are officials in other regimes to conceal or deceive for illicit purposes. Sissela Bok proposes public debate on the parameters of permissible political deception in *Lying* (New York: Pantheon, 1978), 98–99. On the general problem of secrecy in democracies, see Itzhak Galnoor, ed., *Government Secrecy in Democracies* (New York: Harper and Row, 1977).

109. Compare Martin M. Shapiro, *Law and Politics in the Supreme Court* (New York: Free Press of Glencoe, 1964), 26–27, drawing an analogy between law and politics in arguing for the Supreme Court's need to uphold "[t]he judicial myth of impartiality and nondiscriminatory application of 'correct' legal maxims" on which the Court's political power rests.

110. Joseph Raz, "The Rule of Law and Its Virtue," in *The Authority of Law* (Oxford: Clarendon Press, 1979), 214. In the following discussion, I rely primarily on the excellent analysis in this essay. Other valuable philosophical treatments of the rule of law can be found in Finnis, *Natural Law*, 270–76; Lon L. Fuller, *The Morality of Law* (New Haven: Yale University Press, 1964), 33–94; J. R. Lucas, *The Principles of Politics* (Oxford: Clarendon Press, 1966), 106–17; John Rawls, *A Theory of Justice* (Cambridge: Harvard University Press, 1971), 235–43.

111. See supra, 64–65.

112. Fuller was aware of this point. But because he treated law as a uniform substance, undifferentiated into decision rules and conduct rules, he considered the point to be an argument for limiting the clarity of all laws. Recounting the legislative experience of the early Communist regime in Poland, Fuller said: "It was discovered ... that making the laws readily understandable to the citizen carried a hidden cost in that it rendered their application by the courts more capricious and less predictable. Some retreat to a more balanced view therefore became unavoidable." Fuller, *The Morality of Law*, 45.

113. See Raz, "Rule of Law," 226.

114. See Fuller, *The Morality of Law*, 33–41; see also ibid., 49–51 (on promulgation); ibid., 63–65 (on clarity).

115. Jeremy Bentham, "A General View of a Complete Code of Laws," in *The Works of Jeremy Bentham*, J. Bowring, ed. (Edinburgh: W. Tait, 1843), 3:155, 161.

116. Jeremy Bentham, "Rationale of Judicial Evidence," in *Works*, 6:191, 508.

117. In addition to insisting on the clarity and simplicity of all laws, Bentham argued for the publicity of legislative proceedings. See "An Essay on Political Tactics," in *Works*, 2:299, 310–17, and of judicial proceedings, see "Bentham's Draught for the Organization of Judicial Establishments," in *Works*, 4:305, 316–18.

118. Raz, "Rule of Law," 220.

119. For this group of arguments, see especially Friedrich A. von Hayek, *The Road to Serfdom* (Chicago: University of Chicago Press, 1944), 72–87; Rawls, *A Theory of Justice*, 235–36; Raz, "Rule of Law," 220–22.

120. Raz uses the image of entrapment in this context. See Raz, "Rule of Law," 222.

121. See Fletcher, *Rethinking Criminal Law*, sec. 10.3, pp. 811–12.

122. See supra, 54–62.

123. See Immanuel Kant, *Groundwork of the Metaphysic of Morals*, trans. H. J. Paton (London: Hutchinson, 1948), 62–66, 99–95.

124. These duties include the moral duty to obey the law, whenever such a duty exists.

125. Compare Rawls, *A Theory of Justice*, 242, arguing that because the value of the rule of law is related to liberty, the rule of law can be curtailed, when necessary, on liberty's behalf.

126. Raz, "Rule of Law," 213–14.

127. See Fuller, *The Morality of Law*, passim

128. "Violence" is used here in its ordinary sense to denote any intense physical force. There is also a narrower, legal sense in which violence signifies "unlawful exercise of physical force"; that definition obviously does not apply here. See, e.g., *The Concise Oxford Dictionary of Current English*, 5th ed. (Oxford: Clarendon Press, 1964), 1453. Robert Paul Wolff argues against the latter, narrower usage in "Violence and the Law," in *The Rule of Law*, ed. Robert Paul Wolff (New York: Simon and Schuster, 1971), 54, at 59–62.

129. Joseph Raz, "The Institutional Nature of Law," in *The Authority of Law*, 103, at 112.

130. I do not mean to suggest that any particular forms of punishment, least of all the more extreme and brutal ones, are necessary.

Though the rhetorical force of the view I express is enhanced by the fact that fairly brutal punishments abound in all important legal systems, the logic of this view would not be impaired in a system that used much milder punishments.

131. This dilemma is clearly expressed in *State v. Abbott*, 36 N.J. 63, 174 A.2d 881 (1961), a case dealing with the question whether the law should require that a person under attack retreat, if he can do so safely, rather than use deadly force in self-defense. In opposition to the rule requiring retreat, the court noted, was the view that (1) "[t]he law of course should not denounce conduct as criminal when it accords with the behavior of reasonable men," and that (2) "the manly thing is to hold one's ground"; whereas proponents of the rule, the court observed, maintained that (3) "right-thinking men agree" that "it is better that the assailed shall retreat than that the life of another be needlessly spent," and that (4) "a rule so requiring may well induce others to adhere to that worthy standard of behavior." Ibid. at 69, 174 A.2d at 884. The dilemma faces with full force someone who, together with other "right-thinking" people, subscribes to (3) and who also believes (consistently) in both (1) and (4) in a community in which belief in (2) is widespread.

132. See also Guido Calabresi and Philip Bobbitt, *Tragic Choices* (New York: Norton, 1978), 24–26, 78–79, 95, describing situations in which the value of honesty competes against and sometimes loses to other values in what the authors call "tragic" social contexts.

133. Walzer, "Political Action," 64, 65.

134. Obviously, many other pertinent and important issues are not even raised here. Prominent examples would be the complex and crucial role played by lawyers in regard to acoustic separation, and the relation of selective transmission to various theories of democracy.

CHAPTER THREE

IN DEFENSE OF DEFIANCE

Attitudes to authority vary. Authority often attracts allegiance and compliance, but it also provokes defiance and resentment. Philosophers who affirm authority and spell out the conditions of its legitimacy articulate the former, positive, attitudes to it; whereas those who deny the very possibility of binding authority and proclaim philosophical anarchism of one sort or another give vent, and priority, to the negative attitudes. It is of course possible that one or the other of the opposing camps has it right, so that the reactions to authority that underlie the other camp's views should be dismissed as irrational and aberrant. But the conflicting attitudes, as well as their theoretical expressions, persist, suggesting that a different approach may be called for. We should perhaps recognize the validity of both sets of attitudes, and acknowledge the conflict itself as an essential aspect of authority that an adequate theory should accommodate and explain. We need, in other words, an account of authority that incorporates the partial insights of both warring camps: one that validates authority's appeal, while also making good sense of the impulse to escape it.

My proposal for meeting this challenge is simple. Authority usually comes clothed in coercion. Although it is of the essence of authority that it appeal to our voluntary obedience, it is a characteristic of all important authorities, most prominently the state, to use coercive means to back up this appeal and to secure compliance. I will argue that our conflicting attitudes toward authority mirror an inner tension within authority itself between these two elements: *normativity* and *coercion*. To make good on this suggestion we must seek an account of authority's normativity—of the nature of its appeal to voluntary obedience—such that the use of coercive means will be seen to undermine that appeal.[1]

1. Normativity and Coercion: The Disjunctive View

I have spoken so far about attitudes to authority, but for present purposes I could have just as well spoken about attitudes to law. The state is by far the most important source of authority, and it exercises its authority predominantly through the legal system. By restating the issue of authority as the issue of obedience to law, I can tap a discussion that has taken place mainly within jurisprudence concerning the law's use of coercion and the meaning of law's normative appeal. In drawing on this discussion, it will be useful to distinguish three views on the relationship between normativity and coercion: a reductive, an additive, and a disjunctive view.

The reductive view can be traced back to Bentham, and then further to Hobbes, but the most influential formulation of this view that directly spawned modern treatment of the subject is that of J. Austin.[2] His is the much discussed and much maligned command theory of law. Stated in the way most congenial to our present concern, its main claim is that the normativity of law is entirely a matter of law's coerciveness. To be under a legal obligation is simply to be the target of a threat of sanction. The reductive view has been subjected to sustained and well-known criticisms that I need not rehearse here. Suffice it to observe that this view lacks the resources to even make intelligible, let alone affirm, law's presumption "to designate by rules certain types of behavior as standards for the guidance . . . of the members of society"[3] and people's widespread belief that such rules may indeed be "binding" upon them.

Austin's reductive theory has been largely superseded by what I shall call the additive view, the most influential version of which is H. L. A. Hart's. Hart took pains to distinguish, as well as relate, law's coerciveness and its normativity. Both the distinction and the relationship are expressed in the locution "norms backed by sanctions": law's normativity in this view must be understood independently of and in contrast to its coerciveness. Normativity is a matter of voluntary obedience; it invokes and relies on people's disposition, whose nature and sources may vary, to follow legal rules.[4] Coercion and normativity are portrayed as two separate but complementary strategies that the law employs to secure the individual conduct that it desires. The idea of a norm backed by a sanction is not unique to law. Many other authorities seem similarly to regulate behavior by combining a normative "ought" statement with a coercive threat; witness the parent who tells his or her child,

"Clean your room or I'll spank you!" In analogy to the case of legal rules as construed by Hart, the child too is now supposedly faced with two separate but mutually supporting motivational structures: one signaled by the imperative, "You ought to clean your room," and the other conveyed by the threat, "If you don't clean the room, you'll be spanked."

Against this additive account, I propose a disjunctive relationship between norms and sanctions. On this view, sanctions cannot be simply appended to antecedently and independently existing norms without affecting them. Rather than being just complementary and mutually reinforcing devices, normativity and coercion are also at odds with each other. My aim, accordingly, is to display the different ways in which backing imperatives with sanctions detracts from the normative force that an authority's utterances might otherwise have.

Although the disjunctive view of the relationship between norms and sanctions helps explain some widely shared attitudes toward authority, the intuitive appeal of the view itself is uncertain. It will be easier to elicit the requisite intuition and to make better sense of the disjunctive view by using an indirect approach. I will thus first illustrate and explain this view as it applies to requests, rather than to authority. Requests obviously differ from authoritative commands, but they are close enough to make the detour short and worthwhile.

To fix my terms in talking about authority I will use Leslie Green's definition that encapsulates much of the recent discussion of the subject: "A has authority over B if and only if the fact that A requires B to ϕ (i) gives B a content-independent reason to ϕ and (ii) excludes some of B's reasons for not ϕ-ing."[5] This definition characterizes the reason for action provided by authority as source based, content independent, and exclusionary. It is source based in that the very fact that A mandates B to ϕ is a reason for B to ϕ; it is content independent in that the reason so provided by A has nothing to do with the substance or merits of the mandated action: within a certain range (that defines the scope of A's authority) A's utterance would be a reason for *any* action that A mandated; and finally, authority provides an exclusionary reason in that its mandate displaces at least some (and perhaps all) reasons that would otherwise apply to B and might counsel against ϕ-ing.

Although my arguments do not require a corresponding definition of coercion—the ordinary term, despite its looseness, will do—one clarification is in order. Coercion, I take it, is designed to render the decreed conduct nonoptional. By using coercive threats authority does not merely seek to provide its subjects with an additional reason for compliance. To be coercive, the avowed purpose of the threat must be to bring about the commanded behavior independently of the agent's own values and desires. The inner logic of coercion does not contain, accordingly, a limiting principle that sets a ceiling on the threats employed. The constraints on the harshness of penalties actually used by authorities result from considerations that are external to the authority's coercive goals, such as the retributive considerations that ordinarily delimit the permissible severity of criminal sanctions.[6]

Green's definition of authority helps bring out important similarities between authoritative utterances and requests. Requests also provide source-based and content-independent reasons for action. Consequently, many of the difficulties raised by the idea of authority—how can the mere fact that A said something be a reason for doing anything at all?—also attend requests. We can hope, therefore, to gain some insight regarding authority by looking at requests first. Consider a simple request such as "Please pass the salt." By making such a request A provides B with a reason, whose precise nature we must yet consider, to pass the salt. Now suppose that A expands on his request by adding the words "or else I'll break your arm." On the additive view, B is now presented with two reasons for passing the salt: the reason generated by the initial request, and the reason created by the coercive threat. But this analysis is strikingly inadequate. Rather than leaving the first reason intact, the threat clearly seems to undercut the request and to supersede it: the reason that B had to pass the salt prior to the threat has been destroyed by A's threat.

Even though the disjunctive view enjoys intuitive support here, the view is not without puzzle. How is it that merely by adding a motivation for passing the salt, A undercuts other reasons that may have been present for doing so? Why is more, in this case, less?

The question becomes even more pointed when we observe the full force of the disjunctive interpretation of this situation. To see that, we should note the difference between *disjunctive reasons* of the kind that characterize the salt-passing episode, and a more common kind of contending reasons, namely *conflicting reasons*. Conflicting reasons are those that call for incompatible actions. The reasons themselves, however, are cumulative: they apply to the agent and exert their influence simultaneously, albeit in opposite directions. The good flavor and the high caloric content of ice cream are conflicting but cumulative reasons with respect to eating ice cream. Such conflict between reasons is resolved by weight: one reason (or set of reasons) outweighs the other. In the case of disjunctive reasons, in contrast, the reasons themselves, rather than the actions they call for, are mutually exclusive. That my friend is at home is a reason for visiting him, whereas the fact that he is out is a reason against, but the two cannot apply at the same time. The noncumulativity of disjunctive reasons is perhaps even more apparent when the reasons would both call for the same action. That *Gone with the Wind* is playing is a reason for me to go to the local movie theater tonight, as is the fact that *Children of Paradise* is showing. But I cannot have both of these reasons for going to that theater.

An account of the salt-passing episode in terms of conflicting reasons may seem easy. For example, one might suggest that A's threat provides B with a reason against passing the salt because B resents the threat, all the more so for being unwarranted and out of place. This reason now weighs against, and perhaps outweighs, the reason for passing the salt provided by A's request. But this simple explanation does not fit our intuitions in this scenario. The threat does not merely present the request with a new rival (B's aroused resentment) while also supplying it with an ally (B's fear for his arm). Rather, A's willingness to compel B's behavior, a willingness he manifests by use of a coercive threat, extinguishes the normative force his request originally had. It is this intuition that marks the request and the threat as disjunctive. And since the threat displaces or invalidates the reasons for passing the salt provided by the request, it cannot back up those reasons by enlisting B's fear any more than it can outweigh them by arousing B's resentments. The simple explanation I have suggested misses precisely this disjunctive relationship between the two parts of A's utterance. It therefore fails to address the real puzzle.

That A's threat does not simply outweigh the reason for passing the salt created by A's request, but rather nullifies it, seems clear. "A request backed by a sanction" is an oxymoron. The case of authority, I maintain, is similar. "A norm backed by a sanction" presents an incongruity that the prevailing additive conception of authority ignores.[7] This incongruity has also been obscured by a number of influential claims about authority that, if true, would respectively make the disjunctive view seem either trivially true or patently false. The disjunctive view must be first rescued from such an all too easy victory, as well as from an early defeat, before a more affirmative case in its support can be made out.

2. Illusory Victories: Authority and Consent

Authority's normativity implies an appeal to, or reliance on, the subjects' volition or consent, a fact that suggests a rather straightforward incompatibility with coercion. Conceptions of authority that emphasize the voluntarist or consensual element would appear, therefore, to be friendly to my approach. These are, however, false friends, not just because the arguments they provide in support of the disjunctive view are unsound, but also because if the arguments were valid, they would make the disjunctive view seem rather trivial. We must distinguish two ways in which authority can engage its subjects' will: through general acceptance of the authority and through specific acquiescence to its directives.

Consent theories of authority maintain that in order for a putative authority to issue binding directives—in other words, in order for it to be a real authority—it must be willingly accepted by its subjects. Coercive threats, in this view, vitiate the consent on which authority depends. People are not really given an opportunity to extend or withhold their consent to the authority's directives; they are forced to comply no matter what. Consequently they are not obligated by the authority's demands.[8]

There is, however, more than one problem with this argument. First, the premise that authority depends on general consent is problematic at best. Many paradigm authorities—parents, for example—do not purport to be consensual in this sense. Even in the case of political authority, where the idea of consent has been most prominent, consent must be deformed beyond recognition in order to describe an even highly idealized relationship between the citizen and the state. Second, even if general consent is a precondition of authority, it is not necessarily vitiated by sanctions. By accepting the state's authority, as consent theorists claim citizens do, citizens are taken to assume a general obligation to obey, an obligation that the state is entitled to enforce. To suggest that the use of coercive sanctions vitiates the consent necessary for authority would accordingly make no more sense than to maintain that one cannot assume a contractual obligation because coercive measures are available to enforce the obligation if one defaults.

Specific acquiescence to the authority's directives provides the second link between normativity and volition. Here too the road to the disjunctive view looks short. Recall the characterization of normativity as an appeal to the subjects' voluntary obedience. Add to this the realization that coercive threats are designed to secure compliance irrespective of the agent's attitude toward the authority's directives. Put these two observations together, and the disjunctive view will seem to follow. Plainly, voluntary obedience cannot be coercively enforced. By using coercive means authority opts for mere compliance, while removing the opportunity for voluntary obedience that is a necessary condition of its normative appeal.

This simple argument for the disjunctive view fails as well, though its failure is more contingent than that of the preceding one. I will mention two objections to it. The first concerns the coercive measures authorities use. By design or by default (usually by a combination of both) the actual sanctions used by even the most ruthless political regimes fall short of securing full compliance; they leave a motivational gap within which citizens can respond to the law voluntarily. The second objection depends on a view of people's response to motivational overdetermination. When faced with reasons that overdetermine a certain action, it seems that one can, though perhaps only with difficulty and with an ever-present danger of self-deception, ignore some of these reasons and act only on the others. So if one is disposed to obey an authority willingly, one can do so just for the reasons that underlie this disposition, stoically disregarding the evils with which one is threatened if one were to disobey. These two objections are interdependent: the less overwhelming the sanctions, and the less effective in coercing compliance, the easier it becomes to bracket and ignore them in one's practical reasoning and respond only to the normative component in the authority's utterance.[9]

3. Sham Defeats: Instrumental Conceptions of Authority

I turn now to an examination of a family of conceptions of authority that, if true, would make the disjunctive view implausible. This family conceives authority in strictly instrumental terms, endorsing obedience only insofar as it has beneficial consequences. I focus first on a relatively young member of this family that has gained considerable prominence of late. I then expand the discussion to the family as a whole.

Joseph Raz has advanced an account of authority that is based on the notion of *dependent reasons*.[10] He illustrates this notion with the example of arbitration. When a dispute is submitted to an arbitrator, her decision is a reason for action by virtue of the fact that she is expected to consider and weigh all the reasons that apply to the parties under the circumstances, and to properly reflect those reasons in her decision. Similarly, according to what Raz calls *the dependence thesis,* authority can claim to bind people by its instructions only insofar as those instructions purport to reflect preexisting reasons that apply to those people anyway. The point of obeying an authority is that by doing so one increases the overall likelihood of acting on the right reasons.

If this conception of authority were true, the disjunctive view I have described would obviously make no sense. Defying an authority so understood merely because it appended a threat to its instructions would amount to cutting one's nose to spite one's face. The analogy to theoretical authority, drawn by Raz to support the dependence thesis, is telling. Would anything a physician does (threatening you, being rude to you, etc.) ever interfere with the reasons for taking the medication she prescribed, so long as the prescription itself is believed to be medically sound? If the disjunctive view is to be true, there must be more to authority than a strictly instrumental conception allows. This is indeed the case. Out common experience of authority is not fully captured by a purely instrumental account. I will again consider the dependence thesis first and will comment more broadly on the entire instrumental family later.

The first feature of authority that the dependence thesis misrepresents is that an order, like a request, not only reflects but rather changes the balance of reasons that the agent faces. Consider requests first. When A asks B to pass the salt, A may provide B with some dependent reasons for doing so; for example, the request implies that the food is not salty enough and that A likes it saltier. Suppose that these facts, together with the fact that B is seated closest to the salt shaker, are a reason for B to pass the salt to A. The request simply signals the existence of such facts (or the likelihood of their existence) and is in this way a dependent reason for passing the salt. But clearly the request is more than that. Suppose B knows the facts just mentioned: she had just tasted the food, and she is also aware of A's preference for saltiness. Still, the request itself— the very fact that A asks for the salt—is an additional reason for passing it. This additional reason cannot be a dependent reason; it must be an independent one.

The case of authority is no different. Someone who is aware of all the reasons that have led an authority to issue a given instruction is nonetheless in a different practical situation before the instruction is issued and after. The instruction does not simply reflect or replace the extant reasons but adds to them. Suppose that a bill has been passed by a legislature, but that it becomes effective only after a ceremonial signature by a designated dignitary or after publication in an official gazette. One's practical situation differs dramatically before these formalities take place and after them, even though one is fully apprised of the authority's view on the balance of reasons before the ceremonial ratification or the publication. In order to issue an instruction and create a duty, the authority must actually speak in a way that counts as its pronouncement, and this fact is not captured well by the dependence thesis.

Consider now a situation in which a certain rule applies, though the reasons that support it do not. A red light in an empty intersection provides the standard example. Raz tries to reconcile a duty to stop under these circumstances with his instrumental conception of authority by noting that if the driver were to ascertain all the conditions that make stopping unnecessary in this case, he would have to do the same in many other situations, thus forgoing the advantages of authoritative guidance. It is because of all these other cases that one is better off following authority "blindly" even in the deserted intersection.[11] However, this analysis ignores the possibility that the underlying reasons in any given situation may be clear and apparent, and the cost to the agent of considering them then extremely low. In such situations—of which the red light seems to be one—obedience on instrumental grounds is pointless.

However, if we allow that such cases can be excluded from the rule's ambit, we get an intermittent picture of authority, according to which its directives are binding only as long as appeal to the underlying reasons and their direct consideration by the agent are disadvantageous. But such an intermittent conception is at odds with our ordinary experience and the traditional philosophical understanding of authority. Although philosophical inquiry can of course discover that certain attitudes toward authority or beliefs about it—both ordinary and philosophical—are ill founded, we should be hesitant to announce a *conceptual* error that would render the very notion of authority, as generally understood, defective or incoherent.[12]

Another objection to the dependence thesis concerns a ubiquitous disparity between reasons for action that would apply to its subjects and reasons that apply to the authority itself and guide it in issuing its directives. Authorities are often motivated by what we might call *enforcement reasons*. Forbidding any communication among examinees to forestall cheating, and decreeing a uniform speed limit despite relevant variation in the make and condition of cars, driving skills, the urgency of particular trips, and so on, are clear examples. In these cases, the directives take the shape they do in order to facilitate the detection and the adjudication of delinquent behavior. Such directives do not provide dependent reasons that apply irrespective of the authority's instruction: although it is incumbent upon students not to cheat on their exams, a student would not be inhibited from inquiring what time it is were it not for an explicit rule that flatly enjoins any communication among the examinees. Why should one obey such a rule nonetheless? It seems that here the dependence thesis must help itself to some other theoretical device. The most common one, especially in the political context, is the alleged duty to uphold just (and perhaps one could add useful) institutions.[13] But even if we concede such a duty, it seems to fall short of what recognizing an authority is usually taken to entail. Many instances of disobedience would clearly not make the slightest dent in any institution; this would again suggest the intermittent picture of authority that we have just encountered, and the same incompatibility with the categorical demands for unconditional obedience that authorities make.[14]

These observations can be now generalized to cast doubt on any strictly instrumental account of authority. Such an account inevitably introduces a contingent element into the authority relationship. All instruments are fallible, and if authority's claim to obedience depends exclusively on promoting the goal the authority is said to serve, then it is always in principle appropriate to second-guess the authority's directives and to disregard them whenever they are found wanting. Such latitude is not commonly associated with the idea of authority.

Authorities typically demand obedience that exceeds their claims to usefulness. A full account of authority must include a noninstrumental component as well. It is only in light of such a component that the tension between coercion and normativity can be revealed.[15]

4. Authority and Deference

Different suggestions have been made regarding the noninstrumental component in authority, and I will consider some of them momentarily. But ordinary language provides us here with what looks like the most apt and encompassing term. The linguistic key to the authority relationship is the notion of *deference:* those subject to an authority are expected to defer to its wishes and demands. Deference signifies a "submission or yielding to the judgment, opinion, will, etc. of another," as well as an attitude of "respectful or courteous regard."[16] Thus the word captures at once both the "operational" side of the authority relationship—obedience to the authority's injunctions—and the paradigmatic attitude that is supposed to underlie and motivate obedience, namely respect. By issuing a command, authority appeals to, and seeks to activate, this deferential attitude. When the subject responds to this appeal—that is, when the subject counts the authority's pronouncement as a content-independent reason for action—she expresses that attitude.

Deference toward authority can have different sources, three of which have become particularly prominent in discussions of the subject. One is gratitude: since Socrates it has been maintained that obedience to the law is a due expression of gratitude to the state, just as obedience to one's parents can express gratitude to them.[17] Another prominent source of deference is identification. Obeying the law, for example, is said to be a way of identifying with one's society and expressing one's loyalty to it. Finally, the respect conveyed by deference can be a matter of trust: obedience conveys one's belief that the authority will not lead one astray.[18]

These sources of deference are all related in obvious ways to the instrumental dimension of authority. Gratitude, identification, and trust are likely to arise out of one's belief that the authority earned them, supposedly by discharging a useful function in an overall satisfactory way. But it should also be clear that the relationship need not be tight. The attitudes in question are not sustained, and beyond a certain point cannot be sustained, by a constant monitoring of the authority's performance and a detailed reevaluation of its directives. It is for this reason that deference and the respect it conveys plays such a crucial role in an account of authority: they provide the needed material to fill the gaps in the intermittent picture of authority that a purely instrumental account tends to generate. However, even this attenuated relationship between instrumental considerations and deference is not a necessary one. In the case of charismatic authority, for example, one's respectful attitude and deferential behavior can be divorced from any instrumental assessment of the authority's performance relative to some independent evaluative standard.[19] We may of course decry such an authority relationship, but it is a credit to the concept of deference that it permits us to articulate and make intelligible that of which we disapprove.

I have noted earlier the significant overlap between commands and requests: they both issue in source-based, content-independent reasons for action. It should come as no surprise, then, that deference pertains to both. Although the grounds for, and the precise meaning of, one's respectful attitude can differ between the case of authority and the case of requests, abiding by someone's request is as much an expression of deference as obeying a command.

Deference labels the kind of noninstrumental reason that an adequate account of authority must recognize. But deference also satisfies the other condition we set earlier on the reasons for action that authority provides. We searched for reasons that are sensitive to the presence of coercion, thus bearing out the disjunctive view of authority. Deference displays such sensitivity. In the remainder of this article I consider different ways in which coercion is at odds with deferential conformity to authority. In doing so it will be convenient to distinguish the authority's perspective from that of its subjects.[20] In this section I describe two ways in which deference reasons that might lead to voluntary acceptance of authority are undercut by authority's use of coercion. The next section assumes the authority's perspective, arguing that a coercive authority cannot be understood to make a bona fide appeal that its subjects willingly defer to its commands.[21]

Deference and Expressive Reasons

I have characterized deference reasons as noninstrumental, but for the purpose of my present argument a more affirmative feature should be emphasized. Following Professor Raz, we can describe deference reasons as *expressive reasons,* thereby highlighting the fact that obeying an authority (or complying with a request) is a way to express a certain range of attitudes.[22] The expression can be addressed to others, thereby endowing the relevant action (obedience in our case) with communicative significance; but it can also be addressed to oneself and serve as a symbolic affirmation for one's own sake of a certain attitude or disposition.

Now insofar as deference to authority is a matter of acting on expressive reasons, it is quite clear why authority's normative appeal is incompatible with coercion. To be successful in their communicative mission, expressive actions must, so to speak, wear their motivation on their sleeve. Since coercive threats are avowedly designed to compel compliance, they deprive obedience of its expressive or communicative potential. When an authority's directive or someone's request is backed by a sanction, compliance can no longer carry the significance it otherwise would have had as an expression of respect. For all we know—and this includes the agent herself—compliance was motivated by fear of sanction, and is therefore devoid of expressive content. Consider a familiar situation. When facing a red light, with no car approaching, some of the pedestrians intent on crossing the street will invariably jaywalk whereas others will wait dutifully for the light to change. In the absence of coercion the latter group's behavior would be a clear manifestation of respect for the law, in contrast to the former group's blatant disregard for it. But this contrast loses its significance when the difference between the two groups' behavior may reflect a difference in courage—willingness to risk arrest—as much as a difference in respect.[23]

In explaining obedience to authority in terms of expressive reasons we should not assume that in the absence of coercion obedience would be unequivocally expressive of respect. Mixed motives are common, and there is always the possibility that other reasons motivated compliance—a possibility that inevitably detracts from the clarity of the signal conveyed. But imperfect as any medium for symbolic communication is likely to be, a pattern of consistent and unwavering submission to a noncoercive authority will be a relatively clear expression of respect and related attitudes. What distinguishes coercion in this regard from other motives is both its publicity and its intended power. Whereas the existence of some motive other than deference can be always suspected, it is of the essence of coercive threats that they be clearly announced. Similarly, while the role of other motives for compliance is both speculative and variable, coercion is designed, and is known to be designed, to provide a compelling reason for compliance all by itself. Moreover, within a coercive system, voluntary obedience will tend to fail its expressive mission even on the rare occasions in which detection and enforcement seem unlikely and the threat hollow. This is so for two reasons. First, the expressive potential of actions is a matter of their shared public meaning. A coercive system destroys the expressive capacity of obedience, because in such a system obedience will not assume the social meaning that would make it a suitable medium for expression and communication. Second, a coercive system is likely to condition people to a generalized and pervasive apprehension toward the authorities that does not depend on specific calculations of risk of detection in each particular case. This spillover effect of threats further erodes the expressive potential of obedience even when enforcement is unlikely.[24]

Deference and Reliance

There is a second, less direct, relationship between deference and abiding by a request or obeying an authority. This connection too is disrupted by coercion. Consider again examinations. Most would agree that although cheating is generally wrong, cheating under an honor system is even worse. If so, the very fact that an examination is unsupervised is taken to provide a reason for complying with the examiner's instructions. How is that so? The answer I suggest fixes once again on the idea of trust, but this time in the passive voice: the importance of being trusted. By setting up the honor system the examiner puts her trust in the examinees. Their reason for complying with her instructions is the importance of proving themselves worthy of her trust. The relationship between this attitude and deference is this. By taking A's trust in him to be a reason to prove himself trustworthy, B manifests a certain valuation of A and her trust; he implies that the trust is something he values enough to want to justify and uphold.

This reciprocal relationship between trust and deference may be altogether circular or self-referential. After all, the examinees may not value the examiner and may disparage her trust, in which case the honor system does not provide an additional reason for their compliance. But notice how advantageous the other option—obedience out of deference—really is. If B does respect A and values her trust in him, then proving himself worthy of that trust means, metaphorically speaking, scoring points on a scoreboard that is of significance to him. By dismissing the scoreboard and being indifferent to scoring on it, B deprives himself of what otherwise would be a source of value and self-esteem. In other words, the reciprocal relation between trust and deference can be seen as a transaction that creates surplus value measured in the denomination of individuals' self-esteem.[25]

This observation can be now applied to both authority and requests. Starting with the latter, when A asks B to pass the salt, A, like the examiners, puts her trust in him. Cognate expressions, such as dependence or reliance, are perhaps more apposite here than trust, but the basic idea is the same: B's treating A's request as a content-independent reason for passing the salt is a deferential response in which B's effort to justify A's reliance demonstrates the importance B ascribes to that reliance and hence the esteem in which he holds A. A successful requital of A's trust is a source of satisfaction for B and a boost to his own self-esteem, as he proves himself worthy of trust whose source he values. This account of the salt-passing episode provides an obvious explanation of the disjunctive view of this situation. When A supports her request by a threat ("or I'll break your arm") she emphatically withdraws the trust or reliance that is implicit in the request and on which B's deferential response is premised. Passing the salt as a way of upholding A's reliance is now pointless.

Complying with a request is a clear case of proving oneself dependable and trustworthy. But as the honor system demonstrates, authority can also offer an occasion for such a demonstration. The authority's directives can be seen as appeals to people's good will and as attempts to enlist their cooperation in a certain venture. The reason for compliance with such directives is not people's interest in the venture, but rather the authority's appeal to them. This is in line with the source-based and content-independent interpretation of the authority's directive. The authority's appeal is all by itself a reason for compliance precisely because it provides people with the occasion to show themselves dependable and trustworthy. However, as in the salt-passing situation, all this is possible only as long as the authority's normative appeal is not backed by threats. When it is, the authority can no longer be understood as trusting its subjects and relying on their good will. Obeying the authority will not serve to justify the authority's trust, simply because in the presence of coercive threats there is no trust to justify.

5. Authority's Normative Appeal

I turn now to examine the claims made by authority. To talk about authority making a claim is to ascribe certain intentions to it. Specifically, the normative aspect of authority I have described implies a dual intention that every putative authority must have: that its subjects treat its instructions as exclusionary reasons, that is, that they act on the instructions even in the face of contrary reasons that might otherwise prevail, and that they do so voluntarily. Both of these intentions are vitiated by the use of coercion.

The Call for Voluntary Obedience

Authority is said to call for and expect its subjects' voluntary obedience; only because it anticipates some recalcitrance does it add a coercive threat as an "ancillary" motivation for compliance.[26] But this appearance is misleading. By opting for coercion authority reveals a very different attitude than the one ordinarily ascribed to it: voluntary obedience can no longer be seen as its genuine goal.

An example will help clarify this point. Suppose A covets B's watch. Moreover, A would very much like B to give him the watch as an expression of her affection for him. To this end he could drop some hints, send concealed messages through emissaries, and so on. However, A can also obtain the watch by using a coercive threat. A thus has a choice between awaiting a gift and issuing the threat. Suppose he opts for the latter. How are we to interpret his decision? A tempting but erroneous interpretation would be this: getting the watch as a gift is what A really wants; after all, this would satisfy his desire for the watch as well as for a token of B's affection. Obtaining the watch forcibly is only his second-best alternative, chosen because of his suspicion that B may be disinclined to give it to him of her own accord. This interpretation is mistaken because under the given circumstances A cannot be said to seriously want B to give him a gift at all.

To see this consider a second example. You offer an orange to a guest. It turns out he likes the smell of oranges, their taste, and so forth, but he detests their orange color. Suppose he asks you to give him the orange provided you do not include its orange color. This request will naturally be understood as a humorous circumlocution for simply declining the orange. One would not think in this case of seriously ascribing to A a complex, two-tier intention, consisting in a preference for, say, a blue orange and, in default of that, a second-best willingness to forgo the orange altogether. Why? The obvious reason is that we take A to know that the orange color is a fixed property of oranges and that there's no such thing as a blue orange. Not to want an orange orange, no matter how much one appreciates the orange's other attributes, is not to want an orange at all.

Generalizing this example, the following principle can be ventured: A seriously wants X only if A wants X complete with all of X's fixed properties and logical entailments that are known to him. Call this *the principle of comprehensiveness*. It should be now easy to see how this principle helps explain A's attitude toward getting the watch in my previous example. The key is the recognition that the concept of a gift involves essentially the donor's freedom to either give or withhold a particular object. Call this *the indeterminacy factor*. To seriously want an object as a gift is, according to the principle of comprehensiveness, to want the object subject to the contingency that results from the indeterminacy factor. One seriously wants a gift, in other words, only when the benefits of getting a desired object by way of the donor's free choice outweigh the risk of not getting the object at all. When A in our example opts for obtaining the watch coercively, he demonstrates that this condition is not satisfied in this case, and that he does not seriously want the gift at all.

There is an air of paradox in this conclusion, and the following observation should help remove it. The paradox results from our realization that by ignoring the threat and giving the watch to A voluntarily, B would have delighted A. Both his desire for the watch and for a token of B's affection would have been satisfied. Is this not evidence that A prefers a gift after all? However, this suggestion results from confusing the ex post perspective on the transaction with the ex ante one. Ex post, that is to say when B does in fact decide to give the watch to A as a gift, A of course prefers this state of affairs to the alternative. But the relevant perspective from which to assess A's preferences is the ex ante perspective, when those preferences are put to a practical test in determining A's actions. The seriousness of A's desire for a gift should be measured at that earlier time, when the gift option still involves the risk of not getting the watch at all. By resorting to coercion A signals that he is not seriously interested in getting a gift.

The analogy with authority should be now plain. Voluntary obedience to authority is as subject to the indeterminacy factor as a gift is. Once authority resorts to coercion, we cannot impute to it a serious plea for voluntary obedience any more than a serious preference for a gift can be ascribed to A. As with the gift example, authority's readiness to impose upon its subjects the mandated behavior undermines its capacity to make a credible appeal to voluntary obedience, because it reveals authority's unwillingness to assume the risk, inherent in the very concept of obedience, that disobedience might ensue.[27]

Coercion and Exclusionary Reasons

I have so far focused on two characteristics shared by authority and requests: they both provide source-based and content-independent reasons for action. I now turn to the third characteristic of authority, which distinguishes it from requests. Intuitively, the difference is this: in the case of requests it is ultimately up to the agent whether to comply. Although the request is a reason for action, it does not presume to be a conclusive reason. In contrast, authority does not leave its subjects such leeway. A command is meant to be preemptive or peremptory. A more technical way of making this point that has been recently proposed by Professor Raz has become highly influential: authority intends its commands to be not just first-order reasons to act as commanded but also second-order "exclusionary" reasons to ignore at least some reasons that would otherwise apply to the agent and might counsel disobedience.[28] This distinctive characteristic of authority, I will argue, is also defeated by the use of coercive means.

To see how that is, I need to mention two additional observations made by Raz regarding the nature of the exclusionary reasons authority generates.[29] First, "exclusionary reasons exclude by kind and not by weight. They may exclude all the reasons of a certain kind (such as considerations of economic welfare), including very weighty reasons, while not excluding even trivial considerations belonging to another kind (such as considerations of honor)." Second, "there is a minimum that an order must exclude to be an order. It must at least exclude considerations of the recipient's present desires.... [It] is never a justification [for disobeying an order] that the agent had a desire, however strong, for something inconsistent with his following the order." These observations are designed to help us distinguish situations in which one person simply wishes to control the actions of another—as in the proverbial gunman example—from the exercise of authority. The latter involves a more complex intention than a sheer wish for the other's compliance. On Raz's analysis, the authority must intend not only that the subject perform a certain action but that he do so while excluding some putative motivations, specifically his present desires. My aim is to show that on one interpretation, Kantian in spirit, of this complex intention, the latter is inconsistent with the use of coercive threats to enforce compliance.

I begin by noting that Raz's claim that an order must intend to exclude at least the subject's present desires is plausible, but stated by him dogmatically. The mere fact that I am disinclined to obey does seem irrelevant to my obligation toward authority. But why? What is it about present desires, as against the agent's interests, for example, that makes their exclusion a necessary condition of an authoritative order?

A clue to a possible answer is provided by a formal similarity between authority and morality: in the case of morality present desires are excluded from competition with duty as well. Promises are an intermediate category that will help clarify the point. Suppose I have good reasons 'to give you my pen: your need for it, my affection for you, and so on. Clearly these reasons are in legitimate competition with my own fondness for my pen and my desire to keep it. Suppose, however, that I make a promise to give you the pen. I have now assumed a moral obligation to do so, and although the obligation grew out of the preexisting reasons, it alters the situation radically. The promise does not only represent a new reason for giving the pen but, unlike the other reasons for doing so, it excludes from consideration my disinclination: given the promise,

I must now completely ignore my desire to keep the pen. Promises are an intermediate case between authority and morality because here the moral duty is self-imposed: in a sense the agent exercises authority over himself. But the situation is similar in the case of other moral duties and prohibitions that are not self-imposed. The moral injunction against bodily assault does not just outweigh a person's homicidal impulse; it rules such an impulse out of court.

The analogy between authority and morality is helpful because in the moral case we do have at least one powerful explanation of the exclusion of the agent's desires. It is the Kantian distinction between inclination and rational free will, and Kant's identification of moral action with the latter.[30] To act on present desires is to be motivated by inclination, and hence to succumb to deterministic forces that drain the action of its moral worth. One acts morally only insofar as one succeeds in detaching oneself from the passions and is motivated exclusively by reverence for the moral law. "Duty" signifies precisely this tension between inclination and rational freedom and the difficulty that is experienced in subduing the former in order to give rein to the latter.[31]

Kant's moral theory is enmeshed in an esoteric and highly problematic metaphysics, but many of its main insights regarding our moral experience do not depend on this metaphysics. It is this phenomenological insight that can be now extracted from the moral context and applied to the case of authority. As we have seen, when an authority issues an order it intends to exclude (at least) the agent's present desires. The full significance of this intention can be expressed in Kantian terms. By issuing the order authority seeks to suspend the recipient's inclinations and elicit instead behavior motivated exclusively by deference to the authority and its instructions.[32] The fact that the language of duty is used in the case of authority as commonly and as naturally as in morality is of crucial importance. As in the case of morality, the idea of duty signifies here an expectation that one suspend one's inclinations and act instead on a rational recognition of the rightfulness of a certain demand. Seen in these terms, the authority's normative appeal addresses the individual in her capacity as an autonomous moral agent, able to stand apart from, and if necessary to overcome, her psychological impulses.[33]

We should now recall the other observation that we quoted from Raz: exclusionary reasons exclude by kind. This feature is compatible with the Kantian interpretation I have offered. For the reasons outlined, all inclinations, irrespective of their content, are to be ignored. Practically speaking, an authority anxious that its orders be obeyed is concerned with excluding only reasons against compliance, not those that support it. But the logic of authority's normative appeal does not allow for such selectivity. The mode of behavior that authority seeks to elicit—acting on duty out of deference—requires that all inclinations be suspended or ignored. An appeal by authority to its subjects' supportive inclinations to the exclusion of the hostile ones will be unprincipled and self-contradictory. This is, however, precisely what authority does when it backs its orders by coercive threats. Such threats are an attempt to intimidate people into compliance by inducing in them the fear of sanction. As such they appeal to the subjects' present desires. Authority's attempt to activate such inclinations and enlist them in its favor runs afoul of its own call to suspend all inclination that is implicit in its normative appeal.

This inconsistency can be mirrored, and its significance accentuated, in the subjects' response to an authority's threats. The subject may reason, "It would be all right with the authority if I obeyed out of fear. Accordingly, as far as the authority is concerned, it is acceptable if I act on my inclinations, as long as these are the suitable ones; after all, by using threats, the authority itself called forth these inclinations. However, I cannot find any principled ground for following some inclinations (for example, my fear) while excluding others (for example, my disinclination to do as commanded). Insofar as it is permissible for me to act on my fear, it must be equally permissible to act on my other desires, including my dislike for the required action." This line of reasoning in effect invokes the logic of estoppel. By using threats the authority itself transposes us, as it were, from the plane of duty and respect to one governed by impulsions and inclinations, implicitly licensing or endorsing the latter kind of motivations. But it is precisely the exclusion of such motivations that defines the other, more elevated plane. Once authority itself allows for such motivations, it can no longer expect to control, logically speaking, which of them will prevail.[34]

I have reached this conclusion with the help of an analogy between authority and morality, and I can further clarify it by marking an important distinction between the two: authority is source-based, whereas morality is not. Some philosophers, most notably Hans Kelsen, deny the distinction by insisting that the binding force of authority's pronouncements does not really emanate from the authority itself but rather from some other norm, not itself source-based, that empowers the authority to issue binding directives. To think otherwise—to believe that the authority's pronouncements can themselves create duties—is in their view to commit the naturalistic fallacy.[35]

These are some of the stickiest issues in practical philosophy, and this is not the place to address them fully. I will make only two brief points. One concerns the phenomenology of obedience. In the case of parental authority, for example, the overwhelming experience is that of obeying one's parents, rather than obeying an abstract, sourceless norm that decrees obedience to parental demands. At least presumptively, our conception of authority should recognize this experience and accommodate it. Second, even within a Kelsenian framework of the kind I have just mentioned, one should stress the normatively creative role played by authorities. Even if an authority's normative power—its capacity to issue binding directives—is ultimately to be traced to some sourceless norm, authority is nevertheless related to its subjects as an originator of duties, not just as a conduit for them. It would be a mistake to view the authority's act of issuing a directive as merely concretizing a general, preexisting duty of obedience in the way that someone's fainting concretizes the duty of rescue. Legislators and parents are themselves sources of duty-imposing norms in the way that the swooner is not.

The difference in provenance between authority's normative appeal and morality's explains why coercion does not have the same devastating effect on the latter that it has on the former. I have already observed that, strictly speaking, morality cannot be enforced; moral motivation, which is constitutive of moral action, cannot be compelled. Still, this does not preclude any agency from backing moral norms with sanctions. Although sanctions appeal to the kind of motivation that the moral imperatives seek to exclude, this does not loosen the grip of the moral reasons, because their force does not in the first place emanate from the sanctioning agency. In contrast, the reasons provided by authority are source-based: their normative force does originate with the authority and the deference that it commands. So whereas authority cannot disrupt the normative force exerted by morality, it can be estopped through its behavior from claiming exclusionary force for its own demands. Authority's use of coercive threats has just that effect.

The upshot of the two arguments made in this section is that when authority uses coercion it can no longer lay a good faith claim to its subjects' voluntary obedience by demanding that they put aside their own inclinations and act out of deference on the authority's will. Insofar as authority's normative appeal is understood in terms of such a claim, coercion undermines the normative appeal.[36]

Conclusion

I have suggested a construction of authority's normativity and attempted to show how this construction is undermined by the use of coercive means. As is often the case in philosophy, the practical ramifications of my argument are more modest than may perhaps seem. First, on my view coercion is at odds with a capacity that many maintain authorities never possesses anyway: to create content-independent, exclusionary reasons whose validity is not exhausted by instrumental considerations alone. Second, even if authority's normative appeal is understood in terms of deference in the various ways I have described, the realization that coercion weakens or destroys such normativity has only limited consequences. There are many other reasons for complying with authority — notably instrumental reasons — that my argument does not touch, and that in most cases have greater practical significance than deference would have even in the absence of coercion.[37] Finally, my arguments focus only on one kind of use of force by authority, force designed to enforce compliance. Other common uses of sanctions — most importantly as punishment imposed on retributive grounds — are not directly touched by what I have said. The meagerness of practical ramifications should be, however, of little concern. Both authority and coercion are here to stay, so one would be suspicious of a theory that claimed a significantly more radical incompatibility between the two on the practical level than my arguments suggest.

The arguments I have presented, if sound, are important nonetheless. They validate, though with a shift of focus, a pervasive ambivalence toward authority to which I alluded at the outset. They are a reminder of how deeply our normative life — and not just the moral aspect of it — is distorted and subverted by the ubiquity of coercion. Presently we get only rare glimpses of authority without threats. Deferential obedience to parents in adulthood within traditional families is possibly an example. But such glimpses perhaps suggest the feasibility and desirability of creating or expanding pockets of noncoercion where authority relationships can exist that make possible the expression of undisrupted identification with or loyalty to one's community.

The main implications of my comments are less grandiose and optimistic. They come into play in the kind of situation that I have mentioned earlier, such as a red light at a deserted intersection — conditions that make stopping look rather pointless. I have also alluded to, and tried to refute, Raz's attempt to explain stopping in this situation in instrumental terms as the price we must pay for the convenience of not having to ascertain in each case all the pertinent conditions and considerations, even though following authority with such blindness "once in a while . . . makes one look ridiculous to the gods."[38] In my view, instrumental considerations do not extend the reach of authority to all such cases. If our sense that authority applies even in such situations is to be vindicated, we must resort to the kind of explanation based on the idea of deference that I have described. It is here that my arguments make a difference. In the absence of coercion it would make perfectly good sense, despite the impracticality, for the driver to stop at the red light out of deference reasons. However, the driver must realize that because of authority's long hand, extending even in the deserted intersection, holding a club over her head, these reasons do not in fact apply. The driver is free to run the light, and by doing so she will perhaps register a private symbolic protest and give vent, in an innocuous manner, to an abiding exasperation. No other person will know, but the gods will be pleased.

Notes

1. Some terminological clarifications may be in order. First, I am concerned only with practical authority that issues binding imperatives and provides reasons for action, and not with theoretical authority that provides grounds for belief. (For an attempt to collapse the distinction see Heidi Hurd, "Challenging Authority," *Yale Law Journal* 100 (1991): 1611). Second, there is an important ambiguity in the use of the term *authority,* especially in political theory. Many writers distinguish authority by its appeal to deferential obedience that is based neither on coercion nor on persuasion. See, for example, Hannah Arendt, "What Is Authority?" in *Between Past and Future: Eight Exercises in Political Thought* (New York: Viking Press, 1968), 91, at 93; R. S. Peters, "Authority," *Proceedings of the Aristotelian Society,* supp. vol. 32 (1958): 207, reprinted in *Political Philosophy,* ed. Anthony Quinton (Oxford: Oxford University Press, 1967), 83, at 92; Bertrand de Jouvenel, *Sovereignty: An Inquiry into the Political Good,* trans. J. F. Huntington (Chicago: University of Chicago Press, 1957), 33. But *authority* is also used to label the legitimate use of coercion. To avoid the ambiguity, I use the term *normativity* to designate the characteristic that is emphasized by the first sense of *authority,* i.e. the appeal to deferential obedience. This permits me to discuss normativity and coercion as a relationship between two aspects of authority. On the ambiguity in the use of *authority* see R. B. Friedman, "On the Concept of Authority in Political Philosophy," in *Authority,* ed. Joseph Raz (New York: New York University Press, 1990), 62.

2. John Austin, *The Province of Jurisprudence Determined* (New York: Noonday Press, 1954).

3. H. L. A. Hart, *The Concept of Law* (Oxford: Clarendon Press, 1961), 38.

4. "To command is characteristically to exercise authority over men, not power to inflict harm, and though it may be combined with threats of harm a command is primarily an appeal not to fear but to respect for authority." Ibid., 20.

5. Leslie Green, *The Authority of the State* (Oxford: Clarendon Press, 1988), 41–42. "Definition" may overstate what Green's formulation provides, but it is sufficient for my purpose that it focuses on some central characteristics of authority.

6. I do not consider the possible use by authority of noncoercive spurs or inducements, though I believe that some of my arguments would apply, with variable force, to such milder means as well.

7. We are probably less startled by the incongruity between normativity and coercion in the case of authority than in the case of requests,

in part because in the former situation we have become inured to the combination through long exposure to it. "Authority and coercive power are so closely associated in some men's minds that one is often mistaken for the other." John Day, "Authority," *Political Studies* 11 (1963): 265, 257.

8. See A. J. Simmons, "The Principle of Fair Play," *Philosophy and Public Affairs* 8 (1979): 333–37; and Rolf Sartorius, "Political Authority and Political Obligation," *Virginia Law Review* 67 (1981): 3.

9. For a view that the coerciveness of political regimes does not vitiate the consent necessary for political obligation, see Alan Wertheimer, "Political Coercion and Political Obligation," in *Nomos 14: Coercion,* ed. J. Roland Pennock and John Chapman (Chicago: Aldine, 1972), 213.

10. Joseph Raz, *The Morality of Freedom* (Oxford: Clarendon Press, 1986), 38–69.

11. Joseph Raz, "Legitimate Authority," in *The Authority of Law* (Oxford: Clarendon Press, 1979), 24–25.

12. Significantly, it is Raz himself, as well as other theorists laboring to provide an instrumental account of authority, who tries to extend the account to the red-light kind of situation. They are right to do so, I believe, because the main theoretical challenge presented by the concept of authority has to do precisely with the seeming "blindness" and hence the apparent irrationality of obedience to authority. The fact that such accounts fail in this regard leaves an explanatory lacuna that I will address below. Compare also Green, *The Authority of the State.* However, some writers believe that a duty to obey the law, as well as other duties, may have an intermittent shape. See Chaim Gans, *Philosophical Anarchism and Political Disobedience* (Cambridge: Cambridge University Press, 1992), 76–77.

13. See John Rawls, *A Theory of Justice* (Cambridge: Harvard University Press, 1971), 334.

14. Compare Raz, *The Morality of Freedom,* 101–2. With enough ingenuity and sufficient footwork additional instrumental reasons can quite likely be contrived to further narrow the gaps in the intermittent picture of authority to the point where these gaps may look acceptable. However, while sufficient effort and ingenuity can commonly lead from almost any starting point to almost any desired end in moral philosophy, the very ingenuity and effort required to reach the end argue against the adequacy of the starting point and motivate the search for another. Cf. Brian Barry, "And Who Is My Neighbor?" *Yale Law Journal* 88 (1979): 630.

15. Some philosophers maintain that since the use of coercion is necessary for the state's ability to discharge its functions, coercion is part of the instrumental basis of the state's authority. See, for example, Raz's

introduction to *Authority*. If this is the case (an issue that I need not consider here), the disjunctive view points to an insoluble dilemma in the case of political authority.

16. *College Dictionary,* rev. ed. (New York: Random House, 1988). The idea of "deference" has also been traditionally prominent in discussions of authority in political philosophy. See Friedman, "Concept of Authority," 64ff.

17. See e.g. A. J. Simmons, *Moral Principles and Political Obligations* (Princeton: Princeton University Press, 1979), 163.

18. Raz connects the latter two: obeying the law is a matter of identification with one's society because it expresses trust in its institutions. See "Respect for Law," in *The Authority of Law,* 260–61.

19. For a similar point see Steven Lukes, "Perspectives on Authority," in Raz, *Authority,* 213–14.

20. For an elaboration of different "perspectives" from which authority can be considered see ibid. In discussing authority from the perspective of those who claim it and those who accept it I elide the notion of "having authority." My account can be extended to this notion by using the distinction between *de jure* and *de facto* authority. Roughly, one has *de jure* authority when one's claim to authority is well founded; one has *de facto* authority when one's claim to authority is accepted. See Friedman, "Concept of Authority," 56; and Peters, "Authority," 89ff.

21. As I pointed out earlier, when the authority relation depends on consent, the relevant consent is not necessarily vitiated by coercive threats. However, my arguments for the disjunctive view bear on a consensual authority, and point out that certain grounds for accepting authority and acting deferentially on its commands become unavailable when coercion is used. It remains logically possible, however, for someone to consent to authority for reasons that are neither instrumental nor expressive, or for no reason at all, and to use the consent itself much like a promise as the ground for "blind" obedience, even in the presence of coercion. I doubt that such consent is common or rational. However, even such consent would not affect the arguments in the next section that deal with the incongruity between the authority's normative claims and its use of coercion.

22. Raz, *The Authority of Law,* 255.

23. It should be emphasized that I do not claim that acting out of deference in the presence of coercion is impossible, but that it may be pointless. If the point of the pedestrians obeying the law is to convey a certain attitude, obedience under the shadow of coercion is a faulty medium for doing so. It does not matter for this argument (as well as for my other arguments) whether the coercive regime is accepted by the pedestrians themselves as necessary or beneficial.

24. The contrast with morality is instructive here. At least within the Kantian tradition an action has moral value only when it is done out of the right kind of motivation. In this sense moral behavior cannot be enforced. However, backing a moral duty by a threat does not necessarily deprive the agent of the opportunity to act morally; she can still act on the moral duty alone by being impervious or oblivious to the threat. In that case the moral value of the action is unaffected by the threat. The threat does, however, make it more difficult to ascertain the action's moral worth. But this is only an epistemological, not a moral, problem. In the case of expressive actions such as obeying authority, the epistemological problem assumes the substantive significance described in the text.

25. Although violators of an honor system are sometimes severely punished, to be consistent with the spirit of the honor system, such punishment is best interpreted as retributive rather than as deterrent and coercive. As I make clear later, my arguments in support of the disjunctive thesis do not apply to the use of sanctions for purposes other than coercion. However, if violations of an honor system are in fact detected with some regularity and harsh penalties are imposed, the retributive sanctions may assume a deterrent significance, and the honor system will increasingly resemble a supervised exam.

26. The view of sanctions as having only an "ancillary" function in the law's guidance of behavior is emphasized by Hart in *The Concept of Law*, 38.

27. A crucial element in my gift-giving example is that A employs coercive means *before* B has had a chance to give him the watch voluntarily, thereby knowingly destroying the preconditions for a gift and thus demonstrating a preference for simply getting the watch. The same sequence is typical of authority. Authorities do not first wait for voluntary compliance and use coercion only later against the recalcitrant. (Such a strategy could be used only once anyway.) Rather, authority issues its coercive threats concomitantly with the imperatives, thereby expressing preferences analogous to A's in the gift situation.

28. The concept of exclusionary reasons is elaborated in Joseph Raz, *Practical Reason and Norms* (London: Hutchinson, 1975).

29. Raz, *The Authority of Law*, 22–24.

30. Kant, *Groundwork of the Metaphysic of Morals*, trans. H. J. Paton (London: Hutchinson, 1948).

31. Kant's view implies that where moral action is concerned, even benign inclinations such as love or compassion should be brought before the court of practical reason since they too, like their noxious counterparts, can lead one astray; e.g., by making one unduly solicitous toward one's beloved at the expense of a more deserving stranger.

32. We must of course be careful to distinguish here between causal reasons and cognitive reasons. Desires can apparently be both: they can be direct, causal determinants of action; but they can also figure as elements to be considered in one's practical reasoning. Whereas exclusionary reasons may seek to exclude desires in both of these senses, my Kantian interpretation fixes most clearly on the first. It is less clear what the Kantian perspective would have to say on the exclusion of desires as reasons in the second, cognitive sense.

33. To extend the Kantian account of moral duty to the case of authority is of course not to resolve the difficult questions as to when, if ever, an authority's presumption to create duties so understood is justified, and whether obedience to authority for the sake of duty alone can ever be required by, or even be compatible with, morality.

34. We often experience threats as a challenge or a dare. The present account helps make sense of this reaction.

35. Hans Kelsen, *General Theory of Law and State* (New York: Russell and Russell, 1961) and *Pure Theory of Law,* 2d ed. (Berkeley and Los Angeles: University of California Press, 1967).

36. It might be thought that the state addresses its threats only to recalcitrant citizens, while speaking in purely normative terms to the law-abiding ones. But this would be a delusion. No matter how small the number of recalcitrant citizens because of whom coercion is employed, given the generality of the law, everyone's behavior falls within the scope of the threats. There is, however, one possible rationale for the state's use of sanctions that would pertain even to a community entirely composed of law-abiding citizens. According to this rationale, even such citizens may refuse to obey unless assured that others will obey too; hence sanctions are needed to provide such assurance. (See, for example, Rawls, *A Theory of Justice,* 240.) Would such purely reassuring sanctions interfere with normativity too? We must distinguish three situations. In the first, call it the *mutual suspicion scenario,* all citizens are in fact law-abiding but each suspects, and is known to suspect, that others may not be, and is therefore reluctant to obey unless reassured of the others' compliance. Since in this situation sanctions are not generally perceived as performing only an assurance function, all my arguments for the disjunctive view would still apply. The second situation is one of *perfect mutual trust:* each citizen is law-abiding and believes that others are too. In this scenario coercive threats would not be used, as the need for mutual assurance does not arise. The third situation is characterized by *imperfect mutual trust.* With some simplification, the following conditions hold of each citizen C: (1) C is law abiding; (2) C believes (correctly) that everyone else is law abiding too; (3) C believes (wrongly) that others may suspect that some citizens are

not law abiding; (4) C believes that as a result of their belief those others may themselves disobey the law; (5) C may disobey the law as a result of condition 4. In this situation a regime of sanctions is in fact needed to secure obedience by providing assurance, even though once such a regime is in place, everyone's obedience is, and is known to be, voluntary. Since no one is even ostensibly subject to coercion, this scenario falls outside the disjunctive thesis. It should be noted, however, that even such a regime of putative threats can impair normativity unless people hold an additional, counterfactual, belief: namely, that had condition 1 not held, government would not use coercion simply to deter violations. Otherwise, the mere fact that government does not have an occasion to use real coercion would be of little significance. Government would still be perceived as willing to appeal to people's inclinations when necessary (my fourth argument); and it would not be seen as genuinely relying on the citizens' good will and cooperation (second argument). Only the first argument would not apply: as long as condition 2 holds, the existence of threats is generally believed to provide assurance only, and so it does not attenuate the expressive significance of people's obedience.

37. Compare M. B. E. Smith, "Is There a Prima Facie Obligation to Obey the Law?" *Yale Law Journal* 82 (1973): 950, which maintains that whether we recognize a general moral duty to obey the law makes little practical difference.

38. Raz, *The Authority of Law*, 25.

PART 2
BASIC VALUES

CHAPTER FOUR
CONCEPTIONS OF CHOICE
AND CONCEPTIONS OF AUTONOMY

Freedom of choice is an important liberal ideal, both in itself and as a constituent of the ideal of autonomy. Choice and autonomy in this way mutually reinforce one another: we value autonomy in part because of the freedom to choose it validates, and we value free choice in part because it contributes to our autonomy. However, the conception of choice that plays this normative role largely originates in the theory of rational choice, the area in which choice received greatest attention and was given the most detailed and rigorous articulation. That conception of choice, at least in its broad outline, is often taken for granted in normative discourse in general, and in discussions of autonomy in particular. The basic tenets of rational choice theory have been subjected to thorough and well-known criticisms,[1] but these focus for the most part on the descriptive inadequacies of that approach.[2] My interest is rather with the normative aspect of rational choice—with the kind of ideal of free choice it projects and with the role it plays in shaping conceptions of autonomy. I begin by observing some "inherent frustrations" that are bound up with the dominant conception of choice. In the second section I point to a number of familiar experiences from which I extrapolate a conception of choice I call *willing* that is diametrically opposed to the dominant conception. In the third section I present some considerations that make willing a more suitable conception of choice than the dominant one for constructing an adequate account of autonomy. I conclude, in the final section, with a few comments on the relationship between the two conceptions of choice I distinguish.

125

1. Frustrations of Choice

The conception of choice codified by rational choice theory—call it *choosing*—does not have a single canonical form, but the following features are sufficiently common. First, choosing requires a *choice-set:* a number (at least two) of options among which the agent must choose. Second, choosing depends on the agent's *preferences:* these are comparative evaluative attitudes which permit the agent to rank various options in terms of their relative desirability. Third, choosing consists in a process I call *selection:* it involves evaluating the choice-set in light of the agent's preferences, ranking the options accordingly, and picking out the leading option. Finally, choosing involves *opportunity costs,* roughly the value to the agent of the opportunities forgone in favor of the selected option.[3]

This is of course an idealized version of choice, and it is idealized in two very different senses: both in the sense of being an *ideal type,* and also in the sense of presenting these features as an *ideal,* that is, as a measure of rationality and a key to freedom and autonomy. As an ideal type we can easily recognize in the four elements I have listed a rough approximation of some familiar choice situations: poring over the restaurant menu or staring at the shelves of a department store come readily to mind. But these experiences should also alert us to some abiding frustrations that ought to chill our willingness to embrace choice, so understood, as an ideal in terms of which we lead and assess our lives. Though my present comments will be too cursory to count as a critique of this version of choice, they should nonetheless suffice, I hope, to motivate the search for an alternative conception that I conduct in the next section.

It is true of course that we find many of our ideals frustrating: they are too hard to attain, they conflict with other ideals, and so on. But choice as I have just described it is defective in a more fundamental way: it is an *inherently frustrating ideal.* By this I mean an ideal whose pursuit involves a sacrifice or a violation of values that are underwritten by the ideal itself. (By underwritten I mean values that are part of the ideal or are presupposed or entailed by it.) I value choice because it puts me in control and it lets me have what I want. The lure of choice lies in the wealth of options presented to me, all conceived as so many sources of potential gratification, and in the fact that it is up to me how to shape my life from those materials in the most satisfying way. It is some such picture that lies at the bottom of choice's attraction, and it is in its light that choice's inherent frustrations must be understood.[4] The seeds of frustration are present in each one of the four elements of choice I have listed.

Consider the idea of choice-set first. On the assumptions of the choice model, the value of things for me is uniquely and exclusively determined by my *preferences*—by a thing's location within a ranking relative to the other members in the choice-set. But this condition is not satisfied with regard to the choice-set itself. Ex hypothesi the chooser does not get to determine—to choose—the composition of the choice-set: if she did, then the more inclusive set out of which the "choice-set" was selected would be the real choice-set. To get off the ground, the process of selection must presuppose a set of conditions—that is, a choice-set—that violate the only method of valuation recognized by the model of choice, namely conformity with the agent's preferences. Consequently, choosing must take place in a field of nonchoice, that is against the background of what from the perspective of choosing is an arbitrary or coercive delimiting of options and possibilities.[5] Indeed, even the very imperative to choose appears within this picture as a constraint or a restriction—it is not itself the product of our preference ranking.

I turn now to the kind of valuation implicit in choosing. Choosing is based on preferences that are essentially comparative attitudes, and the valuation that issues from them is therefore necessarily relative. Since as already mentioned the process of selection takes place within an artificially delimited choice-set, the potential for frustration inherent in this aspect of choosing is obvious. To say that I chose correctly can only mean that given the choice-set I made the best selection; that is, that the selected item or option is better than its competitors. This is the most I can hope for. My confidence in the item's superiority is, however, qualified by my awareness that my judgment is incomplete, since it does not extend to the items not included in my choice-set. Moreover, even my confidence regarding the superiority of the chosen item within the choice-set is precarious. In the nature of things I shall experience (possess, use, follow) only the item I chose, and not the forgone items. I can never be certain, therefore, that I have chosen correctly. No matter how pleased I may be with my choice, my satisfaction is always liable to be marred by the lurking suspicion that some other options would have been better after all. Even if I do not in fact envisage any possible improvement over the chosen item along the dimension on which its satisfaction is measured, a choosing mentality makes room for anxiety that my contentment merely signals failure of imagination: had I been presented with or given the experience of additional options to those that were included in my choice-set, I would have found them more satisfying or fulfilling than my present fantasies reveal.

The point again is not psychological but logical, concerning the internal structure of choice, as presently described, seen as an ideal. There is an ineliminable tension in this picture between the method of valuation by preferences and the idea of a choice-set. As we saw, the value for the agent of any item is uniquely fixed by its location in the agent's overall ranking of the members in his choice-set. The agent is best off, and rational, when he picks out the highest ranking item. But which is the highest ranking item is determined, in part, by the composition of the choice-set. Given an expanded choice-set it is in principle always possible that different items would rank even higher, and thus the agent would be better off choosing *them*. In other words, the idea of preferences does not have an internal limiting principle or any natural stopping point. Instead it points to a potentially infinite series, along which value—always a relative matter—keeps increasing, a series that is arbitrarily cut off by the boundary of the choice-set. But in this picture, that boundary, no matter how determined—be it by human, natural or even metaphysical factors—does act as a limitation or constraint by frustrating the potentially higher values and satisfactions that would be made possible by extending the preference ranking beyond the boundary line.

Consider finally *opportunity costs*. I use the term in a nontechnical sense, to convey the idea that every choice is made at a cost: the loss of the forgone opportunities that the making of any given choice allegedly entails. This is a reminder of the negative aspect of choosing—to select one item also means to give up all the other valuable options included in the choice-set. On the model of choice we are considering, the fact that choice involves the forgoing of valuable options is not as it were an external, contingent constraint, the product of distressing though perhaps ineliminable scarcity or what not; it is once again part of the logic of choice itself, a consequence of what would seem to be necessary conditions of adequacy on the composition of the choice-set. Let me divide the claim that choice necessarily implies the need to forgo some valuable options into two parts.

First, is it necessarily the case that when I select an item from the choice-set, I must have given up some *valuable* options? After all, it may be thought, perhaps there was nothing attractive in the other options, so that forgoing them involved no sacrifice on my part. The condition of adequacy for a choice-set that provides a negative answer to this query is that the choice-set must consist of elements suitable for the purposes that motivate the choice. If the menu I am given consists of one chicken dish and many kinds of different pebbles, I would be hardly given any choice in selecting my meal. Moreover, my designation of any given item as the best, and selecting it for this reason, strictly depends on the composition of the choice-set that happens to be available to me: each item in my preference ordering could find itself in the leading role if the items ahead of it were not included in the choice-set. But this means that each item must possess some desirability characteristic, which can feed my disappointment at having to give it up in favor of the preferred item.

As to the other claim, it can be asked, must selection really involve giving up any options at all? Could the choice-set not ideally include itself as a member, so that I might choose to have all the items on the menu without having to give up anything at all? The answer is that even in this case choosing must involve a certain sacrifice. This conclusion follows from a second condition of adequacy of the choice-set: its members must not only all have *some* desirability characteristic but they must have *different* such characteristics. If the items on the menu all have the same taste, nutritious value, and so on, and they differ only in some irrelevant respect, for example, that they are made of numerically distinct, but qualitatively identical ingredients (I can choose between a Sarah Steak, cut from the cow named Sarah, an Abigail Steak, cut from that cow, etc.) the choice I am given is of course specious. So for the choice-set to include itself and remain a genuine choice-set there must be some desirability-characteristic that pertains to the individual items but that does not pertain to their combination: for example, the advantage of not overly gorging oneself. So by choosing the entire choice-set, that is, by ordering everything that's on the menu, I forgo the dietary advantages of a more modest meal.

To extend the model of choice that I have presented to important aspects of our lives is therefore to subscribe to the grim image of the choosing agent as carrying behind him an ever-growing trail of closed options and forgone opportunities; or, to revert to the economic jargon that I have used, we get the picture of the individual who over a lifetime accumulates a vast negative account of opportunity costs.

A natural response to these charges against choosing is to raise on its behalf the defense of necessity: insofar as there is room for frustration along the lines that I have indicated, it will be thought, it results from features of the world and properties of human beings; roughly that given people's desires on the one hand, and the world's limitations, both physical and metaphysical, on the other, people's reach is bound to be greater than their grasp. Far from being the source of this ubiquitous frustration, choosing is a mode—arguably the best mode—of coping with it. Moreover, some even make a virtue out of this necessity. On Bernard Williams' view, "The fact that there are restrictions on what [the agent] can do is what requires him to be a rational agent, ... and it also makes it possible for him to be one. We may think sometimes that we are dismally constrained to be rational agents, and that in a happier world it would not be necessary. But that is a fantasy (indeed it is *the* fantasy)."[6]

Against this I want to suggest that we can imagine aspects of the world, or domains in our lives, that are largely free of the frustrations that I have described, and that what makes this appear mere fantasy is our entrapment by the choice model that I have outlined. The best way to demonstrate how a particular conception of choice, and not just human nature and the limitations of the world, bears responsibility for the ubiquity of those frustrations is to contrast the conception of choice so far discussed with another conception of choice. This I do in the following section.

2. Choosing and Willing

The paradigmatic choice situation—choosing a dish from a restaurant menu—serves no doubt as an apt metaphor for many occasions in which it seems natural to describe our behavior in terms of a choice-set, preferences, selection, and opportunity costs. But other choice situations have a radically different structure which does not fit into these categories.

Consider first an idealized version of moral choice as depicted by Kant. On his view our moral experience does not consist in scanning a more or less arbitrarily delimited range of acceptable moral options and then picking out the most attractive member in the set. When we are in the grip of moral truth, we are moved by its intrinsic value, rather than by its comparative advantage over other acceptable alternatives. Moral choice consists, according to Kant, in my embracing a particular maxim and a course of action that falls under it. So long as I willfully embrace the correct maxim, I behave both freely and rationally: consideration of other options does not add to my freedom and to my rationality, just as failure to address or consider such options does not detract from them.

Consider next the two following schematized accounts of A's entering into an intimate relationship with B. One account would follow the logic of the rational choice model. A has selected B as her mate. To make the choice significant, she must have had an adequate sample of eligible men to choose from. She considered them all and picked out B as the best of the lot, thereby revealing her preference for him while at the same time turning down C, the second runner-up, as well as all the others. The second scenario tells a radically different story. A simply fell in love with B. Her love for him is not a matter of favorable comparison with other men, nor does it imply a rejection of other eligible though somewhat less desirable suitors. Instead it expresses a response by A to what she perceives as B's uniqueness and an implicit valuation of him as possessing the kind of perfection that excites A's love. Though both stories seem to make sense in this context, the second account will be recognized by many, I suppose, as more suitable for the kind of choice concerned than the first account seems to be. And though the latter story is no doubt an idealized version of A's attitudes, it is an ideal in the light of which many people construe and enact their romantic engagements.

My third example draws attention to the kind of choices, and the kind of freedom, characteristic of various creative pursuits. Here too the choice one exercises and the freedom one enjoys are not typically in the form of selecting the most preferred option out of an available choice-set. My authorship of this article is not primarily a matter of my selecting this topic over other contenders, nor of my selecting the ideas in it from a bunch of other ideas that I judge inferior and reject in favor of the ones here presented. The idea of an article as well as the ideas in it often present themselves to the writer as possessing a certain intrinsic merit, as sound and as worthy of publication, and he records them accordingly. Needless to say it is not part of this picture that the creative process need be smooth and linear. Quite the contrary, it is more likely to be full of false starts and blind alleys. The point however is that these starts are false and the alleys are blind; they are not second-best options rejected in favor of seemingly superior ones that happened to be in the vicinity.

Despite the extravagant simplifications, the three examples I have given—of morality, love, and creativity—should perhaps suffice to point to a kind of choice—and correspondingly to a conception of freedom, autonomy, and rationality—quite different from that depicted in the preceding section. To distinguish the rational choice model from the kind of choice implied by these examples I will call the latter *willing,* and will contrast it with *choosing,* of which the restaurant menu is the paradigm. To bring out more clearly the contrast between willing and choosing, I will describe willing in terms of four elements, all contraries of the defining characteristics of choosing listed in the preceding section.

First, unlike choosing, willing does not require a choice-set. The object of attention and valuation is a single item. Second, willing does not rely on preferences, but on what I call *values.* My use of the term does not fully coincide with either the ordinary or the philosophical usage (neither of which is very clear anyway); but *value* does have connotations that contrast with those associated with *preference,* and on which I want to capitalize. Preferences, we have seen, are only intelligible in regard to a multiplicity on items; there can be no preference for a single item as such. Values are (or generate) pro-attitudes that can have a single item as their object. Furthermore, since preferences are (or issue in) relative valuations, they admit of a *degree* of satisfaction: higher-ranking items satisfy a particular preference more than lower-ranking items do. Values do not have such a dimension: different items either do or do not satisfy a value, but they cannot do so more or less. We can say that unlike preferences that are a matter of comparative valuations, values issue in *categorical* valuations. Such valuations imply the uniqueness of the evaluated item and deny in principle its fungibility;[7] thus the process of willing consists in what I call *election* in contrast to the process of selection that I have described in the case of choosing. Election is the application of a value to a given item and the determination of whether or not the item satisfies the value. Finally, willing does not entail any opportunity costs in the way that all choosing does. When A elects B as her lover—when she falls in love with him—she does not forgo any other potential lover, because insofar as B's election is concerned, no one else is in the running.

The absence of opportunity costs exempts willing from one of the cardinal sources of frustration inherent in choosing. Similarly, since election involves categorical valuation that focuses entirely on the intrinsic merits of the elected item, its validity for the agent is not qualified by the vagaries of the composition of the choice-set as in the case of selection. This is of course not to say that willing promises fewer frustrations and greater overall satisfaction than choosing. It is easy to imagine any number of situations in which the opposite is more likely to be the case. Still, the difference between these two interpretations of choice is that in the case of willing, frustration and dissatisfaction are contingent—the products of the values one has and of how accommodating the world is to them; whereas in the case of choosing, as we saw, frustration issues from the very logic of choice and thus inheres in the ideal itself.

Willing seems to be mainly at home in the case of the rather high-minded choices encountered in areas such as morality, love, and creativity that I have mentioned. But I would like to suggest that even the restaurant can sometimes be the theater of willing rather than of choosing. I can sometimes approach the restaurant menu with a very specific craving for lobster: I am not really interested in what's on the menu, other than to verify that lobster is still on it. It is not quite the case that at this point I prefer lobster to all other foods: I do not consider any other food at all. If you tried to dissuade me by highly recommending, say, the squab, you would be as likely to spoil the experience as to improve my choice. I may now find myself approaching the choice in an altogether different mode. Initially, that is before your polite suggestion, I would have ordered lobster with a special kind of exuberance. Now, after you recommended squab, I may merely *select* a dish, beset by doubt whether the other one (as well perhaps as other items on the menu too) would not be better after all. Whatever my preference may turn out to be, I will not have satisfied my craving.[8]

Craving is an oft-experienced and an ill-understood attitude. My description of willing is too crude to count its application to the case of craving as an adequate analysis of the latter. Still, associating craving with willing, and through it with the other, more high-minded, cases in which election takes place, locates craving I believe within the right paradigm. Moreover, extending the paradigm of willing to the case of craving demonstrates that willing is much more pervasive, and mundane, than my initial examples suggest. Many situations can be approached in the mode of choosing or of willing. When buying a painting, I may ponder a number of an artist's works, and see which one pleases me most. But I can also, walking through a gallery, "fall" for a certain painting, with a compelling sense of "That's it," or "I've got to get it."[9] The same can be said with respect to more ordinary objects such as clothing, cars, or furniture. In each of these cases I can approach a particular item and elect it by way of a categorical valuation which addresses its unique, intrinsic value. I find in it a perfection or an incontestable suitability which, because of its uniqueness, is not threatened by its implicit competition with other contestants.[10]

A Comment on Freedom of Choice

I have been using the locution *free choice* casually, but in fact the relationship between freedom and choice raises a widely debated question. Suppose that I am constrained to do what I intend (desire, choose) to do anyway: is my freedom of choice impaired? Our intuitions seem to be split. On the one hand, it is felt, how can I be said to freely choose X, when X is the only thing I can do? On the other hand, what more can a person want than to do precisely what he wants to do (or to have precisely what he wants to have, etc.)? There are a number of issues hidden here, and what I will say will certainly not put them all to rest. But I believe that some light can be shed on this question, as well as on the distinction between choosing and willing, if we relate the question to the distinction.

The feeling that in order to freely choose X I must be able to choose not-X too is much better supported by the model of choosing than that of willing. Even if my only options were X and not-X, these are still *options* that may, depending on my attitude, define for me a choice-set. That is, I may approach them in the spirit of selection: compare their relative merits and opt for the superior one, possibly beset by frustration that my options are so few and by doubt whether the one I have selected (say X) is indeed the superior one (i.e., in this case, better than not-X). This would be the spirit in which A might decide to marry B, the only eligible bachelor, rather than not marry him and remain single. This would then be a case of choosing, though with the choice-set sharply restricted. "Take it or leave it" are still options, between which a process of selection, albeit an impoverished one, can take place. But meager as the choice-set is, it is essential that it contain more than one item. As we saw earlier, on the rational choice model the existence of more than one option is constitutive of choosing: marriage cannot be a matter of A's choosing unless she prefers it, and therefore selects it, over at least one other option. Things look quite differently when we move from choosing to willing. In that case, to stick to the same example, A's decision to marry B consists in a categorical affirmation of that marriage. Such a categorical affirmation renders all other options irrelevant: those regarding other potential suitors, if there were any, as much as the "not-marry" option.

To recapitulate: whereas the opportunity not-to-X is constitutive of the agent's capacity to choose X under the choosing model, that opportunity, like all other options, plays no role within the model of willing. Insofar as willing is concerned, the opportunity "not to X if I want to" is not necessary for my capacity to choose X. Rather such opportunity is only conditionally related to willing in the following way: if I elect not-to-X then the opportunity not to X is a condition of my freedom of choice with regard to X-ing (or, more precisely, with regard to not-X-ing).[11]

Of course, the "sour grapes" syndrome and related psychological phenomena make us rightly suspicious of the person who embraces wholeheartedly the only option open to him. But the suspicion may be ill-founded after all. The person's willing of that option may in fact be authentic and freely formed, the product of neither manipulation nor self-deception. When does genuine choosing *or* willing take place is not a simple question, and often (perhaps always) we cannot be confident about the genuineness (whatever exactly that means) of a person's preferences *or* values.[12] But no matter how doubtful we may be concerning one's willing the single option one has, there is no logical connection, as there is in the case of choosing, between the number of options and one's willing affirmation of the one elected.

The point I have just made is a limited one; it only demonstrates that it is important for discussions of the question posed at the beginning of this section to be sensitive to the conception of choice about which the question is posed: whereas on one conception the option not to do as one chose is a conceptual requirement of choice itself, on a different conception of choice such an option is quite irrelevant. But this still leaves open the question whether the concept of *freedom* imports by itself, independently of any particular version of choice, such a requirement. But though limited, the point is I think important. When we use the composite locution *freedom of choice,* the significance of options seems to leap at us, as it were, from both conjuncts. But this I tried to show need not be the case. Choice may be meaningful without being "free" in the sense of freedom that implies the availability of alternative options. Even if we decide to withhold the adjective *free* from choice that consists in willing the only option one has, it should still be recognized that much of importance depends on our conative and evaluative attitudes even to those aspects of the world and of our lives to which no alternative exists.

3. Autonomy and Choice

As I have already indicated, the ideal of autonomy, as commonly understood, is bound up with the idea of choice.[13] There is indeed an obvious intuitive link between the two. The core idea behind the ideal of autonomy is that of the self-governing person, who can effectuate his will and thus exercise control over his life. The autonomous person, to use the familiar metaphor, is an author of his own life. Choice comes naturally into this picture as the concrete embodiment of this ideal, as the medium within which one's wants can be best satisfied by the active operation of one's will. But though that much is common ground, most writers on autonomy remain rather vague on the concept of choice they employ. Still, references to options and opportunities abound, and the specter, faint as it may be, of the rational choice model can be often discerned in the background. My aim in this section is to look more explicitly at the relationship between conceptions of choice and conceptions of autonomy. More specifically, I will suggest a number of considerations against choosing and in favor of willing as the conception of choice most appropriate for an ideal of autonomy. It will be convenient for this purpose to distinguish *choice autonomy* from *will autonomy*. These labels are mere shorthand for conceptions of autonomy in which the agent's choices are assumed to take the form of choosing or willing respectively. I view the two conceptions of autonomy that I distinguish mainly as heuristic devices, designed to facilitate the consideration of various strands in the discussions of autonomy that, given the vagueness of the underlying concept of choice employed in them, are often interwoven in the writings of a single author. I should also say at the outset that there is obviously more to autonomy than choice—of either the choosing or the willing variety. My discussion of autonomy is therefore partial, and it touches only on the contribution made by different conceptions of choice to more comprehensive notions of autonomy.

I will advance three considerations against choosing and in favor of willing as the conception of choice suitable for autonomy; they concern the relationship between moral and personal autonomy, the relationship of autonomy and commitment, and the relationship of autonomy to personal identity.

Personal and Moral Autonomy

The most prominent exponent of the idea of autonomy is no doubt Kant, and the present-day importance of this idea is to a large measure due to him. But Kant was interested in moral autonomy, and as already noted his picture of moral choice had little to do with choosing—with an agent selecting a preferred option out of a given choice-set. Quite to the contrary, moral action is marked by an inner necessity when the will is guided inexorably by a moral maxim relevant to the situation at hand. The relationship between the will and the moral law is analogized by Kant to the relationship of physical objects to the laws of nature: not to follow a law of morality is no more an option for the will than resisting gravity is an option for an apple. My aim is not to enter into the esoteric metaphysics that underlies this picture, but only to underscore the phenomenological validity of Kant's insight: it captures the sense of inevitability that is an important aspect of our moral experience. Once we realize what our moral duty in a situation is, we also appreciate that the moral course is in an important sense nonoptional.

The experience of ineluctability in morality is so pervasive that we may be blind to it. Though I dislike my dean and aspire to succeed him, the option of killing him, even if I could do so with impunity, does not so much as present itself to my mind. Even if I do fantasize the perfect murder in gory detail, it carries no psychological reality for me: it does not present a genuine option. But the fact that not killing the dean, come what may, is my only option in this situation does not vitiate my moral autonomy: it would seem utterly perverse to maintain that my moral autonomy would be increased if killing the dean were a real option for me, so that my having spared him could be described as a matter of choosing, that is, the product of my having selected the more benign option out of a choice-set that included the noxious one too.

Evidently, a conception of autonomy that emphasizes the importance of options and the agent's choosing among them is quite at odds with this depiction of the moral experience and hence with Kant's idea of autonomy that is grounded in it. This has led some writers to draw a sharp distinction between moral autonomy, as conceived by Kant, and "the very indirectly related notion" of personal autonomy.[14] It is of course no fatal objection to a theory of autonomy that it makes the concept branch off into two purportedly unrelated notions: there may be indeed no common denominator to the various philosophical (let alone ordinary) uses to which "autonomy" is put. But it is equally clear that an understanding of autonomy that did not treat the concept homonymously and that would instead uncover the common roots of "moral" and "personal" autonomy, if such can be found, would run deeper and would be preferable on familiar metatheoretical grounds.

More important perhaps, an ideal of personal autonomy focused on choice understood in terms of preferences and options would not just leave out moral autonomy. The experience of inner necessity that is central to Kant's theory of moral autonomy extends beyond morality and is familiar to us in many other areas. Consider again the experience of falling in love. One feels powerfully, even irresistibly drawn to another person. And yet, this sense of ineluctability is fully compatible with wholeheartedly embracing the experience as something welcome and utterly willed. The creative process too, as already mentioned, is marked by a struggle "to get it right." When we hit the nail on the head, either in having a perspicuous idea or in coming up with a happy phrase, we feel very much in their grip. But being carried away by a flow of creativity, far from vitiating our authorship gives us the strongest and happiest claim to it. Finally, even when we descend once again from these lofty heights we encounter ineluctability in the more mundane circumstances represented by my craving for lobster.[15]

These examples underscore the fact that we commonly construe and experience values of all kinds, both high and low, as *forces* that exert their influence on us, draw us to certain things and repel us from others, presenting certain actions or objects as uniquely and indisputably appropriate. The recognition in an object or a course of action of a certain merit or perfection that makes it, in a certain respect (moral, aesthetic, prudential, etc.) incontestably suitable under the circumstances is a phenomenon that extends far beyond morality and pervades our lives.

If these observations are correct, then moral choice is not as unique as Kant makes it seem. This suggests that Kant's conception of autonomy too, at least in broad outline, need not be confined to the moral domain. One (I think welcome) result of replacing "choosing" by "willing" as the key to autonomy is to present morality as a paradigmatic but not unique arena within which autonomy characterized along Kantian lines is displayed.

Autonomy and Commitment

Intuitively, it seems that the person who enters into serious and enduring relationships and who undertakes and carries out long-term projects is a paragon of autonomy, not its antithesis. Commitment need not perhaps be a condition of autonomy: we may want to allow that one can be autonomous while being thoroughly frivolous in one's relationships and undertakings. But it seems that we should at least insist that the concept of autonomy be neutral with respect to commitment, not hostile to it. The choice conception does not pass this test. It fails it on both conceptual and psychological grounds.

The conceptual point is simply that commitment involves, ex hypothesi, foreclosing a certain number of options. If autonomy is based on choosing, then commitment must be seen as a constraint on one's autonomy, albeit a self-imposed one, not as its manifestation. This statement needs clarification. The claim is not that the choice-loving person would never embark (qua choice loving) on long-term projects and attachments, nor that he is always ready to be sidetracked from his commitments by *any* attractive opportunity that may come his way. The choosing agent may rationally (i.e., consistently with the logic of the rational choice model) commit himself to ignore an entire class of options that he considers inferior to those contained in another class, if the very consideration of specific options contained in the inferior class is inconsistent with the exercise and enjoyment of the superior options. To illustrate: in order to enjoy the benefits of an exclusive intimate long-term relationship with B, it is sensible for A to renounce the possibility of having an affair with other men. This is so because she ranks an enduring, exclusive involvement more highly than such love affairs, and the latter are inconsistent with the former. But suppose now that A meets C, who presents himself as a prospect for a long-term, exclusive romantic engagement. Here A's commitment to the relationship with B collides head-on with her valuing choice, which requires that she keep the option of a relationship with C open, and feel at liberty to consider whether he is superior to B as a romantic partner. The decision regarding C is of the same kind as, and should therefore be allowed to compete against, the initial decision regarding B. If A treats the former decision (the "commitment") as foreclosing the latter, she has shrunk the size of her choice-set, she has reduced her options, and has (on the choice conception) thereby curtailed her autonomy.

This conclusion is further corroborated by the relativity of valuation that characterizes choosing. The judgment involved in selecting X (the project or relationship to which I commit myself) pertains only to the choice-set within which I established X's comparative superiority. So if I later encounter an item that was not a member in the original choice-set, then ex hypothesi I have not yet made any judgment concerning its merit relative to that of X. This gives me an excellent (though of course not necessarily conclusive) reason to review and perhaps revise my initial selection. Though the existence of such a reason need not undermine my commitment to X (assuming I made one), it is very likely to weaken it.

The psychological connection between choosing and commitment mirrors this conceptual relationship. Though in principle one could go full steam into a project or relationship even if one were ready to back out when a better opportunity came along, this is not likely to be the case: using much steam will tend to look wasteful in light of the perceived tentativeness of the investment.

Though willing does not of course guarantee the constancy required by commitment—one can always change one's mind—willing is, for reasons that should now be obvious, fully compatible with enduring commitments. It is therefore more suitable in this respect than choosing for a role in accounts of autonomy.

Autonomy and Personal Identity

I turn now to the relationship between choice and personal identity. I will claim that choosing is a poor model for important, identity-shaping choices, so that when it comes to such choices one's authorship of one's life, and hence one's autonomy, are inadequately portrayed by the picture of selecting from among a set of options.

Instead of going to law school I could have gone to medical school, or joined the navy, or taken up the violin. I could have been a physician, a sailor, a violinist. On the choice conception of autonomy in order for me to be the autonomous author of my life some such propositions must be true. But can they be? On certain assumptions, which I shall spell out momentarily, the thought that I could have been a physician (or a sailor, etc.) simply makes no sense. If these assumptions are true (and I shall not argue here their validity), then I cannot understand my autonomy retrospectively as a matter of having chosen important aspects of my life from among a variety of options and opportunities.

To make the point I must distinguish between two contrasting views of the relationship between a person, or a self, and his or her life. On one view the self is separate from its life: personal identity is fixed antecedently to or independently of the person's life. On this view the claim that a given person could have led a different life makes perfectly good sense. The other view—call it the *constitutive view*—holds that a self is constituted or shaped by its life,[16] so that personal identity is inseparable from the person's life. The constitutive view can have an extreme version, according to which no counterfactual thought about a person's life can ever be intelligible—every departure from the actual course of one's life must involve a change in identity, and thus no longer be a counterfactual about *this* person's life. But the view is more plausible in its more moderate version: the answer to the question who I am is given in terms of only the important aspects of my life, not in terms of every detail of it. My identity would survive relatively minor variations from my actual life, but not major ones. In talking about the constitutive view I shall from now on refer only to the moderate version.

Now on the constitutive view in hindsight options have very little meaning for me. In an important sense the significant options that "I" have had—for example, of being a sailor—were not *my* options, because having followed any option other than the one I did would have resulted in an identity different from mine.[17]

It may be objected that though I could not have *been* a sailor, I could have nonetheless made the choice of *becoming* one; and that by choosing law school instead I have decided to become a different person. But this objection seems to fail because of the following consideration. "Can choose X" obviously entails "can carry out (or attain) X." It would make no sense to say that I could have chosen filet mignon if the restaurant were out of it or if I could not afford it. So the following argument seems sound:

> I could not have been a sailor;
> "can choose X" only if "can carry out X";
> hence,
> I could not have chosen to become a sailor.

There is an air of paradox in this conclusion. After all "choosing to go to law school" is an event within *my* life, and at the time this was a genuine choice (putting of course aside questions of determinism, which are not here at issue). Call the guy who twenty-odd years ago hesitated between law school and the navy A. It is indisputably true that A had a choice between going to law school and joining the navy. The following argument thus seems also valid:

> A had a choice between law school and the navy;
> A could have become a sailor;
> I am A;
> therefore,
> I could have chosen to become a sailor.

How are we to reconcile these contradictory conclusions? A full consideration of the matter would take us too far afield, but let me make one suggestion. "I could have been a sailor" (or "I could have chosen to become a sailor") can be interpreted in two different ways: either as a report in the past tense referring to an historical state of affairs, or as a tenseless statement of a counterfactual about myself. Some sentences of this form are amenable to both interpretations. If I go on vacation to London, and it constantly rains, I can say: "I could have been in the Bahamas instead," referring to the fact that my travel agent raised that possibility, that seats on the airplane and a room in a resort were available, et cetera. But I can also be making the counterfactual claim that had I made the right choice, I would now be basking in the sun.

My claim regarding statements of this form that pertain to important, identity-forming—what I call *constitutive*—factors is that such statements are amenable only to the first, the historical, interpretation but not to the counterfactual one. The distinction has this significance. In the case of my spoiled vacation, it makes perfectly good sense for me to regret my choice and to feel that I am missing out by not being right now, as I might have been, on the sunny beach. But given the relationship between one's identity and one's life that I assume, such attitudes would be incoherent in the case of the constitutive choice. The life of a sailor that I am imagining could not have been truly *mine*, because the subject of that life would not have been *me*. Comparing my actual life as, let us say, a lawyer to the life of a sailor would not be very different from my comparing it to the life of a medieval knight or to that of a Hebrew prophet. All three comparisons may perhaps help me assess my own life, but it would make no more sense for me to regret not *being* a sailor than to regret not living any one of the other lives I mentioned, no matter how superior to mine I judge all three types of life; being a sailor has not been an option for *me*, and thus not something that *I* can miss not being, any more than is the case in regard to being a knight or a prophet.

Now these reflections are all retrospective. The prospective situation at the time of the constitutive decision looks markedly different. When I contemplate the possibilities of law, the violin, or the navy, I must view each option as genuinely mine. I have every reason for wanting to have as good a future as possible, and there is no denying that whichever course I follow, *my* future is at stake. Nonetheless, the retrospective reflections that I have recounted bear importantly on the prospective decision. By anticipating those reflections the agent may reassure himself that in opting for, for example, law school, he is not denying his future self the benefits of being a violinist or a sailor. He is not denying them since in the future he will not be able coherently to see himself as *deprived* of those options, no matter how attractive either one may then seem to him. What will eventually matter and be of lasting significance is only the option chosen, not the ones forgone.

The comparison to the choice of a vacation will be helpful here. When I anticipate my "vacationing self" I can imagine myself having two sets of evaluative attitudes, and in choosing the vacation I want them both to be positive. In the one set belong such questions as whether I am having a good time, whether I am not bored, whether I am enjoying beautiful scenery, and so on. The other set involves comparative attitudes: am I having as good a time as I would have had in any one of the other resorts I could have selected but turned down, is the scenery here as beautiful as it would have been there, et cetera. When I choose my vacation, I may try to secure the best I can an affirmative answer by my "vacationing self" to both sets of questions. But when I make a constitutive choice, such as of a career, the imaginative anticipation of my future self's evaluative attitudes yields quite different results. I can encounter attitudes that correspond to the first set mentioned above: I can envisage myself engaged or bored, fulfilled or frustrated, happy or miserable, and so forth. But in light of the considerations that I have mentioned, I should not find a set of comparative attitudes, consisting of satisfactions or frustrations that result from the favorable or unfavorable reckoning of aspects of my life as against the other lives I could have had but turned down: I lack a standpoint from which I can conduct such a comparative assessment. When I choose my career, I can try to replicate the first set of considerations that determine my choice of vacation by trying to embark on a course that will make me eventually fulfilled and happy. But there will be no corresponding point to my trying to secure my future self a comparative advantage by choosing a life that I will find superior to the alternatives. I must recognize that it will eventually simply not matter whether I selected the best option, because in the day of reckoning the very idea of a best option as applied to constitutive possibilities will have lost its meaning.

Some people elect their careers: they have a vocation, say for art, that they pursue relentlessly and single-mindedly from an early age on. Others select their professions and careers: they examine the options open to them, rank them in terms of their preferences, and pursue the one that looks most attractive overall. The considerations I have described, if correct, point to a sense in which both methods of choice as seen retrospectively tend to converge. With hindsight my authorship of my life consists in both cases in my willful affirmation of the path I follow rather than in my preferring that path to others that anyway would not have been mine. If in canvassing my life I am to find in it traces of my autonomy, these traces must be found as it were within my life, not on its outer perimeter between what it has been and that which it might have been but never was. Autonomy accordingly requires an account of authorship that does not depend exclusively on choosing and on the availability of options. The will conception provides such an account. Election—the categorical affirmation of certain aspects of my life—does not assign an essential role to forgone opportunities. Instead it focuses on my attitude to what are the actual constituents of my life story, a story that fixes my unique identity. The thought that I might have had identities other than mine is in this regard neither more unsettling nor more comforting, indeed it is no more relevant, than is the recognition that there are many other people around.

Summarizing in reverse, I have tried to show in this section that a will conception of autonomy—in which authorship is understood in terms of election rather than selection—gives better expression than does choice-autonomy to the relationship between one's identity and one's life; it accommodates commitments more comfortably than choice-autonomy does; and it can subsume both moral and personal autonomy under a single account. But pointing out some advantages of constructing the ideal of autonomy on the basis of one rather than another conception of choice falls of course far short of actually constructing the ideal in those terms. This however is not my present purpose. But if the considerations that I have presented are sound, they support a general approach to autonomy that, broadly speaking, emphasizes the congruence between one's chosen actions and one's "second order" attitudes and valuations, or, in a somewhat different formulation, one's identification with one's motivations and choices. Though there is already by now a small family of such approaches (and, as one would expect, some family feuds), let me add another formulation of my own.[18] It is much too vague and loose to qualify as a definition of autonomy, but it will suffice I hope as a suggestion of the tie between the group of accounts of autonomy I have in mind and the "willing" conception of choice. On the will conception of autonomy one is an author of one's life—hence autonomous—insofar as one willingly embraces different aspects of it because one finds them meritorious and the life that comprises them to that extent worthwhile.

4. Does Willing Depend on Choosing?

In this section I want to consider briefly a number of ways in which choosing, especially the availability of a range of options, might be thought to play a role even in the context of willing. The most obvious relation of a range of options to willing is this. Recall A who falls in love with B. Though the existence of a choice-set is not necessary for A's election of her partner, it is nonetheless likely to play an important role: the larger the pool of eligible men, the greater the likelihood that B would be among them. However, other methods for securing B's availability would do in principle just as well. An experienced matchmaker who knows A well enough could save her much trouble by introducing to her B and no one else.

The matchmaking method, though, may fail. The opportunity to select B by herself out of a group of eligible men might be a precondition of A's falling in love. She would resent being presented with B by a match-maker or by her parents, and would consequently balk at what could otherwise become a thriving relationship. Indeed, it is even possible to will an item in part because one selected it first. One agonized over the choice-set, carefully comparing its members and weighing their relative worth. Having been finally settled on, this option now has a property it did not possess before: it is one's *choice*. One can now will it—fully and unconditionally embrace it—precisely because of this newly acquired merit. In these ways, willing may appear to depend on choosing.

Notice, however, that this claim does not state a conceptual link between willing and choosing but only an empirical generalization concerning the psychological preconditions of willing. But as an empirical generalization the claim is at least to some degree circular: it is more likely to hold true in cultures that value choosing and perhaps consider it a constituent of personal autonomy. A is much less likely to feel resentful when presented with B by a matchmaker, and therefore less inhibited from falling in love with him, in a culture in which matchmaking predominates, than she would be in a culture in which this is not a common practice. Moreover, even if true, the most the claim establishes is the need for an apparent, not an actual, choice-set. It may be a psychological condition of my craving for lobster that I get to pick it out of the menu: my craving would dissipate if I felt that lobster is being forced on me irrespective of my desires. But this only means that the shrewd waiter, aware both of my craving and of my obsession with choice, would be well advised to present me with the menu, ignoring the fact that lobster happens to be the only item on it that is still available.[19] Finally, I said that it is possible for me to value X in part because it has been chosen by me. But though this combination of choosing and willing is familiar, we are also familiar with the possibility that I value X in part because it has been chosen for me by someone else, for example, by my best friend. In that case my recognition in X of a unique merit and my subsequent election of X will follow upon the friend having selected it for me.

Choosing may be thought to relate to willing in yet another way. Election may underdetermine action and seemingly still leave both room and need for selection. Take the example of falling in love. Suppose that A wants to get married with the man she loves; that she falls in love not with just one man, but with two; and that the only marriage allowed in her society is monogamous. On these assumptions it seems that A must now select one out of the two men she loves. If such situations are thought to be sufficiently common, which they may well be, then choosing would appear as a necessary corollary to the indeterminacy of willing.

It should be first noted that what might perhaps look like an easy way out of the difficulty is not in fact available. It is the suggestion that A simply rank her loves in terms of their intensity. In this way, it might be hoped, the process of election would generate an ordering with a single "winner." This suggestion fails for a reason that I have already mentioned. Insofar as the process of election is concerned, the elected items are all incommensurable with one another: different loves are qualitatively different valuations and as such resist ranking and comparison. (This observation seems to me to underlie the familiar tease often addressed to children who are asked to say which one of their parents they love more. The tease does not merely embarrass the child by asking him or her to divulge a compromising truth; it more likely confounds the child by presenting a conceptual difficulty: each parent is likely to be loved differently, rather than more or less than the other.) The process of election will not therefore yield the requisite ordering. But the persistence of indeterminacy does not imply that choosing should now come to the rescue. For the reasons already considered selection can only undo or supersede the election, it cannot supplement it. In choosing between her two lovers, A must rank and compare their different attributes in light of her preferences. But this is precisely what the conditions of election forbid. The problem of indeterminacy, though, is not unique to willing: choosing can also result in a tie. In both cases resort must be had to some tie-breaking mechanism.[20] My only point here is that just as choosing cannot be expected to break its own ties, it cannot break those of willing either.[21]

Notes

1. The best-known lines of attack are respectively represented by D. Kahneman, P. Slovic, and A. Tversky, eds., *Judgment under Uncertainty* (Cambridge: Cambridge University Press, 1982); and by Herbert Simon, *Models of Bounded Rationality* (Cambridge: MIT Press, 1982).

2. A recent exception that takes a more normative view is Gerald Dworkin, "Is More Choice Better Than Less?" *Midwest Studies in Philosophy* 7 (1982): 47.

3. Summaries of the rational choice model roughly along these lines can be found, for example, in David Gauthier, *Morals by Agreement* (Oxford: Oxford University Press, 1986), chap. 2, and in Jon Elster, ed., *Rational Choice* (New York: New York University Press, 1986), introduction. Other standard elements in the rational choice model are *maximization, completeness,* and *transitivity.* Transitivity does not bear on my argument; the requirement of completeness is implied by the idea of a preference ranking, whereas the goal of maximization is implicit in the process of *selection* as I describe it.

4. By ascribing to choice an inherent propensity for frustration I do not mean to claim that people in fact generally experience all the frustrations that I list. But first, the fact that they do not may be taken as evidence that they do not fully or at all inhabit the mind-set fostered by choosing, or that they do not follow out the logic of choosing either in thought or in practice. Second, people do not always have the psychological states for which they have good reasons. My claim therefore is only that someone who embraces the "ideal type" of choice as I describe it has good reasons for the frustrations that I list.

5. Compare: "In a society in which preferences, whether in the market or in politics or in private life, are assigned the place which they have in a liberal order, power lies with those who are able to determine what the alternatives are to be between which choices will be available. The consumer, the voter, and the individual in general are accorded the right of expressing their preferences for one or more out of the alternatives which they are offered, but the range of possible alternatives is controlled by an elite, and how they are presented is also so controlled." Alasdair MacIntyre, *Whose Justice? Which Rationality?* (London: Duckworth, 1988), 345.

6. Bernard Williams, *Ethics and the Limits of Philosophy* (Cambridge: Harvard University Press, 1985), 57.

7. Though much more needs to be said of the idea of uniqueness in the context of willing, it would perhaps be helpful to relate uniqueness to the notion of incommensurability. Indeed we can think of uniqueness as a form of "radical incommensurability" in which the particular object

of choice is treated as incommensurable with any other object. For an illuminating discussion of incommensurability and its role in practical reasoning see Joseph Raz, *The Morality of Freedom* (Oxford: Oxford University Press, 1986), chap. 13. Still, speaking here about a "particular object" may be inaccurate: willing can have as its object a certain group of items taken as a whole (cumulatively), or it may address the group disjunctively: its members are treated as indistinguishable in the relevant respect, so that each one of them possesses the uniqueness that makes it capable of satisfying the applicable value (craving for lobster, discussed infra, is an example).

8. My disposition to elect a certain item does not entail that I would also select it. It would be therefore a mistake to think of the item the agent would have elected, the lobster in my example, as the item that the agent would have selected out of any choice-set that contained it. But how can the mode of choice influence my eventual decision? One possible explanation (though it is probably not the only one) is this. When I contemplate X in the mode of willing, I respond, inter alia, to the uniqueness that I perceive in it or attribute to it. Such uniqueness can be itself a source of value in various objects, actions and relationships. We may be tempted to say that so conceived, i.e., as unique, X would indeed be the item I would select out of any choice-set that contained it. But of course the attribute, uniqueness, in virtue of which we might believe in the truth of this proposition makes the proposition incoherent: this very attribute removes X from any comparative ranking and undercuts the possibility of preferences applying to it. On the other hand, if I treat X as an object of choosing, that is to say if I do locate it in a ranking among other competing options, it must be then contemplated under aspects common to it and the other contenders so as to make comparison and ranking intelligible. But in this case X will have lost its uniqueness (or at any rate it is not considered in terms of it), and without it X may no longer be the preferred item within the choice-set.

9. Herbert Simon calls this the "aha! experience." *Reason in Human Affairs* (Stanford: Stanford University Press, 1983), 27. Perhaps all I am suggesting here is that this mode of choice should be taken more seriously than Simon's appellation implies. It should be observed that my discussion of willing as an alternative mode of choice is consistent with Simon's view that choosing—especially the exposure at some point in one's life to ranges of options—is necessary for the cultivation of what I call values that eventually issue in willing.

10. These comments may create the impression that by *willing* I mean a more impulsive and spontaneous kind of choice than that involved in choosing. But as the examples of morality and creativity demonstrate, the categorical valuation involved in election can be as much the

product of prolonged deliberation as it may come about by a flash of insight or a sudden surge of desire.

11. Compare Richard Arneson, "Freedom and Desire," *Canadian Journal of Philosophy* 15 (1985): 425, 440–41.

12. This of course is a feature of Kant's theory of moral autonomy as well: no one, not even the agent, can ever be sure that a moral action was autonomously motivated.

13. For choice as constitutive of autonomy in recent writing see e.g. R. S. Downie and Elizabeth Telfer, "Autonomy," *Philosophy* 46 (1971): 293; Gerald Dworkin, *The Theory and Practice of Autonomy* (Cambridge: Cambridge University Press, 1988); Thomas Hurka, "Why Value Autonomy?" *Social Theory and Practice* 13 (1987): 361.

14. Raz, *The Morality of Freedom*, 370.

15. It should not be concluded that every whim or obsession manifests my will and that by pursuing it (or rather by being carried away by it) I exercise my autonomy. At least since Kant it is widely recognized that autonomy can be impaired by factors that we would commonly describe as "internal" to the person as well as by "external" ones. Whether my craving for lobster should be construed as expressing my will or as subduing it depends on whether or not I "identify" with the craving. See Harry G. Frankfurt, "Identification and Externality," and "Identification and Wholeheartedness," both in *The Importance of What We Care About* (Cambridge: Cambridge University Press, 1988). But these issues lie beyond the scope of the present discussion.

16. The variation is meant to accommodate different views of the exact manner in which one's life is essential to one's identity, e.g., by forging a character that is a constituent of the self's identity.

17. On some of the complications that attend this view, and which cannot be considered here, see Bernard Williams, *Problems of the Self* (Cambridge: Cambridge University Press, 1973), essays 3 and 4; and Saul Kripke, *Naming and Necessity* (Oxford: Blackwell, 1980).

18. Examples of the general approach to autonomy I have in mind are Dworkin, *Theory and Practice;* and Robert Young, *Personal Autonomy: Beyond Positive and Negative Liberty* (London: Croom Helm, 1986).

19. A similar reply applies to the argument, made by Jon Elster, that choice is necessary to ward off what he calls "adaptive preference formation": if A is my only option, I may change my preferences so as to favor A as a result of a "sour grapes" kind of psychological mechanism. But here again it is my *belief* that A is my only option which will trigger this adaptive response. Actually having additional options is accordingly not necessary to block the "sour grapes" syndrome, just as the absence of options is not sufficient to trigger it. See Jon Elster, *Sour*

Grapes: Studies in Subversion of Rationality (Cambridge: Cambridge University Press, 1983), 128–29.

20. On the problem of tie-breaking in the case of choosing, see Edna Ullmann-Margalit and Sidney Morgenbesser, "Picking and Choosing," *Social Research* 44 (1977): 757.

21. Compare Isaiah Berlin, *Four Essays on Liberty* (Oxford: Oxford University Press, 1969), li–lii, who overlooks this difficulty.

CHAPTER FIVE
DEFENDING DIGNITY

I will make a few notes in the margins of two large and seemingly unrelated developments that are of vital importance to the criminal law: a growing disaffection with the harm principle and the challenge of multiculturalism. The harm principle presents itself as a morally neutral standard that can set rational limitations on the scope of the criminal law. The disaffection results from a mounting recognition that the pretence of neutrality is specious, the limitations illusory, and that the principle fails to define and properly delimit criminal liability. This conclusion invites a search for an alternative. The difficulty of such a search is greatly compounded, however, by cultural diversity and its normative implications for national legal systems. The approach sought must be able to accommodate a wide range of creeds without slipping into a relativism that condones every atrocity as long as it is underwritten by some culture. This apparent dilemma has long haunted moral and legal philosophy, but its urgency is felt with particular force these days, as multiculturalism is becoming a more pressing and a more widely recognized reality.

The suggestion I consider is the replacement of the harm principle by what may be called the *dignity principle:* the view that the main goal of the criminal law is to defend the unique moral worth of every human being. Duly elaborated, the proposed principle may be able to meet the foregoing challenges: provide a more adequate criterion for criminality than the harm principle, and allow us to insist on law's enforcing a substantive morality while leaving ample yet not infinite room for cultural variation. I do not, however, attempt here the requisite elaboration, nor do I present a comprehensive argument in support of this suggestion. I offer only some preliminary thoughts, and I pursue them using a method that is now more commonly practiced by lawyers than by philosophers, even though its origins are distinctly philosophical: attending to puzzle cases, *aporiae,* and constructing theoretical response to them. I will try to demonstrate that the idea of dignity helps account for our considered judgments in a number of test cases in which the idea of harm fails, and then explain how a dignity-based morality may be able to cope with cultural and moral diversity.[1]

It is important to emphasize at the outset that I do not pretend to invent the suggestion I here examine or draw it out of thin air. Quite to the contrary, the suggestion I explore is a move within a familiar dialectic that has characterized the development of liberal thinking in the recent past. On this view of the matter, replacing the harm principle with the dignity principle is the culmination of what can be schematically seen as a three-stage process. The harm principle was ushered in as part of the rise of utilitarianism.[2] The last thirty years or so have been marked by a mounting critique of utilitarianism and a deontological, mostly Kantian response to it. Much of the opposition between these views has focused on utilitarianism's aggregative approach, criticized by opponents as failing to pay sufficient attention to the separateness of persons or their individuality. But another aspect of the opposition, more relevant to my topic, concerns the basic values that the conflicting views respectively posit. These are ordinarily taken to be individual welfare on the utilitarian side and personal autonomy on the Kantian. The relationship between these two values has become a dominant theme in liberal discourse. However, even a casual reader of the legal and the philosophical literature will have noticed a subtle but significant shift from autonomy-talk to dignity-talk that has been shaping recently on the deontological side of the normative divide, with an increasing emphasis on respect for persons as the preeminent liberal value.[3] The following discussion is part reflection and part elaboration within the field of criminal jurisprudence of this trend.[4]

1. Beyond Harm

Liberal criminal law theory has long been dominated by the harm principle.[5] But the principle was contested from the start[6] and has come under increasing attack over the years. I will not attempt a final verdict, but will only illustrate the kinds of misgivings that motivate a continued search for an account of what criminal liability is essentially about. The harm principle is designed to define the legitimate scope of criminal liability, so it is natural to test it by examining how well it performs this task. My starting points are two seminal articles by Professor Sanford Kadish in which he sounded the alarm against the perils of overcriminalization. Though I find both of these articles compelling, when seen side by side they appear to be pulling in opposite directions in ways that reveal strains in the harm principle. In the first of these articles Professor Kadish criticizes a category of offenses often referred to as *victimless crimes*,[7] which includes such things as consensual deviant sexual practices, gambling, and the use of narcotics, whereas in the second article he criticizes the use of criminal sanctions in enforcing economic regulations.[8] The articles thus present two large areas of criminality as objectionable departures from what is taken to be the legitimate core of criminal liability. What is this core? What makes the departures illegitimate? Kadish's answer to the first question is explicit and sound: "The central distinguishing aspect of the criminal sanction appears to be the stigmatization of the morally culpable."[9] What is wrong with the use of criminal sanctions in the service of economic regulation is simply the absence of moral culpability. But this diagnosis creates a tension with Kadish's criticism of the offenses discussed in the first article, offenses that are designed "purely to enforce a moral code."[10] The moral opprobrium that is fatally missing in the case of economic regulation appears to be the defining characteristic of these offenses; why are they an aberration of criminality rather than at the heart of it? The alleged immorality of offenses that fall in the first category does not seem to give them sufficient liberal credentials, nor does the mere presence of harm in the latter, economic types of offenses make them suitable for criminal prohibition. The challenge posed by Kadish's two articles is how the criminal law can retain a moral content without turning moralistic. We need, in other words, a criterion of criminality that is both *moral* and *critical*: one that can preserve the distinctly moral content of criminal liability without endorsing on purely conventional ground any strongly held popular belief. The harm principle seems unable to meet this challenge.

There is a second and related objection to the harm principle, put forward most recently by Professor Bernard Harcourt.[11] As originally conceived, the harm principle was a limiting principle, designed to stave off the heavy hand of the criminal law and to confine it within narrow and relatively secure bounds. But this no longer seems to be the principle's effect. The limitations it imposes are very feeble; it excludes little by way of conduct deemed to be immoral. In most of the areas in which criminalization on moral ground is debated, it has proved remarkably easy to dress up moral objections to various forms of conduct, such as prostitution or pornography, in their alleged harmful consequences. Moreover, far from limiting the reach of criminal law, the harm principle may have contributed to its expansion. By purporting to sever the connection between morality and law, the principle unleashed criminal liability in broad areas that had been previously closed to it. Once the idea took hold that harm is the gist of criminality, every infliction of harm becomes a candidate for criminalization. Add to this the interdependency and density of modern life that make risk of harm ubiquitous, and you get the specter of an expanding criminal law, threatening to hold all of life in its coercive grip. As against this specter (the year 1984 is, after all, already in our past), some fundamental retrenchment seems needed. And, perhaps paradoxically, safe shelter may be found within morality itself: it may prove easier to contain the criminal law if it is recognized that its paradigmatic function is not the prevention of harm, but rather the enforcement of morality.[12]

But what morality? In moving beyond the harm principle it is important to note that objections to it of the kind I have so far mentioned tend to focus on gray areas at the periphery of criminal liability, while taking for granted that when it comes to core crimes, such as homicide, battery, or rape, the idea of harm predominates: in these cases harm to the victim is obvious and must play a decisive role. By demonstrating the difficulties the harm principle encounters even in these core crimes, we can get a clue as to the general direction in which to proceed. I consider a single, but I think compelling, example: rape by deception. It will help to focus on a specific case. In *State v. Minkowski,*[13] the defendant, a gynecologist, was accused of raping during their medical examinations a number of his female patients, who on recurrent visits had not realized what was going on. Everyone would agree, I suppose, that these women were indeed raped even before finding out about the violations, and this judgment would not be reversed even if the women were never to find out. The obvious difficulty is that in such a case, it would be hard to identify any harm to the women. Since no physical injury is alleged, the harm in this type of situation would ordinarily be psychological. But as long as the victims remain unaware of what had happened, it is plausible to assume that no adverse mental effects occurred either. Yet the difficulty of finding harm does not seem to weaken our conviction that the women were raped all the same. It is easy of course to condemn the defendant's conduct in these circumstances and justify his punishment on various obvious rule-utilitarian grounds. But doing so would miss the target. The crucial judgment I assume is that Minkowski's actions are reprehensible acts of rape all by themselves, and should be treated as such out of concern for the unsuspecting victims despite the fact that their ignorance protects these victims from a hurtful experience and quite apart from any likely future ramifications of condoning Minkowski's conduct.

The Kantian perspective offers here a familiar and attractive alternative to welfarism. Even in the absence of harm, the familiar story goes, the women were wronged, because they were subjected to nonconsensual sex, in derogation of their autonomy. It is sometimes added here, mostly for good rhetorical measure, that rape offends against the victim's dignity as well. But such addition plays no substantive moral role, since implicit in it is the identification of dignity with autonomy: the failure to respect the victims' dignity just consists in the failure to respect their autonomy.[14]

Although such shift from welfare to autonomy, and correspondingly from harm-talk to wrong-talk, seems apt in this case, it will not always avail. Two examples will help make the point. Our attitude toward corporal punishment offers the first illustration. In *State v. Braxton*[15] the defendants were sentenced to thirty years imprisonment on charges of sexual misconduct, but were given by the trial court the option of undergoing surgical castration instead. They would have chosen castration, but the appellate court withdrew the option. Why was this option withdrawn? Since the individuals in question would have consented to the procedure, denying them the option compromises their autonomy rather than protecting it. But the court's paternalistic stance cannot be explained in terms of a concern for the defendants' welfare either: no one suggested that the defendants were mistaken in believing that diminished sexuality is preferable in this respect to thirty years in jail. More generally, we would probably not find *optional* flogging or amputation as forms of punishment much more appealing than mandatory. What considerations then override the defendants' express wishes in such cases?[16]

In my second example, *State v. Brown*,[17] the defendant habitually beat his wife when she drank alcohol, allegedly as part of an agreement to help her overcome her alcoholism. In convicting Brown, the court rejected a defense of consent. How are we to assess this decision? To be sure, it is easy to marshal in its support sound public policy arguments. There is, for example, good reason to be suspicious in general of agreements such as the one alleged. But here again, as in *Minkowski,* we must distinguish the generic offense to which such considerations pertain, from the specific token to which they may not. The judgment I assume is that even if we were to consider this case in isolation and be satisfied that in this particular instance the wife did consent, we would still conclude that the beating is unacceptable and ought not to be condoned. Why?[18]

2. From Autonomy to Dignity: The Case of Slavery

In order to answer this question I will first perform a short detour into neighboring and familiar territory. The institution of slavery has long served in the liberal literature as a stock antiutilitarian example and as a demonstration of the merits of a deontological approach. But on a closer look, slavery threatens to embarrass the deontologist as much as the utilitarian. By revisiting the slavery conundrum we will be better able to assess the role of autonomy within the deontological perspective and see more clearly what elaboration of that perspective is needed to escape the embarrassments it potentially faces.

One way in which slavery serves as a counterexample to utilitarianism is by exposing and targeting its aggregative aspect: as long as enough people are sufficiently benefited by slavery, the institution is justified on utilitarian grounds, no matter how wretched the slaves' lives turn out to be. Utilitarianism is here castigated for its willingness to sacrifice some people in order to benefit others.[19] But slavery presents the utilitarian with an additional embarrassment, more pertinent to our present discussion, in the form of the specter of the happy slave. Here we focus on a particular slave who, we are asked to imagine, is quite happy with his lot. Can we raise any objection to his enslavement on utilitarian grounds?[20] This thought experiment highlights the utilitarian's impoverished conception of value. By limiting the normative inquiry to the slave's welfare, the utilitarian is bound to overlook a decisive moral factor, namely autonomy or freedom.[21] It is the utilitarian's blindness to such values that is responsible for her inability to appreciate the moral unacceptability of the happy slave's situation, giving a decisive moral edge to the Kantian perspective.

But this standard Kantian response to utilitarianism's alleged failings is not as successful as it might first appear. To see this we must inquire more closely into how precisely slavery relates to autonomy. Two different moments should be distinguished. The first concerns the circumstances of enslavement. We ordinarily assume that enslavement itself is involuntary, foisted on the slave through brute force. But what about consensual enslavement?[22] To avoid the unwelcome conclusion that voluntary enslavement is morally sound, it must be maintained that through this exercise of one's autonomy one sacrifices more autonomy than one gains. I am not sure how convincing this argument is in its own terms. After all, every contract involves some restriction on freedom of choice, and yet, since the restriction is self-imposed, contracts are generally perceived as expressing autonomy and promoting it. Should each contract be made vulnerable to an assessment of its overall effects on the parties' autonomy?

Be this as it may, the entire onus of this response to the problem of voluntary enslavement rests on the second moment in the relation of autonomy to slavery: whether or not the slave agreed to the enslavement, the ongoing regime under which he lives is assumed to consist in a severe limitation of his freedom of choice. But here too we must tread carefully.

Is it really necessary that to be a slave one's choices must be severely curtailed? It should first be noticed that the question must be understood as inviting a comparative judgment: everyone's options are limited, so the slave's situation could be distinguished in this regard only if his options were more restricted than those of nonslaves. But that need not be the case. We can easily imagine a nonslave whose options are in fact fewer, say due to severe handicap, than those of a slave whose master, out of benevolence or enlightened self-interest, gives him considerable free rein. It may perhaps seem that the slave's predicament must still be understood in terms of limitations on choice if we focus on the reliability of those options rather than on their number: the nonslave's options, even if more numerous, are precarious since they can be withdrawn at any time at the master's whim. But this response will not do. First, it does not seem plausible to focus here exclusively on the reliability of having the options available to one without regard to their range and significance. If reliability is to be taken into account, it would more likely be part of a calculation of something like the expected value of one's overall choice-set, in which the number and significance of options is weighted by the likelihood that they will not be withdrawn. But if this is the more plausible measure of one's freedom, then we can easily make compensating adjustments in the scenario we imagine, such that the larger number of options available to the slave will be made to offset the greater reliability of the fewer options the handicapped nonslave enjoys. Second, the slave's options need not in fact be less secure than the nonslave's. We can posit a master whose firm, perhaps obsessive character makes it all but impossible for her to depart from her benevolent policy toward her slaves, while imagining the nonslave to be suffering from a progressive congenital disease, likely to bring all options to a terminal end at any time.

If autonomy is to be assessed, plausibly, in light of the actual range of options available to one, and if, also plausibly, the assessment must be comparative, then the foregoing considerations lead us to the specter of the autonomous slave. Just as the happy slave demonstrates that welfare is not the only value in this context, so does the autonomous slave show that neither is autonomy. But is an "autonomous slave" not a glaring oxymoron? Is not loss of autonomy the very essence of slavery? The answer depends on the distinction between *de facto* and *de jure* autonomy. My examples, if convincing, demonstrate that de facto autonomy or its curtailment is not essentially linked to slavery, leaving however the possibility that de jure autonomy is so linked. Someone who enjoys de facto freedom of choice may yet be enslaved de jure. This possibility removes the oxymoronic appearance of the "autonomous slave" figure we have imagined, but it does so by raising a different puzzle: if two people can enjoy in fact the same level of welfare and exercise the same degree of choice, yet one of them be a slave while the other is not, wherein does the evil of slavery lie? Why is the mere de jure distinction important?

It is open to the reader to deny at this point the premise of these questions: since our imaginary slave is no worse off than his free counterpart, there is really no need for us to deplore his "enslavement." What makes slavery in general a heinous institution, the objection continues, is precisely the fact that real-world slaves are in fact deprived of both welfare and autonomy to a shocking degree: stipulate away these incidents, and you have removed those features that make slavery the paradigm of injustice. I think that this objection is misconceived. We view slavery as a paradigm of injustice precisely because its injustice is necessary or analytical rather than contingent and empirical. To describe someone as a slave is ipso facto to view him as the victim of injustice, rather than to invite an investigation into the actual circumstances of his life. Why?

3. The Morality of Dignity

There is an obvious answer, though its import is not always fully appreciated. What remains evil about slavery even in the case of the slave who is de facto free and content is the affront to human dignity: slavery is the paradigm of injustice because it denies people's equal moral worth and thus treats them with disrespect. If this conclusion is sound, then our discussion of slavery demonstrates three moral claims: the independence of dignity of both welfare and autonomy, its priority over these other values, and its meaning-dependence. Nothing short of a complete moral theory would suffice to substantiate and adequately defend these claims. But although such a theory cannot be provided here, its general shape and contours can be at least vaguely imagined if we think of it as a variant of Kant's moral theory. All I can do here is to make a few preliminary comments about each of the claims.[23]

Independence

The possibility of a free and happy slave demonstrates the independence of dignity from welfare and, more significantly, from autonomy as well: one may willingly live a life in which a sufficient range of choices is available, and yet be stripped of one's dignity. This observation runs up against a tradition of thought that closely links dignity to autonomy. Dignity, and the related ideas of equal human worth and respect, are all familiar constituents of the deontological perspective.[24] But as I mentioned at the outset, the dominant trend in the deontological branch of liberalism has been to focus on autonomy. For the most part dignity, if mentioned at all, has been seen as a matter of deferring to people's autonomy, and thus has had no independent role to play.[25] Against this background, the independence claim appears revisionary, and my aim here is to dispel this impression, by relating the claim to Kant's own views.[26] Of course, *dignity* and *autonomy* are not Kant's registered trademarks, and their relationship can be discussed apart from his ideas. But as a matter of historical fact, the liberal deontological strand is heavily Kantian, as is more specifically the close association between dignity and autonomy this strand maintains. It is therefore of some interest to note that Kant's moral theory does not provide adequate support for this association. The appearance that it does results from a key feature of Kant's morality: he holds that human dignity is based on or derives from people's autonomy. It does not follow, however, that respecting people's dignity is just a matter of respecting their autonomy in the way the dominant liberal tradition came to maintain. I will make three points in this regard.

To begin with, as others have noted, Kant links the idea of dignity to a rather specialized and restricted conception of autonomy, roughly the capacity for moral self-legislation. No special connection accordingly obtains on Kant's own view between dignity and autonomy in the broader sense that is of interest to political philosophers and that has to do with people's alleged right to make self-regarding choices by themselves.

Second, dignity does not coincide even with moral autonomy narrowly conceived. Even if moral autonomy is the ground of a person's dignity, it need not also define the subject of dignity or its scope, so that the respect demanded by dignity would be exclusively respect for a person's moral choices. We must be careful to distinguish here two different ideas conveyed by two different locutions: respecting a person's autonomy and respecting a person *for* or *by virtue of* her autonomy. To say that autonomy is the ground of dignity connotes the latter idea: the claim is that dignity is the value a person has by virtue of possessing a certain capacity or having a certain property, rather than that it is the value of the capacity or the property abstractly conceived. The real subject of dignity is the person, not her autonomy. Once pointed out, the difference between the two locutions is quite obvious, so it is instructive to observe why in Kant's own theory this distinction is effaced. The reason lies in Kant's metaphysical doctrine of the *noumenal self*: in the domain of things in themselves, a human being simply is a pure rational free will, and is thus characterized exhaustively by her moral autonomy. To respect the person and to respect her autonomy are, on this picture, one and the same. One can, however, accept that a capacity for moral autonomy is the ground of dignity without buying into Kant's extravagant metaphysics. People can be believed to have dignity by virtue of possessing a rational free will without being thought to be metaphysically identical with such a will. If so, one must recognize that there is more to persons than moral autonomy, and correspondingly more to the idea of respecting a person than respecting her autonomy.

My third point is that the possibility of a conflict between dignity and personal autonomy is implicit in Kant's doctrine of self-regarding duties. One of the implications of the idea of dignity, according to Kant, is that one ought to respect not just others' humanity but one's own humanity as well. This gives rise to duties toward oneself, such as a prohibition against suicide. Since these self-regarding duties obviously constrain one's freedom of choice, they seem to manifest a clear conflict between dignity and personal autonomy. Once again, the metaphysics of the noumenal self and the specialized conception of autonomy avoid such conflict within Kant's own system. Moral autonomy consists in a rational will that is determined in accordance with correct moral principles. These principles, or maxims, supposedly take proper account of the agent's own dignity as well as that of everyone else. In the noumenal realm, complete harmony exists between the demands of dignity, including one's own, and one's autonomy. That in the real world we experience the moral promptings of the noumenal self as constraining, and hence as duties, only shows that our phenomenal self is motivated by what Kant calls "inclinations," the familiar paraphernalia of psychological forces that form no part of one's autonomy in the restricted Kantian sense. However, as soon as we depart from Kant's metaphysics, the picture changes radically. It becomes altogether possible for people to make self-regarding choices, and thus exercise their autonomy, in ways that fail to comport with their own dignity and moral worth.

Priority

The discussion of slavery illustrates not only the independence of dignity from welfare and autonomy, but also the priority it takes over them in case of conflict. But why should we be concerned with expressions of respect or perturbed by manifestations of disrespect apart from their effects on our welfare and autonomy? Separated from these apparently more robust values, dignity may seem rather pale, perhaps even vacuous.

I will make two brief observations in response. The first concerns a consideration that casts doubt on the intuition that individual welfare and autonomy are more likely and attractive foundational or basic moral

values. Even without attempting a general inquiry into what a foundational moral value is, it seems plausible to expect of such a value that it
satisfy a rather weak condition: other things being equal, it ought to
count in favor of an action or state of affairs that it includes or satisfies
or increases that value. Welfare and autonomy do not satisfy this condition. Few would find moral merit in a mass murderer being rewarded
with a Caribbean vacation, even when reassured that no negative consequences will follow (because the reward is secret, the murderer presents no future danger, etc.). Similarly, an intentional killing, which is
therefore an expression of the perpetrator's personal autonomy, is for
this reason morally worse, not better, than an accidental killing.

The second observation is that the value of welfare and autonomy
seems most compelling when considered from the first-person perspective. When thinking about myself, it may make sense for me to take the
view that as long as my autonomy and welfare are secure, I do not need
your respect and do not care about disrespect either. But as soon as I
turn to think about your case, autonomy and welfare lose the urgency
they have in my own situation: your autonomy and welfare do not have
the same appeal to me as my own. This thought need not bother me until
I realize that our situation is symmetrical, and that my autonomy and
welfare need not be of greater moment to you than yours are to me. It
is at this point that the idea of our equal moral worth comes into play,
providing a reason why our autonomy and welfare ought to be of reciprocal concern. So even if our engaging in moral reflection is prompted
in the first place by our concern for our own autonomy and welfare,
we realize in the course of such reflection that in order to secure these
interests we must subscribe to a more fundamental value, dignity, whose
content must be known not to be limited to the importance that each person assigns to his or her own interests. A recognition of the distinctive
and supreme value of our common humanity appears to be a precondition of morality. This, indeed, is Kant's view. In his scheme, all morality
derives from a single master principle—the categorical imperative—
which by enjoining the treatment of persons merely as means rather than
as ends, spells out the meaning or the implications of according dignity
to people. Since all immorality consists at bottom in violations of the
categorical imperative, it is also always a matter of offending against
human dignity.

Meaning Dependence

In what way, though, does slavery offend against the slave's dignity if
in the particular instance it does not derogate from the slave's welfare

or autonomy? The answer I propose depends on the observation that dignity demand that our actions, practices, and institutions convey an attitude of respect to people. There are many ways in which respect can be conveyed, and correspondingly many ways in which it can be withheld. But the main point here is that whether an action, practice, or institution is consonant with dignity is a matter of that action's meaning.[27] How does such meaning accrue?

There are two answers to this question, and the case of slavery illustrates them both. First, an action, or in this case an institution, may offend people's dignity through its overt, explicit content. Slavery does so inasmuch as a complete articulation of the meaning of this institution would involve an explicit denial of the slaves' equal moral worth. But the disrespectful meaning of an action may also be conventional. The convention can be an arbitrary one, as is the case with many insulting gestures. But more likely the conventional meaning attaches to an action by virtue of certain empirical characteristics and consequences it typically has. Following Kant, we can say that the essence of disrespect is a failure to appreciate a person as a being whose value is independent of anyone or anything else, and who should therefore be treated as an end and not just as a means. Exploiting a person for one's own ends by inflicting on him harm or suffering with disregard for his own needs, interests, and desires is the paradigm violation of this imperative.[28] Now ordinarily slavery does just that. Given this record, it is not surprising that slavery should be associated in our minds with indignity. My present point is that although the association has an empirical basis, it need not be limited to those instances in which the empirical conditions obtain. The meaning that attaches to slavery as an insult to dignity is retained even in the situation we imagined, in which the typical derogatory effects on the slave's welfare and autonomy are stipulated away.

4. Dignity and Social Meaning

We can now return to the two puzzle cases, *Braxton* and *Brown,* we considered earlier. The prominent feature of both cases that must play a central role in any account is physical violence. Why is violence objectionable? As we saw, the two most obvious replies—that violence diminishes its victims' welfare and that it compromises their autonomy—are not available to us here, since the physical intrusions we consider involve neither. If these physical intrusions are to be condemned, a different ground for decrying violence must be found. Dignity provides such ground. The fact that physical violence does ordinarily hinder both welfare and autonomy is reason enough to render it a blatant manifestation of disrespect. But as we saw in the case of the free and happy slave, the expressive meaning of violence can outrun the reasons for ascribing that meaning to it. Although for the most part their expressive significance is not attached to actions arbitrarily or at random, the connection between the reasons for ascribing to an action-type its symbolic significance as expressing disrespect and the tokens of that action need not be tight. Once an action-type has acquired a symbolic significance by virtue of the disrespect it typically displays, its tokens will possess that significance and communicate the same content even if the reason does not apply to them. Think in analogy of an onomatopoeic expression such as *buzz* or *crunch*. Such an expression does not denote what it does by virtue of the resemblance in sound, nor is its extension limited by such resemblance. Rather, denotation and extension are a matter of the expression's conventional meaning, even though that meaning accrued to it in the first place due to the phonetic similarity of the expression to at least some of the sounds it came to denote. The relative independence of the expressive component of disrespect I described, and the linguistic analogy I just drew, lead to the following conclusion. As long as certain actions are generally considered to express disrespect, one cannot knowingly engage in them without offending against the target's dignity, no matter what one's motivations and intentions are. One does not have any more control over the meaning of one's violent behavior than Humpty Dumpty had over the use of words.[29]

These observations explain our judgment that the castration proposed in *Braxton* and the beating inflicted in *Brown* involve an affront to the subjects' dignity despite their consent and enhanced relative or long-term welfare: when it comes to the expressive meaning of these actions, the typical case of violence casts its shadow over the exceptional. But this explanation is incomplete. A further question remains to be answered: how widely is that shadow cast? To appreciate the urgency of this question, consider some analogous situations to these two cases. The same surgical castration proposed in *Braxton* could be performed as part of some medical treatment or a sex-change operation. No one, I assume, would then impugn the surgery as involving any insult to the patient's dignity. What distinguishes these medical procedures from the *Braxton* case? After all, the redeeming features of castration in these instances are that it advances the patient's welfare and is done with his consent. If these factors are not sufficient to remove the stain of indignity in *Braxton,* why do they seem to suffice in the medical situation? Why do the negative connotations of physical mutilation not cast their shadow over the meaning that certain medical procedures have? A similar question arises with regard to the *Brown* case as well. Here the most suitable comparison seems to be competitive sports, specifically wrestling and boxing, in which the level of permissible violence far exceeds the level, if any, that would be tolerable in a *Brown*-type scenario. Why, again, does the nasty record of the typical case of violence define the meaning of the beating in *Brown,* but not that of, say, pugilistic violence?[30]

The answer in both instances is quite straightforward. How far the shadow of a typical case will reach in defining the meaning of an atypical one depends in the first place on the way we conceptualize, categorize, and individuate the relevant social practices. The difference between the *Brown* case and boxing is first and foremost a result of the generic distinction we recognize between wife beating and boxing. A "benign" case of wife beating is still a case of wife beating, and it draws its offensive meaning from the typical, nasty cases. But that meaning does not carry over to what we recognize and label as "boxing." Moreover, since within boxing violence is not demeaning to the participants, no disrespect will be conveyed by a boxer's punches even if the individual boxer holds the opponent below contempt and harbors the most degrading attitude toward him. Similarly, the crucial distinction in the *Braxton* case is between the practice of criminal punishment and that of medical treatment. The meaning we attach to the same medical procedure—castration in this case—will radically differ depending on which of these practices provides the interpretive template. The negative connotations with regard to human dignity of physical mutilation extend to even such unusual punitive circumstances as those presented by *Braxton,* but they do not extend to the very different practice of medical treatment.[31]

5. Dignity and Culture

The cases I have discussed so far call for moral assessment within a single culture or moral community. But as I have indicated at the outset, the law increasingly confronts situations that require cross-cultural moral assessment. Within criminal law the issue comes up most pointedly in the debate concerning the *cultural defense* to criminal liability.

It is generally assumed that three different stances are open to the law in such situations: *imperialism, relativism,* and *tolerance.* By imperialism I mean the stance of an assessing culture that makes the assessment exclusively in terms of its own norms, ignoring as irrelevant the different norms of the assessed culture. Relativism is the opposite stance, in which the assessment is conducted in terms of the norms of the culture being assessed. Tolerance is an intermediate stance that arises in the relation between assessment and action: the assessing culture may still conduct its assessment in terms of its own norms, but it will not act on its (negative) assessment out of a belief (whatever its source) that the assessed culture has "a right to be wrong."

The difficulties raised by each of these stances are well known, and I will not rehearse them here. My aim is to point out that a morality of dignity opens up a fourth possibility. Moral assessment of actions that take place within a different culture can proceed on the basis of *our* moral views and yet crucially depend on the meaning assigned by that culture to those actions.[32] Acknowledging this form of dependence is no more a matter of relativism or tolerance than is our going along with the fact that, say, Italians use the phonetic equivalent of the English word *my* to designate "never" rather than the first-person possessive pronoun.[33]

A comparison between two types of cases will illustrate this general point. The first concerns members of minority groups who have sought to defend themselves against charges of violence toward their wives by invoking cultural norms that allegedly permit or encourage such violence.[34] It should be obvious that a dignity-based morality will not support such a defense: the norms relied upon by such defendants embody the subjugation and oppression of women in the respective cultures. The victims' dignity is accordingly trampled by such acts of violence, and whatever the possible relevance of the defendants' cultural background, this background does not mitigate the affront to dignity that the violence involves. Contrast these instances with the controversy surrounding the practice, or rather set of practices, of female circumcision.[35] The social meaning of these practices is not at all clear, is not uniform, and is central to the debate. This social meaning, which determines the practices' bearing on the women's dignity, can be intelligibly assessed only in terms that are internal to the particular cultures concerned.

But such deference to the foreign meaning of an otherwise objectionable action or practice is bound to raise the following worry. Given the foundational role dignity plays within a Kantian morality, it would seem that once we are reassured that the cultural meaning of an action or a practice involves no offense to dignity, we no longer have any moral grounds for complaint, no matter how detrimental to people's welfare or how restrictive of their autonomy the action or the practice may be. Female circumcision is a case in point. Perhaps even more acute examples concern deviant beliefs and practices of some American moral or religious communities. The Jehovah's Witness who denies his sick child a life-saving blood transfusion and the Christian Scientist who chooses for a dying spouse prayer over surgery do not display disrespect for their relatives, so on the proposed account we have no basis for morally condemning these actions despite their catastrophic consequences. But if we cannot morally condemn these actions and practices, are we not then bound to condone them?

There are two reasons why this conclusion does not follow. The first is this. The recognition that an action has an inoffensive meaning within the actor's group does not entail that a municipal legal system must accept this meaning as dispositive. Another cluster of considerations arises, analogous to those that come up in the dispute about bilingualism, that concern the desirability of cultural homogeneity within a state. Such "melting pot" issues are altogether separate from the moral assessment of the disputed actions and practices. Those who insist on English as the dominant language in the United States do not thereby imply that there is something amiss with French or Spanish as such. By the same token, one can consistently maintain that certain practices are inoffensive to their objects within their respective cultures and yet be opposed to such practices in this country. I have nothing to say here about the merits of this position, other than to point out that so viewed, the matter is converted from one of moral philosophy to one of political philosophy.[36]

The second reason is of greater importance. The worry I have mentioned assumes that unless we can morally condemn an action or a practice, we must condone it. However, our options are not in fact so limited. For example, we are greatly distressed by natural disasters though no immorality is involved. So also in the cases I have mentioned: they distress us and may call for remedial action without involving moral criticism. In the Jehovah's Witness and Christian Scientists cases, the parents' or spouses' erroneous beliefs are, morally speaking, on a par with the disease itself: we ought to rescue the sick dependents from their disease as well as from their relatives' wrong-headedness without ascribing to either negative moral significance.

What kind of "ought" is this, however? It may be felt that by portraying the actions whose consequences we are anxious to avert as not being themselves immoral, my account drains our reaction of moral significance as well. Since by being refused proper medical treatment by their relatives the patients in my examples are not being morally mistreated, it may seem a matter of moral indifference whether we save them or not. But here too, the analogy to natural disaster is helpful. Though a natural disaster has no moral significance, being in a position to assist its victims has, since unlike the disaster itself, our subsequent actions and omissions can convey an attitude of respect or disrespect to those victims. Similarly, in the situations I mentioned, distinctly moral grounds exist for preventing actions or disrupting practices that are not themselves immoral. The potential victims' dignity comes into play for the first time, and correspondingly moral considerations arise for the first time, only when we have the opportunity to prevent the harm, rather than when the harm is initially threatened or inflicted. In other words, a doctrine of *negative responsibility*[37] can here fill the normative gap opened up by the expressive conception of dignity I advocate.

What difference does it make that the label *morality* attaches only to our intervention or failure to intervene rather than to the harmful actions or practices that provoke it? For example, what difference does it make that given its social meaning in the culture in which it is practiced, clitoridectomy cannot be deemed immoral, if we may have a duty to prevent it all the same, and be ourselves guilty of moral failure if we do not? Diagnosing the situation the way I propose has at least three significant consequences. First, whether we judge the harmful action to be immoral, that is, disrespectful of its objects' dignity, is likely to affect our assessment of the severity of the harm itself. A blow to the head is likely to involve greater psychological harm if intentionally inflicted by another human being than if caused by a falling stone. Second, the duty to avert immoral action is probably more stringent or weighty than the duty to prevent amoral harm. Finally, intervention in such matters always involves harming in some fashion the perpetrators of the alleged harm, at a minimum by frustrating their desire to engage in the harmful activity, but quite often by doing them greater damage than that. The extent to which such secondary harm is permissible will obviously depend, among other things, on whether or not we hold the perpetrators of the harmful actions we seek to prevent to be morally culpable as well.

These last observations lead back to our point of departure. Criminal law trades in blame and guilt as well as in suffering and violence. If the dignity principle were to replace the harm principle, all offenses would be defined in terms of conduct that is disrespectful of someone's equal moral worth. Given the facts of multiculturalism and moral pluralism, this would create a gap between actions deemed immoral and actions that need to be curbed because of their harmfulness, though no immorality be involved. To properly respond to these realities, a line would have to be drawn between criminal punishment with its attended notions of blame and guilt on the one side, and responses that do not carry such nasty connotations, on the other. In trying to coordinate and accommodate a multiplicity of cultures and creeds, an indiscriminate use of the criminal law as guided by the harm principle often adds gratuitous insult to the inevitable injury.

Notes

1. Even if successful in its own terms, the suggestion I explore would leave out some contested zones of morality, and correspondingly of criminality, such as those concerning the treatment of animals and the environment. I do not touch on these issues, but it should be noted that the harm principle does not directly engage them either.

2. Specifically at the hands of John Stuart Mill, in *On Liberty*, in *Utilitarianism, Liberty, Representative Government* (Everyman edition), 158.

3. See, for example, Charles Larmore, "The Moral Basis of Political Liberalism," *Journal of Philosophy* 96 (1999): 599. Ronald Dworkin uses the phrase "equal concern and respect" to describe liberalism's defining commitment: see, e.g., *Taking Rights Seriously* (Cambridge: Harvard University Press, 1977), 180–83, and 272–78. For another recent variant on this general theme see Avishai Margalit, *The Decent Society* (Cambridge: Harvard University Press, 1998).

4. The idea of human dignity plays a central role in German criminal jurisprudence, though not quite the same role I explore here. For a recent survey see Otto Lagodny, "Human Dignity and its Impact on German Substantive Criminal Law and Criminal Procedure," *Israel Law Review* 33 (1999): 575.

5. The most comprehensive exploration and critique of the principle is by Joel Feinberg, in his four-volume magnum opus, *The Moral Limits of the Criminal Law* (New York: Oxford University Press, 1984–88).

6. James Fitzjames Stephens, *Liberty, Equality, Fraternity,* ed. R. J. White (Cambridge: Cambridge University Press, 1873, 1967).

7. "The Crisis of Overcriminalization," in Sanford H. Kadish, *Blame and Punishment: Essays in the Criminal Law* (New York: Macmillan, 1987), 21.

8. "The Use of Criminal Sanctions in Enforcing Economic Regulation," ibid., at 40.

9. Ibid., 51.

10. Ibid., 22.

11. Bernard Harcourt, "The Collapse of the Harm Principle," *Journal of Criminal Law and Criminology* 90 (1999): 109.

12. See Gerald Dworkin, "Devlin Was Right: Law and the Enforcement of Morality," *William and Marry Law Review* 40 (1999): 927, and responses by Jeffrie G. Murphy, "Moral Reasons and the Limitation of Liberty," ibid., 947, and by Lawrence C. Becker, "Crimes against Autonomy: Gerald Dworkin on the Enforcement of Morality," ibid., 959; Michael Moore, "A Non-exclusionary Theory of Legislative Aim: Taking Aim at Moral Wrongdoing," in *Placing Blame: A Theory of Criminal Law* (New York: Oxford University Press, 1997), 639.

13. 204 Cal. App. 2d 832; 23 Cal. Rptr. 92 (1962).

14. Compare Carolyn M. Shafer and Marilyn Frye, "Rape and Respect," in *Feminism and Philosophy*, ed. Mary Vetterling-Braggin, Frederick A. Elliston, and Jane English (Totowa, N.J.: Littlefield, Adams, 1977), 333, in which the authors diagnose the evil of rape as a matter of disrespect, and view respect as an attitude that relates to the victim's autonomy: "The morally appropriate attitude upon encountering another person is one of respect: recognition of its domain, and deference to its rightful power of consent," 339. For an attempt to construct a comprehensive autonomy-based Kantian theory of criminal law see David Richards, "Human Rights and the Moral Foundations of Substantive Criminal Law," *Georgia Law Review* 13 (1979): 1395.

15. 326 S.E. 2d 410 (S.C. 1985). The eponymous defendant in this case is Brown; I refer to the case by the name of the second defendant (Braxton) to avoid confusion with the other case entitled *State v. Brown* I discuss next.

16. All the court says in explaining withholding the option of castration is that such punishment would be in violation of the state's constitutional prohibition against cruel and unusual punishment. No mention is made of the possible relevance of the defendants' preference in the matter.

17. 364 A.2d 27 (N.J. Super. Ct. Law Div. 1976), aff'd, 381 A.2d 1231 (N.J. Super. Ct. App. Div. 1977).

18. For a related discussion of puzzles to which victims' consent can give rise see Leo Katz, *Ill-Gotten Gains: Evasion, Blackmail, Fraud, and Kindred Puzzles of the Law* (Chicago: University of Chicago Press, 1996), 145–57.

19. See, e.g., R. M. Hare, "What Is Wrong with Slavery," *Philosophy and Public Affairs* 8 (1979): 103.

20. Compare Don Herzog, *Happy Slaves: A Critique of Consent Theory* (Chicago: University of Chicago Press, 1989), preface, where the author raises some of these issues, but eschews the use of the kinds of thought experiments I indulge in favor of an historical study of the idea of consent in liberal theory.

21. The equivocation is deliberate since neither term has a single well-defined meaning. I go on to talk about *autonomy*, using the term in the sense in which it is most commonly used in this context, namely as having to do with choice opportunities among adequate options, though elsewhere in this volume, in chapter 4, I express some misgivings about this conception of autonomy. These misgivings, and the conception of autonomy I elaborate there, would not affect my present point.

22. The locus classicus of this discussion is in John Stuart Mill, *On Liberty*. For a critical commentary of Mill's argument, see Chin Liew

Ten, *Mill on Liberty* (New York: Oxford University Press, 1980), 117–23.

23. The term *dignity*, with its disturbing connotation of (often differential) social status and misleading proximity to *honor*, is an unhappy one. It would be better to speak about *moral worth*, but *dignity* is probably too entrenched. Moreover, the historical, if not philosophical, connections among these ideas apparently run deep and may be hard to disentangle. For an excellent historical study that issues a powerful caveat along such lines see James Q. Whitman, "Enforcing Civility and Respect: Three Societies," *Yale Law Journal* 109 (2000): 1279.

24. There is a rapidly growing literature on dignity as a legal value. Some important essays are collected in Michael Meyer and W. A. Parent, eds., *The Constitution of Rights: Human Dignity and American Values* (Ithaca, N.Y.: Cornell University Press, 1992).

25. But the tradition has not gone unchallenged. On the independence of dignity from the value of choice, see Robert Goodin, "The Political Theories of Choice and Dignity," *American Philosophical Quarterly* 18 (1981): 91; on the independence of dignity from consent, see R. George Wright, "Consenting Adults: The Problem of Enhancing Human Dignity Non-Coercively," *Boston University Law Review* 75 (1995): 1397.

26. See mainly his *Groundwork of the Metaphysic of Morals*, trans. H. J. Paton (New York: Harper and Row, 1964). For a commentary that stresses the role of dignity in Kant's thought, see Thomas E. Hill Jr., *Dignity and Practical Reason in Kant's Moral Theory* (Ithaca, N.Y.: Cornell University Press, 1992). I focus here on Kant's *moral* theory, which has exerted the greatest influence on contemporary liberal thinking and is directly relevant to the question of criminalization. I do not deal accordingly with Kant's political writings and specifically with the (possibly less attractive) role that the idea of dignity plays in them. On the latter see for example Michael Meyer, "Kant's Concept of Dignity and Modern Political Thought," *History of European Ideas* 8 (1987): 319.

27. A considerable legal-philosophical literature has grown in recent years discussing some or all of the four interrelated notions mentioned in this paragraph: dignity, expressive value, respect, and meaning. For some salient examples see the following: Elizabeth Anderson, *Value in Ethics and Economics* (Cambridge: Harvard University Press, 1993), 17–43; Anita Bernstein, "Treating Sexual Harassment with Respect," *Harvard Law Review* 111 (1997): 445; Lawrence Lessig, "The Regulation of Social Meaning," *University of Chicago Law Review* 62 (1995): 943; Cass Sunstein, "The Expressive Function of Law," *University of Pennsylvania Law Review* 144 (1996): 2021; Richard L. Abel, *Speaking Respect, Respecting Speech* (Chicago: University of Chicago Press,

1998); Richard Pildes and Elizabeth Anderson, "Slinging Arrows at Democracy: Theory, Value Pluralism, and Democratic Politics," *Columbia Law Review* 90 (1990): 2121. Particularly pertinent here is the view advanced by Professor Benjamin Sendor as an account of the *mens rea* requirement in criminal law. According to Sendor, the point of the requirement is "to acknowledge the importance of the meaning a person conveys to other people through conduct. The meaning relevant to criminal law is the respect a person shows for legally protected interests of other people or the community by acting in a way that avoids injuring those interests." "Crime as Communication: An Interpretive Theory of the Insanity Defense and the Mental Elements of Crime," *Georgetown Law Journal* 74 (1986): 1371.

28. But there may be other ways in which the imperative can be violated. For some interesting suggestions see Martha Nussbaum, "Objectification," *Philosophy and Public Affairs* 24 (1995): 249.

29. "'When I use a word,' Humpty Dumpty said, in rather a scornful tone, 'it means just what I choose it to mean—neither more nor less.'" Lewis Carroll, *Through the Looking-Glass* (New York: St. Martin's Press, 1977), 131. On variations in the social meaning of violence see Dov Cohen and Joe Vandello, "Meanings of Violence," *Journal of Legal Studies* 27 (1998): 567.

30. Though the court recognizes that the participants' consent is a defense in the case of sports such as football, boxing, or wrestling, no convincing explanation is given as to what distinguishes these cases from the instant case.

31. Like many other concepts in this area, the concept of harm is elastic and can be stretched to cover the violations of dignity I distinguish. Indeed the idea of "dignitary harm" has taken hold in the law, especially in tort. Still, there is a natural understanding of harm that ties the term to a diminution of welfare. This is also the sense of harm within the harm principle in light of the principle's utilitarian origins. Insisting on this more restricted use of *harm* serves clarity and specifically helps pose the question of whether welfarism provides an adequate moral basis for criminal law. For a lucid discussion of the various issues that are involved in a welfare-based moral theory see L. W. Sumner, *Welfare, Happiness, and Ethics* (Oxford: Oxford University Press, 1996).

32. The "our" here simply refers to those who subscribe to the morality of dignity to which I allude.

33. For a suggestion along similar lines see Thomas E. Hill Jr., "Basic Respect and Cultural Diversity," in *Respect, Pluralism, and Justice: Kantian Perspectives* (New York: Oxford University Press, 2000), 59.

34. E.g., *People v. Chen*, no.87-774 (N.Y. Sup. Ct. Dec. 2, 1988); cited in Doriane Lambelet Coleman, "Individualizing Justice through

Multiculturalism: The Liberals' Dilemma," *Columbia Law Review* 96 (1996): 1093, at 1102–3.

35. Or *genital mutilation*, or *clitoridectomy*—even the terminology here is highly contested. Some of the voluminous literature on this subject is cited ibid. at 1111–13.

36. And becomes highly charged. For one heated exchange see Coleman, "Individualizing Justice through Multiculturalism," at 1098, and Leti Volpp, "Talking 'Culture': Gender, Race, Nation, and the Politics of Multiculturalism," *Columbia Law Review* 96 (1996): 1573, esp. at 1594–1600.

37. But the doctrine would have to be elaborated and qualified in ways that take account of the well-known critique of such a doctrine in the context of utilitarianism by Bernard Williams, "A Critique of Utilitarianism," in J. J. C. Smart and Bernard Williams, *Utilitarianism: For and Against* (Cambridge: Cambridge University Press, 1963, 1991), 93–118. It should be noted, however, that the objections raised by Williams do not apply for the most part to the case in which the government's negative responsibility is concerned, which is the central case of interest to us here in discussing the limits of criminal law.

CHAPTER SIX
HARMFUL THOUGHTS

If there is one article of faith all liberals share, it is quite definitely an aversion to thought control. This aversion is closely linked to another fundamental liberal tenet, the harm principle: law should concern itself exclusively with preventing harms that people may inflict on each other; people's thoughts ought to remain their own affair. Although the inviolability of thoughts and the harm principle reinforce each other, the connection between them is not as simple as may appear at first sight.

In a well-known article,[1] Professor Herbert Morris probes one dimension of this connection: the interest that criminal law may take in thoughts consistently with the harm principle. From the fact that thoughts are not harmful by themselves, Morris points out, it simply does not follow that the harm principle will not authorize their legal suppression. After all, the law commonly punishes conduct that is not by itself harmful, when the conduct increases the likelihood that harm will occur. One example, given by Morris, is of reckless behavior that may be punished even when it does not result in any harm. Precautionary prohibitions, such as gun control, are another. Finally, and most pertinently, attempts are commonly punishable in the absence of harm. The same logic that licenses legal intervention before the criminal act is fully consummated would also seem to apply to the even earlier stage in the criminal sequence at which the criminal intention is formed. To be sure, intentions present special epistemological problems. But here they are shielded from punishment by their inaccessibility rather than by their harmlessness. Conduct is still called for, not by the harm principle, but rather as an evidentiary imperative. The difference is not only of philosophical but also of practical significance: for evidentiary purposes mere verbal behavior, such as a confession, will do. The conclusion that the harm principle might be in principle consistent with the punishment of thoughts is striking, perhaps scandalous, and Professor Morris proceeds to hedge and qualify this conclusion in many subtle and interesting ways.[2] My aim is not, however, to examine Professor Morris' conclusions, but rather his basic premise: that unless acted upon, thoughts by themselves can have no extrapersonal effects, so that if thoughts are of public, specifically legal concern, it is only because of their link to harmful action.[3]

The same premise underlies other legal areas as well. The thoughts Morris focuses on are for the most part intentions, and the only way they supposedly can affect others is by being carried out. But intentions are not the only kind of potentially harmful thoughts, and executing intentions not the only way by which that potential can be realized. Think of areas such as defamation and hate speech. Here the potentially harmful states of mind are not intentions, but rather beliefs, opinions, and emotions, and the harmful behavior in which they issue is typically speech that expresses those states of mind. Speech, accordingly, becomes in these cases the agent of harm, its regulation licensed by the harm principle. Of course, regulation of speech conflicts with another liberal commitment, to freedom of speech, leading to a wide-ranging debate concerning the permissible constraints on harmful expression. But all parties to the debate seem to take for granted that the potential for harmfulness of the states of mind in question is only realized when those states of mind are publicly expressed.[4]

I question this assumption. Though the assumption is quite entrenched, part of the very "grammar" of mental states, I argue that it rests on untenable beliefs and is inconsistent with other shared judgments and usages in neighboring linguistic fields. I conclude that thoughts can have extrapersonal effects, including negative ones, all by themselves, unaided by action of any kind, executory or expressive. The argument is laid out in the first four sections. The fifth section examines some of its normative implications, specifically with regard to the controversy over the legal treatment of hate speech. The point I raise has broader philosophical ramifications as well: it bears on the limits of individualism by suggesting what I believe is a novel, I call it "active," form of externalism about the mind. I deal with these issues in the final section.

Before I proceed, it is worth pointing out that my main claim is not as striking as may appear at first sight. First, we are often intensely and legitimately interested in the states of mind of other people quite apart from their speech and behavior: Does she love me? Do these people think well of me? Does the physician think I am in good health? Indeed, even when such queries are ostensibly answered by the respective people's reassuring speech and behavior, we may not be quite satisfied: we sometimes worry about the sincerity of their avowals, thus confirming that it is the others' thoughts themselves, rather than their expression, that is of primary significance to us. To be sure, our interest in others' thoughts does not show that those thoughts by themselves affect us: I may be interested in the preservation of the rain forest or in whether there is life on Mars, and yet logging operations in the one case or protozoan stirrings, or their absence, in the other will not by themselves be thought to affect me one way or the other. Still, the reminder that an interest in others' thoughts is pervasive makes the claim about the extrapersonal effects of thoughts seem less far-fetched. Second, other writers have maintained that people's thoughts can be evil, thereby making the world a worse place, and that thoughts can wrong others and perhaps even harm them.[5] As they stand, these judgments appear dark and mysterious, but they express an intuition that even to a secular morality some thoughts can be by themselves of extrapersonal interest and concern.

1. The Argument from Knowledge

The most likely basis for the assumption that one person's thoughts by themselves cannot affect another is probably the alleged inaccessibility of the other's mind. Unless the other person manifests her thoughts by speech or action one cannot know them, the argument goes, and what one does not know cannot affect one. In syllogistic form:

> What one does not know cannot affect one;
> in the absence of any external manifestation, another's thoughts
>   are not knowable;
> hence,
> in the absence of any external manifestation, another's thoughts
>   cannot affect one.

Call this the argument from knowledge. As it stands, the argument is obviously fallacious, since the first premise is clearly untenable: unbeknownst to me, there may be at present a cavity in my tooth, causing decay that will eventually result in acute pain. Surely the cavity is affecting me even though I do not know about it or, indeed, even if I never realize that a cavity will have been the reason for my toothache. The same could be said of thoughts as well. If you punch me in the face, the intention that led you to do so is obviously harmful to me though I never learn what it was. To avoid this all-too-easy refutation, the first premise must be amended by adding the proviso "unless it has consequences that one does know," and correspondingly the second premise must preclude knowable consequences. But even with these amendments the premises will not withstand scrutiny.

Starting with the second, it is not always true that we cannot know through reliable inference another's thoughts. If I see you standing in front of an elephant cage with your eyes wide open, in broad daylight, with the right orientation, and in the absence of any unusual circumstances, I will conclude, with practical certainty, that whatever else may be in your mind at that moment, there is an elephant-thought in it. I could also attain such knowledge by myself planting the thought in your mind by telling you, under ordinary, auspicious auditory conditions: "Think of an elephant." Indeed, far from requiring interpersonal communication in order to be acquired, knowledge of others' minds in circumstances such as these is a precondition of the acquisition of language and of the very possibility of successful communication.[6] Minimal information about the other person concerning her eyesight in the one case and hearing ability in the other will normally suffice for the kind of rudimentary knowledge of her thoughts here involved. But the better we know someone, the more elaborate the thoughts we can confidently ascribe to her on the basis of the external circumstances we know her to be in. Occasionally we can be even better at divining another's state of mind than he himself is. Psychologists and parents are among those who tend to exaggerate and capitalize on this possibility.

Shaky as the second premise turns out to be, it is the first premise that seems to me the argument's weaker link. This premise conjures up a conception of humans as essentially psychological beings whose welfare and well-being is at bottom entirely a matter of the quality of their experiences. It is for this reason that things which do not eventually induce any experience in me cannot be said to have a bearing on me. Such a conception of the self has of course played a prominent role in moral philosophy as the springboard of utilitarianism, at least in Jeremy Bentham's classical version.[7] One way, accordingly, in which we can challenge the first premise of the argument from knowledge is by recalling arguments made by utilitarianism's critics to discredit this underlying conception of the self. Let me just mention one well-known argument to that effect: Robert Nozick's thought experiment of the "experience machine."[8] He imagines a device to which you can hook up via electrodes stuck in your brain that will provide you in the course of a lifetime with a constant stream of pleasurable experiences of whatever kind you choose in advance. Such a device is the fulfillment of the utilitarian's dream, and yet it would seem to strike most people as a nightmare. To those who respond to the prospect of an experience machine with horror rather than delight, the thought experiment demonstrates that there is more to our lives than the experiences they contain. We can formulate this conclusion in a way more congenial to our present purpose. Those aspects of our lives that the experience machine cannot in principle replicate are the ones in which we are vulnerable to being affected by things quite apart from the experiences, if any, those things induce.

The experience machine provides an indirect line of attack on the argument from knowledge by challenging a conception of the self and a related conception of value that seem to underpin its first premise. A more direct line of attack involves looking at some counterexamples: situations in which we strongly incline to say that one is affected by an event of which one does not know. Consider two legal cases first. In *Breithaput v. Abram*[9] a blood sample was taken at the police's behest from an unconscious driver suspected of drunk driving. Were his constitutional rights infringed? Though the Supreme Court divided on this issue, no one doubted that the needle prick, though administered to an insensate person and thus having no experiential effects, affected Breithaupt, thus triggering an investigation into the scope of his constitutional rights. The second case, *People v. Minkowski,*[10] involves rape by deception. On numerous occasions, the defendant, a gynecologist, had sexual intercourse with his patients, unbeknownst to them. Though the physician was eventually found out, all would agree, I suppose, that the patients had been raped even before their suspicions arose, and whether or not they would have ever discovered the truth.

These cases are naturally seen as involving a violation of the respective victims' autonomy: it is after all an *involuntary* drawing of blood in the one case, and *nonconsensual* sex in the other. But appeal to the victims' autonomy begs the question here. People do not in general hold a veto power, not even a prima facie one, over actions they would not approve. To engage their autonomy, the action in question must first be said to affect *them*. But then, if the individuals do not even know about the actions, in what sense can they be said to be affected by them? On what ground is their assent required? A simple answer to these questions is readily available, though. We recognize that the respective victims of the two cases were affected, because their bodies were affected. A bodily intrusion by itself counts as affecting the person though no experience be involved. Despite its obviousness, the significance of this answer should not escape us. It implies a conception of human beings and what might be said to affect them that runs counter to what the argument from knowledge assumes. It does so by identifying an aspect of persons—their bodies—that can be the locus of effects on them without their knowing it and without any subsequent experiences. By generalizing these examples we get an expanded notion of effects and potentially of harm. Just as experiential effects impinge on a person's mind, other effects impinge on other aspects or constituents of the person, such as her body. Moreover, though embodiment is an obvious aspect or property of the self, thus providing a natural arena for nonexperiential effects, it need not be the only one. What counts as affecting the person, and as potentially harming her, must ultimately depend on the picture of the self we have and on what other aspects or constituents it might be thought to comprise.

2. The Argument from Causation

By demonstrating that we can be affected without being aware of it, the examples I have just considered help refute the argument from knowledge. But they also suggest an alternative basis for the belief that thoughts cannot have extrapersonal effects. These examples fit into a familiar paradigm, namely a commonsense causal paradigm: X can be said to affect me insofar as there is a physical causal link between X and an aspect or constituent of myself. These examples fit this paradigm particularly well, since the constituent they concern is the body, and X is a physical object or event impacting the body no differently than the proverbial billiard balls hitting against each other. Indeed, once we discover this causal paradigm at work in the cases just considered, instances of experiential effect can be assimilated to it as well: our experiences are simply one kind of result that external factors can cause in us. Our psychological makeup is in these cases the aspect of ourselves in which the effect takes place, and communication the typical form that the causal chain assumes. But now the belief that uncommunicated thoughts cannot by themselves affect us will seem to rest on a different and if anything firmer foundation than that suggested by the argument from knowledge. The reason that thoughts cannot affect us, and a fortiori cannot harm us, it will now seem, lies in their lack of direct causal efficacy outside the agent. How can one person's thoughts affect another if they cannot causally engage with her?

We reach accordingly the second argument for the belief that a person's thoughts cannot directly affect anyone else, the argument from causation.

> For X to affect A, X must have some causal efficacy with regard
>   to A;
> thoughts by themselves are causally inert with regard to other
>   people;
> hence,
> a person's thoughts by themselves cannot affect other people.

Is this argument sound? The second premise seems to me unassailable. This is so quite trivially, since to speak of a thought "by itself," as it exists in a person's mind, is to cut it off simply by stipulation from any causal chain that could possibly lead to another person. The first premise may seem to be just as firm. Does not "affecting" entail, analytically, causal efficacy on the part of whatever does the affecting? But as some familiar examples demonstrate, the first premise is nonetheless false, in that we do commonly judge a person to be affected by a thing or an event, even though no causal chain, as ordinarily understood, runs from the one to the other. Consider the father whose child is killed, unbeknownst to him, say, in a car accident.[11] It would be natural to report in these circumstances that something terrible happened to the father. But why? How can a car accident that resulted in one person's death be said to affect another person, who, let us assume, lives in a far-away land, and does not even know about it? Clearly, unlike the cases of unknown direct bodily impact I mentioned earlier, there is no causal relation between the accident and the father in this case.[12] Of course, the father has a deep concern for and an abiding interest in his son's welfare, quite independently of what he learns about it.[13] But as we saw earlier, such concern and interest are insufficient to ground the judgment that the son's death affects the father: recall the earlier point about a corresponding concern for the rain forest one might have. It may be tempting to distinguish the case of the father from that of the rain forest by invoking here the notion of "having an interest": though I may be avidly interested in remote deforestation, I cannot be said to have an interest in it, whereas the father does have an interest in his son's longevity. The distinction is sound, but not very illuminating. In the order of explanation, "being affected by" seems to be a more basic and broader notion than that of "having an interest in." To buttress in a non-question-begging way the judgment that something terrible happened to the father when the son was killed, we need some plausible account of the possibility of one thing's affecting another without a causal chain that starts from the one and terminates in an alteration in the latter.

3. Effects and Relational Properties

The Eiffel Tower is 984 feet tall and made of steel; it is in Paris and is illuminated by floodlights every night; it is the tallest structure in Paris and, some believe, the ugliest.[14] These salient properties of the Eiffel Tower fall into three categories: the first two properties are *intrinsic properties,* since describing them does not involve any other objects; whereas the other four are *relational,* since their descriptions do mention or imply other objects. Among the relational properties, in the last two the relation involves a comparison between the tower and some other objects, so I will call these properties *comparative properties*.

The properties I have listed vary in significance: the tower's height is probably more important than its material composition (up to a point: it would have been an altogether different kettle of fish, so to speak, if it were made of cheese), and the latter is perhaps more important than its nocturnal illumination but not quite as important as its general location. Such rankings of properties in terms of their relative significance is natural and common, attesting to some shared background understanding, of a roughly pragmatic nature, about the kind of thing the Eiffel Tower is. Though many of the true statements about the tower describe its properties, attention to our ordinary tower-talk reveals that not all do. This is particularly evident with regard to relational facts: that I climbed it in 1972, and its distance from Mars. Why don't these facts ordinarily count as properties? The answer probably lies in the same criterion of pragmatic significance we just mentioned and in light of which the tower's properties can be ranked. Understanding the kind of thing the tower is also implies the kinds of statements it may be profitable to make about it with any regularity. When they fall below a certain threshold of pragmatic importance, true facts about the tower no longer count in everyday discourse as properties at all.[15]

How can the Eiffel Tower be affected? Clearly, changing any of its properties would count as affecting the tower. These effects could take place with regard to the tower's intrinsic properties—it would be shortened if its legs were sawed off—as well as with regard to the relational properties. Notice however that unlike the intrinsic properties, the relational ones could change in two very different ways. Take the tower's municipal location. That could change if the tower were extracted from Parisian soil and moved to London. But the tower could also lose its Parisian address while standing still, if the rest of Paris were to be moved a hundred miles down the Loire valley. Changing the tower's relational properties without causally affecting the tower itself need not, of course, be as fanciful as that. Consider the other relational property I have mentioned: being illuminated at night. The tower could be affected in this regard if it were moved over to a dark corner of the city, out of reach of the floodlights. But a much less fanciful way in this case of changing the same property would be to simply turn off the lights.[16] The same is obviously true regarding the comparative properties as well: by sawing off its legs the tower would no longer be the tallest structure in Paris. But the same change in this comparative property would be effected if a taller building were erected on the other side of town. The respective effects on the tower of each respective member in the pairs of procedures we imagined are the same: in the first case it ceases to be in Paris, in the second, it winds up in the dark, and in the third it is no longer the tallest. Yet the causal chains that led from each member of the pair to the corresponding effect are, as far as the tower is concerned, radically different. The first procedure in each scenario involves a causal chain that terminates in the tower itself, whereas in the second procedure the causal chain evades the tower, engaging instead with the other objects—call them *the relational terms*—on which the tower's respective relational properties depend.

The case of human beings, to which I now turn, is not essentially different. We too have relational and comparative properties, as well as intrinsic ones. In describing a person it would be natural to list such intrinsic facts as his height or intelligence, as well as relational properties such as marital status or nationality, and comparative ones: being a valedictorian or the best lawyer in town. Consequently, we too can be affected by things that are not causally linked to us but rather to the relational terms. Consider the case of Bob, who is married to Mary. A serious quarrel causes them to separate. A separation could be a protracted and gradual process, but to simplify matters, assume that this one was abrupt and final, so we can date it with precision. If the separation took place, say, on Monday at five, then, all would agree that Bob underwent an important change of status at that time: all at once, he went from being married to being separated. But notice that the causal chain leading from the quarrel to the separation can take two different paths. In one scenario, Bob packs his belongings and leaves in anger, determined never to return. But alternatively, Mary may be the one to leave, with Bob staying put, neither initiating nor desiring nor executing the separation. We can even imagine that Bob is not at home, but at work, when the separation takes place, so that he does not find out about it until later.

A similar account applies to the example of the bereaved father we discussed in the preceding section. The question how a car accident that takes place in a faraway land can be said to affect the father can be now easily answered in terms of the relational nature of the property of being a father. It is this property that makes the father vulnerable to effects due to causal chains, in this case of a fatal nature, that terminate not with him but with his distant son. This account also helps distinguish the case of the father from that of an interest in the rain forest with which I have contrasted it. Remote deforestation will not be said to affect me no matter how interested I am in it, since no corresponding relational property links me to the rain forest. Why not?

I have mentioned earlier the important role supposedly played by a vaguely defined pragmatic background in constraining the kinds of properties ordinary speech acknowledges. It is safe to assume that in selecting the kinds of properties it is sensible to ascribe to human beings, account is taken of people's typical interests. But though the link between interests and properties may be close, it is neither tight nor direct. Our judgment in a particular case that an individual has been affected will be mediated by our general understandings of what counts as a relational property and its relational term. The availability of standard terms and set phrases such as *father, spouse,* or *widow* that embody putative properties seems relevant (though not dispositive) here. To be sure, being a parent or a spouse is ordinarily bound up with numerous and highly significant causal and experiential effects on the persons concerned. These facts are doubtlessly relevant to these terms' evolution, but they need not be present on each occasion of the terms' employment. It would be altogether natural, for example, to refer to a man's death as an event that befell his wife by reporting that "she was widowed," even if she had never heard about the event, and despite our belief that she would not have cared one bit if she had. By contrast , the death of this woman's favorite movie star would not by itself be said to affect her in any way, no matter how distressed she would have been by it (though her distress when she does find out is of course an effect on her). Our ordinary conceptual framework places some things about which one may care a lot, the rain forest was my other example, outside the range of a person's relational terms, so that their fate will not by itself be described in terms that imply an effect on the individual concerned.

4. The Extrapersonal Effects of Thoughts

Recognizing the pervasive role that relational properties play in ordinary speech explains how a person may be affected by a thing that is not causally linked to him when that thing is instead causally linked to a relational term. But this account may seem not to advance my main claim much. Although we may have now somewhat weakened the grip of the argument from causation, we have not weakened it enough: applied to the case of thoughts, our model would allow that one person's thoughts can affect another without engaging causally with her, as long as those thoughts do engage causally with a relational term that defines one of her relational properties. Since thoughts have no extrapersonal causal efficacy, however, they cannot do that: they are no more capable of causally engaging with any relational term than they can causally affect directly the other person herself. Having posed the problem in these terms, the solution, or rather solutions, seem rather obvious. First, although a thought cannot causally affect any relational term that is external to the thinker, the thought itself can simply *be* another's relational term. Second, the thinker can be the relational term that defines another's relational property. Since a thought affects the person whose thought it is, by affecting the thinker the thought will have affected the other as well. I have just given an example of one person serving as the relational term that fixes another's relational property: the son to his father. Hence the judgment that the accident that killed the son affects the father as well. But other effects on the son, short of death, could similarly be said to affect the father. Suppose that the son barely survived the car accident, remaining however in a permanent vegetative state. That too, I believe, could be credibly described as a disaster that befell the father, even if he never learns about the event. In a similar vein, imagine now a third scenario: the son, whom the father remembers as a sunny, cheerful lad, has sunk, perhaps due to a car accident, into acute depression, and is relentlessly tormented by suicidal thoughts. Clearly there is no fundamental difference as far as effects on the father are concerned between this scenario, which has to do entirely with the son's state of mind, and the preceding, more physical affliction. In this case, the son's state of mind, his thoughts, can by itself affect the father because of the fact that the subject of those thoughts serves as the relational term that constitutes the father as such.[17]

Two clarifications are in order. My argument throughout depends on certain shared linguistic intuitions I assume. I cannot convince the reader who does not share them or at least the belief that others do. But there is one possible reason to doubt these intuitions to which we ought to be alert. There is some tendency, I believe, to withdraw one's assent to the judgment, say, that a disaster struck the father whose son died, when the explicit question is posed as to whether the father can be said to have been "affected" or "harmed." This tendency, moreover, seems to increase the more attenuated the effects on the son himself are. Such a tendency does not seem to me to detract from the force of my argument. We know from the outset that we are in general in the grips of a causal paradigm: this is after all our putative explanation of the prevailing belief that thoughts can have no extrapersonal effects. When verbs such as *harm* and *affect* that bear their causal connotations on their sleeve are brought to our attention, we resist the implication that they may apply in the absence of a familiar causal pattern. The relevant responses that ought to guide our investigation are accordingly the ones we can imagine ourselves giving to circumlocutions that are more likely to catch us unawares, while on a linguistic cruise, so to speak, and philosophically innocent. Would it not be altogether natural to report about the father whose son had been run over by a car, that "something awful happened to him" and then add "but he never learned about it"? Such a description would seem clearly in place in the event of the child's death, but it would seem also appropriate, perhaps with a bit more straining, in the second scenario of vegetative survival. Acute depression would probably raise even greater doubts.

These doubts lead to my second clarification, which is to recognize that we are faced here with a sliding scale, and to indicate that nothing in my argument depends on the precise cutoff point at which ascribing to the father effects that derive from mishaps that befall the son would seem linguistically natural. My argument only depends on the realization that in our example, as far as effects on the father are concerned, there is *in principle* no difference between the son's dying or becoming vegetative or depressed. In the absence of knowledge on the father's part, there is no direct causal link between him and any one of the tragic events. The same relational logic that licenses describing the first two events as affecting him seems to apply to the third case in which the son's mental states are involved.

In the examples I have just considered, it is natural to think of the son as the relational term that fixes the pertinent relational property, fatherhood, by virtue of which changes in the son's states of mind can be said to affect the father. The son's state of mind, his depression, does not directly involve the father; it can be said to affect the father only by virtue of a prior and independent connection that binds the two of them together. But in other cases the bond between the people concerned is at least in part a matter of the contents of their reciprocal states of mind. Then the thoughts themselves can be plausibly seen as the relational term that defines a relational property in another.

Most people would probably agree that being a cuckold is undesirable even in those instances in which one never finds out about the spouse's infidelity. This judgment can be analyzed along by now familiar lines: being a spouse is a relational property, one of whose ramifications, defined in terms of the other spouse's behavior, earns the aggrieved party the said sobriquet. We do not have an analogous single English term to describe the condition of the victim of unrequited love. But the situation seems to me relevantly analogous. Consider Joe, who has been married to Jane for many years. Joe is deeply in love with his wife and has always believed that his feelings were fully reciprocated. But they were not: Jane in fact despises Joe, meticulously maintaining a deceptive facade, perhaps for the children's sake. Now Joe's situation may be plausibly viewed as worse than that of the betrayed husband: it is quite possible, for example, that given the choice, Joe would prefer an occasional fling by an otherwise loving wife to a wife who despises him but remains faithful all the same. Those who know the truth about Jane's feelings will judge correctly that without even being aware of it, Joe is trapped in bad situation. The account we suggested in the case of the cuckold would seem to apply here as well: the relational property of being a spouse makes Joe directly vulnerable to Jane's feelings of which he knows not, just as he is vulnerable to aspects of his wife's behavior of which he remains ignorant. In the marital context, some of each spouse's feelings as well as behavior are themselves relational terms whose content plays a direct role in the other spouse's life. Moreover, although the marital relation makes this example more compelling, it is not strictly necessary. We can imagine other scenarios of unrequited love, in which a lover's life will be plausibly said to be marred by the loved one's feelings, whether he knows them or not. Such feelings may turn him into a *disappointed lover,* with the italicized expression denoting not the lover's own state of mind, but the actual state of affairs. There is no point in spinning out such additional scenarios. What is important to acknowledge is that the more attenuated the relationship between the parties, the less likely we are to ascribe relational properties to them that derive from that relationship, and consequently our tendency to view their states of mind as affecting each other will be correspondingly attenuated.[18]

The romantic domain is of course not the only one in which one's thoughts can serve as the relational term for another's property. Let me consider a different kind of example. Consider a young and insecure painter, who desperately aspires to be a "real artist," that is to say someone whose paintings have genuine artistic value. Whether or not this painter is indeed a real artist is doubtlessly an important fact not just to him but about him. But what determines whether one's art has genuine value? This is obviously a difficult question to which many different answers have been given, but one plausible answer points to the experts' opinion. Ordinarily this supposes a consensus or preponderance of views among a group of experts. But suppose that in our case, only one person's judgment counts: because the area is so esoteric that experts are rare, or because of this critic's stature as the dominant and noncontroverted authority. To be appreciated by this critic, on these assumptions, is tantamount to being a real artist. If being a real artist would be a property of the painter, then on this account it would be a relational property, constituted by the critic's opinion. The latter's thoughts thus play the part of the relational term that defines another person's relational property. Suppose now that the critic's initial reaction to the painter's work is enthusiastic, but that later, after further observation and reflection, her enthusiasm sags and she dismisses him as a failure. On the assumptions concerning artistic merit that we have made, it would be natural for someone familiar with the critic's change of heart to describe the situation as follows: "It had seemed for a while that this painter had really made it as an artist, but then he turned out to be a flop." Notice that the accuracy of this description does not depend on the critic's disclosing her opinion to anyone else. Even if the painter were to spend the rest of his life under the illusion of artistic success, by his own criteria the truth of the matter would be that he was a failure.

As this story again illustrates, it is possible for thoughts themselves, rather than the person holding them, to be the relational term that fixes a property of another person. But treating a single critic's opinions as the relational term that constitutes someone as an artist is admittedly artificial: artistic merit is ordinarily determined not by a single authority, but is rather a matter of some collective determination. To take account of this fact, we must distinguish two kinds of relational properties: individual and collective. An *individual relational property* is one in which the relational term is or makes essential reference to another individual; in a *collective relational property*, the relational term is or makes essential reference to a collectivity. My extant examples, such as being a parent or a spouse, belong to the former category; ethnic or racial properties, being French or Caucasian, illustrate the latter.[19]

As the examples of race and ethnicity suggest, some of a person's most important characteristics, those that form what is often loosely referred to as her social identity, are collective relational properties. Now many of these properties are not exclusively or even primarily a matter of other people's thoughts. But some are: reputation, popularity, fame, prestige, are all important aspects of one's social identity that are for the most part constituted by others' opinions. Some collective relational properties, perhaps all those just listed, only require that the views on which they depend be held distributively: there must be a sufficient convergence of opinion, but the opinions themselves can be held individually, without any reference to the fact that others hold them as well. Though communication obviously facilitates such convergence of views, it is not, strictly speaking, necessary: the convergence can occur spontaneously, in response to some salient characteristics of the person concerned or some events that involve him. It is enough, for example, for a person to acquire a reputation for heroism if everyone in town watches him save a child from a burning building: no public communication is required.

Other collective relational properties require that the underlying views be held jointly, that is with a reciprocal awareness that others hold them as well. Consider authority and leadership. To be an authority in a certain professional area, one must be recognized as such. For the most part, the recognition consists not just in convergent beliefs concerning the putative authority's high professional skills but also in the belief that others hold similar views. Here communication is more imperative than in the case of the distributively held beliefs, but it is not mandatory either. As we saw in our earlier discussion of the alleged inaccessibility of thoughts, we can know each other's thoughts with practical certainty in the absence of any communication, by observing each other observe some salient properties or events. Think, for example, of the charismatic leader of an informal group. One can attain spontaneously such a position without any communication among the members of the group, if the following two conditions are satisfied: most members are captivated by the leader's charisma, and they believe that the charisma is so overpowering that it is practically certain that most others will be similarly impressed.[20]

I have earlier distinguished comparative properties from other relational properties and will now indicate how comparative properties provide an additional avenue through which people can be affected by others' thoughts. To recognize this possibility we only need remind ourselves that we commonly ascribe to people mental properties, such as being smart or imaginative, and that such properties often give rise to comparative properties: being the smartest kid in class or the most imaginative member of a department. To acquire or lose such a status is often of considerable importance. One way in which such changes can take place is through an improvement or a decline in the quality of one's own mental processes. But the other way in which one will attain or abdicate such a comparative position is through mental changes in others. Joe may no longer be the most imaginative member of the department because he grew duller over the years. But he may have also lost the title because Mary has recently flourished in this respect. Obviously, these judgments assume a sharp separation between matters of fact, including inner, subjective fact—for example who, Joe or Mary, has in fact a richer imagination—and the epistemological question of how do we tell. The latter, unlike the former, does for the most part depend on expression and communication. But even here the dependence is only partial. For other members of the department to be able to tell who is most imaginative, both Joe and Mary must publicly display their imagination. But for Mary herself to know the truth about Joe's comparative standing in this regard, no manifestation of her imaginativeness is required: since she has firsthand knowledge of her own imaginative life, she can reach a confident conclusion about Joe's standing with only his publicly manifesting his imagination.

Two other points concerning comparative properties. Some readers may have doubts as to whether these are genuine properties of the individuals to whom they are ascribed. That a change in others counts as a change in such a property may increase such doubts. It may perhaps serve as some reassurance of these properties' good standing that many indisputable properties that do not have a comparative form are in fact comparative properties in disguise. Seemingly noncomparative adjectives such as "tall" or "slim" or "smart" do imply a reference group that supplies them with a baseline and a metric: a particular society, or some specific subgroup, or, quite commonly, humanity as a whole.[21]

The other point is that although many comparative properties are well established, the analysis I have here proposed does not equally illuminate all of them. Suppose Johnny had been for quite a while the saddest kid in his class, his sadness a source of consternation to his teachers, parents, and friends. Then one day a teacher reports to the parents that Johnny is no longer the saddest kid in the class. This piece of news would ordinarily come to them as a great relief, so the parents would be justly dismayed to learn that all the teacher meant was that another child, even sadder than Johnny, had just joined the class. This example ought to alert us once again to the significance of the ever-present pragmatic background against which the judgments ascribing both properties and effects are made. The aspect of that background that is relevant to the present point is the qualified validation pragmatic considerations provide to a competitive dimension in human affairs: the more legitimate, salient, and important the competitive aspect is with regard to the assignment of a given comparative property, the less it is likely to matter whether the change in that property is a product of a change in the subject himself or in the others to whom the subject is compared. Sadness is clearly not a characteristic with regard to which competition is encouraged or accepted. Consequently, what really matters about Johnny's sadness are internal changes in him rather than comparative judgements that reflect shifts in other people's moods.[22]

5. Some Normative Implications

As I mentioned at the outset, thoughts can obviously originate harmful causal chains whose middle terms are actions or speech, thus creating a prima facie tension between the harm principle and the liberal commitment to the inviolability of thoughts. But a strategy that mitigates the tension seems available in these cases: the inviolability of thoughts can be preserved without condoning any of their undesirable consequences by focusing all political and legal attention not on the thoughts but on their overt, public manifestations. If my argument is correct, however, such a strategy is not always availing: we may not be always able to prevent the negative consequences by suppressing public manifestations of thoughts because in some cases there may not be any such manifestations. This leads to the conclusion that in being committed to the inviolability of thoughts, one must do so not because thoughts can have no negative effects on their own but despite the fact that they can. There are indeed familiar and weighty arguments that I need not rehearse here pointing out the dangers of any attempt at thought control. We must, however, recognize that the Inquisitorial specter is a real one, as are many other antiliberal ghosts that always lurk in the attic. Their presence is after all what gives liberalism its point and its agenda. In the present case, as in the others, one can only hope, if one is a liberal, that these ghosts will be held at bay by the power of argument and by the strength of commitment, rather than by denying the ghosts' existence.

My main aim in this section is not, however, to consider such general matters, but to focus instead on a more specific implication that my argument has on the current debate concerning *hate speech,* that is, the injurious expression of prejudice and hatred toward the members of vulnerable, usually minority, groups. To what extent do the undeniably negative effects of this kind of speech justify legal inhibitions in possible derogation of free speech concerns? Somewhat paradoxically, I think, recognizing the possible harmfulness of thoughts suggests an argument in favor of a more permissive approach to speech in this area.

I start with an analogy. Recall the example of the father whose son is killed. Should the father be informed? The news will be to him a source of great, perhaps devastating pain. And yet most would agree, I believe, that he ought to be told. Even those who disagree with the conclusion will likely perceive that there is at least a genuine dilemma here, both horns of which have to do with concern for the bereaved father. But what precisely is the nature of this concern? One horn, as we have just seen, is straightforward: the father's experiential well-being will obviously be seriously set back by the disclosure. What's on the other side? It is natural to invoke here the father's right to know. But what is the basis for such a putative right? Autonomy seems a likely candidate, and it might seem to counsel disclosure in two different ways. Neither, however, seems to me entirely satisfactory. The first rests on the view that autonomy requires a capacity to make rational, and hence fully informed, practical judgments. Here autonomy is linked to the prospect for some action, but in the situation we envisage none is likely: there is nothing the father can do about the tragic event, and the validity of his claim to be told the truth does not seem to depend on his engaging in some mourning rites or the like; stipulate those away, and the right to know seems to remain intact. Autonomy can enter in another way, though: we assume that given the choice, the father would have wanted to know the truth, so by telling him we are serving his autonomy simply by satisfying his own presumed wishes. Putting aside the question whether and when satisfying someone's wishes is a matter of her autonomy, this consideration in favor of disclosure is unsatisfactory for another reason. It makes perfectly good sense in this case to maintain that the father ought to want to know the truth, even if we believe that he in fact would not. To be sure, our belief that he would not is itself a reason against disclosure, and this perhaps out of respect for his autonomy. But even here the reason need not be dispositive, and at any rate the question remains as to why it might be felt that the father ought to prefer to be told.

Though autonomy does play an important part in these matters, it cannot tell us the entire story. The locution I have used—knowing the truth—will seem to provide a clue to the missing parts, but unless we are careful the clue may mislead. Aren't we all committed to the truth, and is that commitment not enough to argue in favor of disclosure? But this of course will not do as a basis for the father's alleged right to know: he has no comparable claim, mercifully, with regard to the myriads of other deaths that occurred around the world that same day, nor for that matter with regard to most other events. It might be suggested that the claim to knowing the truth is limited to events that are of concern to the person, and that unlike his son's death, all these other deaths are of no concern to the father. But as we saw earlier in a somewhat similar context, "being of concern" will not do here either: the father may have an avid concern regarding the future of the rain forest with no resulting claim to be briefed about any untoward logging that goes on. A person does have a right to know the truth, but the scope of the truth in question is narrowly circumscribed; it is narrower even than what is to him of interest or concern. It is the truth about the person himself and his own life that seems pertinent here. An apt expression that seems to capture the point is that one ought not to live a lie. Why not? This, I think, is no longer a matter of autonomy, but a matter of dignity, and hence a matter of respect: willingness to face up to significant truths about oneself, painful or otherwise unpleasant as that may be, bespeaks self-respect, just as respect for another's dignity counsels disclosure of such facts even when distressing.

Though the balance of considerations may vary in the other scenarios I have discussed earlier—such as the betrayed spouse and the failed artist—the basic dilemma they pose is the same: it is the choice between avoiding psychological pain and hurt feelings on the one hand and respecting a person's dignity-based right to know all significant self-regarding truths on the other. A crucial aspect of this dilemma is of course the scope of self-regarding truths: which facts are self-regarding? The answer, as we saw, depends in part on what we consider our relational properties to be, and hence on what things we take to affect us by affecting our relational terms.

Now obviously not everything other people think about us can be said to affect us. Thus by the criterion I propose, we do not have a general prima facie claim to know such thoughts no matter how understandably curious about them we may be.[23] But as I have indicated earlier, on some occasions other people's attitudes toward us do serve as the relational terms that fix important features of ourselves. Particularly relevant here are the attitudes held by a community or a society that defines aspects of its members' social identity. If, for example, a community despises some of its members and holds them in contempt when acceptance by that community constitutes an aspect of their social identity, those members are negatively affected even if the attitudes remain latent and their objects bask in illusory acceptability. They live a lie, and their dignity is trampled. Our attitude toward hate speech in circumstances such as these, I suggest, ought to resemble the dilemma I have just described in the case of the bereaved father and the related scenarios. Though the speech be offensive and painful, it is for the most part just a messenger of bad tidings. Gagging the messenger will not make these tidings go away, nor does it neutralize their poisonous effects.

It is sometimes advisable to state the obvious in these sensitive matters. Nothing I said implies that those who engage in hate speech ought to get any credit for honesty or for respecting the targets' dignity: typically nothing will be farther from their minds; their goal is to add the injury of hurt feelings to the insult of bigotry and hostility. Nonetheless, public policy toward hate speech ought to recognize that within the nasty social situation in which it is likely to occur it plays a more ambiguous role than we often realize. If we recognize that the attitudes that hate speech expresses are, if pervasive, by themselves destructive of an aspect of their targets' identity, and if we also believe that the situation is only exacerbated by the indignity of illusion, then despite the obvious hurt, by bringing things into the open, hate speech performs a redeeming function as well.

6. Thoughts and Individualism

The normative implications I have mentioned, though hopefully of some interest, are not, however, the main intended payoff of the position I have outlined. Only rarely do other-affecting thoughts remain utterly unexpressed, and even when they do, other considerations are likely to overshadow and overwhelm the practical significance of my point. My argument, if correct, does however have a broader philosophical significance quite apart from such direct normative and practical ramifications. The broader significance concerns the limits of individualism, and it may be best brought out by relating my argument to another line of thought with which I think it has much in common. Individualism means different things to different people, but here it stands for a picture of the mind as a self-contained entity that is enclosed within (the brain of) each individual human being. So described the picture is vague, but not so vague as to prevent recognizing some well-known objections. The specific objection with which I would like to associate my argument is mostly the joint product of two writers, Hilary Putnam and Tyler Burge, who through a number of famous thought experiments have argued for what has come to be known as "meaning externalism": the view best summarized by the slogan that "meanings are not in the mind."[24] I cannot here even begin to do justice to the intricacies and complexities of the issues involved. But the main point is rather simple. It depends on the observation that our use of language is commonly based on an incomplete understanding of the terms we employ. Since our use of terms is as a matter of course based on only partial understanding and mastery of them, the only way in which meanings can be attributed to us must incorporate the way these gaps in our own understanding are filled in by factors outside of us. These factors are of two kinds: facts about the environment and facts about usage in the relevant linguistic community. The main emphasis in this line of reasoning, at least as developed by Burge, is that these factors determine the content of the agent's mind without causally interacting with her: we can imagine two agents whose inner composition and causal histories are identical, and yet the contents of their minds will be said to vary depending on the natural and social environment in which we imagine them to be.

This brief sketch of the meaning-externalist position will suffice to enable me to draw the following three connections to my argument. First, both views point out breaches in the cocoon in which on the individualist picture the mind is enveloped. Through these breaches the mind transacts with the world outside of it without the mediation of any causal chains. The second connection is by way of contrast in the direction of these noncausal transactions in which the mind is involved. Meaning-externalism highlights the mind's passive susceptibility to external factors: the world, we can say, participates noncausally in constituting or fixing the content of the mind. My argument documents the logical possibility of a more active externalism: the mind can have direct, nonmediated, and noncausal effects on the world outside of it.

Third, the connection between the breaches in the individualist picture highlighted by Putnam and Burge on the one hand and the breaches that I have documented on the other is not coincidental. One way to see how the two views relate is to think of meaning-externalism as at least in part an elucidation of the semantics of terms such as *meaning* and *content.* In a similar vein, mine may be seen as an argument about the semantics of *effect* and related expressions, such as *disaster* or *mishap*. What we find in both cases is that many of our ordinary concepts organize reality in "relational" packages, that is, packages that cross-cut with concepts that form individuals, by combining elements, including mental elements, of different individuals. And since the former types of concepts have in general as much (or as little) warrant as the latter, there is no general reason for privileging the ones that track the boundary of a single individual over those that do not. Indeed, given how pervasive and intermixed both types of concepts are, the very idea of a "boundary of an individual" is thrown into question.

Notes

1. Herbert Morris, "Punishment for Thoughts," in *On Guilt and Innocence* (Berkeley and Los Angeles: University of California Press, 1976), 1–29.

2. For some further reflections on this theme see Douglas Husak, *Philosophy of Criminal Law* (Totowa, N.J.: Rowman and Littlefield, 1987), 97–99, 103–5.

3. For an explicit statement of this assumption, see, e.g., R. A. Duff, *Criminal Attempts* (Oxford: Clarendon Press, 1996), 313–14: "even practical thought [deliberation, intention-formation, choice] does not, by itself, impinge on the world: it must be translated into action; and we can say that it is by action (as distinct from mere thought) that agents impinge on or make a difference to the world."

4. See, for example, Joseph Tussman, *Government and the Mind* (New York: Oxford University Press, 1977), 88.

5. See e.g. Joel Feinberg, *Harmless Wrongdoing* (New York: Oxford University Press, 1988), 23–24; Husak, *Philosophy of Criminal Law,* 105; Duff, *Criminal Attempts,* 314.

6. See, e.g., Willard Van Orman Quine, *Word and Object* (Cambridge: MIT Press, 1960), chaps. 1–2.

7. Jeremy Bentham, *The Principles of Morals and Legislation* (New York: Hafner Press, 1948), 1.

8. Robert Nozick, *Anarchy, State, and Utopia* (New York: Basic Books, 1974), 42–45.

9. 352 U.S. 432 (1956).

10. 204 Cal. App. 2d 832; 23 Cal. Rptr. 92 (1962), discussed in chapter 5.

11. The example is discussed by George Pitcher in "The Misfortunes of the Dead," *American Philosophical Quarterly* 21 (1984): 183; and by Joel Feinberg, *Harm to Others* (New York: Oxford University Press, 1984), 90–91.

12. Pitcher, "Misfortunes of the Dead," diagnoses the problem this case poses in similar terms. I propose a different solution from his, though the two, I think, are consistent. Mine, however, leads more directly to the claim I seek to establish concerning the extrapersonal effects of thoughts.

13. For a discussion of "vicarious harms" along such lines see Feinberg, *Harm to Others,* at 70–79.

14. Guy de Maupassant famously stated that the tower was his favorite lunch place in Paris, being the one place from which the tower could not be seen; he is also said to have left Paris permanently to avoid looking at the tower.

15. So I do not mean to raise the separate question whether there is a useful logical or ontological sense that would admit the "properties" ordinary speech implicitly excludes, or, for that matter, exclude "properties" that the latter takes for granted.

16. This example is actually somewhat out of date: the external floodlighting was replaced in 1986 by a system of illumination that is within the tower's structure. The change corroborates my main point: the significant property of the tower in this case is its being illuminated at night; it does not seem to matter much, relative to this property, whether the light comes from within, making it an intrinsic property, or from without, thus rendering it relational.

17. Feinberg considers a similar case and reaches a similar conclusion: the wife's sinking into a depression can all by itself count as a harm to her loving husband. The reason for Feinberg lies simply in the intensity and duration of the husband's love, which give him a vicarious interest in his wife's well-being. But here again the account seems to leave a conceptual gap: no matter how intense and enduring my love or admiration for, say, Queen Elizabeth, her mood swings, of which I know not, will hardly be said to affect me. See Feinberg, *Harm to Others,* 71.

18. Cases of this kind are also sometimes discussed in connection with the concept of happiness. See, for example, Richard Kraut, "Two Conceptions of Happiness," *Philosophical Review* 88 (1979): 167–97.

19. These two categories are not exhaustive: physical objects, such as geographic locations, can also play the part of a relational term. They are however irrelevant to our present concerns.

20. Indeed, strictly speaking, the second belief may suffice to establish a leader, and it need not even be a true belief. The putative leader may possess a salient characteristic, an imposing appearance perhaps, which on close inspection is not charisma, but resembles it sufficiently to lead most members of the group to believe that the others are bound to be misled by that characteristic into believing that she is charismatic, and hence view her as the leader. Notice that for such mental bootstrapping to successfully establish someone as a leader actually requires the absence of any communication among the members. In the terminology I propose, what we witness here is a situation in which the convergent thoughts of a group of people, uncommunicated and unexpressed, serve as a collective relational property of the putative leader, by constituting her as the group's leader.

21. Compare David Hume, "Of the Dignity and Meanness of Human Nature," in *Political Essays,* ed. Charles W. Hendel (Indianapolis: Bobbs-Merrill, 1953).

22. I have distinguished relational properties from comparative ones, but some properties are a composite of both. Being a popular member

of the class is, as we saw earlier, a relational property that depends on what the other members of the class think of one. But being the most popular member is also comparative. One can accordingly lose this accolade in three different ways: through a change in the person herself, becoming, say, mean and nasty; through a change in the others' attitudes—they simply grew tired of her; or by the fact that a new member, more attractive than the heretofore favorite, joined the group.

23. Hence, the examples recently adduced by Thomas Nagel to demonstrate the perils of excessive candor in social interactions fall outside the purview of my argument. See his "Concealment and Exposure," *Philosophy and Public Affairs* 27 (1998): 3, 10–17.

24. The main papers are Hilary Putnam, "The Meaning of 'Meaning,'" in *Philosophical Papers* (London: Cambridge University Press, 1975), 2:215; and Tyler Burge, "Individualism and the Mental," *Midwest Studies in Philosophy* 4 (1979): 73–121, and "Other Bodies," in *Thought and Object,* ed. Andrew Woodfield (New York: Oxford University Press, 1982), 97.

PART 3
BOUNDARIES OF SELF

CHAPTER SEVEN

RESPONSIBILITY AND THE
BOUNDARIES OF THE SELF

Legal responsibility is not imposed in a moral or a social void. Although the ascription of responsibility is more structured in law than it is in general outside of it, no sharp conceptual division exists. To understand legal responsibility, we must understand responsibility. The most important source of such understanding is morality. Blaming—that is, ascribing moral responsibility for the negative effects of one's behavior—has come to be understood in terms of what I call the *free will paradigm*. In the free will paradigm, responsibility is grounded in the agent's capacity to choose her actions freely. This understanding of responsibility arises most prominently in criminal law, in which the clearest example is the traditional definition of first degree murder based on premeditation and deliberation. The law deems that any emotional agitation, any heat of passion, clouds judgment and impairs self-control and thus reduces responsibility.

Important as moral responsibility is to legal responsibility, however, it cannot be the whole story. First, the legal structure of liability cannot be more sound than its philosophical foundations. And these foundations—insofar as they comprise the idea of free will—are notoriously shaky.[1] Try as it may, the law cannot ignore the ubiquitous specter of determinism. Concessions to determinism are as inevitable as they are perilous: they are steps down a slope that, despite enormous philosophical effort, remains a slippery one.[2]

Second, and relatedly, it is equally difficult to deny or ignore the importance of character traits in both legal and extralegal ascriptions of responsibility. Explaining an action in terms of the agent's character

ordinarily corroborates rather than defeats the ascription of responsibility. The role that character plays in explaining action and in grounding responsibility, however, is a notorious source of embarrassment for
the free will paradigm. If my action of stealing your money is a product
of my greed, it is not simply a matter of the free exercise of my will,
and accordingly my responsibility should be mitigated or extinguished.
It takes considerable footwork to avoid this conclusion, but even if the
effort is deemed successful, the very need for it is an embarrassment to
a voluntarist conception of responsibility.[3]

Finally, just as moral responsibility is not the whole of responsibility
outside of law, legal responsibility is not coextensive with blaming. For
example, in tort law, holding someone responsible need not connote
any moral failure. Ascriptions of strict, vicarious, and collective responsibility fall outside morality and involve no blaming. Yet the free will
paradigm exerts its influence even here, albeit in a negative way. We
tend to think of such forms of responsibility, somewhat apologetically,
as exceptions to the free will idea. As seen from the voluntarist perspective, the picture of responsibility is that of a core and a periphery.
The conception of responsibility as based on freely chosen actions
applies to the core, but it leaves the rather large periphery unexplained.
Moreover, from this perspective the relationship of core to periphery is
unclear: what, after all, do the various cases of "deviant" responsibility
have in common with the core cases characterized by the agent's free
choice?

In what follows, I propose to answer this question. I also respond
to other difficulties with the dominant conception of responsibility. The
response is not a solution to, but rather an evasion of, the problems
endemic to the free will paradigm. My aim is to provide an alternative unitary account, in light of which we can make sense of much
responsibility-talk without encountering the problems presented by the
voluntarist perspective. To introduce this response, however, I must first
draw attention to a second prominent feature of the dominant conception of responsibility.

Theoretical discussions of responsibility have traditionally taken the
subject of responsibility as given and have explored the conditions under
which the relationship of responsibility occurs. I argue, however, that
this traditional approach assumes a simplistic conception of the relationship between responsibility and its subject. Implicit in this approach is
a conception of the human subject—the self—as possessing some important, immutable attributes to which the law responds, of which free will
is most prominent.

The view of the self as a fixed entity defined prior to and independent of social relationships, however, has come under increasing attack.[4] I sketch an alternative in part 1. My sketch draws on a tradition that denies the existence of important fixed human characteristics from which significant normative consequences follow. The concept of self that I use asserts instead the contingency of the self, and hence its "plasticity." However, this contingency and the many ways in which the self can be "filled in," or instantiated, are themselves aspects of the human subject that are of critical normative and legal importance. They permit us to understand the potentially dynamic and dialectical relationship between the law and the nature of its subjects. Specifically, this conception of the self permits us to articulate an alternative to the free will paradigm of responsibility, which I call the *constitutive paradigm*. Whereas the free will paradigm treats responsibility as a matter of what we choose to do, the constitutive paradigm treats responsibility as a matter of what and who we are. The latter view enables us to reinterpret disputes about the ascription of responsibility as reflecting the plasticity of the self and as involving a negotiation over the self's relevant boundaries. The constitutive paradigm also provides a common denominator for the various forms of responsibility we recognize. Volition is one element in our conception of the self, but not the only element; thus, volition is one ground of responsibility, but not the only ground. Accordingly, volitional responsibility is a special case—albeit a particularly important one—of constitutive responsibility. Like volitional responsibility, other forms of responsibility help identify and forge different constituents of the self.

In part 1 I accordingly outline conceptions of responsibility and self that depart from standard approaches, laying a framework for my discussion of the relationship between the two concepts. Parts 2 and 3 use the proposed theory of self and responsibility to analyze some persisting puzzles concerning the attribution and denial of legal responsibility. Part 2 demonstrates that familiar forms of responsibility that appear deviant from the voluntarist perspective, such as strict, vicarious, and collective responsibility, can be accommodated within the constitutive paradigm as manifesting different aspects of the self. Part 3 discusses legal defenses that deny or diminish responsibility. As commonly understood, these defenses run up against the problems inherent in the free will paradigm. By transposing these defenses into the constitutive framework, we can reinterpret them as involving implicit claims regarding the self's proper boundaries. Finally, part 4 focuses on certain distinctive features of the legal context and examines their bearing on responsibility and self. I argue that legal responsibility tends to constrict the self's boundaries and to encourage the enactment of a reduced and shriveled self.

1. The Constitutive Paradigm

The Dual Structure of Responsibility

Ordinary linguistic usage often reveals deeper philosophical truths. This section draws attention to the ambiguity of ordinary responsibility statements such as "A is responsible for X" that conceals an important shift of meaning in the use of such propositions. Although it is important to distinguish the two meanings, it is equally important to note that both meanings are ordinarily conveyed by the *same* linguistic form. The close relation between the two senses of ordinary responsibility statements provides the linguistic clue to the interpretation of responsibility I propose.

The discussion will be more focused if we consider the concept of responsibility through the somewhat distorting, but magnifying, lens of a stipulative definition of responsibility as "consciousness [of] being the incontestable author of an event or an object."[5] Under this definition, when I take responsibility for a broken vase, I confess my "authorship" of the unfortunate event: I broke it. More generally, X in "A is responsible for X" stands for an object or event of which A is the author. Although this understanding comports with common usage, it is plain that not all phrases of this form fit this analysis. Suppose that my child broke the vase rather than I. You may still be able to pin me down by saying, "You are responsible for your children (or for your children's behavior)." In this statement, X (my child) is not the object of which I am asserted to be the author. Instead, X designates the *ground* of my responsibility for a certain object or event (the broken vase).

Consider another pair of examples: (1) "A is responsible for the car accident," and (2) "A is responsible for her negligent driving." Once again, in (1) X designates the event whose authorship is ascribed to A (the car accident), whereas in (2) X refers to an aspect of A (A's negligent driving), by virtue of which she is considered the author of that event. As these examples show, the expression "responsible for" may pertain either to the object of responsibility (the broken vase or the car accident) or to the subject of responsibility, in whom the expression identifies the basis of the authorship of certain objects or events (one's child or one's negligent driving).[6] I call the two senses of the expression "responsible for" *object-responsibility* and *subject-responsibility*, respectively.[7]

How are we to understand these pairs of statements? By assuming or refusing to assume object-responsibility for a certain object or event, I own up to or disown that object or event; I claim or disclaim authorship of it, and in so doing, I use the object or event as a reference point in relation to which I draw my boundaries as subject. Much like the painter whom we know only as the Master of Flémalle, that is, as the creator of certain masterpieces, so also the subject's identity derives from the objects and events deemed to have been authored by her. Consequently, by assuming responsibility for an object or event, I also implicitly affirm a certain aspect of myself as a viable source of *my* authorship and implicitly assume subject-responsibility as well. To use the previous example, by assuming object-responsibility for the car accident, I am identifying with my negligent driving; I implicitly acknowledge my negligent driving as an aspect of myself, by virtue of which the car accident is properly ascribed to me.

Subject-responsibility may sometimes be assumed explicitly too. For example, I may explicitly acknowledge my responsibility for my negligence. Suppose I am at a dinner party, and the host urges me to stop drinking because I will be driving home soon. I can respond by saying, "Don't pester me so much; *I* am solely responsible for my drunk driving. It is really none of your business." I have taken subject-responsibility for my drunk driving. I identify it as an aspect of myself and hence as a responsibility base, which makes me liable to bear certain object-responsibility, primarily responsibility for a car accident if I were to be involved in one.

In short, my suggestion is that the structure of responsibility and its meaning are to be found in a relationship of mutual implication between object- and subject-responsibility. The ascription of object-responsibility implies a certain responsibility base and hence a certain subject-responsibility. Conversely, the ascription of subject-responsibility designates a responsibility base and hence a range of object-responsibility for objects and events that emanate from that base. The ascription or assumption of responsibility, we said, is a two-sided operation, oriented simultaneously toward both the object and the subject of responsibility, through which the subject of responsibility is in part constituted or determined. But what does this constitution or determination of the subject amount to? How does the ascription of responsibility help draw he subject's boundaries?

There are additional difficulties we must attend to. The ambiguity of the expression *responsible for* is often innocuous; we readily know whether it refers to the object of responsibility or to an aspect of the responsible subject. In our example, the statement that A is responsible for the car accident clearly carries the object-oriented meaning. Such clarity does not always obtain, however. In many cases, the same responsibility ascription can be interpreted in terms of both kinds of responsibility that we have distinguished. Consider again the statement, "A is responsible for her negligent driving." This statement can clearly carry the subject-oriented meaning: it identifies in A the source of author-ship of the accident. But it could also be taken in the object-oriented sense: we may focus on negligent driving as the event whose authorship is in question. By affirming A's responsibility for the negligence, we imply some other aspect of A (for instance, her lack of dexterity or her absent-mindedness) as the ground of her responsibility for the negligent driving.

What are we to make of these two interpretations? One interpreta-tion designates negligent driving as a constitutive element of A, and thus as a responsibility base, whereas the other describes it as an external event whose authorship by A needs grounding in some other responsi-bility base. To say that A is responsible for her negligent driving in both of these senses seems to imply that negligent driving both is and is not a constitutive element of A. Have we reached a contradiction?

Such questions require us to turn to a consideration of the human subject. The conception of the self that I now outline permits us to answer these questions and to make sense of the conception of respon-sibility I propose.

The Contingent Self

It is easy of course to contrive an ad hoc conception of the self that would fit any set of propositions about responsibility, or for that matter about anything else. To be of interest, however, the proposed conception must have sufficient credentials of its own, independently of its capacity to buttress the theory of responsibility in whose support it is enlisted. The conception of the self that I adumbrate satisfies this condition by drawing on a long if quite variegated philosophical tradition. Rather than claim originality in my depiction of the self, I must therefore insist on the lack thereof. The more independently grounded and familiar, even platitudinous, the features of the self I list, the firmer the support they provide for my approach to responsibility. The derivative nature of this part of my argument also accounts for the dogmatic or peremptory fashion in which I posit my preferred conception of the self. The argu-ments for the various components of this conception are not mine, but instead are to be found in the voluminous literature in which these com-ponents originate. My aim is to take advantage of whatever light already exists in these sources and train it on the subject of responsibility, with the hope that some illumination of this subject will result.

Although the following conception of the self, I call it *the contingent self* (obviously, the label is not original either[8]), draws on a large and in-creasingly salient philosophical tradition, it stands in opposition to what appears to be the dominant commonsensical conception and perhaps the prevailing philosophical conception too. It would be accordingly best to introduce the contingent self by way of contrast with the dominant conception. Human beings are commonly conceived as intelligent animals, or, a bit more abstractly, as organisms with certain distinguishing properties. On this view, the difference between a human being and, say, a cat, is of the same kind or order, although not quite of the same magnitude, as the difference between a cat and a giraffe. The contingent self departs from this common picture, claiming that it hides rather than reveal, as a good picture should do, human beings' most distinctive and significant characteristics. Attending to those characteristics involves a shift in both perspective and terminology. The picture of human beings as a distinctive type of organism depicts them from the same angle from which all other organisms, and for that matter all other objects, are depicted, that is by observing them from the outside, as it were. But as the tradition on which I draw insists, the best way to capture the gist of humanity is by adopting an internal perspective; by looking at a person from the point of view of being one. The corresponding terminological shift that marks this transition in perspective is the use of the term *self* as signifying a conception of human beings that privileges and accentuates the first-person perspective. (In the nature of things the latter is no more than a tendency: there are no strict uniformities in usage in this area).

Many different thinkers and even schools of thought focus on the self in the sense and in the way I have just indicated, so that in outlining the main features of the contingent self, I must be highly selective, though, as I said, not inventive. The origin in modern times of the tradition of thought I wish to highlight is obvious, though. Since Descartes the human organism, or more simply the body, ceased being the obvious starting point for an understanding of the self.[9] By embracing and exploring the first-person point of view, Descartes not only problematized the self's relation to the body, but more significantly for my present purposes, he gave birth to a wider range of philosophical views that take something like a phenomenology, or subjectivity, or consciousness, or self-awareness, to be the more appropriate starting point. The crucial observation is that there is something it is like to be a human being, a certain stance or orientation which we are uniquely capable of, and which involves a reflexive element that allows each self to recognize itself as such. That stance or orientation, that self-awareness, is itself a defining characteristic of the human. This stance or orientation is not, however, a brute or pure feeling of some sort but is rather marked by its intelligibility: it has content or meaning. What content or meaning is that, and where does it come from? There are again different versions of the answer on which I focus, but its most resounding formulation is the existentialists', specifically Sartre's.[10] The basic idea is that we create ourselves through the meanings we create. Who is the "we" in this description? There are, broadly speaking, two different possibilities, and both seem to apply. "We" can be here understood both distributively and jointly. Each person is at least part author of her own identity through the way she lives her life. This is the idea of *self-constitution*. But this process is conducted in terms of units of meaning that are jointly provided, most significantly through language, by collective endeavors such as culture and society. This is the idea of *modularity*. The self, we can say, is constituted by a phenomenology that is given its content and intelligibility by language and other systems of meaning that as such are irreducibly social.

Of the many interpretations of the phenomenology of self-constitution I refer only to one: the self's ability to identify with various elements and thereby integrate them into itself, or to detach itself from them by objectifying them and holding them at a distance. Different writers have described such identification and detachment in the various dimensions along which the self can be constituted, such as the mental, the physical, and the social. Let me give an example of each.

Professor Harry Frankfurt, among others, emphasizes our capacity to identify with, or to distance ourselves from, various mental characteristics or events.[11] For example, I can treat a particular desire as irreducibly me and consider its satisfaction as self-fulfillment, or I can view the desire as an alien, external force that impinges on me and whose satisfaction is my defeat. Sartre and Merleau-Ponty provide the best-known phenomenologies of physical self-constitution.[12] Normally, when I write, my hand is simply part of me—it is fully absorbed into the writing subject that I am at this time. But my identification with my hand can also extend to my pen: it, too, is just a transparent continuation of my bodily existence as a subject engaged in the endeavor of writings.[13] Conversely, just as I may incorporate my pen in my physical space, I can also remove my hand from it by temporary detachment. For example, by self-consciously observing and contemplating my hand, I can objectify it and create a distance between myself, the observer and contemplator, and my hand. Finally, Erving Goffman has observed a similar variability in the social dimension of the self. His concept of *role distance* describes our capacity either to identify with social roles or to detach ourselves from them and enact the roles self-consciously, as if from a certain distance.[14]

Such identifications and detachments as well as other forms and instances of self-constitution do not occur in a void. Just as identification and detachment represent the active aspect of the self's determination, so *modularity* represents the social constraints within which that determination takes place. Crudely put, the self must build itself using available, that is, socially and culturally provided, building blocks; it must constitute itself in terms of prepackaged units of signification and meaning.[15] Such social construction is most evident in regard to the social roles that a person assumes. Insofar as being a waiter or a parent are aspects of the self, such roles involve a diverse and complex set of expectations, modes of behavior, responsibilities, emotional responses, and so on, all of which mold the self and participate in its constitution. The modes of acquisition and integration of such roles are also for the most part culturally or socially prescribed. Whether one becomes a waiter by choice or by birth, the training one undergoes, the amount of time one spends in that role, and the importance one assigns to this role relative to other aspects of one's life are all matters of social practice: they are the ready-made strings attached to the role by means of which the individual who takes that role links it to the rest of his or her person.[16]

Similar observations apply to other aspects of the self. To have a character, to give another obvious example, is to acquire a set of intelligible behavioral dispositions, where intelligibility is a matter of shared existing patterns and understandings. The process of acquisition is one in which one's dispositions are systematically molded by and are responsive to preexisting norms and expectations. Even the body's participation in the self is shaped and mediated by the applicable units of meaning. Different body parts are irreducible sites of social meanings that are constantly activated in daily life. For example, we take it for granted that what is done to the body is done to us, but the ways we interpret what was done and experience it crucially depend on the significance with which different organs are vested: compare the touching of genitals to the touching of hand or hair.

The approach to the self along such lines raises acute problems regarding the self's unity and identity. *Unity* describes the relationship among the self's different aspects or components by virtue of which these are the aspects or components of a single self. *Identity* provides the criteria for drawing the boundary of the self and for determining whether any particular item belongs to it. Questions of unity and identity are relatively easy to resolve on the ordinary picture of human beings as intelligent animals. As in the case of human beings' less mentally advanced counterparts, such as cats and giraffes, the body, with its clearly demarcated boundaries and spatiotemporal continuity, provides both common sense and the philosophers who adhere to it with a relatively stable and nonproblematic reference point for such determinations. But when we think of the self as a field of phenomenology and meaning, the questions of unity and identity arise in full force. My aim here is not to present any of the numerous answers that have been attempted, but to mention the general shape of the answer I favor. Following Derek Parfit's seminal work on the self, my suggestion is that both the unity and the identity of the self ought to be seen in *scalar* rather than in binary terms.[17]

Parfit is concerned for the most part with the self's continuity over time. On his view, such continuity is a matter of degree, so that a former self can be more or less connected to a later one; there is no deep fact of the matter as to whether two temporally bound selves are stages of a single one or not. My aim here is not to repeat or examine Parfit's arguments, but only to point out their potential relevance to a more comprehensive picture of the self. The same scalar picture that applies to the self's temporal continuity would seem to apply to the issues of unity and (compositional) identity as well. On this view, the question whether something is a part or an aspect of me does not present at a deep level a genuine binary option, and it need not have a single correct answer. Parfit suggests that we can nonetheless preserve the binary logic that he associates with the concept of identity, by legislating a clear-cut if somewhat arbitrary criterion in light of which binary determinations concerning personal temporal identity can be made. Doing so, he maintains, is harmless as long as it is also held that, our ordinary beliefs to the contrary notwithstanding, "identity is not what matters." He advocates accordingly revising the prevailing attitude toward the self by diminishing the normative significance we attach to its identity. It seems to me that we can turn with equal plausibility in the opposite direction: retain the ordinary normative significance we attach to our compositional identity, while allowing that due to the self's scalarity, a looser concept of identity may be appropriate to it, one that accommodates a high degree of fluctuation and indeterminacy in its composition and boundaries, and allows for variation in the degree to which different items are said to participate in the self or be attached to it.

All I have done in these cursory remarks is to indicate a few scattered tips of some very large icebergs. Rudimentary and vague as this picture of the self must remain here, I hope that it has enough definition and sharpness for the purpose at hand: to clarify my claims concerning the constitutive role of responsibility and make good sense of them. The gist of the picture, as it bears on responsibility, can perhaps be best summarized as follows. In dealing with the self, law confronts a subject whose properties and composition are neither fixed nor stable, but are instead determined by and fluctuate in response to shifts in the social, including legal, practices in which it is implicated.

Self and Responsibility

We can now connect the dual conception of responsibility introduced in the first section with the contingent self described in the second. The discussion should clarify how the dialectic interplay between ascriptions of subject- and object-responsibility participates in drawing the boundaries of the self. I do so in two steps. I first use the conception of the self to clarify the relationship between subject- and object-responsibility I have outlined earlier. I then show how constitutive responsibility provides a more encompassing perspective than the free will paradigm and is better able to cope with the difficult instances of responsibility I listed at the outset. By the end of this section, constitutive responsibility should be focused enough to allow its application in part 2 to a number of more specific, and problematic, ascriptions of responsibility.

Earlier I claimed that a relationship of mutual implication exists between subject- and object-responsibility; consequently, every attribution of responsibility plays a role, direct or indirect, in drawing the self's boundary. A clearer understanding of this claim is now possible. Due to the self's plasticity, A in the formula "A is responsible for X" does not provide a fixed point of departure for an analysis in which A's relationship to an object or an event is ascertained. When I assume responsibility for breaking a vase, I perform an act of self-constitution: I implicitly identify with some aspect of myself by virtue of which I am the vase-breaker. The constitutive significance of this assumption of responsibility varies depending on whether I assume responsibility because I broke the vase deliberately, inadvertently, or because my child broke it. Each of these possibilities involves the acknowledgment and activation of a different *responsibility base*. In each case I identify with a different source of the object or event (the broken vase) as being the basis of *my* authorship of it and hence as a constitutive element of myself.

As we saw, interpreting the assumption of responsibility as an instance of self-constitution does not suggest that it is completely up to the individual what stance to take relative to a given event or object. It suggests even less a decision on the individual's part that consciously links her response to some overall conception of herself. The response to the broken vase is most likely to take the form of a certain experience, such as mortification or shame. Such an experience is probably the most compelling way of "existing"[18] my authorship of an event and of recognizing myself as implicated in the situation that precipitated it.

The role of such an experience in assigning responsibility must be qualified in two ways, however. First, the experience does not occur in a personal vacuum. One's prior history of reactions, identifications, and detachments is likely to manifest itself in the specific, momentary reaction. Indeed, if one's reaction departs too far from the pattern characteristic of one's self, the departure itself provides a reason for discounting the event as an aberration and hence for detaching one's self from it.[19] Accordingly, the experience I associate with the responsible stance is not a sufficient condition for responsibility.[20] Second, the experience I have described is not strictly necessary for responsibility either. The reasons are symmetrical to those in the first qualification. My momentary failure to react responsibly can be discounted as a lapse or aberration when judged by reference to past occasions, on which the responsibility base that seems to be presently at issue was in fact reflected in my responses.[21] In such a case, the experiential gap in my response can be bridged by extrapolating from the overall picture of my self.[22]

I have focused so far on the assumption of responsibility, and I must consider now the ascription of responsibility as well. The relationship between assuming and ascribing responsibility reflects the interplay between self-constitution and modularity. The assumption or denial of responsibility is an instance of self-constitution in which the self draws its own boundary by identifying with or distancing itself from a putative responsibility base. However, such assumption or denial of responsibility is shaped in anticipation of and in response to the ascription of responsibility by others. This reciprocal relationship between the assumption and the ascription of responsibility is mediated by the existence of widely shared social conventions and understandings regarding the attribution of responsibility, which are themselves articulations of a shared public conception of the self. The self's modularity—the correspondence between socially sanctioned conceptions of the self and particular selves in that society—secures a high degree of fit between assumption and ascription of responsibility. But the fit need not be perfect. The ascription of responsibility may sometimes reflect an aspect of a shared public conception of self while ignoring the particular subject's deviant self-constitution, or it can assume the individual's perspective despite its departure from the socially sanctioned self.

The conception of self I have sketched also allows us to understand the ambiguity of some responsibility-statements, such as "A is responsible for her negligent driving," which can be interpreted in both the subject- and the object-oriented way. How can the same item appear as both subject and object; how can it both be and not be part of A? The solution to this puzzle rests in the self's scalarity, and in the realization that the structure of responsibility simply mirrors the structure of the self. When we think of the self as scalar, we can imagine it as projecting out from a relatively cohesive core with gradually decreasing density. No sharp and durable boundaries exist between subject and object.

Some putative constituents can be located closer to the self's "core" and thus be more completely and permanently bound up with it. Others will occupy the "periphery," where they become increasingly detached from the self and correspondingly more objectlike. Inasmuch as the structure of responsibility reflects this picture of the self, the distinction between subject- and object-responsibility is also gradual and relative. Negligent driving may serve as a responsibility base—and thus as a constitutive element of the self—relative to an event outside the self's boundary (for example, the car accident). It can also be seen as an object external to the self for which authorship derives from constitutive elements of the self that lie closer to its core and that are, relative to the negligent driving, more firmly bound up with it.

It adds to the complexity of the situation that such scalarity occurs and fluctuates in time. The assumption of responsibility typically derives its content from the particular engagements of the moment in which it takes place. When I run over a pedestrian, this event occupies my attention as the overwhelming object of my responsibility, and my stance toward it is determined by my awareness of my negligent failure to notice the red light in front of me. On another occasion, however, when my spouse tells me that I have just run a red light, I probably focus on this episode of negligent driving as the object of my responsibility, and my stance toward it is determined by a surge in my awareness of my history of carelessness and inattention.

In summary, the scalarity of the self suggests that whether we think of a given item as a responsibility base or as an object of responsibility depends on whether the judgment of responsibility relates that item to more central or more peripheral elements in the self's geography. Moreover, as a result of the self's capacity to detach itself from any particular element of its constitution and temporarily objectify it, an item with which I identify at one time may on a different occasion appear as an external object whose authorship by me is at issue.

I have listed at the outset the main difficulties that a voluntarist conception of responsibility faces: determinism, character, and "devious" forms of responsibility such as strict, vicarious, and collective. I will now discuss the way a constitutive conception of responsibility responds to these difficulties. I start by demonstrating how the constitutive approach can accommodate character as a central factor in ascriptions of responsibility. I then show how the same account applies to voluntarist responsibility itself while avoiding the determinism trap. Finally, I extend the proposed account to what I view as the most inclusive category of responsibility: responsibility for self. As I demonstrate in greater detail later on, what I called the "devious" forms of responsibility are easily explained as instances of this inclusive category.

The philosopher who was probably most acutely aware of the tension between character and a voluntarist conception of responsibility is Aristotle.[23] His well-known solution is the idea of "responsibility for character." In Aristotle's view, people are responsible for their character traits because people form their own characters. Thus, even if my actions are determined by my character traits, I bear responsibility for these actions since I myself chose and developed those character traits. But the solution is not convincing. As a descriptive matter, few people seem to forge large regions of their character in a way that would satisfy even the most minimal conditions of voluntarist responsibility, that is, as a matter of deliberate and free choice. Moreover, important character traits are formed in early childhood, before the person has acquired the qualifications for bearing voluntarist responsibility. If responsibility for character is to be acquired later in life, however, and as a product of decisions made in adulthood, these decisions will have been shaped at least in part by those earlier character traits, thus losing in whole or in part their voluntarist basis. There is also a conceptual difficulty with Aristotle's attempt to incorporate character into a voluntarist perspective. It arises if we think of character, quite plausibly I believe, not just as an optional feature of responsibility, but as necessary to make choice intelligible and human action possible. If so, the choices that allegedly form one's character *must* presuppose some preexisting character traits, either innate or the products of early education. If, by contrast, the person were to forge his character freely, ex nihilo as it were, then on the present assumption the actions and processes of character formation would be unintelligible.[24]

We can diagnose the source of difficulty in Aristotle's position by applying to it the distinction between the two senses of responsibility. In my terminology, responsibility for character is construed by Aristotle as a matter of object-responsibility: I am the author of my character; hence, my character is seen as a product—an object for which I take responsibility. On this interpretation, my character is not who I am. I relate to it from some deeper or central point of view with which I identify, namely my will, whose activity progressively forges my character. However, the idea of responsibility for character contains an important insight that is better brought to light by transposing it from the voluntarist paradigm to the constitutive paradigm of responsibility. Seen from the latter perspective, responsibility for character should be interpreted as asserting not object-responsibility, but subject-responsibility. On this interpretation, responsibility for character is not derivative from voluntarist responsibility, but is coequal with it. I am responsible for my character in the sense that my character's emanations are manifestations of me. I am their author, and hence, bear object-responsibility for them, because I *am* my character. Responsibility for character does not rest on some "deeper" self that somehow creates a bond of responsibility between itself and the character. To the contrary, asserting subject-responsibility for character affirms my identity with my character as that by virtue of which I am the author of certain objects and events.

This reconstruction of the idea of responsibility for character can now be used as a model for recasting the meaning of voluntarist responsibility itself. Responsibility for voluntary actions can be also interpreted in both the object- and subject-regarding sense. I am object-responsible for the consequences of my actions, such as an injury that I have intentionally inflicted, simply because I identify with my actions. I take them to be the most important mode of my authorship of objects and events—hence my subject-responsibility for my actions. Suppose, however, that the action itself (the blow I inflicted) is the event whose authorship is in question. I am object-responsible for my actions because I am their author, and that because, being voluntary, my actions issue from and express my will. This last step amounts to our accepting subject-responsibility for the will. By accepting such responsibility for the will, we simply affirm the will as a constituent of the self, a constituent whose operations are the grounds for our object-responsibility for voluntary actions and their consequences.[25]

It is crucial to observe that on this construal, for the will to serve as a responsibility base it need not be free in the metaphysical, antideterminist sense. Construing responsibility for our volition as a matter of subject-responsibility is accordingly a variation on the compatibilist view, according to which responsibility for voluntary actions is consistent with determinism.[26] On my version of this general position, responsibility for voluntary actions simply marks them as constituents of the self. It expresses the self's identification with a certain range of events, roughly characterized by the absence of external coercive circumstances and by an *experience* of free choice. Such responsibility is accordingly validated not by the reality of the choice (and hence the refutation of determinism), but by the reality of one's identification with it. By "identification with our choices" I simply refer to the stance that we ordinarily take toward the products of what we designate as our "voluntary actions," namely that of being their "incontestable authors."

Transposing voluntarist responsibility into the constitutive framework also opens up the possibility that candidates other than the will may be eligible as potential constituents of the self and therefore as bases of responsibility. As we have seen, this possibility is fully realized in the case of character traits. We commonly hold a person responsible for an action precisely because it exhibits her character. We need not stop here, however. Will and character do not exhaust the composition of the self, and they are not the only possible bases of responsibility. Instead, by extrapolating from the discussion of will and character, we can now formulate the most inclusive category of responsibility within my proposed framework: responsibility for self.

The idea of responsibility for self has been introduced into contemporary philosophy by Charles Taylor in a form that places it squarely within the voluntarist paradigm. According to Taylor, we are responsible for ourselves (our selves) because of our alleged capacity, through "deep reflection," to examine, challenge, and ultimately transform even the deepest recesses of the self.[27] Taylor's account accordingly tries to ground responsibility for self in our freedom to choose who we are and thus to be our own creators.[28] We are the authors of our own selves, and hence, in my terminology, we are object-responsible for them. This conception of responsibility for self bears obvious resemblance to Aristotle's version of responsibility for character, and it raises similar difficulties. Object-responsibility for the self casts the self in the role of an object; but this deprives the relationship of responsibility of its subject. To assume the responsible stance toward my own self, I must detach myself from it in its entirety, objectify it, and consider myself as its author. I can succeed in transforming my self into an object of responsibility only at the cost of eliminating the "author" from the scene.

Of course, we can imagine the process of self-constitution described by Taylor in piecemeal rather than global terms. Although I cannot detach myself from my entire self, given the self's contingency I can do so with respect to each segment, one at a time. By identifying each time with one subset of its constituents while revising some others, the self can incrementally transform itself in its entirety; by the end of the day, *all* of the self's elements will be of its own creation or authorship. Incremental self-constitution makes sense, however, because it supposes that, at any given stage, a subject exists that is not undergoing a transformation at that stage. This implies that the entire series of transformations must be launched by a preexisting subject whose constitution—itself not of the self's making—must shape the incremental constitutive steps that follow. To be sure, this process may come full circle and eventually transform or replace the constituents of the initial, launching self. But no matter how large the circle, the nature of all the transformative steps will still depend on the constituents of the starting point.

As in the case of character, we can make better sense of the idea of responsibility for self by transposing it into the constitutive paradigm and by using the notion of subject-responsibility. Object-responsibility for any aspect of the self presupposes the prior notion of subject-responsibility for the self. To be the incremental author of my self and thus bear object-responsibility for it, I must be subject-responsible for the self to whom my authorship is ascribed.

The notion of subject-responsibility for the self is not only primary, but also in a certain sense trivial. The self, being simply who I am, is trivially the ground of my responsibility, namely that by virtue of which I am the author of anything at all. Responsibility for self in its subject-oriented meaning merely restates the basic view of the self as the ineliminable subject. This restatement is a useful one, however. It serves as a reminder of an important normative implication of ascertaining the boundaries of the self. Everything encompassed within the boundaries of my self serves as a possible ground of my authorship of objects and events and hence as the potential source of my object-responsibility. Conversely, the contours of the self can be determined from the kinds of object-responsibility that we bear. Focusing on specific responsibility bases and on the resulting types of object-responsibility consequently provides concrete guidance with regard to the boundaries of the self and the corresponding contours of responsibility. The preceding discussion of responsibility for volition and for character presents us with a model that can now be extended by considering other constitutive elements of the self and the forms of responsibility that they create.

2. Ascribing Constitutive Responsibility

The task of this part is to investigate ascriptions of responsibility as revealing different conceptions of the self's constitution and boundaries. Volition and character traits, discussed in the preceding section, belong to the mental aspect of the self. In this part, I consider three additional dimensions along which the self can be constituted: the spatial, the temporal, and the social.[29] The spatial dimension refers to our capacity and propensity to identify with certain physical objects, including prominently, but not exclusively, our bodies. The temporal dimension may be understood in a number of different ways, but I mean to emphasize the idea of biography: a diachronic string of events that are not just mine, but are irreducibly me. Finally, the social dimension refers to the way in which social roles serve as building blocks of one's self.

Under the constitutive view of responsibility, each of these dimensions behaves in a way similar to that of volition and character traits. Each can serve as a responsibility base on which subject-responsibility is predicated, thus giving rise to certain kinds of object-responsibility. Put another way, we can understand the ascription, or assumption, of

responsibility as an affirmation of our spatial, temporal, and social identity; conversely, we may construe denials of responsibility as an effort to
disown a particular segment of one of these dimensions. In this part, I
show how the constitution of the self along each of the three dimensions
organizes a different category of responsibility: the spatial dimension
refers to strict responsibility; the temporal dimension helps account for
responsibility for actual harm; the social dimension is the basis for
collective responsibility. In part 3, I illustrate the use of "distancing
devices" as defenses against the ascription of responsibility in all three
dimensions.

The Spatial Dimension:
Responsibility for Body and Other Objects

Responsibility for Body

At a party, A is engaged in a heated conversation. He does not notice
that a glass of wine has been placed next to him. Suddenly, upon hearing someone call his name, he inadvertently knocks over the glass.
Even if A could not have been any more careful than he was, it would
be perfectly natural for him, as well as expected of him, to feel some
embarrassment and to offer to wipe away the spilled wine. By his attitude and behavior, A takes responsibility for the spilling of the wine,
just as the others' expectation ascribes to him such responsibility. He
presents himself, and is perceived as, the author of this event. This
object-responsibility implies a certain subject-responsibility. The most
natural locus of responsibility in this case is A's body; A takes responsibility for his body, including its unintended, inadvertent gestures. By his
embarrassment and willingness to undo the damage, A meets the social
expectation that he own up to his bodily movements as to an aspect of
himself, and hence as a responsibility base that gives rise to object-
responsibility. By his responsible stance, A reclaims his body from the
status of a mere object that he most of the time successfully manipulates
and invests it instead with the significance and meaning of an aspect of
himself as subject.[30]

The law of torts often imposes what it terms *strict liability* in circumstances that resemble this incident. Such liability is commonly supported by various policy considerations. Beyond policy, however, on
my interpretation strict liability is also a move within the game of self-
constitution that incidents such as the wine-spilling inescapably excite.
I comment later on the peculiar nature of the legal intervention in this
context,[31] but I now extend the discussion to some other cases of strict

liability. The interpretation of the wine-spilling case as an attribution of subject-responsibility for the body will serve as our model as we examine these other cases.

Responsibility for Property

Tort liability often extends beyond the unintended consequences of one's bodily engagements. The famous tort cases involve escaping water[32] and straying animals,[33] but for our purposes a more mundane example will do. An unexpected wind blows a vase out of my living room, and the vase lands on a passerby's head. Even if I had not myself placed the vase or been otherwise involved, I would be mortified more intensely than, say, my neighbor, as we both helplessly watch the vase traveling toward the passerby, and I would be expected and inclined to rush to the rescue with greater urgency than any Samaritan who happened on the scene.

Notice first how closely the phenomenology here resembles the wine-spilling case: just as bodily involvement was the source of responsibility for the wine-spilling, ownership of the vase links me inexorably to the passerby's injury. Put differently, my reaction to the passerby's injury enacts an intensified momentary identification with my vase, which is very similar to the way A's response to the wine-spilling enacted his identification with his body. In the language of responsibility, this description marks me as subject-responsible for my vase and as object-responsible for the passerby's injury.[34]

This conclusion finds support in two different philosophical traditions. The first conceives property as an extension of the self.[35] The view of the self that I have presented, with its emphasis on the self's plasticity and indeterminacy, is plainly hospitable to that conception of property. The second is represented by a number of writers, mainly existentialists, who have emphasized important similarities between the self's relationship to the body and its relationship to other physical objects. Recall the depiction of my relationship to my pen in the discussion of *identification* in part 1: in the course of writing, my pen, like my hand, is fully absorbed in "me," as a transparent part of the integrated whole who is the writing subject.[36] Similarly, when I walk through a door—to use Merleau-Ponty's example—I do not stop to measure the distance above my head to verify that I can clear the door safely. This immediate, unreflective security in the spatial location of my body parts is an aspect of my identity with them. The same would be true, however, even if I wore my hat while walking through the door. The hat would not normally present me with a new problem of clearance. It would be fully and transparently absorbed into "my" space and would provide me with an immediate and integrated knowledge of my increased height.[37]

Vicarious Responsibility

Vicarious responsibility is a form of strict responsibility in which the responsibility base is another individual, such as one's child[38] or employee.[39] We can therefore analyze it on the model of responsibility for body, described in the present section, and also on the model of collective responsibility that I discuss later on. The phenomenological basis for vicarious responsibility is amenable to either interpretation.

Consider again the wine-spilling example. Our intuitive response would not change much if it were A's infant rather than A who inadvertently overturned the glass. A should still feel somewhat embarrassed and offer to wipe the spilled drink. The propriety of A's response would not depend, it seems, on the presence of any of the policy considerations that supposedly justify holding parents accountable for their children's mischief. A's response to the accident that his child wrought would be appropriate regardless of the child's exemplary education or A's lack of opportunity to restrain his child and avert the accident. Moreover, A's response is likely to have the phenomenological quality that I have associated with the responsible stance, and it will closely resemble his mortification stemming from his own spilling of the wine. These remarkable similarities between the two wine-spilling scenarios can be explained by the same underlying structure of responsibility. Just as the object-responsibility for the spilled drink in the one case implies subject-responsibility for one's body (and thus a view of oneself that incorporates the body and its unintended manifestations), so the same object-responsibility implies subject-responsibility for the child, and hence a conception of the self that extends to one's children.

Although it is easier to think of children as extensions of the self than to think so of employees, one can nonetheless imagine a plausible case involving employees. Consider a great artist who regards his apprentices as participants in what remains throughout *his* enterprise; or the devoted surgeon who treats the members of her trained team as extensions of her own well-honed skills. The painter takes full object-responsibility for the painting and the surgeon for the operation simply because each is subject-responsible for his or her team: their respective identities as master painter and expert surgeon are constituted in part by the roles played in their professional lives by other individuals. In many other less dramatic instances of employer-employee relationships, however, the collective responsibility account presented below is more suitable. No matter which version we choose, the result is an account of certain cases of vicarious responsibility in terms of an expanded conception of the self.

The Temporal Dimension:
Actual Results as Constitutive Events

A and A' shoot at V and V' respectively. A's bullet hits V and kills her; a sudden wind diverts the bullet of A' and saves V'. B and B' both knowingly drive cars with faulty brakes. A pedestrian crosses the street in front of B's car, the car does not stop, and the pedestrian is killed. No pedestrian tries to cross in front of B'. These are standard examples of one of the most perplexing issues in law and morality: A' will be held responsible only for attempted murder and in most jurisdictions will be punished less severely than A, and B' may not be held liable at all. But what accounts for this difference between the treatment of A and A' and between B and B'? The source of this familiar puzzle is the claim that the different results in the two pairs of cases are an external fortuity that should have nothing to do with our evaluation, and hence treatment, of the various protagonists.[40] Note that the attack on the distinction is double-barreled: it claims that the actual consequences are both fortuitous and external to the agents involved. I address these two points separately as I consider the puzzle.

The first point is that the diversion of A's bullet by the wind was totally fortuitous. This point draws its force from our widely shared yearning to purge our life—at least our moral life—of the incidents of luck. As some writers suggest, however, fortuity may not defeat even moral responsibility.[41] With the possible exception of the most ardent Kantians, everyone must admit the inevitability of at least one kind of fortuity: the circumstances of birth and upbringing that to a large extent determine who we are—what Professor Bernard Williams calls constitutive luck.[42] No moral judgments and no ascriptions of responsibility would be possible if they depended on first removing all the incidents of such fortuities. Therefore, the sheer luck that determined the different courses of events in my examples is not as alarming as it may seem at first. Once we realize that the role played by fortuity in all aspects of our lives, including the moral aspect, is inescapable, the issue is no longer whether luck can enter our moral judgments, but rather when it should and when it should not.

This conclusion leads to the second standard objection to the moral relevance of actual harm. The fortuity of the victims' death or survival is allegedly external to the respective actors; such a fortuity is far removed from the kind of constitutive luck, internal to the agent, that must bear on the agent's responsibility. In light of the conception of the self that I have outlined, however, this argument fares no better than the first. Its weakness results from an oversimplified conception of the self's boundaries. Once we recognize that drawing the self's boundaries is highly problematic, no simple interpretation of the internal-external metaphor is available or can be assumed. It becomes possible that the victim's death or survival is internal to the agent and constitutive of his self.

But how can the victim's death or survival affect the constitution of the actor's self? Here, too, the distinction between subject- and object-responsibility proves helpful. Consider A shooting at V. When we raise the question of A's responsibility for V's death, we think in terms of object-responsibility: V's death is the event whose authorship by A is asserted. In this understanding, the victim's death is clearly posited as an event external to A, and our attention is drawn to certain aspects of A himself that make him responsible for V's death, primarily A's intentional act of shooting at V. Since these aspects are equally revealed in the case of the intended victim's miraculous survival, insisting on actual fatality as a distinguishing factor appears arbitrary.

This picture changes radically, however, when we realize that the statement, "A is responsible for V's death" can be used to ascribe subject-responsibility instead of object-responsibility. The entire episode of killing V (which involves, of course, the fact of V's death) can be incorporated in our conception of A's self, and serve as a responsibility base in some other attribution of object-responsibility to A. To see this more vividly, imagine V's widower blaming A for the widower's devastation and agony: "You are responsible for all this suffering." If A were foolhardy enough to inquire why, a natural answer would be, "Because you are responsible for my wife's death." The initial accusation here is a matter of object-responsibility. The second statement, made in support of this accusation, is about subject-responsibility; it identifies "killing V" as the relevant aspect of A, by virtue of which the widower's ensuing misery can be rightfully placed at his doorstep.

This attribution of subject-responsibility to A correctly captures the phenomenological quality of the situation. In the imaginary confrontation with the widower, "having killed V" is likely to be the most prominent and relevant element in A's biography. This entire event (and not just some mental part of it, such as A's intention to kill V) gives rise to A's shame and remorse when A confronts the widower's grief. Support for the subject-oriented interpretation of A's responsibility can be found also in the ease with which V's widower could have explained his grievance against A in an alternative form. Instead of saying, "You are [subject-]responsible for my wife's death, and that is why you are [object-]responsible for my misery," the widower could have simply retorted: "You are my wife's killer!" My point here is that this statement can be taken quite literally as an attribution of a certain identity or characteristic to A—that of being a killer. This linguistic form is not at all surprising. Being a killer is in fact a recognizable social role, and as such it is a natural candidate for participation in the self's constitution. Because one's victim must actually die for one to be a killer, the fortuity of whether this happens becomes a piece of *constitutive* luck.

It should now be clear how this second construal of the ascription of responsibility to A for killing V successfully distinguishes this case from the case of A'. The present construal converts V's death from a fact that is external to A to one that is internal. V's death or survival can play a legitimate role in various judgments of A in ways that a purely external fact cannot.

The present account not only helps make sense of practices such as criminal punishment that differentiate between A and A', but also throws light on our hopelessly conflicting intuitions on the matter. Both the view that V's death or survival is an external fortuity that should have no direct bearing on our assessment or treatment of A and the opposite intuition that the victim's actual fate heavily influences our attitude toward A make a strong claim on our allegiance. This ambivalence, however, is not just a matter of confusion or indecision. The conflict reflects the corresponding viability of the two pictures of the subject of responsibility that these intuitions respectively assume. Seen in one context and at a particular moment, V's death can be perceived as an external event that A brought about; in a different context and time, that same event is seen as part of A's biography, an ineluctable fact within A's boundaries that constitutes his identity as a murderer.

The Social Dimension: Collective Responsibility and Social Role

Unlike individual responsibility, collective responsibility draws immediate attention to the problematic nature of its subject. Accustomed to an individualistic moral ontology, we normally talk about individual responsibility as responsibility simpliciter and add the explicit designation of a subject only when we speak of "collective" responsibility.

The dispute over the proper subject of collective responsibility has traditionally been between two opposing approaches. One, a nonreductionist or holistic approach, perceives collectivities as irreducible ethical entities capable of "authoring" objects and events the way individuals do; they are therefore the primary bearers of direct responsibility for those objects and events.[43] The second, reductionist approach views collective responsibility as a species of vicarious responsibility. The only real entities in this view are individuals: collective actions and their consequences are always fully reducible and in principle traceable to those of particular individuals. By ascribing responsibility to a collectivity, we implicitly hold some individuals responsible for the actions of others.[44]

The difficulties with both these accounts are well known. The nonreductionist view cannot adequately explain the repercussions on the collective entity's individual members that often result from holding the collectivity responsible.[45] The reductionist account avoids this difficulty by explaining collective responsibility in individualistic terms. Its model of vicarious responsibility, however, severs the direct relationship between the subject and the object of responsibility and renders highly problematic both the grounds for ascribing responsibility to a particular individual and the meaning of the responsibility so ascribed.[46]

My purpose is not to critique these two traditional approaches to collective responsibility. Instead, I present another account of collective responsibility, according to which the subjects of collective responsibility are individuals whose responsibility, however, is primary and direct rather than secondary or vicarious. The key is to recognize that one's social identity is a genuine constituent of the self[47] that can serve as an individual responsibility-base for the group's collective endeavors.

An athletic team provides a standard illustration that will serve my approach as well. Every player on a baseball team is likely to use the first-person plural pronoun in speaking about the team's victories or defeats, even if he did not participate in the game in which the victory or the defeat took place. By doing so, the player fully identifies with his role as member of the team. Consequently, he feels pride or shame with regard to the actions of other players as if these actions were his own. By talking about the victory as "our" victory, the player experiences and enacts what may be called the "collective moment": he subscribes as an author to an event whose intelligibility as a game or a victory or a defeat depends on the existence of a number of similarly situated individuals, team members, who interpret the consequences of other individuals' actions as their own. In my terminology, the player thereby assumes subject-responsibility for his role that serves as the basis for ascribing to him object-responsibility for the relevant events.

By generalizing this example, we can extend the analysis to more complicated cases, such as that of being an American.[48] To be an American is to espouse and enact a self that defines itself, in part, by implicit reference to multitudes of other individuals, their language, practices, expectations, history, and culture. Being an American is accordingly something for which one bears subject-responsibility. To assume subject-responsibility for being an American is simply to acknowledge one's American identity as a constitutive element of oneself. Every ascription of subject-responsibility, however, implies some object-responsibility as well. Subject-responsibility for being an American implies object-responsibility for certain objects and events. What are they?

The answer is much more complicated than it is in the case of the baseball player, because the collective identity of an American is more complex: its ingredients are less clearly defined, and it mediates a collectivity composed of a vast number of individuals. We should therefore expect neither uniformity nor clarity concerning the scope of responsibility involved. Whatever the variability and ambiguity, however, there must be some objects and events—the space shuttle and the Vietnam War are perhaps good examples—that are so prominently linked to American identity that virtually every American sees herself as the author of at least some of them and feels pride or shame with regard to them. Denying responsibility for all such objects and events is tantamount to repudiating one's American identity altogether.[49]

Collective responsibility for certain objects and events does not presuppose the individual's positive evaluation of them. One bears collective responsibility even with respect to objects and events toward which one has a negative attitude and despite one's efforts to prevent them. Indeed, such efforts may be motivated precisely by an individual's awareness of the responsibility he or she will ineluctably bear if the object or event materializes. In this vein, Americans' belief that they bear special responsibility for the Vietnam War may explain why it was natural that many Americans should be more actively opposed to the war than, say, the English.[50]

The law, especially criminal law, professes an individualistic ethic that allegedly precludes any form of collective responsibility.[51] But the law's practices belie this profession. Although little uniformity exists in this area, "The notion that one is responsible for the substantive crimes of fellow conspirators in furtherance of the conspiracy has often been expressed in the cases."[52] Similarly, "the established rule" of accomplice liability is that it "extends to acts of the principal in the first degree which were a 'natural and probable consequence' of the criminal scheme the accomplice encouraged or aided."[53] According to both doctrines, a defendant can be held liable for criminal offenses in which he did not actively participate. Still, despite persistent criticism,[54] the doctrines of conspiracy and accomplice liability (and related ones, such as the felony murder rule) die hard; their survival attests to their intuitive grip. It is worth trying to articulate the underlying intuition even if we do not ultimately find it a sound basis for criminal liability.

Consider Rudolph Kessler, who waited in the escape car outside a tavern while his two unarmed companions entered the building to commit burglary. His companions were surprised by the owner inside the tavern, and one of them shot and wounded the owner with a gun taken during the burglary.[55] Can Kessler be convicted of both burglary and attempted murder?

I now add a further, imaginary segment of the story. The same evening, after the burglary but before his apprehension, Kessler meets his girlfriend. He excitedly recounts to her the day's adventures, which culminate with the owner's unexpected intervention: "Everything seemed lost at that point; but then we got this guy's gun and we hit him pretty hard. We nearly killed him. Then we ran away." What additional light does this fictitious narrative cast on Kessler's responsibility? The key is that it is altogether natural for Kessler to use the first-person plural pronoun in describing the situation. Kessler's pride in what he considers the group's successful operation and his adoption or ratification of the various actions as his own are constitutive moves that warrant his usage. By adopting the responsible stance toward the offenses committed, Kessler occupies the collective moment relative to the other accomplices. When the law holds Kessler liable for the shooting, it takes him at his own word: the word "we" that we can imagine him uttering proudly to his girlfriend. The law thereby confirms the social understandings that license Kessler's first-person plural recounting of the story. This conclusion seems to capture the intuitive underpinnings of the court's decision and the doctrine it exemplifies.[56]

Our analysis cannot stop here, however. The ascription of legal responsibility can be seen as at least partly self-defeating, in that it motivates a redrawing of the self's boundary in a way that eliminates or attenuates the basis of the ascription. To see this, we must modify the previous scenario. Kessler no longer makes it safely to his evening date. Instead, he and his friends are intercepted and arrested at the scene of the crime. The first person to whom Kessler tells his story is the police officer, who has just read to him his Miranda warnings. We can expect a very different version than before. With the prospect of an extended jail sentence looming ominously before him, Kessler will attempt to flee responsibility altogether. He will at once abandon the collective standpoint and withdraw from his role by proclaiming defensively: "But *I* did not shoot the owner!" I comment in part 4 more generally on this possible effect of the legal context on Kessler's reaction. Here I merely point out how the inner withdrawal and the flight from responsibility in the face of its legal consequences complicate the account I have offered.

3. Denying Constitutive Responsibility

The binary structure of responsibility that I have described implies a correspondingly binary structure of defenses against it: defenses can seek to deny either subject- or object-responsibility. For example, when charged with responsibility for the broken window allegedly smashed by a ball thrown by his daughter, A's statement, "I am not responsible for the broken window" may mean, "It was not my daughter who threw the ball." This assertion denies A's object-responsibility for the damage by severing the alleged link between the responsibility base (the daughter) and the event (breaking the window). At the same time, it implicitly concedes, or at any rate does not challenge, A's subject-responsibility for his daughter's conduct. Alternatively, A's denial of responsibility may mean: "My daughter is the one who should pay for the window; she is now an adult, and I am no longer responsible for her." Here A denies his subject-responsibility by attempting to sever the link between the putative responsibility base (his daughter) and himself.

This example is a simple one because in it the separation between the two kinds of responsibility is sharp and the distinction between their respective denials is therefore clear. In other cases, the situation is murkier: the same denial of responsibility can be interpreted as addressing either object- or subject-responsibility. The former interpretation is more common, but it often leads to unresolved difficulties. By emphasizing the latter interpretation, we can avoid some of these problems. The previous example suggests the general structure of defenses as I interpret them: they deny a particular assignment of object-responsibility by disavowing its putative responsibility-base. Defenses can be seen as *distancing devices*—refusals to identify with some potential constituents and grounds for placing those putative constituents outside the self's boundary. Inclusion and exclusion are not, however, the only possibilities in this context. Given the self's scalarity, we can think of defenses in continuous and relative terms: they can consist in decreasing the degree of identification with a particular element without completely eradicating it, which would attenuate but not completely avoid responsibility.

As with the ascription of responsibility, its denial can take place along the different "dimensions" of the self. Accordingly, my discussion of defenses follows the same division as the preceding discussion of responsibility ascriptions.

Involuntariness, Provocation, and Bodily Distance

Although the body is commonly a basis of responsibility, we can sometimes successfully distance ourselves from aspects of our bodily existence and deny the responsibility we would otherwise bear. The device most commonly used is the idea of disease. *Regina v. Charlson*[57] provides a vivid illustration.

The defendant hit his ten-year-old son over the head and threw him out of the window.[58] The cause of this otherwise inexplicable behavior,

Charlson maintained, was a brain tumor. Charlson's defense, involuntariness,[59] is often interpreted as amounting to a total denial of responsibility equivalent to the statement: "I didn't really do it." This construal can be read with two different intonations. The more common emphasizes the word "do." On this reading, Charlson denies object-responsibility for the child's injury by attempting to refute his authorship of it. This attempt raises formidable difficulties. It invokes action-theoretical issues regarding the necessary constituents and the proper analysis of human action.[60] It also raises the free will conundrum by calling for an investigation of the counterfactual question whether Charlson could have behaved otherwise.

It is possible, however, to read Charlson's "I didn't do it" with an intonation that stresses the "I," as in, "It was not really *me* who brought about the injury, it was the tumor." This defense consists of two steps. The first seeks to lodge the causal origins of the child's injury in the tumor. The second step requires us to view the tumor as an external and intrusive agency rather than as part of Charlson himself. Charlson is not subject-responsible for his tumor—it is simply not part of him.

What makes this reading of Charlson's defense especially compelling is its graphic imagery. The tumor presents a clearly demarcated, detachable, and hostile object in Charlson's body. It is easy to think of the causal chain traced back to the tumor as sidestepping Charlson himself. To appreciate the force of this metaphor, consider some variations. Assume that the effect of the tumor in Charlson's brain was to create what legal doctrine calls "an irresistible impulse." Charlson's defense of involuntariness would probably still lead to an acquittal.[61] Consider now the case of Karlson, who is charged with rape. Suppose that Karlson raises a defense of involuntariness and maintains that he was overcome with such uncontrollable lust that he, like Charlson, acted out of an irresistible impulse. Why does Charlson's claim of involuntariness seem plausible whereas Karlson's seems frivolous and perverse?

It is tempting to solve the puzzle and dismiss this example by distinguishing it from Charlson's case on evidentiary grounds: we simply do not believe that Karlson could not have controlled his sexual impulse, no matter how powerful it may have been, and we are unpersuaded by the alleged causal connection between the sexual urge and Karlson's violent behavior. But this attempt to convert the issue into an empirical matter is deceptive. The notion of irresistible impulse is obscure, and in trying to clarify it, we easily experience the vertigo often felt in the vicinity of the free will–determinism dispute. If we are nonetheless willing to accept the involuntariness hypothesis in the Charlson case, it would seem dogmatic to disallow a jury to entertain "a reasonable doubt" under some circumstances (no matter how extreme) concerning the voluntariness of the rape. Our adamant refusal to allow for such a possibility seems to rest on a deeper foundation than a mere difference in credibility between the two claims.

Such a foundation can be provided by the radical difference in the relationship between the respective sources of the alleged involuntariness and the self. Unlike a brain tumor, the sexual drive is commonly perceived as an important constituent in our picture of the self. Its hormonal or other physiological underpinnings, far from undermining this perception, ground it in a widely shared image of the "lived body," itself an indispensable element in our prevailing self-understanding.[62]

The contrast between Charlson and Karlson, however, must be seen against the background of the self's plasticity and contingency. Although it takes some effort, we can imagine a self for whom the sexual drive is an intrusive external force no different in kind from the pernicious emanations of a brain tumor. The effort needed to imagine such a self, however, is evidence that our culture (by which I mean at least contemporary Western culture) does not encourage the enactment of such a self. Hence the relative ease with which Karlson would be held responsible: "I am not responsible for my sexual drive" is simply not a viable argument in our culture. One of the ways in which this culture helps constitute a self that inexorably integrates the sexual drive but not a brain tumor is by ascribing responsibility for the former while withholding responsibility for the latter.

Even within our culture, the contrast between the brain tumor's relationship to the self and that of the sexual glands, even though a sharp one, is not absolute. This contrast is mitigated by the ambivalence regarding the relationship of eros to self that characterizes the history of sexuality in Western culture. I do not address this ambivalence here, but one current manifestation of it bears directly on our discussion of the Karlson hypothetical and somewhat qualifies our conclusions: the attitudes and practices pertaining to child molesters. Although they would not have a valid legal defense if prosecuted, these offenders are quite routinely permitted to undergo a voluntary rehabilitative procedure in lieu of criminal prosecution.[63] Much like Charlson's tumor, their sexual drive is seen as an aberration or even as a disease. It is perceived (although with some ambiguity and uncertainty) as an alien presence that should be removed and discarded rather than affirmed as an aspect of the self.

Similar issues of self-constitution come to the fore even more explicitly in the case of the partial defense of provocation. Consider *Bedder v. Director of Public Prosecutions*.[64] Accused of murder, Bedder, who was sexually impotent, claimed that his victim—a prostitute with whom he had attempted in vain to have sexual intercourse—had provoked him

by jeering at him and by hitting and kicking him. The issue raised by
Bedder's defense was whether the "reasonable person" standard, used to
determine whether sufficient provocation existed to reduce the charge
from murder to manslaughter, should include the physical peculiarities
of the accused, in this case, Bedder's impotence.

To sustain a defense of provocation, the defendant must satisfy two
tests: a subjective one, that the defendant acted "under the influence
of extreme mental or emotional disturbance,"[65] and an objective one,
that a reasonable person would be similarly provoked in the same circumstances. The free will paradigm easily explains the subjective standard: heat of passion detracts from rational self-control and therefore
diminishes responsibility. This account, however, leaves no room for
the objective component in provocation. If what we measure when we
assess the severity of the killing is the degree of composure and self-
control, the causes of the reduced self-control should be irrelevant to our
judgment.

The commentary to the Model Penal Code's manslaughter provision
suggests a different account. The "essential rationale for the law of provocation" is supplied by the observation that "some instances of intentional homicide may be as much attributable to the extraordinary nature
of the situation as to the moral depravity of the actor."[66] By counter-
factually casting the morally wholesome reasonable person in the defendant's circumstances, we can assess the degree to which the killing was
the product of the defendant's moral depravity. For this test to perform
its assigned task, however, we must assume that the "circumstances" or
the "situation" in which the killing took place and the defendant's
"moral depravity" are mutually exclusive and jointly exhaustive factors.
Only with this premise can placing the reasonable person in the defendant's "situation" reveal the role that the defendant's "moral depravity"
must have played in the homicide.

As *Bedder* vividly reminds us, however, the external circumstances
of the action together with the person's traits and characteristics in
which his moral depravity resides do not exhaust the causal factors that
might lead to an action. Instead, the idea that there are morally reprehensible characteristics of the person implies a third group of factors,
namely morally indifferent personal characteristics that are not the
seat of moral depravity. As a result, the counterfactual thought experiment required by the reasonable person standard is ill suited for the task
of separating out and assessing the factors that define the defendant's
"moral depravity."

The discovery that the reasonable person standard malfunctions is
not new. It baffled the Royal Commission on Capital Punishment, which
ultimately adopted the test despite misgivings about its fairness.[67] A

leading commentator described it as "paradoxical."[68] Professor George
Fletcher maintains that "[t]he basic moral question in the law of homicide is distinguishing between those impulses to kill as to which we as a
society demand self-control, and those as to which we relax our inhibitions." Resort to the reasonable person standard, he argues, is an attempt
by courts and commentators "to evade this moral issue," an attempt
symptomatic of "the general decline of moral thinking in the analysis of
liability for homicide."

Professor Fletcher links his construal of the role played by the reasonable person standard in Anglo-American jurisprudence to the latter's

> unresolved anxiety about sociological and psychological determin-
> ism that leads many people to believe ... [that] [i]f we know every-
> thing about the defendant, we will invariably excuse him.... If
> the defendant's head injury or impotence is considered in assessing
> the likely behavior of a reasonable person, then why not consider
> his irascibility, greed, jealousy or even his wickedness as a person?

Professor Fletcher has no difficulty sorting out the various factors
involved:

> The obvious difference between the irascible man and the impotent
> man is that, absent a documentable psychological impediment, we
> properly expect people to control their anger as we expect them to
> control greed and jealousy. Therefore persons who are irascible,
> greedy or given to jealousy hardly warrant preferential treatment in
> the assessment of their conduct. These are character traits for which
> people are properly held accountable, not excused. Yet no one is to
> be blamed for impotence, and therefore it is a feature of the defen-
> dant that must be considered in assessing whether he was ade-
> quately provoked by taunting or teasing related to his impotence.[69]

The "deterministic anxiety" that Fletcher mentions is serious, however,
and it does tend to shake one's confidence in the sharp division between
the two sets of factors drawn in the quoted paragraph. Indeed, as soon
as we depart from the view that self-control is the only measure of culpability, we are hard-pressed to explain why being cursed with excessive
jealousy, for example, is morally worse than being afflicted with impotence when the two misfortunes both result in homicide.

This difficulty helps explain the temptation to evade the moral issues,
framed in the idiom of free will, in this area. But we are still left with
the puzzle of what exactly this evasion accomplishes. After all, even the
most severe critics of the reasonable person standard do not maintain
that its use is the equivalent of throwing dice or measuring the length of
the judge's foot. If the reasonable person standard does not successfully

assess the defendant's moral turpitude, what does it measure instead? Although the counterfactual thought experiment mandated by the reasonable person standard does not help us draw the "internal" line between the person's morally relevant and morally indifferent characteristics, it does help us gauge the self's outer perimeter by drawing the line between the self's constituents (whether or not of moral significance) and elements that are external to the self and fall outside its boundary.

We can also now see why this inquiry is not just a hollow exercise (as throwing dice would be) even as it evades the *moral* questions. In the present account, the reasonable person standard helps us assess *responsibility*. Factors contributing to the homicide that are external to the defendant—circumstances that surround him rather than traits that constitute him—mitigate the defendant's responsibility for the killing. If the factor under consideration is determined to be outside the boundaries of the self, the "moral" question, as understood by critics such as Fletcher, may indeed be avoided: the defendant's responsibility should be reduced by the fraction that can be attributed to the external source. We then need not confront the difficulty of identifying morally reprehensible traits with which a person may be helplessly and inescapably burdened.

This account brings into sharper focus both the decision in *Bedder* and the criticism of it. When we transpose *Bedder* from the voluntarist paradigm into the self-constitution paradigm, we can clearly identify the main issue it raises: the relation of impotence to the self. To benefit from the defense of provocation, Bedder must distance himself from his impotence and portray it as an affliction that impinges on him rather than as a trait of himself. Similarly, by rejecting this defense, the House of Lords placed impotence on the self's side of the divide between Bedder and his "situation."

Seen in this light, at issue in *Bedder* was a choice between two characterizations of Bedder's affliction: *disease* and *handicap*.[70] The relevant difference between the two concepts can be best described in terms of *coping*.[71] A disease is something with which one copes. Consequently, a disease is vanquished by being cured, that is, removed or extinguished. A handicap, in contrast, is a condition or factor in terms of which or by means of which one copes. Unlike a disease, a handicap is vanquished by being integrated with a person's life and absorbed into the background of attributes that shape and condition a particular form of life. We need not delve further into the phenomenology of disability; for our purposes, the difference between a disease and a handicap can be indicated (and perhaps somewhat exaggerated) by pointing out that a wheelchair may provide the paraplegic with a form of mobility that is similar in principle to walking for other people. For the permanently disabled person, the wheelchair is absorbed into the background of capabilities that are simply taken for granted. By means of these capabilities, one copes with whatever obstacles one encounters as one moves along. In contrast, the crutch is a constant impediment to the mobility of a broken-legged person; it is one of the obstacles to which he must pay careful attention and against which he must constantly cope until his leg heals.

We can now appreciate both the plausibility and the pertinence of the Lords' determination in *Bedder* that, in applying the objective test of provocation, impotence should not be ascribed to the reasonable person. The decision implicitly classifies impotence as a handicap rather than a disease. As an enduring, pervasive, and possibly incurable condition, impotence may well qualify for that classification. Characterizing impotence in this way also has important implications for the question of responsibility: if impotence is a constituent of Bedder's identity, he is subject-responsible for it and hence is object-responsible for its external manifestations. Accordingly, when Bedder cites the role that impotence played in the killing, he merely identifies another responsibility base rather than lodging part of the responsibility for the killing in an external source as he hopes to do.

To say that the Lords' approach to Bedder's impotence is both plausible and pertinent, however, is not to stem the dissatisfaction with their decision. After all, the critics' main complaint is that the decision fails to come to grips with the distinctively *moral* aspects of the situation. This may be true. Still, we now have a better understanding of the Lords' evasive move. As we have observed, given the dominance of the free will paradigm in our moral thinking, an assessment of blameworthiness would have to be conducted exclusively in terms of freedom and self-control. A consistent application of these ideas to the present case would not have permitted a different interpretation of the objective test and of its protagonist, the reasonable person, but would rather require that the objective test be eliminated altogether.

Duress and Temporal Distance

My next example involves the temporal dimension, specifically the train of constitutive events that make up one's biography. The defense of duress performs a role in the temporal dimension that is similar to the role that the defense of involuntariness performs in the bodily dimension. First, however, I expose difficulties with the conventional view of duress that my alternative account can avoid.

Unlike the defense of involuntariness, the defense of duress does not suggest a total lack of choice. Instead, the defendant points to a severe limitation of choice caused by a serious threat made against him. His capacity to choose the preferred path has been overwhelmed, the defendant maintains, by dire circumstances. The source of this plea's exculpatory force is open to two interpretations. One interpretation is that the defendant does not deny responsibility for the offense, but appeals to our compassion aroused by his predicament. The second is that duress resembles involuntariness in its attempt to disconnect the offender from the offense: the effacement of choice due to the dire circumstances is sufficiently dramatic, the argument goes, to warrant exculpation.[72]

Both of these construals provide plausible accounts of the defense of duress. Yet both are vulnerable to the same objection. Think of D, a hopelessly unemployed teenager, uneducated, raised in a broken home, whose only viable escape from a bleak future of destitution is membership in the neighborhood gang. Is his criminal activity any less compelled than, for example, the false medical certificate provided by Dr. Toscano under extortion in *State v. Toscano*?[73] If extortion provides Dr. Toscano with a defense of duress, should not a similar defense be supported by D's extreme deprivation?[74]

The two interpretations of duress mentioned above do not provide a compelling explanation for the law's negative answer to these questions. If compassion rather than sanction is the proper response to Dr. Toscano's predicament, a similar attitude seems all the more called for in D's case. Insofar as Toscano's choice was overwhelmed by the dire circumstances created by the threats, D's choice is similarly affected; he also faces a radically impoverished choice-set, and he tries to divert the blame for the crime from himself to his extreme life-situation. Yet Toscano has a valid defense of duress, whereas D (or D's lawyer) would probably not even consider raising one. Of course, allowing people in D's situation to escape liability may impair law enforcement to an extent that excusing someone like Toscano does not, but this result only bolsters the arguments of critics who attack the integrity of the duress defense. The limited reach of the defense, they maintain, cannot be justified on principled grounds, but only by considerations that are at best prudential and at worst cynical.[75]

Here again, my aim is not to assess the competing arguments, but rather to examine what new light my approach can throw on the issues. My suggestion is to consider duress as concerned with subject-responsibility. By denying responsibility for the fraudulent certificate he provided, Toscano may be interpreted as trying to repudiate or disown the entire episode that led to the criminal event. This is the temporal analogue to Charlson's attempt to detach himself from the physiological source—the brain tumor—of his criminal behavior. In somewhat similar fashion, Toscano attempts to bracket the extortion as a detachable temporal segment that should not be counted as part of his biography. His grounds for doing so are clear, although not necessarily compelling. The circumstances that gave rise to the defense were so dramatic, overpowering, and incongruous with the rest of his life that they render the entire episode a disruption rather than a manifestation of his true identity.

This interpretation resonates with some familiar intuitions. We sometimes express a similar sentiment when, baffled by our own unexpected response to some highly unusual circumstances, we exclaim: "That wasn't really me!" This exclamation does not necessarily establish the discontinuity between the unexpected behavior and the self. It may equally betray a failure in self-knowledge; the unexpected conduct may turn out to be highly revealing about some hidden or novel aspect of the self. However, the conception of the self that I espouse is hospitable to the other possibility as well. Under certain conditions, the individual's repudiation of a particular episode may be genuine, and he may be successful in disassociating himself from it.

It is now easy to see why the defense of duress may succeed in Toscano's situation but can hardly apply in the gloomier case of D. Unlike Toscano, who wants to deny subject-responsibility for a single, temporally localized occurrence that can plausibly be seen as tangential to his life, D must repudiate poverty and desperate aimlessness that define every chapter of his life. He cannot refuse to take responsibility for them (by fending off his object-responsibility for their criminal consequences) without thereby disowning lasting and pervasive parts of the self that he consistently inhabits and enacts.

I have two concluding observations. First, I have not considered whether a self that recoils from its social and economic circumstances and consistently treats them as external encumbrances is possible. My analysis implies only that such a conception of the self is not a common one and that, at least in the ordinary case, applying duress to D requires that he disown a greater part of his life and his identity than he should be expected to do. Second, the refusal to treat D's predicament as a case of duress is undeniably harsh. My account of this harsh result, however, reminds us of one of the deeper horrors of social and economic deprivation: that such deprivation is not just a highly undesirable situation for people to be in, but it also participates, as other social circumstances do, in the very constitution of their selves.

Official Duty and Role Distance

Almost everyone would agree that an executioner (to take a dramatic example of official duty) is not guilty of murder. The conventional account of this conclusion, however, is not altogether satisfactory. According to this account, the executioner is protected against charges of murder by a defense of *justification*. His defense is thus no different in principle from that of self-defense; in both cases, what would otherwise be criminal behavior is justified because, under the circumstances, it comports with overriding social norms.[76] This explanation seems unexceptionable as far as it goes, but it does not go far enough. Classifying official duty as a case of justification fails to capture an important difference between the executioner and the killer in self-defense.

By interposing a justification defense, the self-defender concedes his responsibility for the killing. It is precisely because of this responsibility that the self-defender must demonstrate that the killing was justified. This position is not the only one open to the executioner, however. Rather than claiming to be a justified killer, he may deny being a killer altogether. He may attempt to avoid any personal responsibility for the killing. The idea of social role serves as his vehicle toward this goal.

The present point can be understood as the reverse of my account of collective responsibility.[77] I have described how by assuming a role and identifying with it I can become subject-responsible for it and through it become object-responsible for other people's actions and their consequences. The case of official duty marks the opposite movement: rather than being a responsibility base, the social role is now used as a buffer against responsibility.

This movement is well captured by the concept of *role distance* that we encountered earlier:[78] the self can assume a detached and instrumental attitude toward a particular role and can perform it in an alienated fashion. Central to the interpretation of the official-duty defense is the experience of impersonality that we commonly associate with carrying out such a duty. The official's comportment and attitude toward the objects of her duty can be colloquially transcribed as saying: "I have nothing personal against you." This message is reinforced by the formal insignia of the official role, such as the uniform or the judicial robe. These trappings convey the message of impersonality not only to the objects of the official role, but also to its subjects.

My interpretation of the executioner's defense as a denial of subject-responsibility is corroborated by the following hypothetical. Suppose that the executioner fails to show up for the execution because of a bout of moral qualms or a common cold. The execution is postponed, but on the following night the executioner, now fully recovered, breaks into jail and kills the convict. The executioner is clearly guilty of murder, and not merely of a disciplinary offense of spoiling the official ceremony and disrupting orderly procedures. Viewing official duty as a justification does not fully account for this dramatic shift in the legal understanding of the executioner's action. The belated killing of the prisoner is no less justified than his scheduled execution would have been the day before. The killing, however, has to be carried out by an official and in her capacity as such.

To be sure, not all public officials maintain role distance in the ways that I have intimated. But the law is unfazed by such variation. By recognizing official duty as barring responsibility, the law codifies a specific conception of the self, regardless of whether this conception applies in each particular case. In doing so, the law is offering its servants a version of the Faustian bargain. This version may not seem more attractive or wholesome than the original one, but it may nonetheless be the lesser of inevitable evils. Detachment may be the self's preferred strategy for dealing with "dirty hands" types of situations, in which social norms call for the performance of horrifying or otherwise repugnant tasks.[79]

4. Dilemmas of Legal Responsibility

I have thus far treated law as part of the larger social arena in which the self's boundaries are negotiated. I conclude by speculating about how some distinctive features of the legal context might bear on the relationship between self and responsibility that I have depicted and how they create a serious dilemma, perhaps even a paradox, of legal responsibility.

We may begin by observing that we commonly expect the law to comport with our ordinary notions of responsibility. The law is expected to reinforce people's sense of responsibility by making an explicit public pronouncement on specific instances of responsibility and by dramatizing the significance of responsibility through severe sanctions. The legal recognition of my authorship of a certain object or event is thus supposed to strengthen my identification with the appropriate responsibility base.

Legal support for ordinary notions of responsibility may backfire, however. While trying to reinforce our sense of responsibility, the law may in fact weaken it. The drastic consequences commonly attached to legal responsibility provide a potent incentive to recoil from responsibility. We have already seen that one of the strategies for avoiding responsibility—and sometimes the only viable one—is to deny subject-responsibility by repudiating that aspect of the self which is the basis for the ascription of legal responsibility. For example, when driving a car, I hit a pedestrian; I am so mortified by the drastic legal ramifications (in addition to my horror at the sight of the harm I have wrought) that I immediately and instinctively try to convert my intoxication from a responsibility base (as in *in vino veritas*) to an excuse: due to my unusual state, it was not really me who hit the pedestrian. I am not the author of the event. Such avoidance of responsibility can also take a more general form. If we learn that the law applies some of its most draconian measures to the operations of our free will, we may respond by progressively contracting the latter's domain. We may increasingly describe actions in a deterministic vocabulary designed to place them at the periphery of the self or even completely outside its boundaries.

A second, perhaps simpler, way that legal responsibility may lead to minimalist forms of self-constitution is to deter people from participating in the forms of life that give rise to those responsibilities. Of course, this result is sometimes the explicit goal of legal sanctions; the law tries to dissuade people from becoming murderers or arsonists. In other cases, however, a similar result may be unintended and unwelcome. If the mishaps associated with driving, performing surgery, or running a corporation carry with them severe legal repercussions, I may decide to give up driving, to stop practicing medicine, and to stay away from the boardroom. Such a decision can be personally rational and even socially desirable. Still, by avoiding responsibility bases they might otherwise occupy, individuals draw the boundaries of their selves more narrowly than they otherwise would have done.

We do find in the law, however, an opposite tendency to the one just described. But this tendency too may contribute to the shrinking of responsibility and self. Aware of the severity of its coercive measures, the law is frequently reluctant to impose liability even when nonlegal responsibility obtains. The law's reticence can assume two different forms: it can take a narrow view of object-responsibility by denying (or ignoring) authorship when it generally would be thought to exist, or it can adopt a minimalist approach to subject-responsibility that recognizes only narrowly drawn responsibility bases. An example of the former strategy is the Anglo-American approach to the Good Samaritan issue. Many people would be astonished to learn that the person who deliberately refrains from pulling the drowning child out of the pond is not legally responsible for the child's death.[80]

Criminal law provides a large-scale example of the second way in which the law tends to hedge its drastic measures by insisting on a narrowly delineated responsibility base. The core of criminal law doctrine, centered around the concept of *mens rea* and the variety of criminal excuses, probably comes closer than any other set of social practices to an instantiation of the Kantian conception of the responsible human subject as the noumenal self, characterized exclusively by a rational free will unencumbered by character, temperament, and circumstance.[81] Criminal law's preoccupation with rationality and free choice, no matter how compromised these concepts are in theory and how diluted in practice, represents a remarkably narrow view of the constituents through which individuals become the responsible authors of objects and events.

   Highlighting this narrowness, however, is not a criticism of criminal law. Such a criticism would require, among other things, an examination of the goals of criminal punishment, which is not my present aim. Moreover, given the consequences of criminal responsibility—brutally coercive measures—a narrowly drawn responsibility base is hardly distressing. My point is rather that by establishing and enacting a socially salient set of practices that embody a narrow responsibility base, the criminal law helps inculcate a conception of the human subject commensurate with such a minimalist responsibility base.

   The dilemma of legal responsibility should now be clear. When the law attempts to support our ordinary sense of responsibility, it provides us with a potent incentive to flee it. On the other hand, when legal responsibility is narrowly circumscribed, it codifies and presents us with a shrivelled public image of our selves. In either case, the law poses the danger of constricting responsibility and hence of shrinking the self.

   Why, though, is the contraction of responsibility and the shrinking of the self a danger to be avoided? An attempt to answer this question would take us too far afield. Moreover, some may even doubt the premise upon which this question proceeds. In stormy waters, they may point out, the temptation is great, and often justified, to dump some cargo to save the ship. We may nonetheless get an intimation of a possible answer to this question if, staying with the same metaphor, we observe that in the case of the self, there is no ship-and-cargo; it is all ship, or perhaps all cargo. If we dump too much, the voyage may indeed become easier, but it may hardly be worth making.

Notes

1. For a leading contemporary philosopher's testimony that the free will–determinism problem is far from solved, see Thomas Nagel, *The View from Nowhere* (New York: Oxford University Press, 1986), 110–37. Nagel also believes "that the problem of responsibility is insoluble, or at least unsolved." Ibid. at 120.

2. Consider Professor Packer's blunt move to short-circuit the whole issue: "Very simply, the law treats man's conduct as autonomous and willed, not because it is, but because it is desirable to proceed as if it were." Herbert L. Packer, *The Limits of the Criminal Sanction* (Stanford, Calif.: Stanford University Press, 1968), 74–75.

3. See, e.g., Michael S. Moore, "Choice, Character, and Excuse," *Social Philosophy and Policy* 7 (1990): 29; and Peter Arenella, "Character, Choice, and Moral Agency: The Relevance of Character to Our Moral Culpability Judgments," *Social Philosophy and Policy* 7 (1990): 59.

4. Notable recent examples include Michael J. Sandel, *Liberalism and the Limits of Justice* (New York: Cambridge University Press, 1982); and Roberto M. Unger, *Passion* (New York: Free Press, 1984). For a related criticism of legal scholarship for its failure to consider the law-creating subject, see Pierre Schlag, "The Problem of the Subject," *Texas Law Review* 69 (1991): 1627.

5. Jean-Paul Sartre, *Being and Nothingness*, trans. Hazel E. Barnes (New York: Washington Square Press, 1956), 707. I borrow Sartre's definition without subscribing to all his views on responsibility. Note that under Sartre's definition, the ascription of responsibility is independent of its possible incidents or consequences such as moral censure or punishment. For an example of the contrary view that collapses responsibility into its incidents, see Fitzjames Stephen, *A History of Criminal Law* (London: Macmillan, 1883), 2:183: "[T]he meaning of responsibility is liability to punishment."

6. H. L. A. Hart draws attention to the ambiguity of responsibility statements, although he construes it quite differently. See H. L. A. Hart, *Punishment and Responsibility* (Oxford: Clarendon Press, 1968), 186, 196–97.

7. A sense of responsibility that corresponds to what I call subject-responsibility is suggested in Joel Feinberg, "Collective Responsibility," in *Doing and Deserving* (Princeton: Princeton University Press, 1970), 222, 250–51; and Eugene Schlossberger, "Why We Are Responsible for Our Emotions," *Mind* 95 (1986): 37. An account of responsibility for emotions that is based on what I call object-responsibility may be found in Edward Sankowski, "Responsibility of Persons for Their Emotions," *Canadian Journal of Philosophy* 7 (1977): 829.

8. See, e.g., Richard Rorty, *Contingency, Irony, and Solidarity* (Cambridge: Cambridge University Press, 1989), esp. chap. 2.

9. René Descartes, *Meditations on First Philosophy*, in *The Philosophical Writings of Descartes*, trans. John Cottingham, Robert Stoothoff, and Dugald Murdoch (Cambridge: Cambridge University Press, 1984), 2:1.

10. Most prominently in *Being and Nothingness*.

11. See Henry G. Frankfurt, "Identification and Externality" and "Identification and Wholeheartedness," both in *The Importance of What We Care About* (Cambridge: Cambridge University Press, 1988), 58, 167.

12. "This is why my body always extends across the tool which it utilizes: it is at the end of the cane on which I lean and against the earth; it is at the end of the telescope which shows me the stars; it is on the chair, in the whole house; for it is my adaptation to these tools." Sartre, *Being and Nothingness*, 325. Compare Merleau-Ponty's view: "To get used to a hat, a car or a stick is to be transplanted into them, or conversely, to incorporate them into the bulk of our own body.... It is literally true that the subject who learns to type incorporates the key-bank space into his bodily space." Maurice Merleau-Ponty, *Phenomenology of Perception*, trans. Colin Smith (New York: Humanities Press, 1962), 143, 145.

13. John Dewey gave a similar description: "A piano player who had perfect mastery of his instrument would have no occasion to distinguish between his contribution and that of the piano. In well-formed, smooth running functions of any sort—skating, conversing, hearing music, enjoying a landscape—there is no consciousness of separation of the method of the person and of the subject matter. In whole-hearted play and work there is the same phenomenon." John Dewey, *Democracy and Education* (New York: Macmillan, 1916), 195.

14. Erving Goffman, *Encounters* (Indianapolis: Bobbs-Merrill, 1961), 85–152; and "The Underlife of a Public Institution: A Study of Ways of Making Out in a Mental Hospital," in *Asylums: Essays on the Social Situation of Mental Patients and Other Inmates* (Garden City, N.Y.: Anchor, 1961), 171, 318–20. See also chapter 1 supra.

15. The primary modern text on the social origins of the self is George H. Mead, *Mind, Self, and Society* (Chicago: University of Chicago Press, 1934). For a more recent statement, see Peter L. Berger and Thomas Luckmann, *The Social Construction of Reality* (Garden City, N.Y.: Doubleday, 1966), 173–80.

16. To say that the self is constructed of modular units is not to suggest any particular degree of uniformity of such units, nor to claim that any such unit cannot unravel into smaller units of modularity. For example, although a large modular unit under the description *Orthodox*

Jew is available, it does not follow that one must espouse it in its entirety or not at all. One can pick subunits out of this package that are themselves modular. However, identifying and applying the appropriate means and criteria of such selective self-definition are difficult issues that I cannot discuss here.

17. Derek Parfit, *Reasons and Persons* (Oxford: Clarendon Press, 1984), part 3, esp. 199–306.

18. Sartre uses this peculiar verb in reference to the relationship between consciousness and the body: "It would be best to say, using 'exist' as a transitive verb—that consciousness *exists* its body." Sartre, *Being and Nothingness,* 329. Conscious states, such as pain, are also "existed" by consciousness. Ibid. at 338.

19. The occurrence of such an aberrant reaction, however, may assume different significance over time. For example, if such "aberrations" recur, they may have to be incorporated into the ever revisable picture of the self and thus change its constitution.

20. Obviously, an experience of shame is not a sufficient condition for responsibility when the experience results from a factual mistake: as it turns out, it was not really me who overturned the vase; it was the wind, or someone else.

21. Here again, the simplest case is one that involves a factual mistake: I did not notice at first that it was my hand that overturned the vase.

22. As in the corresponding situation mentioned in note 19 above, persistent failure to assume a responsible stance under similar circumstances will eventually be incorporated in the composition of the self and will suggest a revision of its boundaries.

23. See Aristotle, *Nicomachean Ethics,* book 3, chap. 5.

24. For an interpretation (or rather a reconstruction) of Aristotle's theory of moral responsibility that tries to avoid this problem, see T. H. Irwin, "Reason and Responsibility in Aristotle," in *Essays on Aristotle's Ethics,* ed. Amelie O. Rorty (Berkeley and Los Angeles: University of California Press, 1981), 117, 126–44.

25. This is in one sense Kant's own solution; roughly, we are responsible not because we "will our will" but because we *are* our will as noumenal selves. See Immanuel Kant, *Groundwork of the Metaphysic of Morals,* trans. H. J. Paton (London: Hutchinson, 1948), 101–2; see also Allen W. Wood, "Kant's Compatibilism," in *Self and Nature in Kant's Philosophy,* ed. Allen W. Wood (Ithaca, N.Y.: Cornell University Press, 1984), 73.

26. See, e.g., Alfred J. Ayer, "Freedom and Necessity," in *Philosophical Essays* (New York: St. Martin's Press, 1954), 271; John V. Canfield,

"The Compatibility of Free Will and Determinism," *Philosophical Review* 71 (1962): 352.

27. Charles Taylor, "Responsibility for Self," in *Free Will,* ed. Gary Watson (New York: Oxford University Press, 1982), 111, 112.

28. See ibid. at 126.

29. These "dimensions" should not be reified and rigidly separated. They are merely heuristic aids meant to facilitate a mental grip on the unitary category of the self. As explained below, the same phenomena can sometimes be explained by reference to different dimensions of the self.

30. This is not to say that people are responsible for all the effects traceable to their bodies. In part 3, I illustrate some of the ways in which one can try to avoid responsibility by distancing oneself from certain aspects of one's bodily existence.

31. See part 4.

32. See *Rylands v. Fletcher,* 3 L.R-E. & I. App. 330 (H.L. 1868).

33. See *Page v. Hollingsworth,* 7 Ind. 317 (1855).

34. The language used by the court in an old case to explain the defendant's tort liability for his straying animals is instructive on this point: "[W]here my beasts of their own wrong without my will and knowledge break another's close I shall be punished, for I am the trespasser with my beasts." William L. Prosser, *Handbook of the Law of Torts,* 4th ed. (St. Paul: West, 1971), 496 (quoting 12 Hen. VII, Keilway 3b, 72 Eng. Rep. 156). On the identification of the owner with his slaves and property in old tort law, see John H. Wigmore, "Responsibility for Tortious Acts: Its History," *Harvard Law Review* 7 (1894): 315, 330–37.

35. For a succinct statement see Rudolph von Jhering, *The Struggle for Law,* 2d ed., trans. John J. Lalor (Chicago: Callaghan and Company, 1915), 59: "Property is but the periphery of my person extended to things." For a recent exposition of this perspective, see Margaret J. Radin, "Property and Personhood," *Stanford Law Review* 34 (1982): 957, 959. I elaborate my own version of such a theory in chapter 9.

36. See supra, note 12 and accompanying text.

37. See Merleau-Ponty, *Phenomenology of Perception,* 143. In chapter 9 I propose a more elaborate picture, in which identification with the body and other objects is not based directly on the phenomenology described here, but is linguistically mediated by the use of the concept "I."

38. Although the common law does not generally recognize parents' vicarious liability, many jurisdictions have statutory provisions to this effect. For a survey, see Note, Emogene C. Wilhelm, "Vicarious Parental Liability in Connecticut: Is It Effective?" *University of Bridgeport Law Review* 7 (1986): 99, 121–24.

39. For one commentator's testimony of the difficulties encountered in this area, see George P. Fletcher, *Rethinking Criminal Law* (Boston: Little, Brown, 1978), sec. 8.5, p. 649: "Tort scholars have been puzzled for decades to explain the tort rule in employer liability cases."

40. For a comprehensive examination and rejection of the different arguments that might uphold the relevance of actual harm, see Stephen J. Schulhofer, "Harm and Punishment: A Critique of Emphasis on the Results of Conduct in the Criminal Law," *University of Pennsylvania Law Review* 122 (1974): 1497.

41. See, e.g., Thomas Nagel, "Moral Luck," in *Mortal Questions* (New York: Cambridge University Press, 1979), 24; Bernard Williams, "Moral Luck," in *Moral Luck* (Cambridge: Cambridge University Press, 1981), 20.

42. See Williams, "Moral Luck," 20–22.

43. See, e.g., Feinberg, "Collective Responsibility," 248–51; Thomas R. Flynn, "Collective Responsibility and Obedience to the Law," *Georgia Law Review* 18 (1984): 845, 846–52; Virginia Held, "Moral Responsibility and Collective Action," in *Individual and Collective Responsibility*, ed. Peter A. French (Cambridge, Mass.: Schenkman, 1972), 101, 108–9.

44. See, e.g., Feinberg, "Collective Responsibility," 233.

45. "From our attribution of an action, and moral responsibility, to a collectivity, it does not follow that the collectivity's members are morally responsible for the action of the collectivity." Held, "Moral Responsibility," 109 (footnote omitted).

46. Thus, some writers deny the intelligibility of collective responsibility altogether. See, e.g., H. D. Lewis, "The Non-moral Notion of Collective Responsibility," in French, *Individual and Collective Responsibility*, 119, 121–32. Note that Lewis speaks only about responsibility "in the proper ethical sense," ibid., 121, rather than in the more general sense addressed in this article.

47. See, e.g., John P. Hewitt, *Self and Society: A Symbolic Interactionist Social Psychology* (Boston: Allyn and Bacon, 1976), 91–95.

48. My discussion focuses on the social or cultural meaning of "American identity," not on the formal meaning, as with citizenship requirements.

49. The collective identity I describe admits the possibility of *alienation*: one can be distanced from a role with which one is generally expected to identify. Moreover, alienation here is not at all a negative term. Depending on the nature of the role, one may be better off, ethically speaking, being alienated from it than identifying with it. This point is elaborated a bit further in chapters 1 and 8.

50. See Stanley Bates, "My Lai and Vietnam: The Issues of Responsibility," in French, *Individual and Collective Responsibility*, 145, 155–57, 161–63.

51. "[I]t is of the very essence of our deep-rooted notions of criminal liability that guilt be personal and individual." Francis B. Sayre, "Criminal Responsibility for the Acts of Another," *Harvard Law Review* 43 (1943): 689, 717.

52. Wayne R. LaFave and Austin W. Scott Jr., *Handbook of Criminal Law*, 2d ed. (St. Paul: West, 1986), sec. 6.8, p. 588 (footnote omitted).

53. Ibid. sec. 6.8, p. 590 (footnote omitted).

54. See, e.g., Phillip E. Johnson, "The Unnecessary Crime of Conspiracy," *California Law Review* 61 (1973): 1137.

55. *People v. Kessler*, 315 N.E.2d 29, 30–31 (Ill. 1974).

56. This does not amount to an endorsement of the decision or the doctrine. Responsibility, in the sense discussed here, is a necessary but not a sufficient ground for criminal liability; the latter also requires blame. The conclusion that the defendant is not responsible for an offense precludes liability, but finding responsibility does not by itself authorize criminal punishment. Further conditions of blameworthiness must be satisfied, but they fall outside my present topic.

57. 1 W.L.R. 317 (1955).

58. Ibid., 317.

59. Ibid., 322–24.

60. Criminal law theory casts this issue as a dispute over the adequate definition of "act"—that is, whether the definition should include a reference to the element of voluntariness. See, e.g., Herbert Morris, *Freedom and Responsibility* (Stanford, Calif.: Stanford University Press, 1961), 105–7.

61. There are in fact references in the decision to the impairment of Charlson's self-control as a result of the tumor. See *Charlson,* 1 W.L.R. at 320–22.

62. The relationship between sexuality and the self has important constitutional ramifications. See *Bowers v. Hardwick*, 478 U.S. 186, 203–13 (1985) (Blackmun, J., dissenting). In arguing against the constitutionality of a Georgia statute criminalizing sodomy, the *Bowers* dissent relies on "[t]he fact that individuals define themselves in a significant way through their intimate sexual relationships with others." Ibid., 205.

63. For data concerning the treatment of child molesters in a number of jurisdictions see Josephine Bulkley, ed., *Innovations in the Prosecution of Child Sexual Abuse Cases* (Washington, D.C.: American Bar Association, 1981), 9–134.

64. 2 All E.R. 801 (H.L. 1952).

65. *Model Penal Code,* sec. 210.3(1)(b) (Proposed Official Draft 1962).

66. *Model Penal Code and Commentaries,* part II, sec. 210.3, at 56 (Official Draft and Revised Comments 1980).

67. Royal Commission on Capital Punishment, 1949–1953, *Report* (London: Her Majesty's Stationery Office, 1953), 52–53.

68. Glanville L. Williams, *Textbook of Criminal Law,* 2d ed. (London: Stevens, 1983), 548.

69. Fletcher, *Rethinking Criminal Law;* the quotations are from sec. 4.2, pp. 247 and 249, and sec. 6.8, pp. 513–14.

70. The ordinary use of these terms only roughly approximates the conceptual distinction I want to make.

71. For the centrality of the notion of "coping" in Heidegger's conception of the self, see Hubert L. Dreyfus, *Being-in-the-World* (Cambridge: MIT Press, 1991), 67–75.

72. These two interpretations of duress are elaborated in Fletcher, *Rethinking Criminal Law,* secs. 10.3–10.3.4, pp. 798–810.

73. 378 A.2d 755 (N.J. 1977). Dr. Toscano, a chiropractor, was charged with aiding the preparation of a fraudulent insurance claim by making out a false medical report and was convicted of conspiring to obtain money by false pretenses. Toscano claimed that he had been under threats to his own and his wife's safety. The conviction was reversed on appeal.

74. Judge Bazelon has argued for an expanded insanity defense that extends to extreme social deprivation. See David L. Bazelon, "The Morality of the Criminal Law," *Southern California Law Review* 49 (1976): 385, 394–98; see also Richard Delgado, "Rotten Social Background: Should the Criminal Law Recognize a Defense of Severe Environmental Deprivation?" *Law and Inequality Journal* 3 (1985): 9, 12.

75. See Mark Kelman, "Interpretive Construction in the Substantive Criminal Law," *Stanford Law Review* 33 (1981): 591, 643–44.

76. Blackstone, for example, lists the execution of condemned criminals as the first item in his discussion of justified homicide; self-defense appears later in that discussion. See William Blackstone, *Commentaries on the Laws of England* (London: T. Cadell, 1791), 4:178.

77. See supra, 221–24.

78. See supra, 206 and chapter 8 below.

79. On law's "dirty hands," see pp. 75–76 supra. Compare Nagel, "Ruthlessness in Public Life," in *Mortal Questions,* 75; Williams, "Politics and Moral Character," in *Moral Luck,* 54; Michael Walzer, "Political Action: The Problem of Dirty Hands," in *War and Moral Responsibility,*

ed. Marshall Cohen, Thomas Nagel, and Thomas Scanlon (Princeton: Princeton University Press, 1974), 62.

80. See generally LaFave and Scott, *Handbook of Criminal Law,* sec. 3.3, pp. 211–12.

81. For a Kantian interpretation of criminal law's main doctrines, see David Richards, "Human Rights and the Moral Foundations of Substantive Criminal Law," *Georgia Law Review* 13 (1979): 1395.

CHAPTER EIGHT
INTERPRETING OFFICIAL SPEECH

My starting point is a narrow but persisting problem: the role, if any, of legislative intent in statutory interpretation. But though this is my starting point, it is not my main target. My aim is instead to identify and characterize a wider category of speech—I call it *official speech*—of which legislation forms just one part. Placing the interpretation of statutes in such a broader context puts the ongoing debate in a new light. The contribution is, however, not in the form of added ammunition to one of the contending parties. Rather, my analysis will take us outside that debate, revealing a layer of normative considerations not usually addressed in the current discussion. They concern the ways in which different strands in our interpretive practices help construct various social roles—specifically the role of "official"— and the selves that occupy those roles.[1]

The Standard Sequence and Its Breaches

The question of the interpretive relevance of legislative intent arises against the background of the ordinary relationship between intention and speech.[2] We ordinarily view a speaker's intentions as highly relevant to the meaning of her utterances. Why? A simple answer can be given in terms of what I call the *standard sequence*. On this picture, a speech act consists in a speaker having or forming an intention which she proceeds to express or convey by an utterance. This can be schematically represented as $S \rightarrow I \rightarrow U$, where S is the speaker, I the intention, and

U the utterance. The standard sequence embodies what has become one of the central elements in the analysis of speech acts: the condition of sincerity. Both the meaning and the significance of this condition are most famously highlighted by John Searle.[3] As he points out, saying, for example, "Thank you, but I'm not really grateful," does not involve a logical contradiction, yet is linguistically odd. The oddity results from the implicit background assumption, labeled the *condition of sincerity,* that saying "thank you" is ordinarily designed to express the speaker's gratitude.

The condition of sincerity describes the standard speech situation from which there are many deviations, and speech act theory spends considerable effort analyzing and documenting them. Insincere speech is thus widely recognized, commonly diagnosed as a lack of correspondence between intention and utterance: as in saying "thank you" without being grateful, or as in dissembling more generally. Such cases of insincere speech can be seen as disruptions of the normal connection between intention and utterance. In terms of our notation they can be accordingly rendered as $S \rightarrow I -/\rightarrow U$, where the broken arrow signifies the lack of correspondence between the speaker's state of mind and what she says. However, as the notation clearly suggests, there is a second, though I think a less well recognized, way in which the standard sequence can be disrupted, one in which the breach in the sequence occurs, as it were, between the speaker and the intention: $S -/\rightarrow I \rightarrow U$ in our notation. I will label a speech act that fits this description *detached speech.* Detached speech, I argue, provides the key to understanding official speech and the role of speakers' intentions in interpreting it. But what kinds of speech acts fit this description? And what exactly is meant by a separation between the speaker and the intention? To answer these questions we need to consider some examples.

The AT&T Operator and Detached Speech

As an occasional user of the services of AT&T, the reader may have observed that the operator invariably concludes each exchange with the refrain, "Thank you for using AT&T." Now notice that in this case we find an opposite oddity to the one involved in denying one's gratitude subsequent to saying "thank you." It would be equally out of place for an overzealous operator to add the words, "I'm really grateful." Such an explicit affirmation of the state of mind supposedly expressed by the "thank you" expression is as incongruous in this case as its denial would be in the ordinary instance. Why?

Now it should be first noted that this is not a case of insincerity that involves deception of any kind. The operator does not pretend to be grateful while failing to possess that state of mind. Indeed, the explicit affirmation of gratitude would be just as inappropriate even if while speaking to the customer the operator did in fact experience a surge of gratitude. It seems, in other words, that the operator is not in violation of the condition of sincerity, but rather that this condition does not at all apply to him. What accounts for its suspension?

It might be suggested, in response, that the condition of sincerity is not really suspended here at all, but that it is merely displaced. According to this suggestion, the operator does not speak on his own behalf but rather on behalf of someone else. He engages in what I will call *representative speech*. Given his representative capacity he is simply the wrong person in whom to search for the intentions that animate the speech in question. Now, as a general proposition, this suggestion is quite plausible. Take a simple example: R reads to A a thank-you note she received from S. If R were to interrupt the reading and add the words, "and I'm really grateful," referring to herself, we would think her deeply confused. But it would be altogether appropriate for her to interject the phrase, "and he is really grateful," referring to S, on the evidence, let us suppose, of the large bouquet that accompanied the note. Some speech situations, in other words, may present a question as to who is the real speaker whose intentions ought to control the interpretation of a given utterance. But they are not exempt from the condition of sincerity. Once the real speaker is identified, the standard sequence would be restored and the condition satisfied.

Plausible as the suggestion is in the simple case, it does not seem to apply to our main example. If we try to track down the origin of the operator's speech, we are most likely to be led to an AT&T public-relations office or to an advertising firm. Someone in some such outfit must have come up with the idea that a standardized display of politeness on the operator's part would enhance AT&T's public image. The idea quite likely needed and received the approval of someone in the corporation's management, whereupon the appropriate instruction was inserted into the operators' manual. The most important aspect of this hypothetical scenario is that at no point does it involve anyone's actual gratitude that the operator's utterance would purport to express. It may seem, though, that this search for the real speaker, on whose behalf the operator utters the "thank you" refrain, overlooked the most obvious candidate, namely the AT&T corporation itself. Doesn't the operator simply speak for the corporation? However, ascribing the speech to the corporation does not restore the standard sequence in this case. No matter how sanguine one may be about the agency of collective entities, one would be hard put to impute to the corporation an actual intentional state of gratitude of which the operator's speech is the sincere expression.[4] Whatever the basis and the meaning of ascribing speech to corporations, such ascription must involve the recognition that it may proceed without anyone's possessing the intentions that the speech is ostensibly designed to convey. The suggestion that the operator is merely a shadow-speaker, thanking on behalf of someone else, does not accordingly remove the difficulty presented by the seeming exemption of his speech from the condition of sincerity. The anomaly of his speech situation requires a different diagnosis, one that acknowledges the breach in the standard sequence that I have mentioned and tries to account for it. To improve the chances of diagnostic success, we need first acquaint ourselves with more symptoms of the problem. The following example should help us do so.

The Juror and Capacity Disclaimers

Consider the utterance "guilty as charged" made by F, the forewoman of a jury stating the jury's verdict to the judge. Suppose that F had been heard earlier to argue to the jury in favor of acquitting the defendant, a view she has not changed. Would this fact vitiate her declaration of the defendant's guilt or at least impugn her sincerity? The answer to both questions is clearly negative. For F's utterance to count as a valid verdict it must be only true that a majority of the jurors voted for conviction;[5] and the only relevant beliefs implicit in F's utterance concern such facts about the jury's vote.

However, this should not be understood as suggesting that F uses the phrase "guilty as charged" in a new sense, namely as meaning "a sufficient majority of the jury voted to convict the defendant." We must draw here a crucial distinction between the evidentiary grounds for a proposition and its truth conditions. The fact that the jury voted the way it did counts as sufficient grounds for F's declaration of the defendant's guilt. Still, the meaning of the phrase "guilty as charged" is not affected by this fact; the phrase retains its ordinary meaning, namely that the defendant is guilty as charged.[6] How are we then to explain the fact that F is pronouncing the defendant's guilt while believing in his innocence? Is she dissembling?

The puzzle arises out of a seeming conflict between what F says and what we have taken to be her actual view as expressed during the jury's deliberations. Let us now probe the latter. Imagine that during a recess in the jury's deliberations F had been heard to divulge to her friend her belief in the defendant's guilt. Would this discovery impugn her sincerity in arguing to her fellow jurors in favor of acquittal? Not necessarily.

When speaking to the jurors, F is bound by legal rules and standards, both evidentiary and substantive, and her position may reflect her conviction regarding the right decision given these legal guidelines. Her acting as a conscientious juror, however, is compatible with her holding the view, expressed during a break, that the defendant is guilty. But even as we acknowledge the compatibility we must also recognize that we have replicated the earlier puzzle, this time arising out of the flat contradiction between F's exculpatory attitude conveyed to her peers and her condemnatory beliefs revealed by the statement to her friend. As before, the puzzle reflects a conflict between what F says (to the jury) and what we *now* take to be her true point of view.

The story need not stop here. F, it turns out, is a newcomer to California, speaking to her Californian friend. The criminal charges in question concern smoking in a public place. F had just moved from another state, say New York, where public smoking, let us assume, is common and generally approved. Finally, F had been earlier heard talking to an old New York friend about those "poor innocents persecuted by the Californians for their smoking habits." Does this additional information render F's statement to her Californian friend fallacious and insincere?

I think there is some doubt here, which further facts would perhaps help remove. But whichever way we lean at this point, this much seems clear. F could easily escape such charges of falsehood or insincerity by appending to her statement of the defendant's guilt addressed to her Californian friend the explanation, "I'm saying this in my capacity as a Californian." A similar qualification—call it a *capacity disclaimer*—would be in order, and is indeed implicit, in the other situations we have imagined: "I'm saying this in my capacity as a juror," or "in my capacity as forewoman." The capacity disclaimer, I suggest, highlights the presence in these situations of the second kind of breach in the standard sequence that I have distinguished, where the speaker is separated from the intention conveyed by her speech. To see how this can be we need to look at an analogical case concerning fictional speech. We must go to the theater.

Fictional Roles

A, an actor in a play, rages against her "husband," played by B, exclaiming, "I hate you!" Now suppose that in order to add conviction to her acting, A can bring herself to a high level of emotional involvement in the play, so that at the relevant point in the plot she is in fact provoked into intense rage. Clearly, her exclamation expresses this emotion. At the same time, it would be ludicrous to conclude that A does in fact hate B, even momentarily. A and B are the best of friends, and their friendship is forged rather than suspended during their common performances. The situation seems clearly to illustrate the kind of disruption in the standard sequence that issues in detached speech: the utterance expresses an intention, but in an important sense the intention does not belong to the speaker. It is also easy to see what accounts in this case for the separation between the speaker and the intention: it is the role that A performs and the fact that she utters her lines in her fictional capacity as B's wife in the play. But though this account seems clearly on the right track, it is not very informative. How exactly does the fact that A performs the role of a wife affect her relationship to the emotion she expresses? What precisely does it mean to say that her speech is detached?

One source of difficulty arises from the fact that A's exclamation of hatred on the stage is accompanied by a surge of rage no different in intensity from what A might feel and express at home. The difference between the theatrical performance and its domestic counterpart is not simply phenomenological. Nor should we say that A is merely performing the *role* of a wife in the theater. The concept of role extends beyond the theater and reaches into the household. There too, to be a wife—or a husband—is to perform a role. The distinction then must be made in terms of some characteristic other than that of occupying a role: perhaps by pointing out that one role is "fictional" while the other one is "real." But describing the two situations respectively in such terms simply restates the puzzle rather than solving it: we want to know precisely what makes one role-performance real and another fictional.

Some easy answers should be dismissed right away. For example, it would be a mistake to emphasize the limited duration of the actors' enactment of their roles as husband and wife. In a long-running play their engagement onstage can outlast in the aggregate some real marriages. Nor is the intermittent nature of the theatrical role of great significance. The real marriage is no different in this regard, and the fact that we think only of the latter as continuous, that is, as persisting even when the parties are off enacting other marriages onstage, is part of the puzzle rather than part of the solution. Next, I want to discard summarily the possible suggestion that the crucial difference between the two kinds of marriage lies in the fact that the theatrical role is scripted and directed by others, whereas the domestic one is not. We can imagine in response an improvised play in which the actors enjoy no less textual and behavioral freedom than that allowed a couple who live, let us say, under the constantly vigilant scrutiny of parents and in-laws. Finally, it cannot be said that the real spousal role differs from the theatrical in the former's greater importance to its occupant. The opposite may well be the case. An actor may value his onstage role as

Desdemona's husband, and Desdemona her role as Othello's wife, much more than they value their relationships with their respective partners at home.

Speech and Self

The distinction we seek is not simple and is likely to involve different kinds of factors. But one way of drawing the line that looks to me promising is in terms of a particular conception of the self. I cannot provide in this space a detailed description of this conception or deploy the arguments that support it. However, the picture of the self on which I rely is familiar, and a rough sketch is all I need. The self, on this view, is at least in part constituted by social roles and mental states.[7] But a self is not merely a concatenation of roles and intentions. To form a single self, a bunch of roles and intentions must be unified in some fashion. A self, we might say, is an integrated set of social roles and mental states.[8] What does the integration consist in? The answer I suggest is metaphorical. The different roles and intentions must form a dovetailing, interrelated, and interacting arrangement that we can imagine as possessing a certain "density" or as forming a "core." Such a spatial depiction of the self makes immediate room for the possibility that a person—by which I mean a human individual as ordinarily understood— may occupy roles and entertain mental states that are too tenuously connected to the elements forming that core to count as parts of the self. Such a possibility, as well as the underlying spatial imagery, is implicit in Erving Goffman's notion of *role distance:* it describes the possibility of enacting a social role without fully integrating it into the self.[9] Analogously, Harry Frankfurt drew attention to the distinction between "internal" and "external" mental states.[10] In both cases a spatial metaphor is used to demarcate a certain boundary line around the self and to separate out some elements that ordinarily would likely be ascribed to the same individual.

The sketch of the self I have drawn so far is static, but in order for it to meet our present needs I must add to it a dynamic component. I will call *identification* the process by which a new role or mental state gets attached to the preexisting constituents of the self. A person identifies with a particular element (a role or a mental state) insofar as this element is allowed to sprout enough connections with existing constituents of the self. The proclivity for identification with any new role or intention can be understood in terms of the dynamic properties of the person's existing roles and intentions: how prone they are to hook up or interact with the new addition. Identification describes, accordingly, an inner or subjective process by which the self is shaped and modified. But the self has also a public, interpersonal existence. The contours and properties of this objective entity are a product of what we may call the process of *interpretation* by others. Just as identification is constitutive of the subjective self, so is interpretation of the objective one. One of the important aspects of interpretation is the interpreter's willingness and ability to connect various roles and intentions, and his decision, in light of his overall interpretive scheme, as to which roles or intentions sufficiently interrelate to form an integral whole and which are distant or external.

Although identification and interpretation are thus clearly distinguishable, they are also obviously related. First, each person has available to her the outside perspective on herself, either by learning how others interpret her or by taking a direct interpretive glimpse at herself from the outside, as it were. Such interpretive input is likely to play a role in the process of her identification. Conversely, one of the interpretive resources likely to have a significant import on interpreting the public self is the subject's own self-understanding. A third reason for the tendency of identification and interpretation to converge is perhaps even more important than the first two. Roles and mental states are shaped by a social and cultural context shared by both the subject and her interpreters. The tendency of such roles and intentions to interrelate or to separate in various contexts and combinations is accordingly a generally known piece of social or cultural data. This tendency is, in other words, part of the shared vocabulary of the self, a shared vocabulary that underlies and to a considerable degree unifies identification and interpretation.

In light of these observations it is easy to see why the interpretation I have described can be labeled *constitutive* interpretation. First, such interpretation is the process by which the public self is constructed. Second, this construction is refracted in the subject's own self-understanding both through her interpretive perspective and as a result of the way in which the properties of the roles and intentions that compose her self and determine its identifications are themselves the products of society's interpretive practices.

Although rough, this sketch of the self can help us now clarify the contrast between the marriages onstage and at home. This contrast is a matter of the different degrees of integration between the respective roles and their associated states of mind on the one hand and the subject's self on the other. Unlike the domestic role, the theatrical one is distant: it is relatively removed or disconnected from the actor's other roles. Similarly, the rage she experiences and conveys on stage is external: it is seen neither by A nor by others as continuous and intertwined with A's other mental states. Evidence for these characterizations can be found in our respective approaches to construing the theatrical and the domestic episodes. In the former case, our explorations would be strictly confined to the theatrical role, implying a sharp separation between this segment of A's life and the rest of it. In trying to understand fully A's onstage verbal assault, we would not deem relevant information such as A's relationship and attitudes to other people or even to B himself. By contrast, all such information would be highly relevant to our understanding of a corresponding domestic feud. We would naturally view the emotional outburst as of a piece with other roles A may occupy, such as a mother or a sister, and as related in important and potentially revealing ways to her other mental states, such as her attitudes toward other people, her aspirations, frustrations, and the like.

Moreover, these contrasting interpretive practices do not only testify to the difference between the two episodes, but they also help constitute it. Our refusal to transgress the boundary of the theatrical role in our interpretation of A's onstage utterance helps constitute that role as distant, just as by not exploring A's mental life on that occasion we help constitute the onstage rage as an external intention, cut off from A's genuine mental self. Finally, these two aspects of our interpretive practice help constitute A's onstage utterances as detached speech. In short, to call an utterance, an intention, or a role fictional is, among other things, to activate with respect to it a set of interpretive practices that help constitute it as separate from the subject.

This conclusion raises the following question: Why do we create and enact such disparate interpretive practices? More specifically, what is the point in separating certain utterances, intentions, and roles from their subjects and in treating them as self-enclosed and detached? The question is obviously much too broad and involved to be adequately treated in this space, but our theatrical example suggests some preliminary points. As the prevalence of gossip columns and voyeurism testifies, people find pleasure in observing others' private lives. The interpretive practice we call "fiction" or "theater" gives us the benefit of a public display of scenes from a private life while controlling most of the potential damage inherent in publicly enacting such scenes.[11] The potential benefits of such an arrangement can be subsumed under three headings. The first concerns reduced responsibility. In our example, A will not be perceived as the offending party when she utters offensive words, and correspondingly she will not be made to bear the personal consequences that might be otherwise attached to her behavior. The second implication of the theatrical role is to reduce vulnerability: the distant role B enacts provides him with a kind of immunity; the insults are hurled at his role, not at himself. Consequently, A and B can remain good friends with no hurt feelings despite the daily display of mutual hostility beheld by a large crowd of observers. Finally, the actors' distant role increases their versatility: they can assume and shed roles at will without deep repercussions and corresponding adjustments in any other parts of the self. By reducing responsibility and vulnerability, and by increasing versatility, the distant nature of the theatrical role can accordingly be said to augment freedom of speech and action: it allows A to do (say) things that might be otherwise inappropriate; it allows B to have things done or said to him that would otherwise be injurious; and it permits both actors to engage in a larger variety of activities than would be otherwise feasible.

Constructing Officials

Every analogy is imperfect—otherwise it would be an identity—and the one between my examples of the theater and the jury is no exception. Nonetheless, our foray to the theater can shed some light, I believe, on the issues raised by our jury example.[12] There we observed that a capacity disclaimer can reconcile apparently conflicting statements regarding a defendant's guilt made by the same person F on different occasions. How does this capacity disclaimer work? Let us consider the first instance in which F, speaking in her capacity as forewoman, pronounces the verdict. In analogy to our theater example, the distinguishing mark of the forewoman role, I suggest, is that it is a distant role. Consequently, although F utters "guilty as charged" with the requisite intention—to convey the belief that the defendant is guilty as charged—that intention is an external one, meaning that the belief in question is not continuous or integrated with F's other beliefs and intentions. These features of the role and the intention define F's utterance as detached speech, similar in this regard to the actor's exclamation onstage.

Drawing further on our discussion of the theater, our interpretive approach toward F's speech can be characterized as a constitutive interpretation. Our refusal to explore the relationship between the belief in the defendant's guilt implicit in F's statement and her other beliefs and intentions is a constitutive move in constructing the role of foreperson as a distant one. The point of such an interpretive practice has also been suggested, at least in outline, by the theatrical analogy. For example, the distant nature of F's role and the correlatively detached character of her speech help mitigate F's personal responsibility for the defendant's fate.

The foreperson case can be now generalized. It highlights a set of interpretive practices that treat official speech as detached by locating its underlying intentions outside the configuration of the speaker's mental states, thereby helping to constitute the role of official as distant. In this way such interpretive practices participate in constructing the familiarly impersonal nature of officialdom. Such construction of the official role diminishes officials' personal responsibility as well as their vulnerability. Things can be done and said by officials and to them without engaging them personally and thus without the costs that such engagement might sometimes carry. The impersonal nature of an official role also increases versatility by reducing the personal costs of being assigned to different tasks and positions or of moving out of the official career into other pursuits.

The forewoman example presents a clear case of detached speech produced in one's capacity as a holder of a distant role. But this clarity is in a way deceptive. It suggests a sharp line between detached and nondetached speech and a correspondingly clear divide between distant roles and roles that are integral to the self, as well as between external and internal intentions. In other words, the example implies a rigid and well-defined boundary of the self by reference to which these binary distinctions can be sharply and confidently drawn. The subsequent stages in our story of F were designed to dispel this impression.

As you may recall, F's profession of the defendant's innocence was made in her capacity as juror. Here we are presumptively inclined to ascribe the speech to her as nondetached and to view the underlying intentions as internal. But as the example suggests, this presumption can be easily rebutted by a reminder that being a juror is an official role of sorts, which F can enact at a distance, forming ad hoc intentions appropriate to the role but disconnected from her other views and beliefs.

We would be, however, less receptive toward a similar use of the capacity disclaimer in the next stage of the story, when F points out that her condemnatory statement to her friend is only made in her capacity as a Californian. We would likely view such a disclaimer as intelligible but jarring. Both components of this mixed reaction are noteworthy. We can imagine treating one's newly acquired California residency as a quasi-official role, mouthing without conviction politically correct opinions and exhibiting upon cue the expected attitudes without integrating them with one's erstwhile New York self. It is, of course, possible that one is simply dissembling. But this would mark one's speech as insincere in the first, straightforward sense that I have distinguished early on. The scenario I have in mind is a different one. F has an image of what is expected of a Californian, and she sets out in good faith to meet the expectations. But this entire package—role, attitudes, and speech— is somewhat alien to her. There is a split or a disjunction between her role as Californian and the other roles and intentions that have so far formed her identity. We can even imagine an extreme case in which over time aspects of F associated with her role as Californian may have grown in bulk and importance and her former New York identify shrivelled to the point where at least over a certain range of issues and attitudes the question who is the real F has no clear answer.

These considerations make F's use of the capacity disclaimer intelligible and under some circumstances credible even in the case of her Californian role. But the circumstances are rare and the invocation of the disclaimer in this kind of case artificial and jarring. The reason is clear. The role of Californian is ordinarily enacted in a nondistant fashion; views and beliefs one holds in this capacity are treated as integral to the self; and one's speech accordingly is construed as nondetached.

These problematic uses of the capacity disclaimer should serve to correct the impression created by the foreperson example and the theatrical analogy that the distinctions I have drawn between kinds of roles, intentions, and utterances are binary and that the self to which they apply is clearly and rigidly bounded. Taken together, these examples reveal a more complicated picture. Roles—and their related intentions and utterances—can be arranged on a spectrum defined by a variable role distance. At one end we will find, among other things, strictly official roles whose bearers are expected to keep them at a distance. The other end is defined by personal roles that are uniformly expected to be an integral part of the self. In between these two poles, matters are more flexible and negotiable. The negotiation concerns the proper relation of a given role with its attendant intentions and utterances to the self, and correlatively the proper way of drawing a given segment in the boundary of the self. The negotiation can arise in different contexts and take many forms, but one of them will be that of a dispute over the interpretive practice appropriate to a given type of utterances, and more specifically over the role of a speaker's intentions in interpreting her speech.[13]

Legislative Intent

Earlier I distinguished three ways in which speech can seem to fail the condition of sincerity: by being deceptive, representative, or detached. All three categories can potentially apply to legislators and influence the way their speech is interpreted. Politicians are notorious practitioners of the noble and not-so-noble lie, and as such their discourse is sometimes deceptive. Legislators also act in a representative capacity, and at least on some conceptions of political representation, approximated perhaps in certain settings, it makes sense to think of the legislators merely as mouthpieces or conduits for someone else. I will not dwell, however, on these possibilities and on their implications for the role of legislators' intentions in interpreting statutes. My main purpose has been to identify and describe the third category—detached speech—as potentially applicable to the case of legislators. What bearing does it have on the role of intentions in statutory interpretation?

Our analysis of detached speech suggests two sets of considerations: reactive and constructive. By reactive considerations I mean the inquiry as to whether the legislative role is generally understood and enacted in a distant or a nondistant manner. Here we are trying to fit the interpretive approach to the social facts.[14] Clearly, if the legislative role is distant and the speech in which it issues detached, then it would make little sense to mine a legislator's mental life that lies outside the boundary of her legislative role for added insight into the meaning of her official utterances. The point can be amplified by contrasting it with a seemingly unexceptionable comment made by Professor Gerald MacCallum in his well-known essay on legislative intent. In arguing for the possibility of imputing intentions to other people, including legislators, MacCallum maintains that doing so "may require a fair degree of intimacy with the person whose intentions are being considered."[15] On the present view, this statement applies to nondistant roles only. "Intimacy" involves close familiarity with someone across a wide range of nondistant roles. Because of the interconnections among such roles, one's speech and behavior in any one of them can be better understood in light of the interpreter's acquaintance with that person's enactment of the other roles. We can more easily and confidently impute an intention to a mother if we know her also in her capacities as, say, wife, sister, and friend. But such intimacy is irrelevant to the construal of detached speech. Since ex hypothesi the intention we impute is unrelated to the states of mind that belong in the core of the speaker's self, intimate familiarity with that core and the roles that compose it is quite unnecessary, and can only mislead.

How are we to assess the distance of the legislative role so as to choose the appropriate interpretive approach? We can think of many kinds of relevant evidence, but let me just give one example. Consider the public-figure exemption that present-day libel law creates for expressions that would be otherwise defamatory.[16] Here we have a legal doctrine that legitimates the exposure of politicians' private lives to public scrutiny. Such a doctrine both reflects and foments the effacement of the boundary between the politician's self and her role, thereby signaling a reduction in the acceptable role distance in this case.[17] An increased willingness to consult legislative intentions in our practices of statutory interpretation would accordingly seem consistent with this piece of evidence.

The constructive considerations that our analysis implies relate to the constitutive aspect of interpretive practices. How widely we cast our net in search of legislative intentions deemed pertinent to the interpretation of official utterances is a constitutive move in determining the relationship of the legislative role to the self. Consequently, in contemplating the adequacy of an interpretive practice we must also examine the normative question: where should the boundary of a politician's self be drawn? What is the desirable relationship between a legislator and his role?

Again, the question is too multifaceted to be adequately considered here. But we can attempt a first stab at it by recalling the kinds of general considerations that we have earlier identified as relevant to the creation of distant roles: decreasing responsibility and vulnerability and increasing versatility. Are such effects desirable in this case? Consider responsibility first. The limitation of responsibility implicit in role distance means that as long as the legislator acts within the confines of the role, he is given personal immunity from the adverse consequences of his official actions and decisions. These consequences can affect him only in his official capacity, and at most will cost him his job, but they will not have direct personal ramifications on him beyond that. Is such a system of limited liability advantageous? The answer depends on many considerations that we cannot canvass here, but we can briefly mention some obvious ones. Should legislators be encouraged to be risk-takers or risk-averse? How adequately can sanctions that are limited to the legislators' role police their conduct? Specifically, is the risk of losing the role altogether—by being removed from office or by failure to get reelected— sufficient to deter official misconduct? Finally, how important is such a limitation of responsibility for recruiting worthwhile candidates to such political roles?

It should be noted that the issue here goes beyond legal liability. Politicians are often faced with the "dirty hands" moral dilemma: they are called upon, sometimes by duty and public interest, to perform morally repugnant actions. If relatively good people are to be attracted to such tasks, some devices may be necessary to alleviate somewhat the moral burden beyond the removal of whatever material or physical sanctions might be otherwise attached to such behavior. Role distance can be such a device. Instituting visible distance between the role and the self can be a way to exempt the politician from some of the moral responsibility for discharging his official duties.[18]

Limiting politicians' responsibility by expanding their role distance can have an additional advantage. Politicians do and say many nasty things to each other as well as to people outside their circle. Role distance and the implicit invocation of the capacity disclaimer may somewhat soften these blows. In the relationship among the politicians themselves these devices can help instill a measure of civility—legislators can go out together for a drink even after the most acrimonious exchanges. In the relationship with the citizenry, legislators' role distance is linked to the ethos of law's impersonal nature and to the ideal of being ruled by laws rather than by other people. For reasons that we cannot even start to explore here, it is sometimes preferable—less injurious to one's self-esteem—to sustain the same insults or aggravations when these are not perceived as directly inflicted by another human being but are instead mediated or authored by an impersonally held social role.

Role distance, we saw, also reduces the role-holder's vulnerability. A distant role helps legislators be thick-skinned about the insults and aggravations to which they are subjected by both their constituents and their peers. A complicated judgment is, of course, required to determine whether it is desirable on balance to fit politicians with such a shield. The kinds of considerations that bear on this question are quite obvious, though, and they resemble those that arise under the heading of responsibility. Vulnerability to insult and aggravation may help keep politicians in line, so the trade-off would seem to be between policing legislators' conduct and providing incentives for good and sensitive people to run for office.

Finally, role distance increases politicians' versatility. It encourages people to make relatively short stints as legislators by reducing the damage to the self that might be otherwise involved in giving up one's office or losing it. The resulting revolving-door politics has its obvious attractions, but also some potential disadvantages, such as reduced commitment and expertise.

Taken together, the three groups of considerations that I have listed should help us select an adequate interpretive practice regarding statutes and other legislative pronouncements. On the present analysis, taking full account of legislative intentions represents a choice, with constitutive ramifications, in favor of effacing the boundary between self and legislative role and integrating the latter into the former. Limiting resort to legislative intentions has the reverse implication, representing a vote for role distance in this case. By a careful examination and weighing of the conflicting considerations we can accordingly hope to resolve the prevailing uncertainty regarding the interpretive relevance of legislative intent, and thus help constitute the desirable relationship between legislators' selves and their roles.

But such a stark choice between identification and distance in the legislative role is not, in fact, forced upon us. I want to mention briefly in closing another possibility. The prevailing indecision and ambiguity in statutory interpretation need not represent uncertainty on the question of role distance, but may rather provide the right answer to this question. To recognize this possibility, recall the scalar aspect of the role-distance imagery. Some roles, we said, occupy a middle ground between those that are detached from the self and those that are bound up with it. One's identification with such roles is typically qualified or selective rather than wholehearted or wholesale. In light of the conflicting considerations I have listed, such intermediate and variable role distance is perhaps the best we can hope for in this case, and a wavering, fluctuating interpretive practice the best way to achieve it. We started this essay by noting the problem marked by the mixed views and practices concerning legislative intent in statutory interpretation. Recognizing the crucial difference between an unresolved problem and one solved by a compromise, we can now see that what we initially took to be the problem may in the end turn out to be part of the solution.

Notes

1. Much of the literature on legislative intent is concerned with the difficulties that result from the fact that the legislature is a collective body. I do not address these issues here; I focus instead on the speech and intentions of single legislators whether or not they are part of a collective legislature, and more generally on single officials.

2. Throughout this essay I use *intention* broadly and interchangeably with *mental state* to include such things as beliefs, emotions, and desires.

3. John R. Searle, *Speech Acts* (Cambridge: Cambridge University Press, 1969), 60–65, and *Expression and Meaning* (Cambridge: Cambridge University Press, 1979), 4–5.

4. I do not mean to suggest here that gratitude is a pre- or extra-linguistic sensation. Gratitude may well be constituted by the relevant social and linguistic practices and is in this sense inseparable from the conventions for expressing it. However, once these practices are in place, they do permit us to entertain, identify, and label a mental state of gratitude, and to interpret utterances conveying gratitude as expressing, in the standard case, that state of mind. My point is that such an interpretation would make no sense in the case of the corporation.

5. For the sake of this example I simply stipulate a majority rule for the jury's decision rather than a requirement of unanimity. Nothing substantive in my argument depends on this stipulation.

6. I do not think that the performative aspect of the forewoman's utterance bears on this analysis, but in any event we can stipulate that aspect away. We can hypothesize that it is only the judge who proceeds to perform the institutional act of convicting the defendant, based upon the forewoman's statement. This would make it clearer that the performative aspect is separate from and depends upon the propositional content of the forewoman's utterance.

7. I do not mean to maintain a sharp distinction between roles and mental states. On the present view the appropriate state of mind under given circumstances is indicated by a role (or by the role's "script") as much as the expected behavior.

8. The primary modern text on the social origins of the self is George Herbert Mead, *Mind, Self, and Society* (Chicago: University of Chicago Press, 1934). For a more recent statement see Peter L. Berger and Thomas Luckmann, *The Social Construction of Reality* (New York: Doubleday, 1966), 173–80. The dramaturgical imagery I employ is closest to Erving Goffman's. The most comprehensive statement of his approach is in Goffman, *Frame Analysis* (New York: Harper and Row, 1974).

9. See Erving Goffman, "Role Distance," in *Encounters: Two Studies in the Sociology of Interaction* (Indianapolis: Bobbs-Merrill, 1961),

and "The Underlife of a Public Institution: A Study of Ways of Making Out in a Mental Hospital," in *Asylums: Essays on the Social Situation of Mental Patients and Other Inmates* (New York: Anchor, 1961). Although I borrow the notion of role distance from Goffman, I modify it for my present purposes and employ it in ways that depart from his own use.

10. Harry G. Frankfurt, "Identification and Externality" and "Identification and Wholeheartedness," in *The Importance of What We Care About* (Cambridge: Cambridge University Press, 1977), 50 and 159.

11. I do not mean to suggest that these benefits provide the main reasons or explanations for the theater, but only that they can be usefully extrapolated from the theater example in order to illuminate the nature of official roles.

12. On the use by sociologists of the theater analogy to explore the nature of social roles, compare E. Burns, *Theatricality: A Study of Convention in Theater and in Social Life* (New York: Harper and Row, 1972).

13. A similarly scalar conception of self is argued for by Derek Parfit, *Reasons and Persons* (Oxford: Clarendon Press, 1984), part 3.

14. Describing the investigation as factual should not of course hide the normative component in it. The way a role is enacted, as distant or nondistant, is itself a normative matter. However, in this part of the investigation we are concerned to find out what norms of distance in fact apply to a given role in a given society, seeking to adjust our interpretive practices to these normative understandings.

15. G. C. MacCallum Jr., "Legislative Intent," *Yale Law Journal* 75 (1966): 745, 773.

16. See e.g. *New York Times Co. v. Sullivan*, 376 U.S. 254 (1964).

17. Compare the increased First Amendment protection given to abusive language directed to police officers as reflecting and encouraging an increased role distance in their case. See *Lewis v. New Orleans*, 408 U.S. 913 (1972).

18. This point can be seen as complementary to Bernard Williams' suggestion that we are better off with politicians who are sensitive to the immorality their task sometimes requires. See Williams, "Politics and Moral Character," in *Moral Luck* (Cambridge: Cambridge University Press, 1981), 54. On the "dirty hands" dilemma in politics, see also Thomas Nagel, "Ruthlessness in Public Life," in *Mortal Questions* (Cambridge: Cambridge University Press, 1978), 75; and Michael Walzer, "Political Action: The Problem of Dirty Hands," in *War and Moral Responsibility*, ed. Marshall Cohen, Thomas Nagel, and Thomas Scanlon (Princeton: Princeton University Press, 1974), 62.

CHAPTER NINE
THE VALUE OF OWNERSHIP

To understand private property, it is generally assumed, we must recognize the contribution objects make to human life. On the prevailing view, ownership is valuable only insofar as its subject matter is of value: in the order of valuation, the value of objects comes first, that of owning them comes second. This assumption correlates with another pervasive premise. It is generally taken for granted that ownership is a right or perhaps more commonly a bundle of rights which define normative relationships among people with respect to an object. These two premises are related through a dominant account of rights, according to which their role is to enhance or protect important human interests by imposing duties and restrictions concerning behavior that affects such interests.[1] On this view, ownership concerns rights designed to protect people's interests in various objects.

But despite an air of obviousness, these two premises do not entirely fit our ordinary concept of ownership. First, ownership can be valuable quite apart from the value of the owned object, and it can be the source of an object's value as well as derive from the latter its own value. In reversal of the first premise, the value of ownership can be primary, the value of the object secondary and derivative. Second, observing the role ownership plays in ordinary normative discourse reveals that ownership does not just label some rights with regard to an object but that it also names a relationship to an object that forms a basis for claiming that some such rights ought to exist. In reversal of the second premise, ownership of an object can precede and underpin claims of right regarding the object.

I illustrate and substantiate these claims in part 1. If true, these claims pose both a conceptual and a normative challenge. The conceptual task is an account of ownership that goes beyond the privileged opportunity it provides to take advantage of an object and benefit from it. I offer such an account in part 2. Part 3 takes on the normative issue: it demonstrates how the proposed account explains ownership's capacity to endow objects with value they do not otherwise possess, and to serve as the basis for claims of right with regard to an object.[2]

My main conclusion can be briefly stated. At its core our ordinary concept of ownership does not just designate rights regarding objects but also an ontological relationship to objects that is only partially and contingently related to those rights.[3] This relationship resembles our relationship to our body: in both cases ownership is grounded in the use of the personal pronouns *I* and *me* to allude to the respective items, and is revealed by the similar role that the possessive pronouns *my* and *mine* play in our body-talk and in our property-talk.

A few prefatory comments are in order. Given the amount of speculation generated by this topic in the past, it may be doubted that yet another theory in this area is what the world most urgently needs. As against this, the puzzles I discuss in part 1 present what I believe is an unanswerable challenge to the dominant approaches to property, and despite the vast literature, it seems to me that no satisfactory theory that successfully tackles these problems exists. I will not however try to establish the latter claim by engaging critically with predecessors. This would make my argument inordinately long and unnecessarily tedious. There is a second shortcut I must indulge in order to avoid the same perils. Many forks mark the philosophical road I will take in constructing my approach, and for the most part I will make the requisite choices, say between realism and antirealism or conceptualism and anticonceptualism, without so much as acknowledging them. This is just as well since as often as not the choice is motivated largely by my destination and by my general sense of direction. I do not think that any of my implicit philosophical positions are extreme, though, so I can hope that the resulting approach will be of interest even to readers who would have taken a different turn at various junctures.

As I have just pointed out, the theory I propose takes seriously the ordinary use of the pronoun *my* and associates the concept of ownership closely with it. This invites the following two methodological observations. First, the connection between possessive pronouns and ownership is obvious and close and has teased theorists in the past. The tease turned into frustration, because of the notorious promiscuity of these possessives. My approach is related but significantly different, in that my primary focus is on the personal pronoun *I* and its distinctive role in the constitution of the self. Ownership, I claim, can be best understood when the meaning of the personal possessives is related to and is derived from the meaning of *I*.

Even so, and this is the second point, it remains undeniably true that the pronouns on which I focus are in fact used much more widely than just to denote ownership. Thus neither attention to ordinary speech, nor indeed the other considerations I present in part 2, entail my theory or otherwise compel its adoption. All I can show by direct argument is that the theory is optional, in that it is consistent with usage, providing a possible interpretation of relevant segments of it, as well as with pertinent philosophical views. It remains up to us, however, to follow the option and subscribe to the theory or not. A crucial factor in making this decision are the puzzles I discuss in part 1, and the ability of the proposed theory to solve them, demonstrated in part 3. In this way, the puzzles form an integral part of the argument in favor of my approach, and are not just a lure or a bait for getting the reader's attention. Thus the argument resembles in its logical structure a Kantian deduction, in which we are invited to accept certain propositions on the joint ground that they are not contradicted by other true beliefs, and that they help make sense of important attitudes or experiences that otherwise appear senseless or mysterious.

1. The Puzzles of Ownership

I begin with a common though largely tacit picture that informs our thinking about property. Property rights regulate human relationships concerning objects. Such relationships need regulating because of the benefits people derive from objects. If it were not for these benefits, no one would care about objects, nor would there be any need to regulate relationships concerning them. To be suitable for property rights an object must hold the promise of some potential advantages.[4] These advantages can vary: they can be instrumental, aesthetic, sentimental, symbolic, and so on. Let me call the sum total of the potential advantages associated with a particular object, *object value*.[5] Property rights can be seen as determinations about how the object's potential advantages will be enjoyed and hence who will reap the object value. This picture naturally induces a reductionist, "bundle" view of ownership.[6] An object is likely to have numerous potential advantages, and it will be possible to contrive various ways of enjoying them. Consequently, multiple ways of combining advantages with ways of enjoying them exist. As we proliferate such bundles and distribute them among different individuals, no particular individual stands in a qualitatively distinct relation to the object. "Ownership" simply names one such bundle, its value consisting in the sum of potential advantages and modes of enjoyment that the bundle contains. What, after all, could be left of the idea of owning an object once all the specific advantages that can be gained from that object have been enumerated?

But the picture is incorrect. It starts to disintegrate as soon as we recognize instances in which ownership pertains to objects that have no advantages to offer on their own and whose object value is therefore nil. Such instances of ownership are rare, but they can be found, not surprisingly, in the context of collecting—not surprisingly, since collecting is a practice that particularly accentuates the value of ownership for its own sake. Although many collectibles, such as works of art, are a source of gratification outside of collecting, others are not: think of sea shells, bottle caps, or better yet, apricot pits.[7] Collectibles like these starkly represent a wide gap between object value, which here approaches the vanishing point, and *ownership value*, the value of owning these items, that can be quite considerable. Collecting worthless items involves a reversal of the logical relationship between ownership and value implied by the standard picture: to delight in the particular heap of otherwise useless items, the collector must recognize them as belonging to her. She does not value owning these items because she values the items, but the other way around: she values the items because she owns them. Ownership is logically prior to and is presupposed by the value to the collector of the collection.

This reversal poses an obvious challenge to the standard picture. The point of the rights and protections that are said to constitute ownership supposedly derives from the advantages that objects promise. But where the object has no value of its own, these components of the bundle are pointless. Consider, for example, the right to use the owned object. The owner of a collection of apricot pits would typically enjoy some privileged and protected access to them: she can look at them or touch them whenever she pleases. But if, as we assumed, apart from being hers the pits by themselves hold no attraction for her, so that she would derive no pleasure from seeing other piles of pits even once, why would the prospect of repeatedly observing this particular pile count as an improvement? Similarly with the other main components of the bundle, immunity to deprivation and, relatedly, a right to transfer: the collector cares about her ability to hold onto or transfer at will a given pile of apricot pits only if she recognizes the collection as hers. In short, the rights and protections that are the incidents of owning the collection are valuable only because of some prior relation to the objects that these incidents by themselves do not explain.[8]

The collecting cases we have examined are extreme, but this should not blind us to their significance.⁹ They present in a pristine form a pervasive phenomenon. In the case of the worthless collection, ownership value is easy to recognize because it stands alone as the exclusive value of ownership. Once ownership value is revealed in its pure form, it becomes easier to spot in more common situations in which it is less clearly visible. Unlike the collector's pits, cars and homes are sources of pleasure and utility. But these constituents of their object value do not exhaust the value of owning such objects. It is particularly notable that people often take pride in their own cars and homes that they do not take in those belonging to other people, even if, say by borrowing, they can otherwise enjoy these items to the same degree. Such disparate attitudes, even if not universally shared, are quite intelligible. But why is it appropriate that *I* take *pride* in the car I own? There are two different questions here, and an adequate account of ownership must answer them both. One question is why pride is the proper attitude, rather than, say, just pleasure in the car's appearance or the exhilaration of driving it. The other question is why should I, the owner, rather than someone else, such as a borrower, be entitled to take pride in this particular vehicle? Or, what amounts to the same question, what is it about my relation to the car that singles me out as the proper recipient of admiration that this car provokes?¹⁰

We have seen so far that ownership of objects can have value that is unaccounted for by the contribution that the objects themselves make to our welfare. We encounter a correspondingly puzzling phenomenon on the negative side of the normative scale: trespassing on someone's property is commonly viewed as per se wronging the owner, even if no setback to any of the owner's interests is involved. The most natural basis for this judgment points to the owner's autonomy. But why precisely is the owner's autonomy at stake? A simple answer is that due to the ownership, the owner's consent regarding matters that touch on her property is required; the nonconsensual handling of or entry into the property is accordingly all by itself a derogation of the owner's autonomy. On this picture ownership extends the scope of the owner's autonomy by making others' behavior regarding the property subject to the owner's will. But this simple answer will not do. Autonomy is, roughly speaking, a matter of having control over (or ability to make choices about) oneself and one's own life. It is an essentially reflexive value. Consequently, extending a person's power or control does not ipso facto augment that person's autonomy. Think of Regina, the reluctant heir apparent, who is forced to accede to the throne. Even though she now exercises a large measure of control over important affairs of state, her autonomy is not thereby expanded, and indeed may be contracted, if she is constrained to dedicate herself to the good of the people and thus, while controlling many other people's lives, is left with little control over her own. If the extended control that ownership involves is to expand the owner's autonomy, this control, unlike Regina's, must be reflexive: the added choices it affords and the consent it calls for must be all self-regarding. But how is one's control over other people's conduct regarding, say, a remote plot of land, all by itself self-regarding?

Ownership, moreover, plays in our normative discourse a role that goes beyond the assertion of rights to protest others' failure to abide by their corresponding duties. In ordinary normative discourse, owning an object can serve not just as the basis for invoking some existing rights but also for claiming additional ones.[11] Suppose that the law affords public access to the beach through Susan's land, or permits ranchers to have their cattle graze on it. It would be altogether natural for Susan to experience these legal dispensations as impositions, and it would seem legitimate, if not always laudable, for her to protest them and try to revoke them, so as to expand her rights in the land. Borrowing a legal term, we can express Susan's special position relative to her lot by saying that she has *standing* to demand rights in it. But why?

Notice that the very fact that blocking public access or stopping the grazing will enhance Susan's interests is not a satisfactory answer. First, they may not. Susan's resenting the intrusions is understandable quite apart from any detrimental effects the intrusions might have on her interests. To be sure, in such a case we might judge Susan to be mean-spirited and selfish. However, mean-spiritedness and selfishness, though deplorable, are intelligible attitudes, quite unlike the lunacy we would ascribe to Susan had she expressed similar sentiments toward the fact that, say, cattle are allowed to graze on the ranchers' own land. Moreover, the intelligibility of the nasty attitudes presents Susan with the opportunity of exhibiting their attractive contraries, such as the generosity of spirit of welcoming the benefits that accrue to others from using her land, an opportunity not available to her with regard to other people's property. But even if removing the intruders would in fact redound to Susan's benefit, her standing in the matter would not thereby be explained. After all, staying for free in a suite at the Plaza Hotel, or a round-the-world flight ticket might benefit her even more, without giving her any foothold to demand either or resent not getting it. What seems distinctive about the public's or the ranchers' rightful incursions into Susan's land is that by virtue of Susan's ownership, these incursions can be seen to affect her directly, even if no violation of her rights is involved. But this feature of ownership is not well captured by the view that ownership is exhaustively constituted by rights. Why does the fact that Susan already has certain rights in the land even tend to give her any special standing to claim that she be given additional rights in it? The puzzle increases when we recall that if Susan had the very same schedule of specific rights regarding the land but without these rights counting as her owning it, the rights by themselves would indeed fail to establish the connection to the land by virtue of which it becomes the basis for Susan's standing to claim additional rights with regard to it.[12]

My final observation concerns the expressive significance of ownership. A well-known decision by the Supreme Court provides a good illustration.[13] Requiring car owners to display license plates containing an ideologically loaded state motto ("Live Free or Die") was held to offend against the First Amendment. The Court reasoned that "the right of freedom of thought protected by the First Amendment ... includes the right to refrain from speaking at all," and that by requiring car owners to "use their private property as a 'mobile billboard' for the State's ideological message," the state violates this right just as surely as when it requires public high school students to participate in a ceremony involving a flag salute.[14] But why would posting a message on someone's property count as the owner's coerced expression? Once again, viewing ownership as a matter of certain rights with respect to an object does not give a satisfactory answer. After all, the allegedly offensive motto is not said to violate any of the owner's property rights, but rather his personal right to remain silent. How does the fact that he has some other rights with regard to the car, rights that are not themselves here at issue, make the car into a medium of self-expression, such that inscriptions that appear on it become attributable to the owner?

The puzzles I have described, of value, pride, autonomy, standing, and expressivity, seem to demonstrate that ownership has normative significance that exceeds the share that it secures in object value. Let me call the overall value of owning an object *proprietary value*. In my terminology, *proprietary value = object value + ownership value*. Sometimes, such as in my example of worthless collectibles, object value approaches the vanishing point, and proprietary value equals ownership value. Other cases are the opposite: ownership value tends toward zero, and proprietary value equals object value. But often, such as in owning a home or a car, we tend to value both the object and owning it, so that proprietary value consists in both. This normative structure reveals a corresponding conceptual one. Just as proprietary value can be unpacked into object value and ownership value, so also the concept of ownership can be divided into a *pragmatic* aspect, which consists in the different ways an individual can benefit from an object, and a nonpragmatic aspect, which for reasons that will soon become clear I call *constitutive*. The bundle theory gives us a plausible account of pragmatic ownership by reducing it to the host of specific ways the owner can enjoy the object value. But the account is incomplete in that it leaves out constitutive ownership and the ownership value to which it gives rise.[15]

2. Ownership and Self-Reference

Can ownership and its value be understood apart from the opportunities to benefit from a given object? I start with an obvious yet noteworthy observation. The puzzles I have listed are all distinctly philosophical puzzles. If confronted with corresponding queries in daily life, the layperson would not so much be baffled by them as by why they are being made, and at any rate would have an easy and quite uniform answer to them. If asked to explain why he cherishes a particular pile of apricot pits, the collector would naturally say: "Why, they're my pits!" A similarly emphatic use of *my* is usually all it takes to explain one's pride in a particular car. This is also the most likely and usually sufficient way for Susan to justify her resentment: "But they're intruding on my land, aren't they?" Finally, if asked why he cares about the message on a license plate or a sticker attached to his car, the car owner would again deem it natural and sufficient to point out that the offending inscription appears on *his* car. These simple answers are not proffered to the philosophical puzzles I have raised and should not therefore be expected to solve them. But the ordinary answers I imagined are highly relevant to solving the puzzles nonetheless. The task is to see what philosophical sense can be made of the use of *my* in these ordinary settings.

Another feature of ordinary discourse is equally significant here. We can easily imagine similar settings in which an emphatic use of *my* is made to assert and defend corresponding claims to the ones we have considered concerning however the body. For example, some people take pride in high cheekbones or shapely calves simply for the reason that these body parts are theirs; and all you're expected to say in support of your request that the person next to you move over is to point out that he's stepping on your toe. This similarity, I maintain, between our ordinary property-talk and body-talk provides a clue to an account of the constitutive aspect of ownership that, as shown in part 3, can solve all the puzzles I have listed in one fell swoop. The analogy between body and property has of course tempted other theorists before. For the most part, their approaches share a starting point and a metaphor. The starting point is the idea of self-ownership.[16] Although self-ownership is not quite the same as owning one's body, when self-ownership is used as a launching pad for a general theory of property, it must at least include or entail ownership of the body as a paradigm case of what owning a physical object amounts to or consists in. From this basic idea, the meaning of owning other physical objects can be extrapolated by means of the extension-of-self metaphor.[17] But the idea of self-ownership is perplexing, and the metaphor of extension of self, though suggestive, is obscure. The goal of a theory is accordingly to spell out the idea and the metaphor and give them a more precise philosophical content. In the next section I suggest an interpretation of the extension-of-self metaphor that focuses on the use of the first-person pronouns *I* and *me,* and draws the boundary of the self by reference to this use. In the remainder of this part I present an account of constitutive ownership that unifies ownership of one's body with that of other objects and that is based on the meaning of the personal pronouns that I discuss first.

Personal Pronouns and the Extension of the Self

A plausible strategy for making sense of the idea that the self can extend to objects beyond the body would consist in two steps: an account that shows why the body is a part or an aspect of the self, followed by a demonstration that the same account or one close enough to it applies to other objects as well. I begin, accordingly, with the question, In what sense is the body an aspect or a constituent of who I am? Now a straightforward, but for our purposes unpromising, answer to this question seems available. The body is constitutive of the self in that human beings are living organisms, and as such no different in respect of their physical composition from cats or cows. The analogy to other animals also suggests, however, why this approach would lead the extension-of-self metaphor to a dead-end. The physical composition of cats and cows is fixed and is coextensive with their bodies. There does not seem to be room for any extension with respect to such natural kinds. The analogy to other animals also reveals the shortcomings of an approach that relates people to their bodies on the same basis as exists in the case of other animals. To think of human beings as organisms is to adopt with respect to them an external perspective. But this perspective misses the distinguishing mark of being human, namely that we essentially relate to ourselves from an internal point of view, from the inside as it were. In other words, essential to being a human being is an awareness of how it is to be one. Although there is no fixed and consistent terminology in these matters, talk of the *self* tends to accentuate the primacy and centrality of the internal, first-person perspective that an adequate understanding of human beings must acknowledge. The real challenge here is to incorporate the view of human beings as living organisms into an adequate conception of self that takes full account of this essentially internal, first-person perspective.

The challenge has not been easy to meet. The main reason is that as soon as we accept the challenge and turn indoors, so to speak, we tend to lose our grip on the body altogether. An account of the self "from the inside" easily becomes an account of the mental, which seems to be the stuff of which our self-awareness is made. We find ourselves drifting in the direction of a Cartesian conception of the self and in the grips of the mind-body problem. Once a mental conception of the self is adopted, resurrecting the body and reattaching it to the self is no easy matter. The difficulty, then, is to acknowledge in our account of the self the first-person perspective without lapsing into a mentalistic view of the self. I will not try to go over the well-known difficulties that arise, but will mention instead one variation on this theme that is of special importance here. A natural and particularly influential way to incorporate the body within a unified first-person conception of the self is by recognizing and exploring the *experience* of embodiment. This is essentially the program of phenomenology: roughly, the effort to understand what the self is by spelling out the experience of being one. Three considerations, however, tell against a purely phenomenological account of the relationship of body to self. First, phenomenology's starting point is essentially Cartesian, so it is naturally heir to many of the problems of the Cartesian view of the self. Specifically, a phenomenological account seems to be faced with the specter of skepticism about the body. This skepticism can be global: an experience of embodiment does not guarantee or entail embodiment; but perhaps more plausibly, and therefore damagingly, it can be local: as phantom pains demonstrate, sensations do not prove the existence of the body parts in which they seem to occur. Second, although we do have distinctive experiences of some body parts, no experiences are associated with many others. If phenomenology were our guide to our physical composition, the result would differ considerably from our actual body. Third, not only does our experience of embodiment not coincide with the body, but phenomenology is ill equipped to capture even our mental life in its entirety. Much of our mental life is submerged below the surface of our awareness and is not experientially present to us. There is at least a need for considerable footwork here in order to incorporate all these regions within a phenomenological picture of the self.

That no firm experiential basis for incorporating the body within a first-person conception of the self can be found illustrates the difficulty of escaping a Cartesian, mentalistic conception while holding onto the first-person point of view. This point of view appears to give us a strong grip only on our mental life. But upon reflection this grip turns out to be illusory too. Mental states do not by themselves and as a matter of course belong to a self or constitute one. The point can be best made by comparing human states of mind to those of animals. Both my cat and I can be cold or hungry or in pain; we can both see the same mouse or dream about one. These sensations, representations, and images, we commonly surmise, are quite similar in the two cases, and yet in my case, but not the cat's, they belong to a self. Why? One answer, Kantian if not quite Kant's, fixes on my capacity for what I shall call *articulate self-awareness*.[18] In my case, each one of the listed states of mind, call it X, is subsumed or subsumable under another thought, namely that "I think (or feel, or experience) X." And it is only by virtue of this second, identifying thought that X can be ascribed, or give rise, to a self. In other words, the crucial feature that constitutes a self is the possession of the concept of one, or, more precisely, the concept "I." By subsuming various thoughts under this concept, I constitute those thoughts as those of a self. But if applying the concept "I" to a bunch of mental states is what converts those mental states into those of a self, then by the same token things other than mental states can be similarly converted into aspects of the self. Specifically, X could be the body or any of its parts. Just as in the case of thoughts, here too, by subsuming the latter under an *I* they become constituents of me as well.

A difference of course remains between the way mental states and the body are respectively subsumed under *I* and thus incorporated into the self, and this difference is responsible for the impression that a first-person perspective is bound to lead to a mentalistic conception of the self. Only in the case of mental states, but not in the case of the body, is the subsumption under *I* inexorable. I cannot help but register the pain I experience as mine. This creates the impression that the *I* already inheres in the pain and is bound up with it in a way that does not apply to the body.[19] But once we conceive of the cat's pain—no less acute but bereft of selfhood—we can pry apart, analytically speaking, the sensation of pain from my awareness of it as mine, thus realizing that the sensation by itself, the pure sensation if you like, does not stand to the self in a fundamentally different relationship than the body: both types of items are aspects or constituents of a self only through the conceptual mediation of an *I*. Mind and body stand on an equal footing relative to the composition of the self inasmuch as both require and commonly receive the endorsement or underwriting of an *I* as the conceptual vehicle by means of which the self is constituted.

I cannot hope to deal adequately in this space with all the issues that this picture of the self raises,[20] but two must be briefly addressed. The first concerns the nature of the first-person perspective whose primacy to our conception of the self I urge. Doesn't thinking of the body as a constituent of the self apart from the experiences with which the body is associated or to which it gives rise amount to abandoning this perspective after all? Haven't we drained the self of its subjectivity, which the first-person perspective is meant to recognize and instantiate? The answer to these worries, suggested by the cat analogy, is that they reflect a prevailing confusion or displacement as to the nature and location of the subjectivity that is distinctly the self's. Once we are led by our reflection on animals' mental life to recognize a gap between being the subject of mental states and being a self, it becomes clear that the distinguishing experience of being a self does not reside in the mental states themselves, but rather in a particular mode of conceiving or relating to them, namely the mode expressed in the application of an *I* to them. The first-person perspective can accordingly hold onto this distinctive stance, call it *identification*, by which a self relates to some properties or occurrences as its own, without limiting itself to the mental or even privileging it.

The second issue I need to address concerns the possibility of misidentification. It has been famously observed that occurrent mental states are immune to such an error by the agent: in reporting being in pain or believing that it is Sunday, there cannot be a question as to who is really having the experience or the belief. In the case of the body, though, mistakes are possible. I may misidentify a bodily event by either failing to realize that it took place in my body or by mistakenly believing that an event in someone else's body happened in mine.[21] Does not this possibility of extending or withholding the *I* in the wrong circumstances belie the alleged priority of the first-person perspective when the body is concerned? Does not the very judgment of an erroneous application of the *I* demonstrate that in this case the third-person perspective dominates after all? Such an objection would miss, I believe, what is meant by associating selfhood with possessing the concept "I." This view is not meant to release the self from an intersubjective reality but rather to ground it in one. In order to be a self one must be in possession of *I*. But as is the case with any other linguistic aptitude, "possessing" a term or a concept is a matter of having a disposition to use it correctly. Such aptitude is properly assessed in light of both actual and counterfactual use. Occasional erroneous applications of a concept can be dismissed as such as long as the assumption can be maintained that the speaker would have rectified her usage had she been apprised of all the relevant facts. One's disposition to use *I* correctly, that is, in line with the applicable social understandings, can accordingly be maintained as a criterion for the composition and boundary of the self so long as that disposition is seen to include counterfactual use, thus allowing us to dismiss or rectify erroneous applications.

We can conclude, therefore, that both mind and body are constituents of the self inasmuch as they are both endorsed or underwritten by a self-referential use of the *I*. Let me now be a bit more specific about what this endorsement or underwriting consists in. To do so it will be useful to distinguish two different notions that are commonly involved in predicative statements: *reference* and *allusion*. Consider the following statements: "The horse has cavities," "The car has a flat tire," and "The game of chess was decided by the brilliant gambit." At least on our commonsensical view of these statements, the terms *horse, car,* and *game of chess* refer, respectively, to a horse, a car, and a game of chess, but allude to teeth, a tire, or a gambit. (It is irrelevant for the purpose of this distinction whether the items alluded to are explicitly mentioned in the respective statements, as they are in the two latter examples, or not, as in the first.) These allusions reveal our beliefs about the constitution of the objects referred to. For the statements to be true, the allusions must hold: the items alluded to must in fact be constituents of the referred objects. Among the many kinds of error to which such statements are prone is a failure of allusion. For example, it may turn out upon inspection that the damaged teeth are in fact dentures, and thus not part of the horse after all. The notion of allusion gives rise to a related idea, namely that of the *scope* of referring terms such as *horse*. The scope of such a term corresponds to the composition of the object referred to. The relation between allusion and scope is simply this: everything we permissibly allude to in speaking of an object falls within the scope of the term labeling it. Since we can speak both about a particular horse as well as about horses in general, allusion and scope pertain both to the singular term and to the general one. So even if my alluding to a particular horse's teeth is erroneous (because it has none), alluding to horses' teeth in general is appropriate, whereas alluding to their wings is not. We can put this by saying that teeth do, but wings do not, fall within the scope of *horse*.

My suggestion that to be a constituent of the self the body must be endorsed or underwritten by an *I* can now be simply restated. All this requires is that the pronoun *I* as we commonly use it allude to the body, so that the body fall within the pronoun's scope. This condition is of course satisfied abundantly. Our self-referential talk (or reflection) is as rife with allusions to the body ("I gained ten pounds") as it is replete with allusions to the mind ("I believe that today is Tuesday"). Such allusions express, as I just suggested, one's identification with the body and provide the basis for seeing the body as a constituent of the self. By thus establishing the grounds for including the body within the boundaries of the self, we have concluded the first step in the two-step strategy that I recommended for interpreting the extension-of-self metaphor. The remaining second step is to demonstrate that these grounds extend beyond the body and apply to other objects as well. This is easy to do; indeed so easy, that some misgivings are bound to arise.

My main task in the remainder of this section will be accordingly to allay such misgivings.

First the demonstration. Consider a simple request, such as, "Please take a picture of me," or a report such as, "I was hit by a car." As we have just seen, *me* and *I* in these utterances refer to me but allude specifically to my body. When I ask you to take a picture "of me," I obviously have in mind a picture of my body. Similarly, when I report that I was hit by a car, the physical contact was between the car and my body. My request for the picture and my report of the accident express, accordingly, my identification with my body, and as I have just argued, that identification is what establishes the body as a constituent of the self. But let us consider now another feature of these utterances. My request for a picture is not normally understood to connote a nude portrait. Similarly, in reporting that I was hit by a car, I may be in fact describing an accident in which my car rather than my body was hit. The personal pronouns, while still referring to me, turn out to allude in these instances to other objects beside my body, and correspondingly, the physical boundary of the self as indicated by these allusions is not coextensive with the body: it includes my clothing in the one case and my car in the other. Moreover, extensions in the scope of the pronouns do not necessarily depend on the contiguity of the relevant objects, clothing or car, with the body. Consider events such as car or horse races, and dog or cat shows. It is natural for the owner to report in these contexts: "I participated in the race" or "I won the competition" even if the owner was not present at the event.[22] Based on the criterion I propose, these self-referential expressions lead to the conclusion that the scope of *I* and hence the boundary of the self may extend beyond the body and incorporate other objects as well.[23]

But as I just said, this simple procedure for extending the boundaries of the self may seem too simple and may appear, if consistently followed, to lead us astray. Using in general our putative allusions as guides to the composition or boundaries of objects would play havoc with our ordinary ontology without any clear theoretical payoff. If by virtue of the allusion of *me* in "Take a picture of me" my clothing is an extension of my self, is the collar not also an extension of the dog due to an apparently corresponding allusion of *dog* in "Take a picture of the dog?" Similarly, when asked at a dinner table to pass the salt, you'll be ill advised to first empty the shaker. Are we to conclude that shakers fall within the scope of *salt,* so that the salt includes its shaker? We must, in other words, beware of what are only apparent or putative allusions that do not carry any implications with regard to the composition of the objects involved, and distinguish them from earnest or literal ones that do have such implications. But how are we to do that? It is natural to suppose that in order to ascertain which allusions are serious and sound we must turn to the items concerned and inspect them directly. Contextual variation in what the terms we use designate is not by itself a safe ontological guide. Reading off the composition of things from the way we talk about them would appear to have matters in reverse.

These are weighty worries, and given the complexity of the issues they raise, I cannot hope to put them fully to rest. But they can, I believe, be significantly allayed. It should be immediately acknowledged that with regard to many terms, most significantly natural kind terms such as *dog* and *salt*, the worries are well grounded. Two features of such terms are particularly relevant here. First, at least according to our commonsense conceptual scheme, endorsed by many though obviously not all philosophical views of the matter, dogs and salt are mind independent: they remain unaffected in their composition or constitution by our beliefs about them, no matter how widely shared. This implies that our dog-talk or salt-talk has no particular authority with regard to the dogs or the salt. Our speech must be amended or interpreted in light of the latest results of inspecting the items themselves. If the inspection yields results that contradict our shared beliefs embedded in ordinary usage, the beliefs will change, and the usage will follow suit or else be interpreted as loose or metaphoric. But this strategy is not always available. Suppose that someone asks you the height of the Empire State Building, and you answer that it is 1,453 feet high. The interlocutor challenges your reply, and upon further inquiry it turns out that you have included in your answer the length of the television antenna on top of the building, whereas your interlocutor maintains that the correct answer should include the 102 floors sans antenna. How is this dispute about the composition and the boundary of the building to be resolved? Surely not by inspecting this particular building nor by studying others. Whether the antenna is part of the building is purely a matter of convention, and the best way to ascertain what the convention is, is by investigating actual usage: do other speakers who refer to buildings allude, when circumstances so require, to their antennae as well? In contrast to the case of the dog's constitution, usage taken as a whole is veridical here: there is no prospect of some future discovery concerning buildings and their appurtenances requiring that we revise our understanding in this area, and correspondingly our usage.

The second, and related, relevant feature of natural kind terms is their social inertness. Dogs and salt are not altered by social practices. So in interpreting what "taking a picture of a dog" means, it is easy to distinguish the practice of photography as it applies to the dog on the one hand, from the dog itself on the other. Similarly, the meaning of "Pass the salt" understood as part of the practice of table manners does not affect the meaning of "salt." But contrast in this respect natural kind terms with social terms, by which I mean terms whose referents are social phenomena, such as institutions, organizations, and so forth.[24] Here, shared beliefs, discursively embedded, are not just veridical with respect to an independently existing reality, as in the case of the Empire State Building, but are constitutive of that reality. Consequently, when the bits of social reality to which these terms pertain are formed by the same linguistic community in which the terms themselves originate, no gap, of the kind possible in the case of natural kinds, exists between the meaning of the terms we use and the reality they designate: the meaning of the terms and these realities are formed and change in tandem by the same social practices and understandings; changes in the one must correspond to changes in the other. Take terms such as *marriage, money,* and *baseball*. The precise content of these terms varies over time, and it covaries with the respective practices to which these terms refer. The covariation is secured by the fact that what is at any time the meaning of "marriage" or "money" or "baseball" and what counts, respectively, as marriage or money or baseball, are one and the same. Now it is clear in light of this state of affairs that the strategy I have recommended of studying the constitution of some things by inspecting the scope of the terms we use to refer to them is quite plausible in the case of social phenomena. Indeed, there really is no fundamental difference between studying the phenomena directly and studying the language used to refer to them, because in either case we will be looking at one and the same thing: the system of shared meanings and understandings that constitute both the semantics of the terms we use and social reality itself.

How does all of this bear on exploring the constitution of the self? The answer depends on what kind of thing the self is. As living organisms, human beings are natural kinds. But as I have pointed out already, that is not the perspective that the idea of self designates. I have so far associated the idea of self with a distinctly human capacity for articulate self-awareness. But there is a second tradition of thinking about the self that I wish now to bring into play: the view of the self as socially constructed.[25] My aim is not to argue for this view, but to point out its relevant ramifications. To claim that the self is socially constructed is in the first place to offer a genealogical or etiological theory of the self. But this is not my main interest in this perspective. Implicit in the view concerning the social origins of the self is a more important claim about the kind of thing the self is. It must be the kind of thing that can at least in principle be constructed by society. The self must accordingly belong to the same category or order of things as social practices, institutions, games, and the like. What category or order is that? For our present purposes the answer focuses on the two features I have associated with natural kind terms, mind independence and social inertness, contrasting the self with such terms in both respects. If the self is an essentially social phenomenon, then no clear line separates the self from the discursively embedded system of shared beliefs and understandings concerning it, or from the various social practices in which it is implicated. The most common way in which these abstract ideas are encountered in our ordinary experience is through the notion of social role. We are quite used to thinking about people's identities in terms of such roles. Roles in this way straddle the divide, and efface the gap, between selves on the one side and social practices on the other. So, for example, how one behaves, what one feels and says in one's capacity as a *spouse,* are at once manifestations of the institution of marriage and manifestations of one's own particular self.

But even if some aspects of the self can plausibly be considered socially constructed, it may seem puzzling how this perspective can apply to the physical extension of the self. Though the issues here are complex, a simple analogy will suffice to make the point. Suppose that in a multipurpose stadium someone asks you to delineate the boundary of the playing field and name its various parts. The question is meaningless unless the interrogator indicates which game he has in mind: say, is it baseball, football, or soccer? The boundary and the configuration of the field clearly depend on the social practice, in this case the game, of which it is a component. Obviously, the game does not bring about physical changes in the ground. Conceived as a physical object, the field does not change from game to game. But to think of it as a playing field is precisely not to think of it in purely physical terms. It is to endow a physical object with a certain meaning or significance, to count it as this or that, in ways that do not simply represent or supervene on its physical properties. The source of this meaning or significance, the origin of this "counting as," is the game we assume as the background to the interrogator's question. Since different games can be played at different times in the same stadium, the boundary and configuration of the playing field will vary depending on the game. So, for example, in relating to the field as a baseball field one would mention the mound as a feature or constituent but ignore the goals, while the reverse will be apposite if soccer were assumed as the background. The same is true of the physical composition of the self. Different social practices invest parts of the body as well as other objects with meaning or significance that is adequately expressed by subsuming in the appropriate circumstances those body parts and other objects within the scope of *I.* To think of the self as socially constructed is, accordingly, to recognize the relevance of social context to its physical constitution just as social roles are seen to bring social context to bear on other aspects of our identity.

It may be objected, however, that even if in principle legitimate, deriving the boundary of the self from the scope of *I* as used in different social settings is unnecessarily circuitous. Why, in charting the boundaries of the self, should we bother to investigate people's allusions in using *I*, rather than simply ask them directly whether this or that is a constituent of them? Moreover, if we pursued the latter course, the answers we would get would likely be quite different from the ones obtained by the roundabout method. If asked, most people would maintain that, say, a hand is part of them but that a car is not. This objection, however, would miss the nature of the present investigation. The concept of self that we are trying to elucidate is a theoretical, not an ordinary, concept, and as such it draws its meaning from the broader theoretical context, in the present case the social construction approach, within which it plays a role. It would be, accordingly, pointless to address to a layperson the question, "Is X a constituent of your self?" Unless philosophically trained, most people would be baffled by such a question. However, the alternative and apparently more appropriate formulation, "Is X part of you?" is not in fact equivalent to the former formulation, but is rather an invitation to use *I* on a particular occasion. People's response to this question would not settle the philosophical one concerning the concept of self and its boundaries. Instead, their response would only supply a small part of the answer to the philosophical question by revealing one segment of the overall picture of the respondent's self, namely, that segment with which the respondent identifies through her use of *I* within the social context defined by a direct scientific interrogation concerning her physical constitution. The respondent's avowals and disavowals under such circumstances have no direct implications concerning the boundaries of her self revealed in different circumstances in which the use of *I* is governed by a different social practice or context.

We can now put together the two approaches to the self I have sketched, articulate self-awareness and social construction, by fixing on the first-person pronoun *I* as the term whose scope as determined by the appropriate social practices and understandings corresponds to and covaries with the composition and boundaries of the self. What distinguishes on this view the self from other social constructs is the fact that the social determination of the self's constitution is mediated by self-awareness that consists in the disposition to correctly apply the word *I*.[26]

Possessive Pronouns and Ownership

I turn now to the notion of self-ownership from which a general conception of ownership will be derived. We must account for the sense in which people own their bodies, and then observe how, by virtue of the extension of self we have so far elaborated, that account applies to and explains the ownership of other objects too. Two earlier observations motivate the proposed account. The first is that we ordinarily use the possessive pronoun *my* to assert claims of ownership and to defend them in the situations that the puzzles described in part 1 represent. Second, the same possessive pronoun performs a similar function with regard to the body as well. To see how these observations yield an account of self-ownership, a third must be added, namely that in self-referential utterances in which allusion to the body is intended, the personal and the possessive pronouns, *I* and *my,* are commonly used interchangeably: the results of a mishap while slicing bread can be reported either as "I am bleeding" or alternatively as "my finger is bleeding." How are we to understand such uses with regard to the body of both types of pronouns?

The first thing to notice is that this use of the possessive pronouns is not unique to talk about the human body but is perfectly general. Instead of saying that the bear is brown, we can say that its fur is, or its color. Cognate expressions, most significantly *have* and its derivatives, are often used to convey the same thought: the bear has brown color or brown fur, just as Paul may be said to have a snub nose. I will call this use of the possessive pronoun, and correspondingly of *have* and cognate expressions, *constitutive,* because it relates a thing to its constituents. This constitutive use of possessive pronouns and their cognates, though pervasive, is obviously not the only one: saying of the horse that it has a good rider or that it lost its rider, does not imply that riders are constituents of horses. But in the case of the body and its parts, the constitutive sense of possessive pronouns and their cognate expressions is clearly at play.

My second observation is equally mundane. There is a perfectly general sense of *own* that corresponds to the constitutive use of possessive pronouns and their cognates. This sense is mostly used to emphasize the reflexive relation of a thing to its constituents: the horse tripped over its own legs or bit its own lip simply highlights that legs and lips are the horse's constituents. By the same token, to speak of my own finger or leg is to highlight the constitutive relation that these parts bear to me. Here again this strong sense of *own* must be distinguished from a weaker sense, at play when relationships to an object that are not constitutive are signified, as in "the horse bit its own rider." But the strong constitutive sense is central and distinctive, as is the corresponding sense of the possessive pronouns and the cognate expressions that I have mentioned.

We can extrapolate from these observations a basic, broad, and rather trivial interpretation of self-ownership, namely as marking the relation of a thing to its constituents. On this interpretation, my owning my body or its parts amounts to no more than the horse's owning its: in both cases the locution marks the respective constitutive relations.[27] But although this sense of self-ownership is not distinctive to human beings, the possibility of deriving from it a general concept of ownership that applies beyond the body is. Only in the case of humans can ownership, in the same constitutive sense, extend beyond the body, because the self, as I argued in the previous section, can so extend. Due to my articulate self-awareness, things other than the body can be mine in the strong, constitutive sense, insofar as I can allude to them by my use of *I;* and insofar as the self is socially constructed, the grounds for my alluding by the *I* to such other objects may be purely a matter of social practice.

The thought that possessive pronouns and their cognates can mark a constitutive relation to objects we own is further corroborated by the use and etymology of the word *property* itself. Ordinary usage and the dictionary distinguish two main groups of meanings of *property:* one concerns such things as the qualities, traits, and attributes of a thing, and the other concerns the ownership of objects that is our present subject matter. (To distinguish the two I will in the remainder of this section capitalize Property in the second sense.) But the relation between the two senses is more than a pun. First, they both have the same etymological source: the Latin *proprias* for "own." Second, the entire battery of terms that we have just encountered, consisting of the possessive pronouns and such cognates as *have, possess, acquire,* and *belong,* pertain both to the relation of a thing to its properties as well as to a person and her Property. If my argument concerning the extension of self in the previous section is sound, then my relation to my properties, such as, say, height, that I mark by the constitutive use of the possessive pronoun, is indeed no different in principle from my relation to my Property, such as a car, that is similarly expressed. Saying about both my properties and my Property that they are mine expresses the same underlying thought, namely that they are candidates for allusion in the proper circumstances by my use of *I,* and hence that they fall within its scope and correspondingly within the boundaries of my self.

These considerations suggest a first, rough approximation of the constitutive sense of ownership. *Ownership, as signaled by the application of a possessive pronoun to an object, consists in the permissible inclusion of that object within the scope of the personal pronouns as used by the putative owner.*[28] The idea of something's being a constituent of me is thus logically prior to its being mine: *myness* is a suspended or potential *meness.* But logical priority should not be confused with temporal priority: an object may become mine first.[29] The conventions for acquiring property can be best understood in this way. By buying a car I make it mine in the sense that I may now allude to it self-referentially whenever I participate in a practice such as a race that calls for or legitimates such use of the personal pronouns. But though this is what acquiring a car means, the acquisition is obviously not annulled if I never enter the car in a race nor participate in any other practice that occasions the *I/me* allusion to it. This relative independence of *myness* from *meness* can be carried a step further. Once practices of acquisition are in place, objects can be acquired even in the absence within the relevant social setting of occasions to apply the personal pronouns to these particular objects. The meaning of ownership, however, does not thereby change. The semantic criterion I propose can be still satisfied in such situations, though in a hypothetical or a counterfactual manner. We can always imagine practices and settings within which what is mine would be appropriately alluded to by *I* or *me*. Such imagination is guided and underwritten by the other cases in which the *me/my* usage applies and by our recognition that it takes only an appropriate social convention, rather than an ontological leap, to bridge the seeming gulf between what is mine and what is me.[30]

Ownership and Identity

Although this account captures, I believe, the gist of our ordinary concept of ownership, deriving a general conception of ownership from our relation to our bodies involves a considerable simplification and idealization. We must now take account of these by attending to some of the complications involved in constitutive ownership of objects other than the body. Notice first that in drawing the analogy between owning the body and owning other objects, I have focused mainly on the link between including an object within the scope of a personal pronoun on the one hand, and including it within the boundaries of the self on the other. But a further question ought now to be considered: What guides or determines the inclusion of different items within the scope of the personal pronouns in the first place? What kinds of considerations fix the socially sanctioned allusions of *I*? Though the topic is very large, a preliminary and schematic overview will help see the difference in this regard between ownership of the body and that of other objects, and to appreciate some of the complications that arise.

We can best see the various grounds on which the personal pronouns encompass objects by dividing objects into three categories: the body and its parts; objects that are attached to the body; and objects that are not. We can also distinguish three broad types of reasons for including a physical object within the boundaries of the self: naturalistic, phenomenological, and pragmatic. Naturalistic reasons relate to a conception of human beings as living organisms. Although, as I argued earlier, this conception does not by itself provide an account of the self, it does play a decisive role in the use of *I* and through it in shaping the self. Phenomenological reasons pertain for the most part to a conception of human beings as agents. There is a host of experiences associated with agency or presupposed by it—spatial orientation, control, and so on—and those too are acknowledged by or incorporated into the use of *I*. Pragmatic reasons conceive human beings as subjects of welfare; the contribution of such reasons to the scope of *I* is mainly oriented toward the promotion of such welfare.

Now the difference between owning the body and other objects can be understood in terms of the relationship between these types of reasons on the one hand and the three kinds of objects I have just distinguished on the other. Most significantly, only with respect to the body do all three types of reasons apply. Since other objects are not part of the naturalistic conception of human beings, their participation in the self can be based only on phenomenological or pragmatic reasons. Both kinds of reasons can apply to the second category, consisting of objects that are contiguous with the body. A number of writers have observed important similarities and continuities between experiences relating to the body and experiences relating to such objects. The experience of mastery and control over body parts that is central to agency, for example, extends to the tools we use as well; spatial orientation that permits one to correctly assess clearance extends to the hat one wears; and so on.[31] These examples also illustrate the obvious pragmatic value of such objects and of our bodily contiguity with them. Finally, when it comes to the third group of objects, those that are detached from the body, phenomenology for the most part plays no role, and pragmatic reasons predominate.

To appreciate the significance of these differences for the idea of ownership, it should be next noted that a conception of property as an extension of self links ownership to identity; in my version, *I* refers to and circumscribes the self, and in doing so it must observe some general imperatives of identity. ("Identity" is used here broadly and loosely to range over such disparate things as physical objects on the one hand and, say, social institutions on the other.) Such imperatives vary greatly, and in the case of the self raise particularly thorny issues, but three rather weak imperatives would seem to apply, at least presumptively, to all types of entities: duration, continuity, and exclusivity. Ordinarily, entities endure for at least some time; they exist during that time continuously; and their existence is exclusive of other things, in the sense that some way is available at least in principle for telling them apart from other things. The reason that such imperatives can be at all stated generally, even if only tentatively and vaguely, is that they do not in the first place derive from the nature of the great multitude and hetero-geneity of things to which they apply but rather from the needs of the mind applying them. Simply put, their satisfaction at least to a minimal degree provides for a mental grip necessary to recognize and individu-ate an entity as such.

Thanks mainly to the naturalistic basis for including the body within the scope of the *I*, the body by and large satisfies these three imperatives of identity as a matter of course. The rules for using *I* in allusion to the body are to a large extent simply parasitic on our ordinary ontology of living organisms. Consequently, ownership of the body persists as long as the owner exists (though for shorter stretches of time in the case of various body parts); is continuous, in that the rules for using the pro-nouns to allude to the body permit their application, actual or counter-factual, at any time, including such times as sleep and unconsciousness, during which no phenomenological basis for such application exists; and there are ordinarily (that is to say, excepting such unusual cases as Siamese twins) no claimants to the body other than the owner.

In the case of other objects, to which no natural ties exist, the situa-tion becomes murkier and more problematic. Our phenomenological and pragmatic encounters with objects that license alluding to them by an *I* may be brief, or intermittent, and, most damagingly as far as iden-tity is concerned, they may conflict. Occasions can easily arise in which multiple potential claimants are in principle entitled to use the *I/my* locutions with respect to the same object. So in order to perform ade-quately the constitutive role I ascribe to them, conventions defining own-ership must deliberately replicate or approximate the three imperatives of identity that the body satisfies as a matter of course. To be the owner of an object, and thus to have this object incorporated within the bound-aries of one's self, one must ideally be able to allude to it by an *I* on an enduring, continuous, and exclusive basis. The ideal is rarely achieved, in part due to the fact that constitutive ownership is often overlaid by other institutionalized relationships to objects that share the same vocab-ulary though not the same meaning. Nonetheless, duration, continuity, and exclusivity are salient aspects of our ordinary conception of owner-ship and are well recognized at least as regulative ideas in the law.[32]

In light of these considerations, the preliminary account of constitu-tive ownership ventured in the preceding section may be now supple-mented to read as follows: *Ownership, as signaled by the application of a possessive pronoun to an object, consists in the permissible inclusion, on a sufficiently enduring, continuous, and exclusive basis, of that object within the scope of the personal pronouns as used by the putative owner.*[33]

Even with these strictures in place, however, the suggestion may seem unsatisfactory: given that property rarely satisfies the three conditions of identity I spelled out nearly as well as the body, the resulting conception of identity would be too unruly to be of much use. I will not try to rebut the objection but only to dull its edge by downplaying its importance. I can do so summarily by enlisting for this purpose the conclusions reached in Derek Parfit's well-known study of personal identity.[34] Like most philosophers who deal with this topic, Parfit is concerned for the most part with temporal identity, whereas our present inquiry primarily raises issues of what we may call *compositional identity,* concerning the composition of the self and its boundaries at any given time. The two issues are closely related, however, in part through the two temporal factors, continuity and endurance, that appear to influence our judgments of compositional identity as well. Now on Parfit's view, temporal continuity is a matter of degree, so that a former self can be more or less connected to a later one; there is no deep fact of the matter as to whether two temporally bound selves are stages of a single one or not. My aim here is not to repeat or examine Parfit's arguments, but only to point out their potential relevance to the present issue. The same scalar picture that applies to the self's temporal identity would seem to apply to compositional identity as well. The indeterminacy and flux we observe in the use of pronouns, both personal and possessive, are consistent with such a scalar view of the self. On this view, the question whether something is a part or an aspect of me does not present at a deep level a genuine binary option, and it need not have a single correct answer. Parfit suggests that we can nonetheless preserve the binary logic that he associates with the concept of identity, by legislating a clear-cut if somewhat arbitrary criterion in light of which binary determinations concerning personal temporal identity can be made. Doing so, he maintains, is harmless as long as it is also held that, our ordinary beliefs to the contrary notwithstanding, "identity is not what matters." He advocates accordingly revising the prevailing attitude toward the self by diminishing the normative significance we attach to its identity. Seen in these terms, my approach tilts in the opposite direction: it retains the ordinary normative significance we attach to our compositional identity, while allowing that due to the self's scalarity, a looser concept of identity may be appropriate to it, one that accommodates a high degree of fluctuation and indeterminacy in its composition and boundaries.

But what precisely is the normative significance of our compositional identity? Why does it matter whether something is a constituent of me or not? In the next part I turn to this question with an eye to solving the puzzles that were presented in part 1.

3. Value and Ownership: Solving the Puzzles

The analogy along the lines I have suggested between body and property as constituents of the self offers quite a straightforward solution to the puzzles discussed in part 1. I shall first outline the general shape of the solution, and consider the specific puzzles next. The general point follows from the observation that the normative significance of the body is not in the first place a matter of whatever rights concerning the body we may be said to have. Rather, the body's primary normative significance is that of a constituent of the self; the rights regarding the body are one kind of normative ramification of this more fundamental fact. But why is being a constituent of the self of normative significance and a source of rights? The answer draws on a battery of what I call *personalized* norms and evaluative attitudes that provide a background or a foundation for much of our moral and more broadly normative life. By personalized I mean norms and attitudes, either self- or other-regarding, that have particular persons as their objects. Obviously not all norms and evaluative attitudes belong in this category: restrictions against deforestation and love of art do not. But some of the most important norms and attitudes, such as dignity, autonomy, and pride, do. By virtue of its constitutive relationship to the self, the body triggers or activates these values (using value broadly and loosely), since by applying to a body these values are deemed to apply to the person whose body it is. Now in light of the considerations presented in part 2, the same is true of property as well. The determination through ownership of the self's boundaries similarly assumes normative significance in light of these personalized norms and attitudes, whose scope tracks the boundaries of self. By fixing the boundaries of the self, ownership helps determine the occasions in which these norms and attitudes are activated and apply.

This is perhaps easiest to see in regard to autonomy. Nonconsensual bodily intrusions are normally wrongful per se, even in the absence of any harm. The wrongfulness can be easily explained in this case in terms of the victim's autonomy. Such intrusions satisfy the reflexive element in autonomy by virtue of the implicit recognition, obvious yet noteworthy, of the body as a constituent of the self and hence as falling within the scope of the person's autonomy. The crucial point here is that a body-affecting action does not have normative significance qua body-affecting, but rather because of its being person-affecting as well: as a matter of course, behavior toward the body counts as behavior toward the person whose body it is. The wrongfulness of harmless trespassing can be now understood along similar lines. Such trespassing too derogates the owner's autonomy. But why is the control ownership affords the owner over, say, some remote land a matter of *autonomy?* Remember that in order for the control over an object that ownership involves to be a manifestation of or contribution to the owner's autonomy all by itself and apart from the contribution to her welfare that is afforded her thereby, the control must be seen to satisfy autonomy's essentially *reflexive* nature. Consequently, the only way in which increasing a person's control over regions external to her would all by itself involve her autonomy is if a corresponding extension of her self is also affected. In other words, ownership must be capable of converting what would have otherwise been other-regarding preferences and choices into self-regarding ones, and it does so by incorporating, in the way I have outlined, the owned object within the boundaries of the self.

The point about standing is similar. Our rights concerning the body are not absolute, but our normative standing exceeds such rights and permits us to claim additional ones. So, for example, in *Breithaupt v. Abram,*[35] the Supreme Court held that no rights were violated when the police ordered that a blood sample be taken from a comatose patient suspected of drunk driving. But even if it is accepted that Breithaupt was neither harmed nor wronged by the bodily intrusion, no one would doubt that Breithaupt had standing to protest drawing the blood. Again, the conclusion may be simply seen to rest on the realization that by affecting his body, the action affects *him,* thus bringing into play the battery of personalized values and attitudes such as autonomy that I have mentioned.[36] So also with regard to property. As we saw in the case of Susan's lot on the beach, one can be normatively implicated with the goings-on on one's property beyond the reach of one's actual rights in that property and in ways that make one's ownership the basis for claiming additional rights and protections. The reason is that through ownership, the goings-on on the beach are deemed to affect one directly in much the same way that body-affecting actions affect one directly even if the actions are unfelt by the person whose body it is, do not harm her, and do not violate any of her rights.

The normative bootstrapping in Susan's case takes place on the basis of some ownership rights she has in the plot. But a similar process can also start at ground level, normatively speaking, creating ownership rights ex nihilo, as it were. When a constitutive relationship a person forms to an object through some facts and practices concerning his interacting with it attains a sufficient level of de facto exclusivity, duration, and permanence, so that it becomes appropriate to appeal to personalized values as applying to that person by virtue of that relationship, a successful claim can sometimes be made for the legal recognition and endorsement of this state of affairs by granting him ownership rights in that object. In such a case, what can be described as a *pure* constitutive relationship to an object, one that is as yet devoid of any rights, precedes and undergirds ownership rights in that object. Law's willingness to grant ownership rights based on *adverse possession* can be interpreted along such lines and so provide the paradigm example.[37]

As I pointed out, autonomy is not the only personalized value that bears on the normative significance of the body and correspondingly of that of property as well. Consider the case of the body first. Our opposition to corporal punishment, for example, is not mostly based on deference to the offender's supposed preferences in the matter: we would not feel much more comfortable with optional flogging than with mandatory flogging. Why? The most natural way of answering this question is in terms of the idea of human dignity. Dignity is bound up with respect: to say that people have dignity is to say that they ought to be respected. Respect is an expressive value, embedded in a system of social meanings. The affront to dignity that flogging involves is a matter of the meaning it carries, and that meaning does not change with a particular defendant's consent. The body serves here as the medium through which a symbolic message concerning the person is registered and takes effect. Now similar observations apply to property as well. Like one's body, one's property is a medium through which respect toward one or disrespect may be conveyed, thus providing an additional arena for affirmations and denials of one's dignity. Consider the following example from a recent novel by Philip Roth.[38] As a defiant act of protest, a disgruntled poor man, evicted from an apartment whose rent he can no longer afford, defecates, before leaving the apartment, in the living room, and proceeds to smear the walls with his excrement. The owner is obviously the intended target of this action. But how is he supposed to be affected by it? Since the narrative context within which this act takes place concerns resentment against the capitalist system, neither the perpetrator nor the reader should be expected to assume that the physical discomfort of coping with the mess would be visited upon the owner himself. It is much more likely in this context that some janitors will be dispatched to do the cleanup. And yet the shocking gesture is rightly perceived as directed against the owner and not against the janitors. Here again, it is the expressive nature of the action that is of primary significance. But why of all people should the expression address the owner? The simple answer is that defecating in someone's living room counts as an expression of disrespect against the person whose apartment it is just as surely as some other actions taken with regard to someone's body count as insults to the person whose body it is. Constitutive ownership provides in both cases the crucial link between the person and the offensive meaning of the actions involved.

By generalizing this example we can now answer the puzzle of value with which we began. How are we to understand the surplus value that owning an object seems to involve over and above the stream of benefits the object provides? The idea of dignity provides at least the beginning or an answer.[39] As a constituent of the self, the body provides an arena in which a person's dignity can be affirmed or denied through expressions of respect or disrespect. On the view I urge, the physical constitution of the self is not coextensive with the body. Insofar as other objects participate in the self's constitution, they too become avenues for the expression of respect or disrespect and are in this sense affected with dignity too. In short, ownership value is our own value extended to various objects.[40]

We can now dispose summarily of the two remaining puzzles, of expressivity and pride, along similar lines. Similarly to autonomy, pride is a self-regarding personalized attitude. It thus applies to the body simply by virtue of the body's constitutive relation to the self. So, for example, whereas there is aesthetic pleasure in observing a handsome face or a well-shaped hand, the pleasure may turn into pride when and only when you realize that it is your own face or hand you are beholding. Pride is here appropriate because of the recognition that the body's attractive features are deemed one's own. If Paul has a snub nose or long fingers, then Paul himself is snub-nosed or long-fingered. On the account I suggest, taking pride in the red sports car one owns is essentially no different: through ownership of the car one becomes, we might say, red-sports-carred.[41]

The matter of expressivity also falls now into place. If freedom of expression includes freedom from expression, then coercing someone into an expressive gesture or forcing him to display a tattooed message would as surely violate that right as coercing him to speak. We can understand in the very same terms what is objectionable in the offending slogan on the license plate discussed in part 1, or, by the same token, in forcing people to fly flags over their homes or display billboards in their yards.

Conclusion

Our ordinary concept of ownership is complex, and we are now in a better position to unravel this complexity. We can do so by reuniting the two aspects of ownership that I distinguished early on: the pragmatic aspect, which I tied to the idea of object value, and the constitutive aspect tied to ownership value. The institutions of private property are concerned for the most part with assigning people pragmatic ownership, consisting in bundles of rights designed to afford the owner a share in the object's value. In doing so, however, these institutional arrangements also participate in forming the social and linguistic conventions that pertain to the use of the personal pronouns and correspondingly to the boundaries of the self. In shaping the use of these pronouns and defining the boundaries of the self, pragmatic ownership gains a new normative significance. This significance derives from those background personalized values, such as autonomy and dignity, whose domain is coextensive with the self and is therefore sensitive to variations in the latter's socially determined composition and boundaries.

Notes

1. Probably the best statement of this approach is in Joseph Raz, *The Morality of Freedom* (Oxford: Clarendon Press, 1986), chap. 7.

2. My discussion is limited to the ownership by an individual owner of physical objects. This leaves out, among many things, important forms of wealth such as ownership of stock, collective ownership of various kinds, etc. Though my discussion bears indirectly on these kinds of property, I do not deal with them here.

3. In his splendid book, *Property and Justice* (Oxford: Clarendon Press, 1996), James W. Harris rejects the distinction between viewing property as involving a person-thing relationship as against a person-person one. See 119–38. But although I find his arguments in favor of the person-thing view generally persuasive, there seems to me to be an ineliminable tension between this view and his conception of ownership as a right.

4. Though this assumption is mostly taken for granted in discussions of property, it is occasionally explicitly stated. E.g.: "property is also a set of interests, for if the things we own become worthless, we no longer have property." Virginia Held, "Property Rights and Interests," *Social Research* 46 (1979): 550, at 550. "In the last analysis both primitive and civilized man will only take the trouble to acquire objects because they have value for him." Ernest Beaglehole, *Property: A Study in Social Psychology* (London: George Allen and Unwin, 1931), at 156.

5. Exchange value, such as that of money, is obviously parasitic on such primary advantages as those I list. However, the concept of object value and the analysis based on it pertain to objects with such secondary value as well.

6. See Wesley Hohfeld, "Some Fundamental Legal Conceptions as Applied in Judicial Reasoning," *Yale Law Journal* 23 (1913): 16; A. M. Honoré, "Ownership," in *Oxford Essays in Jurisprudence* (first series), ed. A. G. Guest (Oxford: Clarendon Press, 1961), 107; Frank Snare, "The Concept of Property," *American Philosophical Quarterly* 9 (1972): 200; Thomas Grey, "The Disintegration of Property," *Nomos 22: Property*, ed. J. Roland Pennock and John W. Chapman (New York: New York University Press, 1980), 69–85; Stephen Munzer, *A Theory of Property* (Cambridge: Cambridge University Press, 1990), 22–23.

7. A study of collecting habits among American children lists about three hundred different items, some quite outlandish. They include, to mention a few, acorns, beans, birds' beaks, cans, chalk, broken dishes, flint, pebbles, rabbit ears, and sticks. See Caroline Frear Burk, "The Collecting Instinct," *Pedagogical Seminary* 7 (1900): 129, at 183–85.

Apricot pits are collected by Israeli kids. I stick mainly to this example not just out of nostalgia, but because in the collecting-of-worthless-objects department it still strikes me as, well, the pits ...

8. Positing, as psychologists sometimes do, a "collecting" or an "acquisitive instinct" as the ostensible basis of the value we seem to find in ownership for its own sake faces the same problem without solving it. Obviously, the idea of an "acquisitive instinct" presupposes that of ownership—to acquire an object is to obtain ownership of it. But if the satisfactions one derives from the object, e.g. from handling it or excluding others from it, depend on having first "acquired" it, what then is the acquisitive instinct a desire for? See, for example, Burk, "The Collecting Instinct"; Leon Litwinski, "Is There an Instinct of Possession?" *British Journal of Psychology* 33 (1942): 28. In later studies, some psychologists have attempted to reduce ownership (or possession) to some other, allegedly more basic, instinct or need, such as "effectance" ("human beings are motivated to produce effects and interact competently in their environment," Lita Furby, "Possessions: Toward a Theory of Their Meaning and Function throughout the Life Cycle," in *Life Span Development and Behavior,* ed. P. B. Baltes (New York: Academic Press, 1978), 1:298, at 312). But first, it is not at all clear how the collectibles I discuss advance such a function; and second, as the interchangeable use of *possession, ownership,* and *property* suggests, this approach does not seem to distinguish ownership, as a qualitatively distinct relation to objects, from simply handling objects in various ways. Some psychologists, though, explain collecting in particular and property in general by the extension-of-self metaphor. See, for example, Russell Belk et al., "Collectors and Collecting," *Advances in Consumer Research* 15 (1988): 548, at 550–51; Gordon W. Allport, *Becoming* (New Haven: Yale University Press, 1955); E. Prelinger, "Extension and Structure of the Self," *Journal of Psychology* 47 (1959): 13. As I point out in the next part, mine is an attempt to give a specific philosophical content to this metaphor.

9. The most extreme cases may be dubbed *fetishism* and thus be deemed pathological. But that would not deprive them of their significance either. The labeling does not resolve the conceptual puzzles; and by exaggerating certain features of the "normal" situation, pathology, here as elsewhere, can be a useful heuristic in studying the ordinary. For a good treatment that downplays the specter of fetishism as sometimes raised in discussions of property see Harris, *Property and Justice,* 256–58.

10. It has been generally recognized that pride is a peculiarly self-regarding emotion. But though this view seems intuitively compelling, giving a precise account has proved notoriously difficult. Three main

suggestions have been made, but none is quite satisfactory. The first, and simplest, is to equate the object of pride with its subject: one can take pride only in (an aspect of) oneself. But unless our ordinary conception of human beings is replaced here by the extended conception of self I later propose, this suggestion is belied by the examples we considered in which property is a source of pride. To accommodate these cases a looser standard has been proposed, requiring only that there be some connection between the object of pride and its subject. But this is obviously too loose: there is some connection between the subject of pride and anything whatsoever, and unless the kind of connection required is spelled out, and its relevance to pride shown, the standard does not advance our understanding much. The third suggestion is indeed more restrictive than the latter, while being more inclusive than the first, and is for this reason the most promising: the objects of pride are the things we own. But as it stands the suggestion begs the question we consider: what is it about the relation to an object we call ownership that would legitimately give rise to a feeling of pride? See Gabriele Taylor, *Pride, Shame, and Guilt: Emotions of Self-Assessment* (Oxford: Clarendon Press, 1985). It should be also recognized that an object we own can be a source of shame, say because of its decrepitude; the issues this raises, however, would seem to be the same.

11. The distinction is less obvious than may first appear. The reason is that a claim of a (new) right often takes the form that when properly understood, the relevant normative system within which the right is claimed already contains the right in question. The convergence between claiming a right and invoking one is most compelling when the discussion concerns some abstractly conceived moral system. To say, relative to such a system, that a certain right ought to exist, is indeed no different from claiming that the right already exists in that system. This is so since there is nothing more to the existence of a right within an abstractly conceived moral system than that the system entails or otherwise implies such a right. But the distinction is significant when the right concerned is a social (and that includes legal) right. The existence of such a right is a matter of the holding of certain facts, concerning for example people's attitudes (such as an inclination to criticize violations of the right) or the content of some official documents (such as that a statute recognizing the right exists). With respect to a social right so understood it is accordingly altogether possible to maintain that some right ought to exist but does not.

12. A well-known observation by Wittgenstein carries the present point to its logical extreme. As Norman Malcolm recounts it, "On one walk [Wittgenstein] gave to me each tree that we passed, with the reservation that I was not to cut it down or do anything to it: with

those reservations it was henceforth *mine.*" Norman Malcolm, *Ludwig Wittgenstein—a Memoir* (Oxford: Oxford University Press, 1967), 31, cited in Bruce Ackerman, *Private Property and the Constitution* (New Haven: Yale University Press, 1977), 233. The intended joke trades on and through exaggeration accentuates the space between our ordinary concept of ownership and the advantages ownership commonly secures.

13. *Wooley v. Maynard,* 430 U.S. 705 (1976).

14. Ibid., 714–15. The latter requirement had been previously held unconstitutional in *Board of Education v. Barnette,* 319 U.S. 624 (1943).

15. What I call the pragmatic aspect of ownership and the related ownership value are close to Marx's notion of *use value:* "The utility of a thing makes it a use-value." Karl Marx, *Capital,* trans. Samuel Moore and Edward Aveling (New York: International Publishers, 1967), 1:36. There is a much more distant and looser correspondence between my constitutive ownership and ownership value and what Marx calls *exchange value* or simply *value.* On Marx's view, through labor, a distinctly human and social value gets embodied in commodities: "the value of commodities has a purely social reality, and ... they acquire this reality only in so far as they are expressions or embodiments of ... human labour" (47). My approach too accentuates the distinctly human value of property and its essential social dimension, but departs from Marx's in other fundamental ways that I will not here try to explore.

16. The origin of the modern discussion of self-ownership is Locke: "every man has a Property in his own Person." *Two Treatises of Government,* ed. Peter Laslett (Cambridge: Cambridge University Press, 1960), II, sec. 27. Though many writers consider self-ownership as involving the body, Jeremy Waldron insists on the importance to Locke's view of the distinction between the person and the body. See *The Right to Private Property* (Oxford: Clarendon Press, 1988), 177–83. For other critical discussions of self-ownership, see for example, J. P. Day, "Locke on Property," *Philosophical Quarterly* 16 (1966): 207; Gerald A. Cohen, *Self-Ownership, Freedom, and Equality* (Cambridge: Cambridge University Press, 1995); Alan Ryan, "Utility and Ownership," in *Utility and Rights,* ed. R. G. Frey (Minneapolis: University of Minnesota Press, 1984), 175–95, and "Self-Ownership, Autonomy, and Property Rights," *Social Philosophy and Policy* 11 (1994): 241; Harris, *Property and Justice,* 184–97. For an attempt to derive property rights directly from rights in the body see Samuel Wheeler III, "Natural Property Rights as Body Rights," *Noûs* 14 (1980): 171. The attempt is unsuccessful for reasons forcefully stated—and sometimes overstated—in David Braybrooke, "Our Natural Bodies, Our Social Rights: Comments on Wheeler," *Noûs* 14 (1980): 195.

17. On the natural-law doctrine of the *suum* as the extension of

personality, see Karl Olivecrona, "Locke's Theory of Appropriation," *Philosophical Quarterly* 24 (1974): 220, at 222–24. See generally Stephen Buckle, *Natural Law and the Theory of Property* (Oxford: Clarendon Press, 1991). The most influential modern theory of this general type is Hegel's, in *The Philosophy of Right,* trans. T. M. Knox (Oxford: Oxford University Press, 1967), 40–57. For illuminating critical discussions, see Waldron, *Right to Private Property,* chap. 10; and Harris, *Property and Justice,* 232–37. A recent revival of this general approach can be found in Margaret Jane Radin, *Reinterpreting Property* (Chicago: University of Chicago Press, 1993), and "Market-Inalienability," *Harvard Law Review* 100 (1987): 1849. In the psychological literature the best-known view along these lines is that of William James: "In the widest possible sense ... a man's Self is the sum total of all that he can call his." *Principles of Psychology* (New York: Macmillan, 1890), 1:292.

18. The Kantian insight on which I draw is famously expressed by his claim, "It must be possible for the 'I Think' to accompany all my representations." *Critique of Pure Reason,* trans. Norman Kemp Smith (New York: St. Martin's Press, 1929), p. 152, B131. Cf., "To be an I, a self, is to have the capacity for reflexive self-reference." Robert Nozick, *Philosophical Explanations* (Cambridge: Harvard University Press, 1981), 78.

19. Recall Lichtenberg's well-known objection to Descartes, that instead of "I think" all that can be legitimately claimed ought to take the form of "It thinks," with "it" used as in "It is raining."

20. A particularly helpful discussion that reaches a conclusion similar to mine can be found in Hans Sluga, "'Whose House Is That?' Wittgenstein on the Self," in *The Cambridge Companion to Wittgenstein,* ed. Hans Sluga and David Stern (Cambridge: Cambridge University Press, 1990), 320.

21. Immunity to such error is associated with the use of *I* "as subject," in Wittgenstein's terminology. See *The Blue and Brown Books* (New York: Oxford University Press, 1958), 66–67. For a clear statement of the issues involved see Sydney Shoemaker, "Self-reference and Self-Awareness," *Journal of Philosophy* 65 (1968): 555.

22. For the phenomenology of the extension-of-body idea, see, for example, Maurice Merleau-Ponty, *Phenomenology of Perception,* trans. Colin Smith (New York: Humanities Press, 1962), esp. 143, 145; John Dewey, *Democracy and Education* (1916; rpt. New York: Simon and Schuster, 1997), 195. But as Kant, among others, was well aware, the puzzle of ownership arises most acutely when there is no physical contiguity with the body: "I do not call an apple mine simply because I hold it in my hand (possess it physically) but only if I can say: I possess it even when I let it out of the hand that is holding it." *The Metaphysical*

Elements of Justice, trans. John Ladd (Indianapolis: Bobbs-Merrill, 1965), 54. Kant's solution is to recognize a noumenal *de jure* proprietary relationship that occurs in the intelligible realm and that involves a union of the subject's will with the object viewed as a thing-in-itself. Ibid., 55–64.

23. Cf. Eddy Zemach, "The Reference of 'I,'" *Philosophical Studies* 23 (1972): 68. The problem of drawing the boundaries of the entity to which *I* refers is also raised in Michael Woods, "Reference and Self-Identification," *Journal of Philosophy* 65 (1968): 568.

24. These comments draw heavily on John R. Searle, *The Construction of Social Reality* (New York: Free Press, 1995); see also Margaret Gilbert, *On Social Facts* (Princeton: Princeton University Press, 1992).

25. The classical text on the social construction of the self is George Herbert Mead, *Mind, Self, and Society,* ed. Charles Morris (Chicago: University of Chicago Press, 1934). See also his distinction between self and organism, on 135–44. On Mead's view of the relation between physical objects and the self, see E. Doyle McCarty, "Toward a Sociology of the Physical World: George Herbert Mead on Physical Objects," *Studies in Symbolic Interaction* 5 (1984): 105. See also Peter Berger and Thomas Luckmann, *The Social Construction of Reality* (Garden City, N.Y.: Doubleday, 1966), 173–80. But for a critical view cf. David Wiggins, "Locke, Butler, and the Stream of Consciousness: And Man as a Natural Kind," in *The Identities of Persons,* ed. Amélie Rorty (Berkeley and Los Angeles: University of California Press, 1976), 139.

26. It may be objected that the proposed conception of the self will play havoc with some fundamental moral and legal understandings. Suppose that I spend an evening at the theater in the company of friends. In the next morning's paper, I read about a death that occurred the previous evening at the race track. Shouldn't I feel secure in my knowledge that my undisputed alibi gives me a metaphysical warranty against any involvement in this nefarious matter? But such confidence would be ill-founded. I may be implicated in the death and indeed held responsible for it if, for example, it was my horse that threw off its jockey or trampled a hapless onlooker. In a legal regime of strict liability my responsibility may depend exclusively on my ownership of the horse, irrespective of how I became its owner, e.g., by purchase or inheritance, or of any failure on my part to properly train the horse or prevent the accident in any other manner. I deal at greater length with these issues in chapter 7.

27. Cf. the view of self-ownership as stated in 1646 by the Leveller Richard Overton, in *An Arrow against all Tyrants:* "for every one as he is himselfe, so he hath a selfe propriety, else could he not be himselfe." (Cited in Day, "Locke on Property," at 219.)

28. As I noted earlier, the use of personal possessives ranges widely and is not limited to ownership. Still, a common semantic marker, fallible but significant all the same, distinguishes and privileges the owner and the constitutive connotations of her use. It is an emphatic use often preceded by *really*. So, for example, I can with perfect legitimacy say that "my plane leaves in five minutes"; but if a misunderstanding were to arise I would clarify: "Oh no, it's not really *my* plane, but just the one I'm about to fly." Bill Gates, by contrast, would aver under similar circumstances: "Indeed, it is *my* plane I'm talking about."

29. The order of acquiring the pronouns by children may be reversed, too. See, for example, the comment by W. C. Bronson, "It is as if 'I' was being partly defined by exploration of the notion of what is 'mine' or under 'my' control." In "Developments in Behavior with Age-Mates during the Second Year of Life," in *Friendship and Peer Relations,* ed. Michael Lewis and Leonard A. Rosenblum (New York: Wiley, 1975), at 145–46. My interest is in the conceptual relation between the pronouns as used by adult speakers.

30. Other people are among the physical objects to which possessive pronouns can refer. Our relationship to other people marked by the use of these pronouns resembles in many ways our proprietary relations to objects. So, for example, I take special pride in *my* child or spouse, and what qualifies someone as one or the other is no less problematic than the proprietary relation to other objects. An extension-of-self analysis suggests itself here as well, though the difference between the case of people and most other objects is revealed in the difference between the respective personal pronouns used in the two cases. When other people are involved, the personal pronoun used is *we* or *us* rather than *I* or *me,* perhaps signaling in this way that the constitutive relationship is reciprocal. This suggestion is complicated, however, by the fact that the plural personal pronouns are commonly used in regard to animals as well. Be this as it may, the question how to best square the relationships with other persons with my present account of ownership is one I leave for another day.

31. See sources cited in note 22.

32. See for example Blackstone's classical definition of ownership as "the sole and despotic dominion which one man claims and exercises over the external things of the world, in total exclusion of the right of any other individual in the universe." William Blackstone, *Commentaries on the Laws of England,* 11th ed. (London: T. Cadell, 1791), 2:2.

33. To criticize, as some authors do, a natural-law approach to property by insisting on the social origins of property is, accordingly, to see only half the picture. See, e.g., Joseph Singer and Jack Beermann, "The Social Origins of Property," *Canadian Journal of Law and*

Jurisprudence 6 (1993): 217, in which the authors take the Supreme Court to task for failing to realize that property is socially constructed. Though I find many of their criticisms sound, from my perspective the authors are themselves guilty of a similar omission in not realizing that so is the self.

34. Derek Parfit, *Reasons and Persons* (Oxford: Clarendon Press, 1984), part 3.

35. *Breithaupt v. Abram,* 352 U.S. 432 (1956).

36. It is natural to speak in a case like this of a prima facie right to bodily integrity as providing the normative backdrop. But though invoking here this right is no doubt sound, unless we are cautious, it may mislead. Talk of the right to bodily integrity may conjure up a picture according to which the body is protected by this right in the same sense in which works of art or forests may be especially protected. In the latter cases, injury to the protected objects is of primary concern; if rights regarding the objects' protection are allocated to, say, a museum or to a ranger, these right-holders are considered the trustees or guardians of the art or the trees. But I am not similarly the guardian or the trustee of a body whose protection is desired for its own sake. The normative status of the body derives entirely from its constitutive relation to the person, and from the latter's normative significance as the object of the background personalized values.

37. Justice Holmes provides a rationale for adverse possession along parallel lines: "I should suggest that the foundation of the acquisition of rights by lapse of time is to be looked for in the position of the person who gains them.... A thing which you have enjoyed and used as your own for a long time ... takes root in your being and cannot be torn away without your resenting the act and trying to defend yourself, however you came by it. The law can ask no better justification than the deepest instincts of man." Oliver Wendell Holmes, "The Path of Law," *Harvard Law Review* 10 (1897): 457, 476–477.

38. Philip Roth, *I Married a Communist* (New York: Vintage Books, 1999).

39. The most influential source of the modern secular conception of dignity is Immanuel Kant, *Groundwork of the Metaphysic of Morals,* trans. H. J. Paton (London: Hutchinson, 1948), 96–97.

40. To say that concerning dignity, no qualitative difference between the body and other objects we own exists is not to deny that important quantitative distinctions can be drawn. After all, such gradations obviously exist with respect to the body itself: compare, for example, the touching of someone's genitals to the touching of hands or hair. In a similar vein, the dignitary aspect of property may vary between the important and the trivial. Even so, it should be acknowledged that the

approach I recommend can be easily enlisted in the service of unappealing ideological commitments, as is demonstrated, I think, by a piece such as James W. Wiggins, "The Decline of Private Property and the Diminished Person," in *Property in a Humane Economy*, ed. S. I. Blumenfeld (LaSalle, Ill.: Open Court, 1974), 714.

41. It goes without saying that ownership of body or of property is not the only basis for pride. I can take pride in a painting I have painted or in a score I have composed. But here the pride originates from my actions and my talents, both of which are undisputed and central aspects of the self. The puzzle of ownership is that owning an object can serve as a sufficient basis for pride all by itself and in the absence of any other contribution of involvement on the owner's part. This is also the main point of the analogy to the body: Paul's pride in his snub nose is entirely a matter of his ownership, and no further contribution or involvement is required or expected.

INDEX

Abel, Richard L., 169n.27
Ackerman, Bruce, 86n.71, 295n.12
acoustic separation: conduct and decision
    rules in context of, 41–44; in defenses
    of duress and necessity, 46–52;
    described, 40–41; determinants of
    degree of, 49–52; effect of lack of, 41;
    in ignorance of the law, 52–54
adjudication 28–32
alienation: distinct from role distance, 18
Allport, Gordon, 294n.8
allusion, 276–78
Anderson, Elizabeth, 169n.27
Arendt, Hannah, 90n.107, 116n.1
Arenella, Peter, 238n.3
Aristotle, 212, 240n.23
Arneson, Richard, 148n.11
Atiyah, P. S., 90n.105
Austin, John, 77n.5, 95, 116n.2
authority: attitudes to, 94; based on
    dependent reasons, 100; and coercion,
    94, 96–7, 99–100, 114; commands of,
    109–13; compared to requests, 107–
    13; consent theories of, 99; deference
    to, 103–5; and exclusionary reasons,
    109–13; instrumental conceptions of,
    100–107; normativity of, 94–95, 98,
    107–13; similarity to morality of, 110–
    12; source-based reasons for, 112–13;
    of the state, 95; and voluntary obedi-
    ence, 107–9

autonomy: choice autonomy, 135; and
    commitment, 138; *de facto* and *de
    jure*, 156–57; freedom of choice in
    ideal of, 125; linked to dignity (Kant),
    157–58; moral (Kant), 2, 136–37,
    158–59; and ownership, 268–70,
    288–90; personal, 136–37; physical
    violence hinders, 161; rational choice
    and, 125; as reflexive value, 268–69;
    relation of slavery to, 155–57; rela-
    tionship between conceptions of choice
    and, 135–43; and roles, 16–17; value
    of, 159–60; will conception of, 135,
    142–43
Ayer, Alfred J., 240n.26

bad faith, 18
Barry, Brian, 117n.14
Bates, Stanley, 243n.50
Bazelon, David L., 244n.74
Beaglehole, Ernest, 293n.4
Becker, Lawrence, 167n.12
Bedder v. Director of Public Prosecutions
    (1952), 227–31
Beerman, Jack, 299n.33
Bentham, Jeremy, 38, 41, 55, 70–71,
    77nn.1,2, 85n.63, 92nn.115,116,117,
    175, 193n.7
Berger, Peter L., 239n.15, 298n.25
Berlin, Isaiah, 149n.21
Bernstein, Anita, 169n.27